and
How It Changed My Life

How I Found
THE URANTIA BOOK
and
How It Changed My Life

Compiled by Saskia Praamsma

Square Circles Publishing, Inc.
Glendale, California

How I Found
THE URANTIA BOOK
and
How It Changed My Life

FIRST EDITION

Copyright © 2001 by Square Circles Publishing, Inc.

All rights reserved.

Many of these stories previously appeared in slightly different form in a privately circulated work entitled *How I Found the Urantia Book*, © 1998 by Square Circles Publishing, Inc. This compilation is a revised and enlarged version of that work.

Cover art: Chick Montgomery

回

SQUARE CIRCLES PUBLISHING, INC.
P.O. BOX 251194
GLENDALE, CA 91225
www.squarecircles.com

ISBN#0-9666705-2-3
Library of Congress Control Number: 2001118266

Printed in the United States of America by
Morris Publishing
Kearney, Nebraska

DEDICATION

*This book of testimonies is dedicated to
the humans and superhumans
whose joint efforts brought us
the Urantia revelation.*

ABOUT THE URANTIA BOOK

What is the Urantia Book?
The Urantia Book is a revelation given to the peoples of our planet, Urantia. It instructs us on God, angels, life after death, the structure of the universe and its divinely planned development, the origin and history of our planet, the life and teachings of Jesus, and our eternal destiny as perfected citizens of a friendly universe. It provides an enlightening picture of reality in which science, religion, and philosophy are unified.

Who wrote the Urantia Book?
It is held by believers in the Urantia revelation that the authors are a corps of celestial beings who were authorized to reveal this information to us. Because such higher beings do not ordinarily communicate directly with human beings, a favorably constituted human conduit—known as "the contact personality"—was used.

How did the Urantia Book come into existence?
No person alive today knows exactly how the Urantia teachings were transmitted to us. The human beings who were most intimately involved with their reception—six people known as "the contact commission"—have all passed on to the mansion worlds and have taken their secrets with them. We are left with some facts, some myths, much conjecture, and a 2,097-page book comprising 196 papers of incomparable beauty, scope and spiritual power.

How do we know the Urantia Book is true?
There is no way to prove scientifically that the cosmic and spiritual teachings of the Urantia Book are true. Each seeker must discover the truth of the teachings deep within his or her soul.

HISTORY OF THE URANTIA BOOK

The following historical outline has been widely accepted by believers in the Urantia Book, though the lack of firsthand documentation makes it impossible to verify its accuracy.

Early in the twentieth century, in Chicago, a man in his sleep began to transmit communications from benevolent celestial personalities. The man became a patient of Dr. William S. Sadler, a well-known psychiatrist and author. The scope of knowledge and depth of wisdom of the communications were so far beyond the ken of this man, that the doctor, a noted debunker of spiritualism, was forced to take the case seriously.

Dr. Sadler, his wife Lena, their son Bill, their adopted daughter Emma (Christy) Christensen, Lena's sister Anna Kellogg and her husband Wilfred Kellogg, became the custodians of the manuscripts and were known as "the contact commission." The man transmitting the information was known as "the contact personality" or "the sleeping subject."

From his wide circle of patients and acquaintances, Dr. Sadler invited a number of individuals to attend weekly meetings at his residence at 533 Diversey Parkway, Chicago. The members of this group, called the Forum, signed a pledge not to tell non-Forumites about their involvement with the unfolding revelation. They studied and discussed the teachings as they were being revealed, and were encouraged to ask questions regarding the material. The content of the Urantia Papers would sometimes be modified by the revelators in response to these questions. In 1955 the completed series of papers was published as *The Urantia Book*.

Many revelations have been given to our world, but the Urantia Book claims to be a revelation of epochal significance, the first of its kind since the days when our Creator Son, Michael, as Jesus of Nazareth, came to reveal the loving nature of God.

ACKNOWLEDGMENTS

I wish to express my gratitude to my co-workers in this endeavor: Matthew Block and Joy Brandt for their editorial assistance; Chick Montgomery for the cover art; Will Sherwood for producing the cover; and Al Loskamp for his legal services. I also salute the late Julia Early Fenderson, a dedicated Urantian and Forum member, who began this project many years ago and whose collection of early accounts, included here, have given this work an historical depth that would not have been possible otherwise. My deepest appreciation goes out to the 324 individuals who shared their stories. I am merely the string that has tied them together.

—Saskia Praamsma

TABLE OF CONTENTS

Dedication v
About the Urantia Book vi
History of the Urantia Book vii
Acknowledgments viii

PART I: FORUM DAYS
Clyde Bedell 1
Ruth Renn 2
Grace Walker 3
Wesley R. James 4
C. Barrie Bedell 6
Katharine J. "Ticky" Harries 7

PART II: 1955-1969
Jacques Weiss 11
Meredith Sprunger 12
Gene Joyce 14
Gus Walstrom 15
Wally Ziglar 16
Ila and Loren Hall 17
Bill Bryan 18
Eldred Cocking 20
Polly Parke Friedman 21
Hal Kettell 21
Beverly Wold 23
James Irwin 24
Bill Hazzard 26
Virginia Lee Hallock 27
Dick Bain 28
Joel Rehnstrom 29
Stefan Tallqvist 30
Mary J. Michael 31

Tonia Baney 32
Jeff Keys 32
JoAnn Eichmann 34
Sara Blackstock 34
Patricia Bedell Martin 35
Pat Fearey 36
Doc Livingston 38
Larry Mullins 39
Dorothy Elder 40
Mo Siegel 42
Kermit Anderson 42
Chick Montgomery 43
Irving Townsend 45
Marilyn Hauck Green 45
Henry Begemann 47
Gary Hall 48
Pat McNelly 48
Will Sherwood 49
Francyl Gawryn 51
Susan Sarfaty 52
Thomas Orjala 54

PART III: 1970-1971
Steven Hecht 55
Robert F. Bruyn 56
Larry Geis 58
David Bradley 61
Denver Pearson 62
Jerry McCollum 64
Philip Geiger 65
Bill Spang 66
Scott Brooks 67
Jim Downs 68
George Coutis 69
Marty Greenhut 70
John Roper 72
Thea Hardy 73

TABLE OF CONTENTS

Ed Owen 75
Russ Gustafson 76
Bob Hunt 76
Philip Calabrese 78
Lyn Davis Lear 79
Denie Schach 80
Jamail McKinney 81
Jeffrey Wattles 82
Stacey Harlan 84
Kelly Elstrott 85
Les Tibbals 86
Stephen Zendt 88
Janelle Balnicke 88
Norman Ingram 89
Gerald Harrison 91
Cheryl Ashiqa Zents 91
Doug Parker 93

PART IV: 1972-1973

Duane Faw 95
Mark Freeman 97
James Woodward 100
Forrest Adkins 100
Peggy M. Johnson 102
Jim Harris 103
Michael Pitzel 104
Al Lockett 106
Gard Jameson 107
K. Brendi Poppel 108
Sonny Schneider 109
Tammy Horton 109
David Glass 110
Ardell Faul 111
Buck and Arlene Weimer 112
Don Tyler 114
Daniel Raphael 115
Claudia Ayers 116

Rob Crickett ... 117
Stella Religa ... 118
Emy Hoy ... 119
Glenn Bell ... 120
Angus Bowen ... 120
Martha Groh ... 122
Lee Armstrong ... 124
Jess Hansen ... 126
Janet Quinn Nilsen ... 126
Donna Oliver ... 128
Susan Hemmingsen ... 129
Kris Reinecke ... 130
Larry Pawlitsky ... 131
Lynn Goodwin ... 133
Darlene Sheatz Criner ... 134
Michael Mann ... 135
Delores Dinsmore ... 136

PART V: 1974-1976

Joy Brandt ... 139
Richard Omura ... 141
Byron Belitsos ... 142
Esther Wood ... 144
Sue Smith ... 145
Jane A. Roper ... 147
Mike Kubik ... 148
Michelle Klimesh ... 149
Roger J. Abdo ... 150
Terry Galvin ... 151
Sioux Harvey ... 152
Robert Burns ... 153
Mario Caoile ... 155
Ruth L. Steach ... 156
Beth Bartley ... 156
Lorrie Shapiro Krasny ... 157
Rosey Lieske ... 159
Jim Lee ... 160

TABLE OF CONTENTS

JJ Johnson 161
Joe Feller 162
Larry Watkins 163
Laurence R. Whelan 165
Sheryl Bellman 165
Karen Farrington Daniels 166
Dolores Nice 168
Chrissy Palatucci Smith 169
Karen Jeppeson 171
Sharon Ziglar 172
Tommy Outerbridge 173
Julianne Clerget 175
Matthew Block 176
Jean Ascher 178
Betty Bright 179
Paula Lynn Sutton 180
Christos Konstas 181
Paula Garrett Thompson 182
Ron Faulk 184
Dave Tibbets 186
Fred Smith 187
Mary Ebben 188
Dennis Nicomede 189
David Robertson 190
Charlie Beyer 191

PART VI: 1977-1979
Charlotte Wellen 195
Jon DeToy 196
Nancy Brown 197
Saskia Praamsma 199
M. (Sek) Seklemian 201
Daniel Love Glazer 203
Dave Holt 206
Cathy Jones 207
Irwin Ginsburgh 208
Dave Weber 209

Donna Maria Hanna 210
Mark Greer 211
Paul Defourneaux 212
Daniel Megow 213
Kathleen Vinson 215
Paul Hall 215
Bruce Carriker 216
John Dupree 217
Laurence Gwynn 218
Liz Engstrom Cratty 219
Brad Wortendyke 220
Joan Batson Mullins 221
Lamar Zabielski 223
Karen Pike 223
Kathryn Pike 225
Sandor Szabados 226
LuAnn Harney 227
Bruce White 229
Sharon Sadler 229
Craig Rohrsen 230
Kitty and Tim Traylor 231
Mike Rayl 233
Gregory McCormack 233
Steve Shinall 234

PART VII: 1980-1986
Barbara Jo Howell 237
Rob Estrada 240
Christilyn Biek 241
Luc Lachance 243
Pierre Girard 243
Michael Mark 244
Helen Markellos 245
Ed Healy 247
Enno Benjamins.. 247
Robert O'Guin 249
Al Aldo 250

TABLE OF CONTENTS

Stephen Thorburn 251
Henry Zeringue 252
Steven McWhorter 253
Michael Hayes 254
Virginia Brown 256
Peter Hayman 257
Ginny McCarty 258
Fred Beckner 259
Lee Colbert 259
Susan Mohr 261
Timothy Nicely 262
Barry Norby 263
Joilin Johnson 265
Geoff Taylor 266
Rick Warren 267
Lee Rauh 268
Gisela Filion 269
Jenni Di Bacco 271
Bill Kelly 271
Gary McSweeney 273
Jerry Dalton 273

PART VIII: 1987-1993
Arley Grubb 275
Juan Jose Martinez Afonso 276
Rob Lawson 277
Mary Huggins 278
Loren Leger 279
Tom Channic 279
Sage Waitts 280
Suzanne Kelly-Ward 282
Robert Schreiber 283
Stephanie Forbes 283
Willis Davis 284
Michael D'Ambrosia 285
Peri Best 286
Susan Kimsey 286

Fred Harris 287
Mike Bain 289
Leonard Ablieter 290
Michael J. Zehr 292
Calvin McKee 292
Billy Burnette 294
Gene Narducy 295
Sherie Crosby 295
Margo Lewis-Sutter 296
Hamid Reza Mazdeh 297
Evelyn Hammond 298
Angel Sanchez Escobar 299
Pat Porter 300
Karrie Hummel 300
Terry 302
Judy Tuttle 302
Lee and Mildred Maxton 304
Allene Vick 305
Don Roark 306
Alba Teresita Rojas Agudelo 307
Holly 308
Jordi Solsona i Estrada 309
Nora and Saed Moakher 310
Donna Brown 311
Diana Elwyn 312
Jeannie Scott 313
Doug Huntzinger 314

PART IX: 1994-1996

John McKinney 315
Beu'lah Mary Omar 316
Bud Hughes 317
Calvin Matthew Gorman 317
Bob Fontana 318
Sybil W. Morgan 319
Gonzalo and Merci Bandera 320
Eduardo Guelfenbein 321

TABLE OF CONTENTS

Alicia Satterthwaite 321
Julie Suga 322
Santiago Flores 324
Phil Kava 325
Charlie Barden 326
Jeff Abercrombie 327
Patrick Maloy 327
Scott Smith 328
Rodger Benjamins 329
Curt Day 331
Linda Barnett 332
Holly Carmichael 332
Shane Borowski 333
Catherine Heyneman 335
David Linthicum 335
Ricardo Franco 337
Pradhana Fuchs 338
Kinda Ford 338
Jeffrey Mason 339
Jaime Andres Cuello 340
Vicki Miller Newby 340
Josefina de Martinez 341
Juan Paulo Vega 342
Diego Gonzales Munos 344
Gustavo Proano 344
Roger in Hawaii 345
Nel Benjamins 347

PART X: 1997-2000
Timothy W. Morris 349
Andrew Gamez 350
Jacob Dix 351
Jim Patten 352
Monti Pagni 354
Shauna Hardway 355
Tom Greaves 356
Judy Kroll 357

Fernando Muldonado 358
Olga Lopez 359
Fernando Risquez 360
Gabriel Lara 360
Albert Oliver 361
Ray Nathan Stephenson 362
Shane Cotner 362
Betsy Berna 364
Therese Logan 364
Cynthia Taylor 365
Costas Diamantopoulos 367
George Benavides 369
Faye Loskamp 369
Al Loskamp 370
Inge Scheumann 371
Lonita Murto 372
Wendy 372
Mark Underwood 373
Brad Trainham 375

Index 377

Part I

Forum Days

CLYDE BEDELL: How can a man or woman be so fortunate as to become intimately associated with an epochal revelation—as every reader-believer of this generation is?

My story begins in Chicago in 1921, when I was 23. I was working at the Walter Hoops Advertising Agency. My best friend there was Lister Alwood, much my senior, and a gifted writer and poet. While at Hoops I also met a lovely creature who joined the company after I did. I asked her for a date, she told me "soon," and I gave her a rain check. But before the rain check could be honored, I left Hoops to join an agency in San Francisco.

After two years on the coast, I received a wire from Alwood urging me to apply for an $8000-per-year job he had applied for unsuccessfully. (I was making only $400 a month, and $8000 was a mint of money at that time!) I agreed to return to Chicago for a personal interview. When I told my boss of my dilemma that good man said, "Go get it if you can, and God bless you. If you don't get it, come back and go to work and forget about it." I got the job.

The first evening back in Chicago I had dinner at Alwood's home. He asked if I would like to attend with him, on the following Sunday, a meeting at the home of a famous psychiatrist—a Dr. William Sadler, a great speaker and teacher. Perhaps there would be some reading, but interesting discussion and conversation for sure. I accepted. Before Sunday came, I had a date with the "Hoops lovely," making the rain check good. We had not corresponded, but I had carefully kept the address.

The first Sunday I was back in Chicago—the last Sunday in September, 1924—I attended my first Sadler Forum meeting. Afterwards I asked the doctor if I could bring a young woman the next time. He consented.

The following Sunday Florence Evans went with me, and from that day to this we have been identified with the Forum that later received the Urantia Papers.

In 1955 Florence and I knew the first Urantia Book would issue from the presses while we were on a round-the-world trip for me to do some work in Australia and New Zealand. Dr. Sadler's brilliant son Bill, a fantastic student of the Papers, agreed to airmail a book to us as soon as he could lay his hands on one. That copy is now so underlined that the underlining has no emphasis. It bears in the front this inscription:

> *"First Urantia Book! Glimpsed in Rome, 11:40 a.m., October 1, 1955. Clyde and Florence Bedell."* An addition reads: *"First reading completed 4/22/56. San Francisco, 10:48 p.m."*

Florence departed this sphere for the mansion worlds in 1979, a week after our fifty-third wedding anniversary.

My life, with the enthusiastic approval of both my sons, is dedicated to help, in every way I possibly can, "promote, improve, and expand the understanding of the peoples of the world of the teachings of Jesus." We should all pray that all people in our movement, from Chicago outward over all the earth, might discover those quoted words from the Foundation's Declaration of Trust.

How many people in a millennium can be early recipients of an epochal revelation? It is our duty to bring its message to all the spiritually deprived people we can reach, in keeping with the character of our book.

RUTH RENN: In my early years it was difficult for me to accept the message of being redeemed by the blood of Jesus. I was constantly on a quest for truth. I searched in many libraries for books that might give me what I wanted and needed. On the radio, Preston Bradley in Chicago came the nearest to imparting the truth I was seeking.

In 1925 I went to the Chicago Institute of Research and Diagnosis on Diversey Parkway for a complete physical examination. One appointment was with the co-owner, Dr. William Sadler, for a psychological test. He asked me many questions regarding my thoughts and desires. The question about religious beliefs was, "Do you believe in a Creator?" The conversation led to truth. I mentioned that I would like to be closed in a room to read and read until I found the truth I was looking for. I remember the doctor's face as I said this. He seemed to have a satisfied spark in his eyes and he nodded his head up and down. Not long after that I received a note in the mail inviting me to attend a Sunday meeting called the Forum at the Sadler home.

One Sunday I persuaded my husband to attend a meeting with me to see what it was about. As we ascended the stairs of the building at 533 Diversey Parkway, my husband made the remark, "You will never get me down here again." We were greeted by Dr. Lena Sadler, the doctor's wife, who said, "These beings told us to build the scaffolding; they would do the rest."

When the meeting opened we were fortunate to hear Paper 1, "The Universal Father." I was astounded. Never had I realized that we could be told so much about God. All the following week I was remembering little snatches of what I had heard about our heavenly Father, his love and mercy. I had found what I had been searching for.

The following Sunday my husband Roy was preparing to go to the meeting with no thought of what he had said the week before about never going again. Our lives were changed from that time on. And, for over sixty years, I have endeavored to be a faithful disseminator of the Urantia teachings.

GRACE WALKER: I was raised in a religious family in the suburbs of Chicago. My father was an evangelical minister, a circuit-riding preacher in his early ministry. Before the Depression, I wanted to be a missionary or a missionary doctor. In college I was exposed to what was called "higher criticism," which questioned the authority of the Bible. This caused me to do a lot of thinking about religion.

Later, I found a book by a German professor that was quite profound. I asked my doctor, Dr. William Sadler on Diversey Parkway in Chicago, if he had read this book because I just felt he knew something. He said he *had* read the book, then added, "I've got something I think you'd be interested in." He told me about the Urantia Papers, and when I showed interest he said, "What are you doing on Sunday? Could you possibly come to the Forum next Sunday afternoon?" Explaining that it would take too long to describe the purpose of the Forum in his office, the doctor invited me to come early. Upon joining the Forum, I signed, at the doctor's request, a pledge of secrecy concerning the Urantia Papers.

I began reading the Papers in 1945. I worked in downtown Chicago, and after work on Friday nights I would take the bus to 533 Diversey. Afterwards I'd take a late train and wouldn't get home until midnight. Reading one paper at a time, I started with the Jesus papers, then began reading from the first part of the book. I was convinced that what I read was true, because the story of Jesus' life as father to his brothers and sisters touched on so many of the same problems I had had in my life.

One time, when I first began to read. I approached Mrs. Kellogg, who was the proctor at the desk, and asked, "Do you really believe all of this?"

"I certainly do!" she replied.

The Sunday afternoon group, which had started as a discussion group, was called the Forum. At the time I began attending it had become an open-house time for readers. I also belonged to a group called the Seventy. There were just seventy people in this group originally, made up of those who had read the Papers in their entirety. Within this group was a school formed to train teachers, which held evening classes at 533. The problem was that there were teachers but no persons to teach at this time. Teachers far outnumbered new readers.

In the Seventy group, each person had to write a paper on a Urantia topic. These were passed by the doctor and read on Sundays.

My parents, who were by then in their seventies, lived next door to me, and they were curious about where I was going on Friday nights and Sunday afternoons. I finally had to tell them a little about the Papers. My dad was skeptical, but my mother was quite open-minded. They both actually held some of the same ideas as the book already.

Living so far away, I wasn't able to keep up with the meetings. I was divorced and had much responsibility. These Papers helped me raise my children. I also learned that with disappointment we have another chance. The Urantia teachings literally changed my life.

WESLEY R. JAMES: I've never had the experience of finding the Urantia Book. That distinction belongs to my grandmother, Elizabeth James, and to my parents, William and Mary James. Because of their efforts the UB has always been a part of my life.

In the late 1920s my grandmother began searching for answers to religious questions that troubled and intrigued her. The answers her Bible and church background provided lacked consistency as far as she was concerned. There were even questions she was told should not be asked, because they showed a lack of faith. She studied the philosophies and attended the meetings of a number of cults and isms that were popular in Chicago in those days, from the Swedenborgians and Rosicrucians to the Silver Shirts of a Dr. Pelley.

At one of these meetings my grandmother mentioned to some people her growing concern that none of the groups she had found thus far had the answers she was looking for. These people—Mrs. Jessie Hill and Fred and Alice Leverenz—suggested she might be interested in a group they belonged to that met on Sundays at 533 Diversey Parkway in Chicago.

After meeting Dr. Sadler and learning about the purpose of the Forum, my grandmother signed the pledge and became a member. Years later as one of the Seventy she was often praised for her prodigious memory and ability to quote verbatim from the unpublished papers which later became the Urantia Book.

The change in my grandmother after she joined the Forum so intrigued my parents that my mother wrote Dr. Sadler asking if they too could become Forum members. In response, Dr. Sadler asked my grandmother if she wouldn't like to have her entire family in the Forum, and so my mother, father, and uncle, Wesley John James, became members.

As our family grew, my parents weren't able to attend Forum meetings regularly. My grandmother almost always came for Sunday dinner after the meeting and would share with us what had been discussed. My oldest brother and I were very young, at most in first or second grade, and it was assumed we wouldn't understand, but I can still dimly recall parts of what was said. I can definitely remember the strange looks and laughs my brother and I got when we told the neighbors' kids that there had once been blue, green and orange people!

Early in her association with the Forum my mother asked Dr. Lena Sadler if they should teach their children the advanced UB ideas before the book was published. Dr. Lena replied that if they didn't, both they and the children would miss the chance of a lifetime. So, although we went to regular Sunday school and church, at home religious questions always received UB-oriented answers.

When I was 15 my grandmother asked me if I would like to become a Forum member. Coincidentally, the Sunday I signed the membership pledge and went to my first meeting, Alfred Leverenz, the son of Fred and Alice, was also attending his first meeting as a new member. While I completed reading all the papers on my own, I can't say I understood a great deal of what I'd read. Even after my grandmother had me memorize the various orders of angels, the names and capitals of the superuniverse divisions, and the difference between "triata" and "ultimata," the teachings still didn't always strike me as true. I was a "UB burn-out" at a very early age!

It was after the book was published and I started attending a study group founded by Al Leverenz, that I began to acquire a fuller understanding of the teachings. It was now possible to read the book as slowly as I wished, and to talk to others in various stages of reading and understanding, and to listen to their stories of how they'd found the book. This is when I more fully began to appreciate the UB myself—not the facts, but the *truths* of the book.

Finding these truths has been an ongoing process. Truth expands as one's ability to comprehend expands, until in eternity we find the Source of Truth.

C. BARRIE BEDELL: World War II was raging, rationing was in effect, and citizens of all ages were pouring all available money into savings bonds and stamps to support the war effort. Signs and posters and radio announcements barraged us with warnings to keep mum about defense activities: "Loose lips sink ships." Everyone was aware of the subversive "fifth column," spies and espionage agents working for the Nazis.

I was in my early teens, a mediocre high school student, obsessed with sports, and reasonably well informed on the progress of the war. At some point—I don't remember exactly when—I noticed that my folks, Clyde and Florence Bedell, would disappear like clockwork every Sunday afternoon and Wednesday evening. I began to question them, "Where are you going?"

"Oh, the Forum," was the usual reply. On Wednesday nights the answer would be, "The Seventy."

"What is the Forum? the Seventy?" I would press them. "What do you do?"

The typical response was maddeningly vague, not at all satisfying to an inquisitive teen: "We read and talk about a variety of subjects."

"Like what?" I would demand.

"We really can't say."

I began to harbor doubts that soon turned to suspicion. Something was terribly wrong. Then one blustery winter night I watched them depart in blizzard conditions. I began to think the unthinkable, that perhaps my parents were involved in something sinister. I came to the terrifying conclusion that they were involved in the Nazi fifth column.

I was greatly relieved when a few weeks later, on my fourteenth birthday, my parents announced: "Now we can tell you what we've been doing every Sunday and every Wednesday evening." They took me to 533 Diversey Parkway and introduced me to Dr. William Sadler, who told me about the Urantia Papers and invited me to attend the Forum. I was excited about what I was soon to experience and, as all who had joined before me, I took an oath of secrecy. It was a pivotal day in my life, for which I will forever be profoundly grateful.

Frequently on Saturdays I went to 533 where I would sit in a small, dark anteroom on the ground floor and read papers one at a time— typewritten manuscripts, each page pasted onto heavier stock, each paper supplied in a kraft envelope handed to me by Christy. Later, typeset galley proofs replaced the typewritten pages. My favorites were "Life Establishment on Urantia," "Government on a Neighboring Planet," and the Adam and Eve saga.

I also regularly attended Sunday meetings upstairs (except when away at school), always greeted by Wilfred and Anna Kellogg. Papers were read by Dr. Sadler or his son, Bill. During breaks I hung out at O'Connells Coffee Shop across the street with somewhat older members Tom and Carolyn Kendall, Nola Evans, Al Leverenz, Phil Copenhaver, Donna and Harry Rowley, and others. My brother Jeff started attending the Forum in 1951 when he was 13 or 14.

Disturbing as it was for a while, I am proud my folks honored their vow of secrecy, as did all but one or two Forum members from the very beginning till the day of publication in October, 1955.

KATHARINE J. "TICKY" HARRIES: I come from a background of Church of England, or Episcopal Church, members and clergy. As a child I was baptized, schooled and confirmed, and later I was married in the Church. I had no difficulty with my very solid belief in God, the Trinity, Jesus, angels, and life after death, and I did not believe in hell.

I wasn't an original member of the Forum, which began in the early '20s, nor were my parents, Lee Miller Jones and Katharine Lea Yarnall

Jones. A number of people had already been there and dropped out before we started.

I was quite young when I began to notice that every Sunday after church, after the "funnies" and Sunday dinner, Daddy would disappear for the afternoon. Daddy had been introduced to Dr. Sadler by Fred Leverenz and had joined the early Forum in 1932. It took him a while, but Daddy finally talked Mother into going with him. For many years thereafter she could not get rid of the feeling that "this is all so wonderful, and I believe it, but how could anything so wonderful possibly be true?" Then one day she realized that she didn't feel that way anymore—she *knew* it was true.

They started taking me with them to 533 Diversey Parkway when I was 11 or 12. Since I was much too young to attend the meetings I would visit downstairs with Mr. and Mrs. Kellogg and read or play games. Many times their daughter Ruth would spend the time with me. What a wonderful person she was! Dr. Sadler had his offices on the first floor and Ruth would take me in to see the lead-lined room which was used for X-rays and show me the specimens in the bottles of formaldehyde. On very warm days (there was no air conditioning then) we would go up to the roof and sit in the sun. Ruth was quite deaf from a childhood illness, but she could lip-read and we never had any trouble talking with one another.

A number of partial papers had been received and typed by the time I started going to the Sunday meetings when I was about 13. They were not complete as they are now in the Urantia Book, but were completed as more and more questions were asked. I remember my father spending many hours typing questions to submit to the contact personalities so that they could give us new information that would be especially meaningful to human beings.

I was not allowed to "join" the Forum until I was 16 (later the joining age was raised to 18). Joining consisted in having a private chat with Dr. Sadler so that he was sure you were truly committed to being a part of the group, studying the papers and attending the meetings every Sunday. There were only three valid reasons for being absent: your health, your family, or your job. And one was never to discuss what was going on or any of the teachings in the Papers with non-members.

Life was very different then from what it is now. On Sundays one went to church in the morning, went home for a big Sunday dinner around noon and then went to Forum still dressed in Sunday Best. That meant silk stockings and dress shoes for the ladies (we didn't have nylon stockings until after WW II), a dress or suit, and for some of them, a hat. The men wore a suit, white shirt and tie.

A paper was read aloud the first hour by Dr. Sadler or his son Bill, followed by a 15-minute break. Refreshments were not provided, so those who wanted to could go across the street for an ice cream or a Coke. The second hour was devoted to questions and discussion.

The room used for meetings was at the front of the building on the second floor, and was originally the living room of the apartment where Bill and Leone Sadler lived with their three children. Dr. Sadler and his wife, Dr. Lena, lived on the third floor. They had an elevator installed which was accessed from the foyer on each floor.

My father, mother and I went to the meetings year after year and during that time my maternal grandmother, Henrietta Lea "Dearie" Yarnall, who was widowed and came to live with us, started going to meetings too. Our group included males and females of all ages and educational levels and different church backgrounds.

While the Forum continued its Sunday meetings, another group was formed of the most committed members, which started meeting every Wednesday evening at 533. It was thought that these people would be the teachers once the book was printed. Attendance was mandatory and it was necessary to sign in each Wednesday. When all of us who wanted to join were counted, it was found that there were exactly seventy names—thus the name of the group, the Seventy.

In the last years of the Forum we would every so often be read a message from "The Boys Upstairs." This is true—it happened! You can imagine the excitement, the butterflies in the tummy—and then the messages stopped.

In the early '50s the plates for printing were ready, the money had been raised, and for a year or more before publication Forumites were asked to "subscribe" to buying and pre-paying for any number of books they would like. After a short period, when no more messages had been received, it was decided to go ahead, and R. R. Donnelley & Sons Co. was given the order to print. On the Sunday after the books were received, they were distributed. Can you imagine what tremendous excitement there was as the people carried them out by the box full on that day in 1955?

My father, along with many others, wrote letters of introduction for the Urantia Book and spent days and weeks wrapping and mailing them to senators, congressmen, members of the clergy and others in places of importance all over the country. We had such great expectations of the wonderful things this book was going to achieve. A few books were returned, unread, and the rest? We heard absolutely nothing!

Work was started by the Brotherhood to set up Urantia Societies, and on June 17, 1956, we met at 533 to sign the charter for First Urantia Society. Mary Lou Hales was chairman of the charter committee, my mother was secretary, and my father, mother, maternal grandmother and I were charter members.

Part II

1955-1969

JACQUES WEISS: Among the persons who were studying the typed manuscript of the Urantia Papers between 1935 and 1955 was a Miss Caroline Brown, a well-informed spiritualist with whom I had long conversations in New York during the winter of 1947-1948. At that time Miss Brown never alluded to the existence of the Papers.

In the early fifties this group received a celestial message stating that because of advances in planetary communications, the number of potential readers had become sufficient to justify the publication of the Papers in English with an initial printing of 10,000 copies, and that a translator in another language would be found to make it a truly worldwide work.

During Christmas time in 1955, as soon as the Papers appeared in English under the title of "The Urantia Book," Miss Brown sent me a copy and hinted that the publication message might be meant for me.

It took me the first months of 1956 to read the book.

Like many French people, I had been searching for a philosophy that could unite science and religion. After a thirty-year quest, I found it in the Urantia Book. Well aware of the difficulty of translating the book into French and publishing it, I nevertheless decided to consider myself, from that time on, as being on a mission. I translated the whole text by hand in twenty-nine large notebooks, constantly receiving immense aid from the invisible world—collaboration, health, inspiration, and money.

When the manuscript was well on the way, I asked my secretary to undertake the typing. Then I wrote to the Urantia Foundation, telling them that I had translated the book into French and requesting permission to publish it. There followed an endless period of negotiations and controls which finally resulted in an agreement for which it was necessary for me to go to Chicago in 1960.

When I arrived there on August 21, Dr. Sadler introduced me to an assembly of around seventy Urantians with the following words: "We received the order to publish the Urantia Book in 1955 because the time had come and because there would be a translator. I introduce to you today this translator, whose potential the spiritual world knew of before the translator, himself, knew of the existence of the work."

Naturally these exceptional circumstances led me to form a great friendship with Dr. Sadler in 1960. He was then 85 years old. In leaving him, I asked for his promise to stay alive until I could come again to see him and deliver to him in person the international fruit of the work. He kept his word.

MEREDITH J. SPRUNGER: My spiritual pilgrimage began at the age of four when I recall saying to myself, "There is something about life that I do not understand, but I'm going to find out." During the years that followed, my life was shaped by a series of peak experiences that led me through academic majors in philosophy and theology preparatory to ordination as a minister in the United Church of Christ.

After years of developing sermons and papers formulating my own spiritual experience that was centered in the religion *of* Jesus rather than the religion *about* Jesus, I realized that a new spiritual approach was needed in mainline Christian theology. I tentatively outlined a couple of books which needed to be written, and after some procrastination, I finally committed myself to the discipline of writing these books. Shortly after making this decision, the Urantia Book was placed in my hands.

In December of 1955 my wife Irene and I had stopped in to visit our friends, Dr. and Mrs. Edward Brueseke, in South Bend, Indiana. In addition to his pastoral activities, Ed served as chairman of a theological commission in the Evangelical and Reformed Church (later united with the Congregational Christian denomination to become the United Church of Christ). During the course of the visit Ed picked up a big blue book and handed it to me, saying, "Judge Louis Hammerschmidt (a member of his congregation) gave me this book. Some businessmen think this is a new Bible." I looked at the table of contents and read chapter headings like "The Messenger Hosts of Space," written by One High in Authority, and "The Corps of the Finality," authored by a Divine

Counselor and One Without Name and Number! As I handed the book back to Ed, we had a hearty laugh about businessmen thinking they had a new Bible. I assumed that that would be the last I would see of the book.

At the time I was vice-president of the Indiana-Michigan Conference and Judge Hammerschmidt was the layperson on our conference board. In January I picked up the judge to attend a board meeting in Jackson, Michigan. During the trip Hammerschmidt brought up the topic of spiritualism, which he did not accept, and was a bit surprised that I had made a study of it. After a pause he turned to me and said, "Say, I've got a book that I would like to have you read and tell me what you think of it." I knew he was referring to the Urantia Book, but to avoid hurting his feelings I replied, "Okay, Judge. Send it to me."

When the book arrived I set it aside, not wanting to waste my time reading what appeared to be either esoteric nonsense or some elaborate system of theosophy. Periodically, I would read a bit in it here and there but I was not impressed. That summer I took it along on vacation but things didn't get boring enough for me to look at the book. In September I realized that I would be in a meeting with Hammerschmidt in October and I had to read something and tell him what I thought about it.

Looking over the table of contents, I saw it had a section on the life and teachings of Jesus. I thought that with my theological training I could make short work of this section. As I started reading I did not find what I'd expected to find—something like *The Aquarian Gospel of Jesus the Christ*, by Levi. The story of the early life of Jesus was more believable than the accounts one finds in the apocryphal stories of the boyhood of Jesus. It was something that might reasonably have happened. As I proceeded to that aspect of the life of Jesus covered by the New Testament I was even more impressed. Some of the traditional theological problems were handled by the events of the story in a way that made more sense than anything I had ever read. I found the Urantia Book's narrative to be solidly rooted in the New Testament realities. There were times when I read with tears streaming down my face. When I finished reading "The Life and Teachings of Jesus" I was theologically and spiritually inspired. Whoever had produced a life of Jesus of this quality, I thought, must have something significant to say in the rest of the book.

Thus motivated, I started with the Foreword and read the entire book. I discovered that the first three quarters of the book was even more amazing and profound than "The Life and Teachings of Jesus"! The teachings of the Urantia Book resonated and harmonized with my experience and highest thinking. The substance of the two books I had planned to write was expressed far better here than I could have possibly done. If this is not an authentic picture of spiritual reality, I said to myself, it is the way it *ought* to be! Science, philosophy, and religion were integrated more effectively in the Urantia Book than in any other philosophical or theological system known to me. There was no doubt in my mind that this was the most inspiring and authentic picture of spiritual reality available to humankind.

I gave copies of the Urantia Book to around a dozen of my colleagues and all of them except one—who admitted that he hadn't read it—confirmed my evaluation of its high quality. Our clergy group spent several years interviewing the people connected with the publication of the book and researching events associated with its origin. Since then I have devoted myself to sharing the Urantia Book with college students and the clergy of mainline Christianity.

GENE JOYCE: In the spring of 1956 my husband and I stopped by to pick up our friends Agnes and Bob so we could all attend a performance of the Theater in the Round at Fair Park in Dallas. I don't remember the play we saw, but I can still recall Agnes's exact words as we entered their house: "Gene, come and see this crazy book a friend of Bob's sent him from Australia!" It was accompanied by a note that read, *"This book has meant so much to me and my family that I wanted you to have a copy,"* and it was signed, *"Clyde Bedell."*

Even without time to peruse the book, I was impressed by its size, the excellent bindings, and the quality of the paper. A quick glance through the table of contents whetted my interest. What was this Urantia Book? Considering what it must have cost to produce a book of such quality, this was no fly-by-night scam. The following day I ordered two copies from the publisher in Chicago—first printings, no less—for $10 each!

It seemed quite a coincidence that scarcely two weeks later, while having dinner with my friend Helen (who was executive secretary to G. B. Dealey, head of *The Dallas Morning News*), she mentioned the word "Urantia." For some time she had been telling me stories about a fascinating man named Bill Sadler who came down from Chicago periodically to visit his business accounts in Dallas. As it happened, Bill was in town and it was part of Helen's job to schedule his appointments while he was here, giving her a chance to get to know him.

Only that morning Mr. Dealey had asked her to find out from Bill some charity or foundation to which *The News* could give money in memory of Bill's son, Billy, who had recently died. After some persistence on her part, Bill Sadler finally said, "Well, if you insist, they could make a donation to the Urantia Foundation."

"Why, Helen, that's the name of that crazy book!" I said, and told her the story about Clyde Bedell sending the Urantia Book from Australia to Bob's family in Dallas.

From the time I was nine years old when my mother died, questions about survival after death and matters relating to religion had been plaguing my mind. I wanted to know why we are here, where we are going, and what is the purpose of it all. Although I believed that Jesus was the Son of God I didn't much like the version of his personality as given in the Bible. Through the Baptists, Presbyterians, Episcopalians, Methodists, Congregationalists and Lutherans, I searched for acceptable answers to my questions. They either didn't have answers or the answers they gave didn't make sense to me.

After reading the Urantia Book for ten years as superb science fiction I decided it was exactly what it said it was and it began to change my life. Jesus as presented in the book was such a revelation to me that it allowed me to come closer to him and to appreciate him as the perfect model of the Father's love. He became my hero and the example of all the attributes I admired and could try to emulate.

The Urantia Book enabled me to abandon anxiety and eliminate my fears. It also helped preserve my sanity when my son Christopher died at 19. I thank our Father for this revelation every day of my life.

GUS WALSTROM: Some boys used to come to the canyon where we lived in Colorado to listen to some occult lectures on Sundays. As we were thirteen miles from Castle Rock and there was nowhere for them to get a meal, we would invite the boys to our house for dinner after the morning lecture. They were students at the University of Colorado at Boulder. They had visited the Urantia Book study group in Denver and were talking about it, and one Sunday in July 1956 Roger Darnell brought with him the Urantia Book all wrapped up like a box of candy.

I started reading it, and by the end of the year I had finished it. My wife Marie read it after I did, and then we asked Roger to bring three more books, which we soon sold. After that we started ordering the books in ten-book lots. A few of us later got together for a Urantia Book reading once a week. From then on we always kept some books.

Through the years we have distributed over seventy Urantia Books. Marie made heavy plastic covers for all the books to preserve the fly covers. Dear Marie, she is now on the mansion worlds.

WALLY ZIGLAR: Back in 1957 my twin brother Richard was attending a flying saucer convention with his friend Max Miller, who had just published the acclaimed *Flying Saucers—Fact or Fiction*. Bored with the lecture, they went next door to browse inside an occult bookstore. It was there that Richard spotted the Urantia Book nestled between several other monumental works, including *A Treatise on Cosmic Fire* by Alice Bailey and *The Secret Doctrine* by Madame Blavatsky. Max said he could get any book for Richard at fifty per cent off list price through his publisher, DeVorss, so Richard bought several, including the Urantia Book.

Only a handful of people were aware of the UBook in those days. I gave the book little notice until my dad, after reading a few chapters, suggested I take a look at it to see what I thought, and left it on the living room coffee table for my comments. At the time, Richard was working on his Master's Degree in psychology at Pepperdine University and I was doing graduate work in finance and real estate at USC. I'd already had the misfortune of reading about fifty pages of the very lengthy *Cosmic Fire* and thought Richard had gone off the deep end; critiquing his spacy books was not exactly what I had in mind for my weekends. None of the other titles caught my interest either, so the Urantia Book sat there for a while.

In the '50s my parents owned a duplex in Hancock Park, a neighborhood in Los Angeles. My grandparents occupied the upstairs unit. It was customary for my grandmother, whenever she was going to a luncheon, to come down to my parents' unit and wait in our living room for a friend to pick her up. One summer day, Maria Culbertson, who had waited years for the Urantia Book to be published and who possessed one of the first copies in Los Angeles, came over to take my grandmother to lunch. Maria tells me that when her eyes fell upon this big blue book resting on the coffee table, she almost had a coronary. She thought she had the only copy in Los Angeles, and so seeing another book only a block away gave her a real adrenalin boost. The idea crossed her mind that it had somehow made *The New York Times* bestseller list without her knowing it, thanks to the advertising genius of Clyde Bedell.

After gathering her senses, she learned from Grandmother that the twins and their dad had recently found the book, not from a bestseller list but from the shelf of an occult bookstore in Fontana, California. Afterwards, Maria called back to encourage me to follow Richard and read the Urantia Book, and that I did in the summer of 1958.

Since then I have read it eight times in its entirety. Over the years I have given the book to many people, some notables being Werner Von Braun, Manly P. Hall, Richard Nixon and my neighbors Will and Ariel Durant. I have had many exhilarating moments and one memorable disappointment: I gave the book to a seminary professor who swore it was demon-inspired. To him the doctrine of Christianity centered on "the blood of Christ shed for our sins," and he judged me to be in strong need of repentance for having read such a powerful work of the devil. I pray for him occasionally.

Together with my brother and dad I have placed numerous books in public libraries and some half a hundred in naval ship libraries where many a sailor has become a captive reader. I have often wondered where those big blue books go when the ships are decommissioned and put in mothballs. It would be nice to have a few of those first printings back.

ILA AND LOREN HALL: In 1957 my husband Loren and I were given a pamphlet by a naturopathic doctor who was treating our little boy who had contracted polio in 1949. The pamphlet advertised a UFO meeting near Mountain View, Missouri. UFOs were something we didn't know much about so we decided to attend the three-day meeting scheduled for that June.

The next year we went again. At that meeting we listened to a talk given by a man from Minnesota who mentioned the Urantia Book, which he'd brought along. As we were loading up the car to start home, I said to Loren, "Wait for me. I just want to look through the books." I went back and on a shelf I saw this big blue book—the Urantia Book.

I opened it to Paper 18, "The Universe of Universes." How great it was reading about all the universes and the inhabited planets! I ran back to the car and told Loren that there was a book in there I wanted.

"How much is it?" he asked.

"Twelve dollars," I told him.

"I don't have that much money with me now," he replied.

"Let me see if I can find the man who brought it," I insisted, "because I have to have that book!" I went back and found him, and the man said he'd mail me the book when he again heard from me. It took me another month to persuade Loren that I really *had* to have that book!

Finally one day the book came in the mail. It was the greatest book I had ever possessed and the truths contained in it thrilled me. From the moment I first opened the Urantia Book at that meeting I knew it was true and I have never doubted it. Both of us have been so thankful ever since for that UFO meeting where I found the book. I believe we were meant to be there.

[Ila and Loren Hall were the backbone of early Urantia organizational activities in the greater Kansas City area, where they opened their home to regional gatherings and sponsored the first Kansas City study group, the Pathfinders. Both have now passed on to the mansion worlds.]

BILL BRYAN: On hot Kansas summer nights, back in the 1930s, my family sometimes slept outside on the hay rack to escape the heat. We would count meteors, study the stars and speculate on whether there were other worlds and, if so, whether they worshipped the same God we did. My parents tried hard to answer our questions but sometimes I dropped off to sleep hearing Mother or Dad saying, "Willie, that's a great mystery. If God wanted us to know, he would tell us."

Time passed and we survived the Depression, dust storms and cyclones. I watched the sky as I worked in the fields, now and then seeing an airplane, and my imagination took wings. Eventually I had my first ride in an airplane and subsequently joined the Army Air Corps

About this time, something happened that changed my life. I was riding the bus home from work one evening reading *Popular Science* magazine and saw some photographs of alien spaceships taken by one George Adamski near Mt. Palomar, California. The idea took root in my mind: We are not alone in the universe!

I don't remember how I learned about the annual UFO conventions at Giant Rock airstrip on the high desert of Southern California near Yucca Valley, but in 1953 I drove out there from Kansas to investigate.

In 1956 we moved to Utah and were able to attend the annual conventions more easily. It was difficult to know what, if anything, to believe. The people who spoke about their contacts were obviously sincere and I was inclined to accept much of what they said at face value; I stored away the remainder for future reference.

It was during our last visit in 1958 that I found the Urantia Book. There, on a table on the runway of that small airstrip, were a number of metaphysical and other books tended by a little old lady from Allen's Book Shelf of Fontana, California. While browsing, I saw a big blue book containing a paper entitled "Government on a Neighboring Planet." I knew I had to have that book! We spent our last $12 for it. It was a first edition, published in 1955.

For almost fifteen years I read it alone, unlearning many things and gaining new insights and appreciation for other aspects of reality. My first-edition UB gave no street address for the Urantia Foundation in Chicago, which made it difficult for me to find other readers. In the late 1960s I moved back to Kansas from the West. I had given up Mormonism and was exploring other organized religions. Naturally, I thought that Christians who loved the Lord would be receptive to the beautiful Urantia revelation, and I like to feel that I have been instrumental to some extent in spreading the good word.

Things happened fast for me in the early 1970s. Imagine my surprise when I finally learned that there were "conventions" nearby where many people came to share the delights of the revelation. The 1971 *Concordex* by Clyde Bedell was a wonderful adjunct to my learning. I began to meet other truth seekers who enriched my life, among them Loren and Ila Hall. The Halls found their first Urantia Book at a UFO meeting in Missouri so we had something in common. I first attended an international conference of Urantia Book readers in Vancouver, B.C. in 1978, where I met Christy, Vern Grimsley and many other early leaders of the revelation. The first regional meeting I attended was at Fountainhead Lodge on Lake Eufaula, Oklahoma. In 1987, I was a founding member of the Heart of America Urantia Society. In 1988, I had the privilege of introducing the book to my present wife, Eugenia.

The Urantia Book has been such a blessing in my life. It answered my childhood yearnings. Through TUB, God is telling me what I had always wanted to know. And I have learned that I am a cosmic citizen on an eternal adventure. Thank you, Lord!

ELDRED COCKING: In the fall of 1959, I picked up a copy of the Urantia Book while browsing in a Chicago bookstore. Over the next five or ten minutes I perused the table of contents and read a few random passages of the text. I concluded that the book was probably just another occult-metaphysical production. I set the book down on the display table and briefly wondered if it would be worthwhile to start reading this weighty volume. The next day I returned to the bookstore with no doubt in my mind. I had definitely decided to buy and read the Urantia Book. It was a decision which was to deeply influence my thinking and actions in the years ahead. What were the determining factors behind this decision? Why was I willing to pay any attention to this strange book? From whence came the urge to become acquainted with the contents of this lengthy treatise by completely unknown authors?

After several decades of reading and thinking about the Urantia Book, I have little doubt that spiritual guidance was the decisive factor in my finding and studying the book, just as it was the same spirit leading which influenced my human mind to persist in a quest for truth over several decades before encountering and receiving the book's revelatory message.

During my long quest for mental and spiritual enlightenment I had learned much about the lives and thinking of spiritual teachers and leaders, philosophers, theologians, and scientists. Most of these personalities and their writings were interesting, a few were inspiring, but—with one exception—none were both inspiring *and* convincing. That exception was Jesus of Nazareth as revealed in the New Testament.

The problem I had with Jesus was the fragmentary, incomplete biblical record of his life and teachings, together with the multiplicity of sectarian interpretations of his message. I believed that Jesus was the greatest figure in human history, even though I realized that I understood all too little of his message and its implications. I longed to know more about this mysterious son of God.

The Urantia Book was a marvelous answer to my felt need for more enlightenment about Jesus and his heavenly Father. Here was a new revelation of Jesus and a vastly improved presentation of his saving message. And the wealth of additional background information about the cosmos and its creator was tremendously impressive and illuminating.

In summary, a persistent hunger for truth led me to find the Urantia Book and stay with it. Spiritual guidance prepared me for the new revelation and ensured my acceptance of this gift from God.

POLLY PARKE FRIEDMAN: My mom, Grace Walker, was a member of the Forum in the '40s, but I wasn't at all interested in her activities at the time. I was an intensely independent teenager who thought her mother was nice but a little wacky for her age.

After college, and two years into a teaching career, I was on the brink of marriage and went into a panic about my decision. Because my mother paid for his services, I went to see Dr. Sadler for advice. He was very formal, just like the psychiatrists in the movies. A large dog, like a Great Dane, stood at his side as a sentinel of affirmation. The doctor told me that my and my fiance's statistics indicated that the marriage would not work out. Again I thought I knew best, and went through with the marriage to show this doctor he was wrong. Alas, years later, the marriage ended as predicted.

In the meantime I moved from Illinois to California and became a Valley Girl. My mom, again on her toes, sent me a copy of the first printing of the Urantia Book in 1955. I put it on the shelf where I stored odds and ends and it sat there for about five years.

Sometime in 1960, while I was experiencing low physical health and mental uncertainties, I took the book down from the shelf, drew the drapes in the bedroom, shut the door, and began to read in secret. I was going to prove this was all a hoax and expose the real writers—whoever they were!

Well, the real truth started slowly to get to me in a big way. It was months before I told my mom, and then only after I had visited the one and only Los Angeles study group, then held in Hancock Park. There I met some beautiful people who, I discovered, were quite normal—at least for L.A.! That was the beginning.

Trying to be cautious, I held off joining the Los Angeles Urantia Society until 1965. It's been surprises and crises ever since, but the teachings have become an inseparable part of me. I'd like to be able to tell Doc Sadler that he was right on all counts, and that I liked his dog. My mom already knows.

HAL KETTELL: Sometime in the early '60s I was working on a fine elderly gentleman in my dental chair. His name was Fred Squires. We talked about philosophy and religion. I was searching even then. In my youth my mother had exposed me to Christian Science; I had been a Sunday school teacher, superintendent, Christian Education chair, elder and trustee of a large Presbyterian church; I had looked into reincarnation,

Edgar Cayce, pyramids, and UFOs, but something was always missing and I was ready for something new. At one point I made the "mistake" of taking my hands out of Fred's mouth long enough for him to say, "I have a book that I think you might be interested in." He then told me a little about it. It sounded quite interesting, so I asked if I could borrow it.

"No way!" he replied, "But you can buy one at the bookstore."

I was not in the habit of buying everything recommended to me in the office, but I guess my guardian angel—or midwayers or my Thought Adjuster—must have been needling me, because I made a trip to Vroman's Bookstore in Pasadena to buy one. At the time, of course, I had no idea that I had a guardian angel or Thought Adjuster, but something motivated me to pursue the issue.

At the bookstore, when I asked for the Urantia Book (Fred had written the name down for me), the salesgirl said, "The *what* book?" When I repeated the name, she said, "Okay, I'll look it up." She soon found that it could be ordered from the publisher in Chicago, but that it would cost $12.50. Feeling like a big spender, and having made a special trip to the store, I told her to go ahead.

In about two weeks I received a phone call saying my book had arrived. "What book?" I asked.

"The Urantia Book you ordered," came the reply.

Well, that was the start of a new adventure into the universe for me. After thumbing through the table of contents and scanning the list of authors with all of their weird names, I decided I had an enormous, expensive, paper-pack of science fiction. I enjoyed science fiction, so I started with the geological development of our planet. It was fascinating, and within a couple of weeks I was hooked on the Urantia Book as fact and not fiction.

Fred subsequently invited me to a study group at Helen Steen's home in Pasadena. Helen, Fred, and Fred's sister Julia Fenderson were all from Chicago and had been a part of the Forum with Dr. Sadler. It was a fascinating study group, whose members prepared charts for daily reading, summaries of the apostles, lists of Jesus' earth family, and some beautiful color drawings of the universes by Georgia Gecht.

After I had read enough to know what it was about, I bought several more first-printing copies and gave them to my relatives. The results were predictable: one fundamentalist sister burned the book, calling it the work of the devil; one brother put it on the shelf of his library, and it was years before he blew the dust off it. So I learned. Now I just occasionally sow a few seeds in the hope that they will take root and grow. Since then, a couple of my siblings have graduated to the mansion worlds, and I'm sure they were surprised on arrival.

Now the blanks in my faith are filled in—the i's are dotted and the t's crossed. I have complete faith and trust in God as my Father and friend as I search to reach him. He is personal and real to me now, rather than a man in the sky with a long beard, waiting for me to make a mistake so that St. Peter can write it down in my book of life. Best of all, the book has given me a real concept of Jesus as Michael of Nebadon, my elder brother and creator. My life is now becoming fulfilled, and I am more at peace with the real world of the spirit. What more can I ask for than to enjoy the journey?

BEVERLY WOLD: The Urantia Book and I came together late in 1962. A copy was loaned to my husband by a Riverside County planning associate as a result of their discussing philosophy and religion on their lunch breaks. The friend had used the Urantia Book as a reference book in a course he took while getting his engineering degree at USC in Los Angeles. I found out later that it had been placed in the university library by Julia Fenderson soon after it was published. So the ripples of this epochal revelation pushed out to be discovered by a truth seeker who was designing parks in Riverside, California. So it was, that my husband brought this big, blue, two-inch-thick, five-pound book home and put it on our bedside nightstand for some shared reading before we went to sleep.

My husband had a busy job, and I was in charge of a large therapy department at what was then Riverside County's largest general acute hospital, with four main treatment areas in various buildings, with quite a large staff of therapists and trained volunteers. I wanted something not heavy but gripping and educational before calling it a day, like an Irving Stone novel—not a 2,097-page gargantuan collection of papers seemingly authored by outer-space entities—but I thought, well, let's give it a try.

It was my turn to read and I let the book open where it would. It spread open at the place where it describes the earth being peopled by red, yellow, blue, orange, green, and indigo races. Well, we surmised that this might be better than Irving Stone, Orson Welles, and a few others collectively. So we started at the beginning. We were greatly inspired and thrilled by the enlarged concept of God—his nature and attributes as set forth in the first three papers. It was like putting flesh and skin on the bare skeleton-picture outline in the Bible.

Often I have read the first and last parts of a book to see if I want to read the in-between. So we turned to Part IV to read about the seventh incarnation of our universe creator, Michael, coming to this earth as a mortal, to demonstrate by his life and teachings the true will of God and God's many attributes, as nearly as mortals are able to grasp. It was about Christmas-time, and reading about the love and compassion of Michael for his creatures was very touching.

It didn't seem to matter who wrote the Urantia Book, for as we read, it filled in all the gaps and unanswered spaces in the Bible about the life of Jesus, his earthly family, and what he did in those missing years before he started his direct ministry to his chosen disciples and the multitudes of his time. And so many other questions were answered in simple, gripping, and eloquent prose. The Urantia Book made the message of Jesus, so sketchy and abbreviated in the Bible, come alive in a vibrant, meaningful way. It gave direction for everyday, present living, and it made the teachings of the Bible understandable, too.

Our spirit guides were lovingly and gently leading us on, for we discovered that some friends in Riverside had also found the Urantia Book through a New Age study group. They had received a notice from Georgia Gecht, then secretary of the First Urantia Society of Los Angeles (FUSLA), of a meeting the first Sunday of the month to be held at a bank in Culver City. We all went to find out more about the Urantia Book from them. Julia Fenderson was at the door, along with others, warmly greeting and introducing people. The meeting was very inspiring, the hospitality so warm and sincere—and no collection plate was passed.

We returned many times and soon started a study group in Riverside. It was the beginning of a long association with FUSLA, multiple associations with Urantia Brotherhood all over the United States and other countries, and deep spiritual experiences, with an expanding knowledge of the journey to eternity as road-mapped in the Urantia Book.

JAMES IRWIN: In 1963 I was working for a supermarket as a part-time stocking clerk in Ft. Lauderdale, Florida. One evening, as I was gathering baskets from the parking lot, a woman approached me and asked, "Is your name James? James Irwin?"

"Yes," I answered, "and how might I help you?"

"Emma wants you to have this," she said, and handed me a large blue book.

"Emma who?" I asked her.

"Emma Christensen," she replied, then turned around and walked away. To this day I have no idea who the person was who delivered the book to me.

When I returned to the store, I opened the book to the first page and wrote Emma Christensen's name inside. I was only 17 at the time, but any book of a theological nature always caught my attention.

Immediately after receiving the book, I began to read it non-stop, day and night, until I finished it. I even took days off from work to complete it.

The Urantia Book has been my companion through all of my life's events. It went with me during my tour in Vietnam, on railroad trips to Japan, Hong Kong, Australia, Thailand, and on side trips to Korea, Cambodia, Laos, and China. (One time it took a side trip without me, but that's another story.) The Urantia Book has served me well these 35 years. Many kind folks have offered to replace it for me, as the cover has long since come off, and pages that came out are tucked inside, but I consider I'm only just beginning to break it in.

Eighteen years after the book had been given to me, I decided it was time to thank "Emma," so I called the Urantia Foundation in Chicago. I knew nothing of the Foundation, Emma, or anything else surrounding the book's origin. The purpose of my call was to thank this kind lady for giving me the book. Although people have since told me that Emma didn't answer the phone at the Foundation anymore by then, on that day she did. I asked if I might speak to Ms. Christensen.

"I am she," she replied.

The next few moments were extraordinary. "My name is James Irwin . . ." I began, but before I could add, "But you probably don't know me," she exclaimed, "Then you got the book?"

"Ahh, umm . . . yes," I replied.

"I'm happy that you called," she said, "even if it has taken you a while."

We talked of many things—the midwayers and their presentiments, the celestial hosts, various spirit beings, Michael-Jesus. She expressed her belief that her time was almost at an end here, and we spoke of the morontia life yet to be experienced.

It has been my privilege, honor, and humble opportunity to have had this book for these many years. I may be deluded, but I am convinced that my Thought Adjuster, guardian angels, and other hosts unknown to me placed these theological concepts in my life's path. Although I never met Emma face-to-face in this life, I look forward to our morontia life meeting. I do not know how Emma knew of me, but I shall always treasure our unforgettable phone conversation. Shortly thereafter, Emma left us to continue on in her life's journey.

Emma was the last living member of the six contact commissioners, and was the individual who typed the entire Urantia Book from the original manuscript.

BILL HAZZARD: In 1966, about a year after I retired as a captain in the U.S. Navy, my late wife Dorothy and I bought a house in Mission Hills, San Diego, next door to a man named Harry Lavoie. Harry lived alone and was a vociferous reader. He would comment to me on things he had read, and I in turn I would comment on things I'd read to him, and we would exchange books. One day he passed the Urantia Book over to me for loan, but without a single comment.

I soon realized the book was something that could not be digested in a short time, and I found it so interesting that I decided I must have a copy of my own. Since a new Urantia Book cost $15 in those days and I was afraid Dorothy would consider that too much, I phoned around to used book stores and located a copy in Hollywood for $9. (Later on I found out that this particular book had been stolen from a man in San Francisco. Among a lot of scribbling in the book, I recognized a name from the Los Angeles readership, and when I showed that person the book, he indeed turned out to be the rightful owner. It had been given to him by his girlfriend in Hawaii. I returned it to him and only then did I buy a new copy for myself.)

I was deeply interested in this book from the word go because it was about theology and many other interesting topics. And while it was in some sense hardly believable because it was so "far out," I took the whole book on faith.

One experience I had had confirmed for me that at least some of it was true. This event occurred in 1918, when I was not quite six years old and living in the small town of Placentia, California, thirty miles east of Los Angeles. Another boy and I were what would nowadays be called "hanging out." When we saw a shiny new car coming into town from the direction of Los Angeles, we both had a primal urge to throw something at it. My friend threw a rock, but I couldn't find a rock so I threw a corn cob. Both missiles landed on target. The infuriated driver stopped the car in the middle of an intersection and started chasing us. The other boy got away and I tried to flee by climbing a small tree in front of my house, a tree that had been planted on my first birthday. The driver was shaking the tree and demanding to know where I lived. Although later I didn't mind disappointing my mother by getting a sailor's tattoo on my arm, at this moment in the tree, not wanting to break her heart, I pointed to a house a couple of doors away. The man departed in disgust, probably knowing I was lying but needing to get back to his car. Immediately I was surrounded by what felt like a golden aura and a comforting feeling, which for years I couldn't understand. But I never forgot the experience, and I puzzled over it for some fifty years until I read on p. 1187 about the arrival of the Thought Adjuster and the birth of the soul.

VIRGINIA LEE HALLOCK: My religious background was eclectic. My father, an intellectual, had been a Christian agnostic but an inveterate searcher for truth. My mother was a Southern Baptist, and it was the Baptist Church and its Sunday school that I had attended in Washington until we moved to Oregon when I was 13. Finding the Baptist Church too conservative, I drifted over to the Episcopal Church most of my friends were attending.

Subsequently, I was confirmed by the Bishop of Eastern Oregon and became a pillar of the Episcopal Church, remaining so for several years. I was president of the Altar Guild, and was the only woman in the state on the Bishop's Committee.

My studies, I must add, had not been confined to Episcopalianism. I had read Emmett Fox, Ernest Holmes, Judge Troward, and had even studied with the Rosicrucians. When I moved to Salem, I visited both Episcopal churches, where I felt the emphasis was more social than spiritual. So, for a time, I church-hopped. I even attended some Baha'i meetings which I thoroughly enjoyed. A friend introduced me to Woodland Chapel, which was a Religious Science church. The minister was a thinker, a real searcher for truth, so I lingered there long enough to take three years of metaphysical philosophy.

On waking one morning I'd meditated as usual and carried a special thought for truth, asking for a more poignant answer than I had heretofore found. Before I even glanced at the morning paper, I picked up the Urantia Book that my friend Marion had left for me the night before. I had known Marion only a few months, but she was a responsive and generous friend. Knowing my interest in religion and philosophy, she had left a stack of books from her own library on my table while visiting me the previous evening.

Scanning the table of contents and perusing it further, I was hooked. I started to read from the beginning, and unlike all the other literature I had assimilated, this book really made sense. I could read, at first, only a few pages at a time. I called Marion and told her that it would take me at least two years to read the book, and that I hoped she wasn't in any hurry for it.

As my interest in the book developed, so did hers, and we decided that I should get my own copy. None of the bookstores in Salem had it in stock, and only one had even heard of it.

The Ruff Times investment group, of which Marion was the leader, met at her house monthly, and at the September meeting one of us mentioned the Urantia Book. Surprisingly, Bob, one of the members, overheard the comment and told us of his long acquaintance with the book. It was through him that we visited a study group in Corvallis and met Julia Fenderson. It has been clear sailing since then.

I am not sorry for my searching and my studying. All the years of various church experiences and omnivorous studying paved the way for my acceptance of the Urantia Book.

The book that Marion lent me, by the way, had belonged to Helen Steen whom Julia Fenderson knew well from their days together in Chicago as members of the Forum. Helen's son had given it to Marion along with other books from Helen's library.

DICK BAIN: I found the Urantia Book in 1966 when I was in my twenties, but I was not looking for it. Nevertheless, it was not an accident; my philosophy professor had assigned a reading from this book. The assignment was to read a section regarding the nature of God, which I did. I was impressed by the quality of what I had read. When I noticed that the book also had some sections dealing with science and astronomy, I immediately had a strong attraction to it. I checked the book out from the college library over the summer and read as much of it as I could while keeping up with my three engineering classes.

I was an avid science-fiction reader, but as I recall the book didn't seem like science fiction or fantasy to me. It had enough of the ring of truth that I decided I had finally found something spiritual that was worth reading. In fact, I felt compelled to read it. During the fall semester I contacted the professor who had given me the Urantia Book reading assignment and learned that he and his wife hosted a study group for this book at their home. When I attended my first meeting, he sold me a copy and I was on my way to becoming a lifelong Urantia Book student.

My relationship with God before the Urantia Book was pretty casual. Yeah, God existed out there somewhere but it didn't much affect me unless I hit a crisis and needed some help. After I read the book, I realized that he's not only *out there*, he's *in here*. One of the book's most profound teachings, for me, is that God, through our Thought Adjuster, is a constant companion and friend. And when I think that everyone I pass on the street has this God presence in them, I am in awe. It makes me think I ought to respect that inner light in each person, no matter what I may think of the person otherwise.

Though it was the science that pulled me into the book, it was the spiritual content that kept me there. I have since found some flaws in the science content, but the spiritual teachings transcend that of any book or philosophy I have ever encountered. I was led to conclude that this book is, at least in part, a revelation, and as such it is the most important book I'll ever read. I remain profoundly grateful to the professor who gave me that reading assignment—Dr. Meredith Sprunger—who has retired from college life but not from promoting the Urantia Book.

JOEL REHNSTROM: For several years I was a member of an international Rosicrucian order. Then, in 1961, I became enormously interested in UFOs as a result of reading George Adamski's *Inside the Spaceships*. I started a small publishing company and had the first four UFO books by Adamski and Daniel W. Fry published in Finnish. Together with other enthusiasts here we then formed the Interplanetist Society and began to collect more UFO information from Finland and all over the world. We were mostly interested in the cosmic messages by contact personalities like Adamski, Fry and others.

In 1965 a Finnish-American lady, who believed she was also a contact person and had written a book about her experiences, brought the Urantia Book to Finland. A few members of the Interplanetist Society may have ordered the book as early as 1965. I opened it in the summer of 1966, became enormously fascinated, skimmed it thoroughly in a few days, and immediately saw that this book really contained the *supermessage*. By this time the Interplanetist Society had many hundreds of members all over Finland. For many of us the UFO interest faded as we began to concentrate on the Urantia Book.

I visited the Urantia headquarters at 533 Diversey Parkway in Chicago early in 1972 and took part in the Lake Forest gatherings in 1980 and 1988. Over the years I became good friends with many readers in Chicago, including Christy [Emma L. Christensen]. I stayed with Christy at 533 and had some good conversations with her during all my trips to Chicago.

In 1968 we started to translate the UB into Finnish, on a voluntary basis and as a group effort. The first translation contract with the Foundation was signed in early 1971, and by 1975 the translation was completed and in mimeographed form. The mimeographed papers had been distributed all along in the translation process to a support group of some one hundred people from all over Finland. We also started to import English-language Urantia Books ten or twenty at a time and soon persuaded the biggest bookstore in Helsinki to stock the book and import it directly. In this way more than a thousand English-language books had already been sold here before the Finnish translation was good enough to be published in book form in 1993.

The translation support group later formed the basis for the Finnish Urantia Society. Most recently I have been occupied as a member of a small team which is translating the UB into Swedish.

STEFAN TALLQVIST: Finland received its first copy of the Urantia Book in the early 1960s. It was sent by Margit Mustapha, a woman from Santa Barbara, California, to a Finnish group calling themselves the Interplanetists. Some of the members of this group who became interested in the Urantia Book were Joel Rehnstrom and Kerstin Dyhr. Rehnstrom very soon started a project to translate the book into Finnish. Others made translations of varying quality at an early stage. Dyhr was the treasurer of a long-established Finnish association for psychic research, Sallskapet for Psyksisk Forskning i Finland r.f., which was founded in about 1908 at the University of Helsinki and is one of the oldest of its kind in the world.

Interested in physics, astronomy and parapsychology, in 1961 I started my studies at the University of Technology in Helsinki and soon joined

Sallskapet for Psyksisk Forskning, later serving as chairman for about ten years. In 1965 I found the Urantia Book through that society and saw it in other places as well. Joel Rehnstrom gave me my first book in 1967 as soon as the second printing appeared. At first I found the book highly interesting, but after discovering what I thought were errors in some astronomical matters, my interest for several years was only mild.

In the early 1970s I worked on my Licentiate thesis in radio technology (antennas) and astronomy, and in 1974 took an active part in the construction of the first Finnish microwave radio telescope. I worked as an engineer and astronomer for a long time. As the years passed I grew to know more about astronomy, and several of the "errors" I'd found in the Urantia Book were vindicated by developing astronomical knowledge. As a result, I became seriously interested in the book, and have been so ever since. Several Finnish newspapers wrote about my involvement with it in the early 1980s, focusing particularly on my model of the electron which I derived from the book.

I have participated in UBook discussion on the Internet since 1993; lately I have been dialoguing with the Skeptics in Finland.

The large amount of scientific material, and the scientific convergence of facts, that I have investigated over the years from a variety of branches of human knowledge, undoubtedly point to the fact that the Urantia Book is a genuine cosmic message to humankind.

MARY J. MICHAEL: In the ninth grade, sometime in the 1960s, I was doing research for a paper on dreams and dream theory. Between Sigmund Freud and Carl Jung, the Cleveland Public Library had planted the Urantia Book. At that time I assumed that the Urantia Foundation was just another research foundation in psychology. Since this book was on the cannot-take-out-of-the-library list, I made little headway in reading it once a month.

In college, I purchased my own copy for the monumental sum of $35. This was a great deal of money for a struggling college student who had tuition, books, rent, food and transportation to pay out of the earnings of her meager part-time job.

It took another few years before I found anyone else who had heard of, much less *read*, this giant blue book. Since that time I have found a sprinkling of people who read the book, a few who study the book, and a very, very, very few who actually try to *live* the book—a most exhilarating challenge

TONIA BANEY: It was 1967 and we were living in Vancouver. One day my husband Steve walked into our kitchen with the Urantia Book opened to the table of contents and his exact words were, "This is what we have been looking for!" He had found the book in a box of books left in our basement by a young man for safekeeping.

When the young man returned we purchased the book for $15 and the shirt off Steve's back—literally! The young man insisted that he have this particular shirt as part of the arrangement. We were thrilled, and have been reading our book ever since.

JEFF KEYS: My childhood ideas about God were characterized by a sense of wonder—wonder about life, wonder about the stars in the skies. And I wondered about that old guy who lived with Bob and Rita across the street, two doors up, when my parents and a couple of the neighbors would say, "God lives there." It didn't take long for me to figure out they were kidding, but you couldn't help wondering what they were kidding about and where God really did live.

When I was about eight or nine, I received a Bible in church for reciting a few of the Psalms. Over the next couple of years I read most of it, and after Sunday school I would try to corner the pastor and ask him questions. It seemed to me that there was something real about God in the stories of the Bible, yet something was lacking: God seemed closer in my sense of wonder than in the Bible.

Every summer I spent a few weeks with a friend and his parents in a house near the beach. On Sunday mornings, the four of us would sit on the floor and read passages aloud from the Bible and discuss what they meant. That experience made God seem more real to me.

Throughout childhood, I had an avid interest in science and science fiction. At 12 or 13, I read about the theory that life could have originated in a "chemical soup." This seemed plausible enough and I had to consider that life might have arisen quite on its own. I then became an agnostic.

My family enjoyed spending a few weekends each year at a desert cabin in Yucca Valley, California; it was a beautiful place, especially in spring. Just a few miles away in Landers was a small airport known as Giant Rock, owned by George van Tassel. Van Tassel claimed to have had considerable contact with extraterrestrials who taught him amazing things, such as the principles of time travel and cell rejuvenation. As you might guess, the chance to go over and eat lunch in his diner and check him out was irresistible to a young boy in the '50s.

Giant Rock covered 5,800 square feet of ground and was seven stories high. Beneath it were cave-like rooms, only one of which was open to the public—an extensive library. It contained primarily books about UFOs; these seemed so at odds with my view of the scientific world that they held no interest. On one occasion, just as my parents were calling for me to leave, I took down a large blue book that seemed different from the others. What I glimpsed in only a few minutes really excited me. It seemed to speak clearly and with authority about the nature of God.

I never went back in that library but I never forgot the experience of feeling assured that it was possible to know something about our Father. Several years after seeing that book, although I didn't remember its name, I began reading many accounts of religious experience by such authors as Jakob Boehme, George Fox, William Blake, and William James. I also read religious classics such as Lao Tzu's *Tao Te Ching* and the *Upanishads*.

Then, when I was 19, a friend came back from Hawaii excited about a book called the Urantia Book. We looked for it in a few local bookstores, but didn't find it, so he ordered it from the publisher, the Urantia Foundation. When it arrived, we eagerly began to read it. I knew I had found something I had been looking for all my life. We showed it to friends in Laguna Beach who owned a bookstore and they ordered it. When it came in, I hitchhiked forty miles to buy the first copy in the store. It was several years before I realized that this was, in fact, the same book I had seen so briefly in that library long ago.

Two years later, I wrote to the Foundation, asking if there were other readers in Southern California. The reply came from a wonderful woman named Julia Fenderson in Culver City, the town where I had lived until I was 16. The letter went to my parent's address, and my mother's reaction was, "Why is Julia Fenderson writing to you?" It turned out that I had known her fairly well when I was in elementary school. She had been in charge of administering IQ and achievement tests for the Culver City school district. Meeting her again, and sharing this book with many other readers, has changed so much in my life since that time. It continues to speak clearly to me about the fundamental questions of human life.

JOANN EICHMANN: I always enjoy telling the story of the most important day of my life—the day I found the Urantia Book. That day stands as an island, everything prior seeming to lead up to it and everything after leading increasingly back into it.

In 1968 I was living in Newport Beach and attending the University of California at Irvine where I was majoring in philosophy. One day, upon arriving home from classes, my next-door neighbor, Ed, met me at my door. Knowing of my intense spiritual quest, he greeted me by saying, "I ran across a book you might find interesting." He handed me the Urantia Book, and the minute I held it in my hands and leafed through its pages something deep within me exploded. I knew of a certainty that this was it—the culmination of my search.

Ed told me someone at the hospital where he worked had bought a first-edition Urantia Book in a secondhand bookstore some years earlier. Although vaguely aware that the book was in some way special, he hadn't read much of it. He loaned it to Ed, telling him that it seemed a difficult book to find and that he wanted it back the next day. I persuaded Ed to lend me the book until it had to be returned. Ed realized how much more all this meant to me than it did to him.

I went into my apartment and proceeded to read for eighteen hours straight, until it was time to go to work and school the next day. Ed arranged that I could borrow the Urantia Book until I was able to acquire my own copy.

For nearly three years I had the book entirely to myself, not knowing another human being on the planet who had also read it. Finally, I wrote to Chicago, was put in contact with Julia Fenderson, and my active involvement in the movement progressed at a steady pace.

SARA BLACKSTOCK: In the late '60s, I was in my mid-twenties and living an alternative lifestyle—to put it mildly. My life was a chaotic mixture of the Urantia Book, LSD, the Beatles' music, and suicidal depression. The book had been given to me by a good friend, Jim Roland, a former nuclear physicist who had "dropped out" because of negative feelings about how that energy was being used. (Jim has long since graduated to the mansion worlds.)

My finding of the Urantia Book wasn't so exciting or unusual, but *after* I found it my life turned upside down. I knew the revelation was what it said it was as soon as I'd read the first few pages, yet I proceeded to go downhill for the next three years. Through my drug-using days (*only* marijuana and LSD!) and through several suicide attempts, I continued to carry the book with me as I roamed the countryside telling people about it. I was a mess, but somehow, by the grace of God, I survived those three years in which I was spinning out of control, with that revelation under my arm.

I was studying, at the same time, astrology, magic, the Tarot, palm reading, the *I Ching*, Egyptian mythology, and all the rest of it, and was becoming increasingly confused. One day, while reading the UB, I came across the section in Part IV where Jesus denounces magic and superstition. As soon as I finished reading these pages, I threw away all of the other books.

And yet, it wasn't until about three years later that I really began to get the message of the book—that God loves you! It was not until then that I began to deeply desire to get in touch with God. After that my life slowly began to turn upwards from its downward spiral. Over thirty years later, the truths, the stories, and the cosmology remain almost a daily nourishment for me.

So much of the Urantia Book is now embedded in my mind, my soul, and my life that I feel the revelation has gone beyond being a book; it has become a living reality that constantly struggles to express itself moment by moment in my life. I doubt that I would be here today if it weren't for the amazing grace of love that flowed, and still flows, from the truths expressed in this living revelation. Thanks to our Father, and to all my brothers and sisters whom I have met through this wonderful gift.

PATRICIA BEDELL MARTIN: I grew up on a dairy farm in a very small community. My parents were not religious and never attended mass at the tiny Catholic church about five miles away, but Grandma did, and occasionally I went with her. As well, non-denominational services were held in the nearby town of Snelling, in the basement of the county courthouse, and often my mother would drop my brother and me off there to attend Sunday school. I loved the hymn singing!

My first serious thoughts and curiosity about God occurred around the age of 13, in the mid 1950s. Up to that time I had taken the necessary catechism classes, but even at that young age I found them to be utterly lacking in meaning. For my 8th grade graduation I requested a Bible—

we did not own one. I now know that my Thought Adjuster had been busy leading me in my first tentative steps to learn more about God. By the time I was 15 years old I knew in my heart that I was not a Catholic. My own sense of what God must be was so much more than the sterile, rigid doctrines that had been preached to me up to that time.

During my first year in college in 1959 I attended the church services of a variety of denominations as I continued to look for my spiritual "home." The next year my roommate introduced me to Jeffrey Bedell, son of Clyde and Florence Bedell. We fell in love and married the following year. Jeff introduced me to the Urantia Book. Clyde and Florence spoke highly of it, and I was very impressed with Clyde's devotion to it. During that time, I would occasionally pick up the Urantia Book, more out of curiosity than anything else, and read at random an interesting paragraph or a few pages. At Christmas and Easter I would read the accounts of the birth and death of Jesus. Nevertheless, it didn't "take" until I was ready.

In 1968 we purchased a home in Chatsworth, California, near a small Congregational church. We began attending the Sunday services. Over a period of a few months, the spiritual truths of the minister's sermons and conversations, combined with the way I saw him living and caring for others, was the catalyst needed to seriously begin my study of the Urantia Book, to learn about Jesus and our Father.

For so many years my patient Teacher was waiting for me to take this superlative book in hand, not to dust it, but to learn from it, to delight in its teachings and satisfy my lifelong quest. What a Godsend! I'm truly blessed and eternally thankful for this great gift.

PAT FEAREY: To one who has been many, the gathering of every multicolored thread of experience to make a tapestry seemed only natural. To one who had peeled layers of insight from many a spiritual onion, a bouillabaisse of many flavors was the obvious next course. To one who had wondered about a music not-quite-heard in the silence of a starry night, a universe-as-symphony seemed not only glorious but logical.

I was ready for the Urantia Book to find me. It was 1968. A metaphysical bookshop in Berkeley had a copy on its top shelf, way up high. I promptly bought it, knowing nothing about it. And, despite good intentions, I read the Jesus papers and little else.

If the Urantia Book found me, did I then find it? Decidedly not. I was not ready to see the love of my life in that guise. I thought I knew how the universe worked after walking down numerous religious paths. I lumped all avatars together, including Jesus. I hated anything that seemed gender-exclusive, after a childhood oppressed by heavy patriarchal assumptions and a young adulthood rich in the finest women's educational opportunities available. Names like "Salvington" made me wince; they seemed so specifically (even suspiciously) Anglo-Saxon, when my ear delighted in the poetry of Sanskrit and in liquid Polynesian syllables.

And though I did not know it then, I had preliminary work to do before I could fully embrace the Urantia Book. I was a student of Hindu psychology at the time, learning from a beloved teacher—a non-guru guru whose message was always *balance*. His proclamation, in the face of an influx of orange robes, beads and sandals in the California of the '60s and '70s, was always: The only real teacher is inside oneself.

I did not, therefore, have the *Eureka!* experience when I first discovered the Urantia Book. I see now that I needed to continue learning from my Hindu mentor and to go to the spiritual community of Findhorn in northern Scotland in 1971 to experience a flowering within myself. I became the first person in the San Francisco area to publicize Findhorn, telling its story straightforwardly in lectures-cum-slides, illustrated with photographs I had taken there. As time went by and I was further away from it, I could no longer present a documentary narrative. Expressing essence became a necessity, and my presentations became more and more an experience of poetry, photography, and music.

To mature, my budding art form needed collaboration with other like-minded souls. It turned out that these early inspirational slide shows were the impetus which led around the spiral again into deeper experiences with the Urantia Book. I made a creative connection with some Urantia Book readers in 1976, working with them on such shows. They then brought me into their San Francisco study group.

Looking back, I can see clearly how one philosophical phase of my life had to end, and another creative phase had to come to a certain level of fruition before the Urantia Book could truly find a wholehearted welcome within my mind and my heart.

Although I began to read the book seriously in 1976, immersing myself in it over and over, ever deeper, I am not at all sure that I have begun even yet to read in earnest, with the sincerity the revelation deserves. One can thrill to its grand sweep, its overarching views, and its satisfying answers to life questions. The more I experience and the deeper I go, the less transformed and the more imperfect I see that I am and have been. I need this beautiful blue star-book as my guide. And, coming from love for the *Bhagavad-Gita* and the *Upanishads*, perhaps it has taken me all this time clearly to see Michael of Nebadon as Jesus of Nazareth, as *real*, as available, and as the companion of my soul.

The world needs the Urantia Book and it needs us to become dedicated "ambassadors of God," ever open to the personal transformation of living the revelation's truth.

DOC LIVINGSTON: Funny that I should remember that night over thirty years ago in 1968 so clearly. I was at a gathering of friends at the Topanga Canyon, California, home of my business associate. He was my partner in an herbal sales and distribution group. (Remember, this was the '60s, folks!) All who were there had been sampling our firm's product for several hours. At that stage in the evening, we were unanimously agreed that our new product would do well in the marketplace. We were singing its praises. It was a jolly, festive moment.

My friend then took me aside and asked me if I would like to check out a book written by Venusians. This person had known me for years and was well aware of my interest in science fiction. He also knew that no other approach would have caught my attention at the time. He took me to his study at the back of the house, sat me down at his desk, and put The Doors' first album on the phonograph. He laid before me a rather large blue book and said, "This will blow your mind!" That was new slang at the time. I asked him what the heck "Urantia" was, and he replied with a knowing smile, "It's the name of the planet we live on."

Well, that surely activated my somewhat befuddled brain synapses and fueled my curiosity. I opened the book to the front and began to scan its contents. Thus was launched a ten-hour reading marathon which became one of the prime moments of my life. With Jim Morrison playing in the background, and surrounded with musk incense and the sweet odors of our herbal product, I began reading one of the few books that has remained a favorite for over thirty years.

My initial impression looking through the table of contents was, "This can't be for real! This sucker was published when I was six years old!" I found it hard to believe that I had not heard of the book prior to that evening. The first section I read was "The Lucifer Rebellion," and it truly did "blow my mind"! I then read "Problems of the Lucifer Rebellion," the Adam and Eve papers, the Melchizedek and religion papers, and finally, "Government on a Neighboring Planet."

When I "came to" around 10 o'clock the following morning and closed the book, I experienced a unique, paradoxical sensation. I knew I should be drained and exhausted, yet I felt so energized. I felt suffused with a sense of other-worldliness, but it was not disassociative, as with chemicals. My overriding realization that day (and to this day, in varying degrees) was that we are all stuck on this "third rock from the sun" together. The brotherhood of man became very real to me that day, and has remained so ever since.

That night I started reading the Jesus papers and finished them, pausing only for sleep and food, in about four days. My view of Jesus was forever changed. What a cool dude! He was nothing like the pious portrayal that had turned me away from the Bible so long ago. My comprehension of his masterful personality is still expanding, and I doubt it will ever stop.

LARRY MULLINS: Clyde Bedell, a man who I consider to be "great in the invisible kingdom," handed me a copy of the Urantia Book in California back in 1968. He was 72 years old at the time and had been acquainted with the Urantia Papers since 1924. I knew Clyde as a pragmatic, tough, brilliant advertising expert, author and businessman, so he shocked me when he said he believed the text had been produced and materialized by celestial beings. This put me off. However, he added a mitigating comment which I recalled later: "But forget all of that. Judge the Urantia Papers by their content. If I told you that I knew for sure they were written by angels, it would be the worst reason of all for you to believe them. There is a part of God in you that will tell you whether they are true or not." I was impressed to some degree by the material, but I was sure I did not need it. I had already settled all of these questions in my mind, or so I believed.

A couple of years later, I watched Clyde give a talk on books for a women's club in Santa Barbara. Clyde had an astounding library, and showed slides of first editions and unusual books, some of which were worth a fortune. He even had handwritten tomes from the Middle Ages. I was a bit surprised when Clyde's final slide showed a copy of the Urantia Book. I was concerned he would empty out the place when he started talking about it. He said, "If I had to relinquish all of these books but one, this is the one I would keep." He said very little else about it but none of the audience left. Nor did anyone seem to care very much.

I thought at the time that Clyde had made a rather radical pronouncement. On that sunny Santa Barbara afternoon I had no idea what lay in store for me. I was about 35, full of energy and confidence. I had no conception that in a few years I would lose Vicki, one of my beloved daughters, and that my wife would die of cancer. I had no idea my life would come apart at the seams and that I would descend into a hopeless, indescribable darkness. It was in this despair that I truly "found" the riches of the Urantia Book.

The Urantia Papers proclaim that personality realities transcend all the other realities. In those days in Santa Barbara I could not have grasped such a philosophical construct. Yet, it is this notion that has assured me I shall see Vicki again; it has taught me to deeply appreciate my new wife Joan and my two other daughters, Kathleen and Michelle. It promises me that one day, in another plane of existence, I will embrace in peace all of those I have loved—and those I have contended with—in my life upon this difficult planet.

The book Clyde handed me many years ago is rather sad-looking today. The pages are marked up and crumbling on the edges, and the cover has come off. I don't use it anymore, because every time I open it more pages fall out of the binding. Yet, I believe its condition is evidence of a noble veneration for the gift Clyde gave me. If I had to give up every book I own save one, I would choose to keep that 1955 copy of the Urantia Book that Clyde Bedell handed me so many years ago.

DOROTHY ELDER: The year was 1968 and I was 37 years old. My life was the picture of tranquillity. I was married with two children ages 12 and 10, lived in a nice home surrounded by camellias, and had lots of family and good friends nearby. But the serene nature of my life was about to change. All of a sudden I was faced with material instability, concern for my children, anxiety, sadness, and an overpowering sense of uncertainty. I had big problems to solve and I was filled with fear.

At about this same time, my mother started telling me about a wonderful book that she had received from a friend. She said that it was written by the angels and told the whole story about Jesus. (I should mention that I was raised in a Protestant home with a mother who had her own liberal interpretation of the Bible.) She said that this book answered all her questions about God and the universe, and urged me to get a copy. But that was the last thing I wanted to do. I feared that if I saw this "revelatory" book, I would know for sure that my mother had lost her grip, and that would mean that the last stable reality in my life was gone. For months she persisted, and for months I politely resisted. I made it very clear that I did not wish to see that book!

Then one day Mother appeared at my door holding the Urantia Book. She thrust it in my hands and told me to sit down and open it. Trapped, I plopped down on the couch, stuck my thumb in the book and opened to "The Young Man Who Was Afraid." I didn't know it then, but that was the defining moment of my life.

I read that section over and over. The phrase, *"Arise, young man!"* (p. 1438), was like a wake-up call to my soul. Then I turned to another page and my eyes fell on these words: *". . . graciousness is the aroma of friendliness which emanates from a love-saturated soul"* (p. 1874). I closed my eyes and just let the beauty of those words wash over me. A sense of peace entered my mind, and once again I turned to another page. For the first time I read the words that would inspire me for the rest of my life: *"Uncertainty with security is the essence of the Paradise adventure . . .* (p. 1223).

I read for an hour without saying a word. Finally, I quietly asked if I could borrow the book. Mother said yes, and left. After three days and nights of reading, I called Mother and said, "Yes! Yes! This book *is* written by angels!"

And that is the story of how the Urantia Book found me. From that point on my life was changed. I was invigorated and uplifted for the challenges of those earlier days, and its inspiration has continued to light up my life on each new day.

My son and daughter began reading the book when I did, and they continue to do so today. We hosted a study group and joined a local Urantia Society. I went to my first Urantia conference in 1969 in Chicago and remember what a thrill it was to be in a room full of people from around the country who were all long-time readers.

I have now retired after many years as a teacher and love having the time to devote to study of the book. My mother's own love, joy and study of the Urantia Book never diminished. I smile up to her now, on the mansion worlds, and utter a prayer of thanksgiving for that day she knocked on my door.

MO SIEGEL: The time was the late '60s and the Vietnam war was tearing America apart. Like many young people, I was in a philosophic crisis, searching for life's meaning. After six years of journeying through various religions, philosophies, and scientific theories, I was strongly encouraged by three friends to read the Urantia Book. They promised that this book blended religion and science into a transforming yet realistic vision of life.

My 1968 Christmas treasure was a Urantia Book under the tree. As the winter snows piled high on the Rocky Mountains outside my window, I sat by the warm fire learning about the mysteries of the universe from the Urantia Book. Life was quickly changing as hope flooded my mind after reading the book's vivid descriptions of life after death and the purpose of our lives here.

And then it happened. I read Part IV, "The Life and Teachings of Jesus." For the first time I found true happiness. From within these pages Jesus came alive and made all things new.

KERMIT ANDERSON: Much of our world view with respect to the great questions of life are "inherited" from our early moral, religious, and philosophical environment. My early environment conveyed to me the moral view that we are all members of the great family of man. Spiritually, however, I had no teaching or direction to follow. My father had suffered at the hands of Roman Catholic nuns in an orphanage for a short time. His experience and the stories he told shaped my early view of religion in a most negative way. My father always asserted his agnostic position regarding the existence of God and felt passionately that one's religion was too important to be left to the choice of another.

In my teenage rebellion I did him one better by going all the way to atheism. As a philosophical materialist I enjoyed poking holes in the religious reasoning of my peers. However, after some poor decisions and traumatic experiences I found myself, 23 years old, anxious and depressed, seeking answers and meaning in astrology, the occult, and drugs.

In a moment of despair one day I asked—or should I say, the question was asked of me—"Who was Jesus?" In light of my past experiences it seemed an odd question to ask or be asked. I picked up a King James version of the Bible and read the synoptic gospels. Perhaps because of its archaic language and terminology, which was associated with a religion I had already rejected, I put the Bible back on the shelf, somewhat disappointed.

About two weeks afterward a friend of mine, Roger Minor, greeted me most enthusiastically with the Urantia Book, saying things like, "This is it! This is the book! It's all here!" Curious, I began to examine it. I bought my first copy a few days later. Little did I understand the significance of the date of my purchase—January 6, 1969, the Day of Epiphany in the Christian Church.

Six months of reading the book led me to my own epiphany. I read that God was real, not just man's invention or the repository of his highest values and hopes. All at once I felt the presence of God. That experience lasted a few hours. During this experience I "saw" the solution of all my personal problems as well as the solution to the problems of the world. Everything was wrapped up in the loving presence that enveloped me. In that marvelous moment I was given the certainty of my own personality survival.

More than thirty years later this survival-certainty is just as vivid and real as it was on that miraculous day. In the matter of a few hours my world view was turned 180 degrees. It took me a number of years to regain my equilibrium and integrate my new orientation to life into all of my affairs. To this day the Urantia Book continues to be my most powerful calling card to sonship with our heavenly Father.

CHICK MONTGOMERY: I was born Charles Montén Montgomery in 1938, to attorney parents. At 13 I was confirmed Episcopalian; I never believed much, but liked the singing. I went to Harvard where atheism was fashionable: man is an accident, evolved from the mud, and consciousness an illusionary adjunct. That philosophy suited me fine. I had no morals, no faith, and a rip-roaring good time.

I dropped out of graduate school in 1963 and hitchhiked around Europe, smoking dope and playing guitar. In a state of open freedom, strolling by St. Peter's in Rome, the thought occurred to me: "Something loves me and, when I find out what it is, I will call it God." I began reading the New Testament, and Jesus became important to me for the first time.

Returning to California in 1964, I sampled various denominations. In the Pentecostal church in Echo Park I answered a call to raise my hand if I was willing to receive Jesus. I felt a great something, and rushed out energized and wept by the lake. On this day, if any, I was "born again." Jesus had broken through my shell and touched my soul.

But faith was elusive. Could it really be true? Is there really a God? A trustworthy God? Five years followed, during which I wrote incessantly about my inner thoughts, took various hallucinogens, delved into astrology and the *I Ching*, and experienced wrenching swings between faith and doubt. Finally, in a silent decision that sounds simple but actually involved great spiritual courage, I declared, "I believe in you, God, but I don't know about this Jesus stuff." It is as though I had cleared the decks for a new spiritual paradigm, for almost immediately, it seems, I was introduced to the Urantia Book.

It was the spring of 1969, and some close friends were celebrating the grand opening of their record shop in Pasadena Old Town. The Beatles' white album was on the racks. I soon found myself in deep philosophical conversation with Kermit Anderson, a tall and gentle total stranger who seemed oddly familiar, and who finally said, "I have a book you might like." I dismissed the idea; people are always recommending books.

Shortly thereafter, at a party in my home, Kermit handed me the Urantia Book. Standing by the fireplace, I opened it at random and read a single sentence. Though I don't remember what page it was, I do remember knowing instantly that this was an important book and that I would read the entire thing. I went to Hollywood and plunked down $12. It amazes me that such truth could be acquired for less than a penny a page.

I struggled with this book, so full of blessing and light, yet of such preposterous claimed origin. I concluded it was too broad and deep, too lengthy and flawless, to be the work of a single human, and doubted that a group of humans could maintain secrecy about such an elaborate hoax. It was too gracious and truth-filled to have been written by anyone who would stoop to pretend to be divine—unless that someone were superhuman and malevolent! Could it be a work of the devil? A printed wolf in sheep's clothing, saying "Lord, Lord," and even quoting scripture, to lure us away from the blood of salvation, into everlasting damnation?

It took me seven years to complete my first (and only) cover-to-cover reading. During that time, all residue of suspicion that the book was of human or demonic origin vanished and was replaced by a great tidal wave of gratitude, blessing, certainty and absolute confidence that the Urantia Book is exactly what it says it is: a revelation of epochal significance. All questions were answered, knowledge integrated, vision expanded and hope confirmed, and I was so relieved to be able to keep Jesus in my faith. Believing these teachings unites me in utmost joy to those within the tiny, embryonic, dynamic, love-filled and growing community of believers who share the special brand of faith uniquely engendered by the Urantia Book.

IRVING TOWNSEND: In 1969 I owned a fabric store on Wilshire Boulevard in Brentwood, a neighborhood in Los Angeles. My bookkeeper was a young woman with two small children. She was going to school part time and working on my books part time to support her family.

We became friends. One evening while she was taking care of her children and preparing to go to dinner with me, she placed the Urantia Book in my hands and said, "Here, Irving. Read this." After reading three pages I realized that this was something I had been searching for for a long time.

I have been reading it all these years. My friend, Diane, eventually got an MA degree in financial planning and has since become very successful.

MARILYN HAUCK GREEN: As an adult I became interested in the study of music. I vowed that when my children were in school and sufficiently independent, I would go back to college and take music courses. In 1968 we moved to Virginia Beach, an occasion which caused me to look again to my goals. Since there was a small college nearby and the time seemed right, I enrolled in freshman courses in the music department.

During Christmas vacation my husband Russ had talked me into going with him to visit the A.R.E. Foundation at Virginia Beach, the old Edgar Cayce sanitarium which looks out upon the Atlantic Ocean. I had avoided this place, not because I'd ruled out the possibility that Edgar Cayce was genuine but because I'd figured that there must be a hundred frauds for every one truth among all the psychic and healing claims. However, Russ persisted, saying that we owed it to ourselves to see something unique right in our home area.

While at the Foundation, I learned of its large library of books dealing with psychic phenomena, fortune telling, prediction, astrology, religious philosophy, and so on. I also visited the bookstore and bought a couple of books for Christmas presents. Russ wrote a check for them and we left. That, it seemed, was that.

By the end of the school year I knew that an occupation in music was not for me. I had been holding off acknowledging that fact, but on the day I returned from my last final, I had to examine what I had been pushing aside. I was quite discouraged that this long-held dream was not valid, and in the course of my mental circles I exclaimed, "Well, God, what am I supposed to do?"

The phone rang. The woman on the other end informed me that she was calling from the A.R.E. bookshop and that the check my husband had written back in December (some five months before) had been dated 1965 instead of 1969. I was embarrassed and promised that I would get right in the car and come out to write her a good check. In five months she had not been able to find me at home because I was attending classes.

On the way to the Foundation I thought over what I'd asked God. I decided that since I had asked, I ought to see whether I had received an answer. The only thing I could think of doing in connection with the A.R.E. was to join the library as an associate and start reading.

Whenever I went back to the library, I deliberately kept an open mind as I searched the shelves. I chose books because they had pretty covers, or were on a subject that intrigued me or covered topics that I knew nothing about. I began to wonder why all the "inspired" authors could not write in simple, understandable English. Apparently their inspiration didn't extend that far. I read great predictions and Buddhist philosophy. A lot of it was obvious pretentious fakery, and some of it was fascinating. By fall, I was a veteran of the card catalogue.

About this time I read a book by a psychic who lived during World War I and the post-war period. In the appendix was an account of a major vision. The main character in the vision was "Urania," a goddess described as a daughter of heaven and earth, of the sun and the moon. The author's description so interested me that I wished to look up more on the subject of Urania. I returned to the A.R.E. library. The card catalogue contained only one book under the letter "U"— "*Urantia Book, The.*"

The library carried only one copy of the Urantia Book, and a non-circulating copy at that. I climbed up the step stool to reach it (it was on the top shelf) and almost fell off when the weight of Big Blue made itself known. That afternoon I sat at one of the oak tables, on one of the hard oak chairs, and started in on the Foreword. I'm not afraid to read long books, but it struck me that it would take me several lifetimes to read through a book of that size and density if I could only spend a few hours a week on it. I put it back and continued my chance encounter with literature.

About two weeks later I approached the checkout desk with my weekly selection. There on the cart of volumes to go on the shelves, was a wide, blue book. The librarian informed me that they had gotten a second copy so that one could go on the circulation shelves. I had seen it twice and decided I ought to check it out. And this time I got beyond the Foreword.

Because the book was on loan from a library, I paced myself at a paper a day to get through it. The librarian allowed me to renew it as long as no one was on the waiting list for it. By November I had ordered my own copy from Chicago, and finished the fourth section reading from my own book. As I read it I knew it was what it said it was. It was as though I had been deliberately primed on the other reading so I would have some similar material for comparison.

We lived in Virginia Beach for another seven and a half years, and I never found another reader except my family members to whom I had introduced the book. In 1976 I finally got to Chicago, visited 533, and met other readers for the first time. I have been reading and discussing the book ever since, and I am happy to report I have many readers to talk to and share with now.

HENRY BEGEMANN: My wife and I found the Urantia Book in a bookstore in Amsterdam. We never go to Amsterdam, if we can avoid it, as we don't like that city—it is the New York of the Netherlands. We went to that shop because we had read about it half a year before when it opened, and it looked attractive. There was one copy of the Urantia Book in the store. Though we knew nothing about the book and even less about the Foundation or the Brotherhood, we were attracted by its size and some things we'd read in it. We decided to buy it, though the price was about US$40. I think it was the only copy for sale then in Holland, and I always felt that we were guided to it.

[Henry devoted the rest of his life on Urantia to working on the Dutch translation. Sadly he passed on to the mansion worlds before the task was completed, but happily his daughter Nienke took over and finished the job. The Dutch translation was officially unveiled in November, 1997.]

GARY HALL: In 1969, at the age of 20, I had come to a point where I needed to make some major decisions about the direction my life was taking. I left Pocatello, Idaho, and went on the road hitchhiking. I traveled up north and then south to San Francisco, where I attended concerts at the Fillmore and explored the ferment that was Berkeley at the time.

After a week or so I headed back north. One evening at around nine o'clock I stood on a corner trying to get a ride out of Woodlawn, California. I went into a service station to get some chewing gum and when I came back out there was a big, tall, long-haired hippie like myself standing on the same corner also hitching north. We introduced ourselves. His name was Michael Bishop and he was from Seattle. We continued on north together through the rainy night and became friends. In Portland we parted company, Michael heading home to Seattle and I to Moscow, Idaho.

A few weeks later I traveled to Seattle to visit him. He was living in a large communal house with about six other people, mostly musicians—a great scene at the time. One night, as I was going to bed on the floor in the basement of this house, Michael handed me a big blue book without saying a word. I started reading the table of contents and knew immediately it was true and right.

As soon as I returned to Pocatello I ordered a copy from a bookstore and have been reading ever since. I lost track of Michael in the early '70s. I sure wish I could locate him now.

PAT McNELLY: I was brought up Roman Catholic in a large family of seven. My mother was deeply religious and a daughter of Polish immigrants, my father a convert from mainstream Protestantism. I went to Catholic grammar schools and was an altar boy. I knew all the rubrics and was proficient in the Latin Mass. I was also a seminarian during my first two years of high school in the early '60s. I sensed that I had some sort of calling or vocation from God, but learned quickly that I was not meant for celibacy or the Catholic priesthood.

After that I attended an all-boys, college-prep Catholic high school and soon lost interest in religion. During the mid-'60s in college, I became an agnostic. I could no longer believe in the dogmas of the Church, and was disillusioned by the world and its absurdities.

Feeling lost, and in an attempt to get control of my life, I left school and joined the U.S. Army in early 1968. After six months of training, I was sent to South Korea. But my spirit had begun to stir. I started reading

Pierre Teilhard de Chardin, Ouspensky, and the *I Ching*. I wanted to find my own way. I wrote volumes and volumes of poetry. And then my world changed.

It was October, 1969, and I was home on leave from Korea after spending thirteen months overseas as a Remote Sensing Imagery Interpreter for the U.S. Army. I was having a conversation with my mother about God and religion, and she said she had something she wanted to show me. She took me into the den to look at a book that she was giving to my father for his birthday in December. She had heard about it from a bookseller in town while attending a faculty party. My father was an avid reader of science fiction and taught the first university course on the subject in the late '60s, at California State University, Fullerton. The subject of science fiction had come up at the party, and this bookseller said he had a book that he wasn't sure was science fiction, called the Urantia Book, that my father might enjoy. My mother bought his last copy, a second printing.

She explained to me that this was a book allegedly written by angels who had all the answers to all the questions mankind had ever asked about God, history, religion, cosmology, life on other worlds and the universe. I paged through it for about twenty minutes and it made a deep impression.

I returned to finish my tour in the Army at Ft. Bragg, North Carolina, and went to a local bookstore to order my own copy, but was told it was out of print. Imagine having just a hint of this revelation, but not being able to get a copy for thirteen months!

When I was finally discharged in January, 1971, the third printing had just come out and I immediately bought my own book. I devoured it in about three months and joined the First Urantia Society of Los Angeles in December that year, after studying under the tutelage of Julia Fenderson, then West Coast Field Representative for the Urantia Brotherhood. The book has answered so many of my questions and has renewed my faith and belief in God, but I have since learned that the real revelation is not in a book, but in the lives we lead.

WILL SHERWOOD: Albuquerque, October, 1962. It was my sixteenth year, and the Month of the Rosary—ugh! My mother had gotten the idea that my sister and I should say the rosary every day, when I wanted to be with my friends. After mumbling through I-don't-know-how-many

Hail Marys, anger building all the time, I stomped out of the house and slammed the front door on my way out of my family's home, saying, "If that's what God is about, I don't want *anything* to do with him!" I'll always remember that late afternoon, the clear, crisp New Mexico sunset. It is forever burned in my memory as the first day of my eight-year-long personal search for truth.

Over the next seven years my journey took me through in-depth studies in astrology, numerology, Tarot, *The Tibetan Book of the Dead*. A little of it made sense, but mostly, reading that stuff was like wading through mud. Hardly any of it was consistent. It just wasn't right, but that's all I could find to study.

One afternoon, late in the summer of 1969, my studies find me together with a group of friends at a reception for some visitors from California. Sitting in a small living room with about a dozen other people, talking about dreams for the future and metaphysics, I overhear someone loudly say, "So you're into reincarnation, are you?"

I look over to see this big blue book being handed to Eddie Chavez, my best friend. I remember thinking, "Great—another big book..." A couple of minutes later, Eddie comes over and says, "Will, you've *got* to read this!" He points me to the first page of the Foreword and the small paragraph on the following page. I am cynical, but I say, "Okay," expecting to find more of the same intellectual mud.

The first sentence grabs me, rivets my attention and focus unlike anything I've ever read: *"In the minds of the mortals of Urantia, that being the name of your world..."* I think, "My God! These people are not from here! They know what they're talking about!"

I am sold. This is the book I have been searching for, period. But there's a catch: When I try to read "Deity and Divinity," I get bogged down and I think, "Guess I'm not ready for this." But I know that this is the highest truth on the planet and know I *must* have the book.

I find it in a metaphysical bookstore, and for another six to eight months, everywhere I go, I tell people about it. I tell them to read the first page of the Foreword. I tell them this is the greatest truth on the planet. I am sometimes even obnoxious about it. It never occurs to me that there might be something easier to grasp further on in the book, so I never even bother to look there.

Fast-forward to the spring of 1970. I am now living in Long Beach, California. I give my little this-is-the-ultimate-truth speech to a lady friend, Ruth Flanders, a.k.a. Ruth Holmes. She reads the first page of the Foreword and declares me full of it. (Remember that I am 23 and she is to a great extent correct.) She decides to prove me wrong and starts reading somewhere in the middle of the book.

A couple of days go by, then I suddenly hear her say, "Will, do you know what this says?" She is obviously excited, impassioned, impressed. I say, "What? What?" and come around to look over her shoulder. She's reading "Religion in Human Experience." My head spins. "You mean there's other stuff in there that I can understand?" So I read the whole book, meet Julia Fenderson, join FUSLA, start a study group, and accept personal responsibility—my journey with the Urantia Book had begun.

To this day, I wonder who those two travelers were who turned me on to to this life-changing book. If you were passing through Albuquerque with the Urantia Book in the late summer or early fall of 1969, please get in touch so I can thank you personally.

FRANCYL GAWRYN: My religious upbringing was a rather sketchy business at best. Our family went to the local community church in Carlsbad, in Southern California, and I vaguely remember hearing my brothers memorizing their Bible verses. My only direct memories of the experience are of the nursery school Bible class, coloring pictures of Jesus holding a lamb in his arms. The feeling of comfort which accompanies these memories has never gone away.

Before it became my turn to begin reading Bible verses, my parents decided to join a Unitarian-Universalist fellowship. My first experiences of God in community with others were largely formed by this Unitarian fellowship, but unfortunately, though they were all delightful and good people, most of them were atheists. Consequently I found God while I was alone, in nature, behind my mother's house in the hills and sagebrush of Southern California—not at all a bad place to find God. Later in life I was surprised to learn that people could really connect with God by going to church!

My turbulent teen years brought me to a very pointed and intense thirst for spiritual truth. I left the Unitarian Church, proclaiming, in my wisdom of sixteen years, that there was nothing spiritual to be found there, and went to find—something.

In December of 1969 I had recently dropped out of high school. I was at the home of a friend when Larry Neff, a musician friend of mine, came in the front door and enthusiastically began to evangelize me about this big blue book. He was so insistent about my reading it that I was sure I never ever wanted to look at it. I did my best to discourage Larry, and had managed to keep him at something of a distance for about a week, when finally, in exasperation, I yelled at him, "Larry, leave me alone and just let me go to hell, okay?"

"There is no hell!" was Larry's retort.

That got me interested. I went to the local mall and found a copy of the book for $12. I opened it and read the first sentence of the first paper: "*The Universal Father is the God of all creation, the First Source and Center of all things and beings.*" This single sentence was deep and sustaining nourishment for my starved and lonely soul. I knew that regardless of whatever else this book might say, it put first things first, and I knew that I wanted it. I bought it then and there.

Since that day, I have found many reasons to appreciate and criticize the Urantia Book, and my understanding of its authority has gone through many permutations. But during and since that time of my life, Jesus remains and increases as a real and living presence for me. The book played a great role in helping me realize his presence in my life, and for this I will always be grateful. It also helped to bring me a comforting sense of the nearness of God's Spirit. It has been a wonderful companion along my journey, and I continue to thank God for its presence in my life. Even more, I am thankful for the people it has led me to—a wonderful community filled with souls who, just like me, are trying to make sense out of this life, and are doing it with a thirst for God's will as guide.

SUSAN SARFATY: From earliest childhood memory, I loved and admired Jesus. I hadn't a clue about who God was, but Jesus was made very real to me by stories I heard that showed the beauty and symmetry of his character. These stories helped set my standards for idealistic living and inspired me to want to be just like him.

Since Jesus traveled and mingled among all sorts of people, learning, teaching, sharing, and loving, this became my dream also. As I grew, I questioned more, and a fuzzy notion of God as primal force, the uncaused cause, began to form in my mind. How this related to Jesus was still a mystery, but I knew Jesus' way was the right way, the way I must live if I wanted to be real.

Increasingly, I placed a premium on connecting with people, places, things and ideas that demonstrated the quality of realness—the quality of flowing naturally and harmoniously from observable universal law; that which is flexible, fluid and open to change; that which is motivated by truth and activated by love, the driving force and powerful bond that holds creation in place.

In search of the reality I felt missing in everyday life, I left home at 16, married and had two children, divorced within a few years, underwent Freudian analysis, explored the inner sanctum of Scientology, and wandered across Europe, the Mediterranean and North Africa, the United States and Mexico. Along the way I examined everything I could find that might light the way to a greater awareness of how the universe really works—Eastern and Western mysticism, metaphysics and occult studies. I lived among the natives, learning the local traditions through their eyes, and sharing my own experiences with them, each of us contributing to a greater understanding between our respective cultures.

My first encounter with the Urantia Papers occurred in 1969 in a little bookshop in Sausalito, California. A friend and I had recently left Scientology, and we were ripe for a different approach, one that might inform and inspire in a more loving way than the one from which we had just escaped. Her brother had told us about the Urantia Book, that it shed new light on mystical truth. So when we saw it on the shelf, we couldn't resist its pull and between us we scraped together the money to buy one we could share.

During my early years with the book, I used to let it fall open where it might and consult the exposed text somewhat as if it were an oracle. I always gained new insight through this process, but it wasn't until I attended my first Urantia conference in 1974, meeting all sorts of wonderful people I liked and respected, who were devout readers (including my soon-to-be-husband, Peter Sarfaty), that I finally undertook to read the entire book from front to back. The story of creation thus presented opened my senses to an exciting new perception of reality, one in which I knew myself to be a beloved citizen of an orderly universe, with a real destiny and purpose, where my contributions could be meaningful and valuable.

My quest to understand ultimate reality has led me through many a puzzling maze, each a unique and thrilling learning adventure. Eventually it brought me face to face with the Urantia teachings, which finally clarified my understanding of the relationship between Jesus and God. At the same time, this amazing synthesis of scientific, religious and philosophical thought has challenged me to consider a whole new universe of questions and discoveries, while also leading me to revel in the refreshing simplicity of Jesus' words to us: "Love one another, even as I have loved you."

THOMAS ORJALA: I was born in 1949 and raised in a poor, rural county in northern Minnesota. My spiritual training was Methodist and I was joyed to know there was a God, but confused by my inability to see him in spite of years of church and Sunday school. My burning question was: If God is omnipresent, where the heck is he? Why is he hiding from me? I found myself depressed and disappointed by life as I graduated from high school.

In hopes of finding some relief, I fled home. I eventually made it to the Haight-Ashbury district of San Francisco and "dropped out" in hopes of finding an identity I could claim as mine. I studied with the gurus of the day: Stephen Gaskin, Yogi Bhajan, Swami Satchidananda, and others. I danced with the Hari Krishnas and Sufi Sam, and sat in meditation at the Zen Center. I joined in Holy Man Jams, shared jugs of wine and joints at Hippie Hill, went to rock concerts with the Dead and the Airplane, and took trips to the mountains to run naked in the woods.

Then, one day in 1969, I met a man with wire-rimmed glasses named Arthur. He had the ability to move through life with a magical ease totally unfamiliar to an introverted farm boy like me. It seemed that whenever a discussion would arise about matters of spiritual importance, Arthur would open his blue book and read from it. I don't recall ever "getting" anything that he said, but I was curious about why he had so much faith in this book. One day I asked to see it.

As I turned the pages and read various paragraphs, I felt the words speak directly to me—to my soul—as if they were alive. In less than ten minutes I knew I had found the answer to the question of my youth. I immediately went to the bookstore and bought a copy.

Now *I* am the guy with the wire-rimmed glasses, daily finding opportunities to share the revelation. Thank you, Arthur, wherever you are!

Part III

1970-1971

STEVEN HECHT: In the winter of 1969-1970, I left my home in Binghamton, New York, and set out on a solo hitchhiking trip across the United States. I had just dropped out of the state university there, in my first year. My explorations in religion up to that time had been Alan Watts's *The Book*, Ram Dass's *Be Here Now*, and the writings of Madame Blavatsky.

While in Berkeley, California, I wandered into Shambala, a metaphysical bookstore, and picked up the Urantia Book. It must have made some kind of impression on me, since a few months later, at the Edgar Cayce library in Virginia Beach, Virginia, I searched out the book again and read newspaper reviews of it from 1955.

During the next few months I had quite an exciting time. I ended up in a "cult" of white Rastafarians (in reality, college students from Michigan) who had spent time in the mountains of Jamaica with a Rastafarian priest named Baz. They had returned to Coconut Grove in Miami, where I met them. A nice Jewish boy from New York, I was temporarily swept away by a heady combination of apocalyptic Rastafarianism, ganja, and trips to the mountains of Jamaica. It's now clear to me that I was searching with determination (and sometimes wild abandon) for a rational and inspiring faith-basis for my life.

A month after ending that adventure, I saw the Urantia Book again in Samuel Weiser's metaphysical bookstore in Manhattan. I can vividly remember running my hand along a shelf of books and finding the Urantia Book right next to *OAHSPE* and *The Keys of Enoch*. I read one sentence from the UB and knew immediately that I had to read the whole thing. It was a relatively inconsequential sentence. It was not the spiritual meaning or significance of the sentence that convinced me, but the syntax and high level of intelligence of the language. Just to make sure, I opened the other two books and found absolutely no call there. Since I didn't have the $16 it cost, I had to borrow the money from my parents. I returned to Weiser's the next day and bought the Urantia Book.

That whole summer I spent three to four hours a day reading the book. I went very slowly and carefully, trying to find contradictions and mistakes. I made sure that I did not move ahead until I understood (at some level!) what I had been reading.

The following summer I read St. Augustine's *Confessions*. In its own way, that book had almost the impact on me that the Urantia Book did. It was while reading that book that I was "baptized in the spirit." It was experienced as an unspeakably sweet sensation in the heart, filling my whole soul. This has been my only extrasensory spiritual experience—and it happened on the New York City subway. This experience is with me always, and is not held in my memory as such, because it does not reside in my mind, but in my soul.

Nine years later I underwent the greatest trial of my life. In 1979 I was diagnosed with end-stage renal failure. I was immediately put on hemodialysis for the next four years. That experience was probably the turning point in my life, for at least two reasons: One, I experienced my mortality at a relatively young age (28); and two, I simultaneously experienced the depth of my faith status with God. I had no fear of death, although I knew I was at death's door. The faith lessons I had appropriated from the revelation allowed me to console my family through this difficult time.

ROBERT F. BRUYN: To tell you the truth, I don't feel that I found the Urantia Book. Rather, it feels as if the book found me through a conspiracy of circumstances that I believe was the work of angels and midwayers.

It was January 1970, a time of turmoil, risk, decisions, and changes. I was in my third year of graduate study in clinical psychology at the University of Kansas in Lawrence. I had just decided to separate from my wife of seven years. I was so unhappy in this relationship that I was willing to give up everything material and even live apart from my precious six-year-old daughter. My first task was to find a place to live. Since it was in the middle of the academic year, few inexpensive apartments were available. I finally found a room—actually a second-story, screened-in porch that had storm windows placed over the screens. The furniture consisted of a small cot, a desk, and a closet. I shared a kitchen and bath with two other students.

Coincidentally, the student living across the hall had discovered the Urantia Book during his four-year stint in the Navy. David Jones had just returned to college following his discharge. (He has his own amazing tale of finding the Urantia Book through a woman in the hills of California, but that's another story.)

One of the first evenings after moving in, while David was making popcorn and I was warming up a can of soup, he struck up a conversation with me. After discovering my field of study, he asked, "What do they teach about God and religion in psychology?"

"They don't!" I answered.

"Well, what do you think about God and religion?" he inquired.

"I'm not sure," I responded. "I think I believe there's a God but I just don't know. . . ."

I had been raised in a very religious family in a small town in Iowa. From an early age I attended a conservative Protestant church where the Bible was interpreted literally. If a person were to doubt one part of the literal interpretation of the Bible, then "you might as well throw out the whole thing." The anatomy courses I had taken in college convinced me of the evolutionary process. *Pow!* Now what do I believe? Not the biblical Adam and Eve story. For about five years I had been living with this unresolved conflict between evolution and the Bible.

That evening, David took the opportunity to suggest that I might want to look at an interesting book he had found while in the Navy, the Urantia Book. He invited me to stop by his room sometime.

It didn't take long before I took him up on it, both of us being somewhat alone at the time. David had a large room compared to mine and he owned a stereo system! All I had were my clothes and books. He began to share some passages from the book. Of course, I was curious about what this book had to say about evolution. Immediately I was impressed. The Urantia Book unified science and religion. I could believe in God *and* in evolution. What a deal! My dilemma was forever resolved. And the book did so much more.

Little did I know that this was just phase one of the conspiracy. *"They [angels] cannot fully control the affairs of their respective realms of action, but they can and do so manipulate planetary conditions and so associate circumstances as favorably to influence the spheres of human activity to which they are attached"* (p. 1256).

With a new semester and a new set of classes, I met a student named Barbara Newsom. We became friends. One afternoon we were at a pizza shop and during our conversation I mentioned that my new friend David had shared a very interesting book that I had not heard of before. "I think it's called *Uracia* or something," I said.

"Not the Urantia Book?!" she inquired emphatically.

Suddenly, I felt overwhelmed. The feeling was somewhat frightening. I stood up and walked out of the pizza place into the parking lot, somewhat dazed. What was going on here? Two new friends who *both* knew of a revelatory book that I had never heard of before?

I came to find out that Dr. Myers of Newton, Kansas, had introduced Barbara's family to the Urantia Book amidst a curious set of circumstances following the death of Barbara's sister. But that's another story as well.

David, Barbara and I met often to read and study the Urantia Papers. The circumstances of our having gotten together felt so much like the work of superhuman forces that we joked about having been "coincidenced"—a term we'd coined.

I soon realized that I no longer had a fear of death. I hadn't been aware of ever having any anxiety or uncertainty about death, so why the sense of peace? Maybe I was experiencing the satisfaction of really believing in eternal survival.

Why was I so attracted to the teachings of the Urantia Book? I'd had so many unanswered questions during my childhood and young adult life that I had just about given up on ever getting answers. Then out of nowhere comes a new revelation that gives plausible answers. For me, what it boils down to is that the Urantia Book just makes sense. Could this feeling be the Spirit of Truth working in our lives?

I cannot begin to describe the many ways in which the Urantia Book has changed my thinking, my decisions, and my life. I am so grateful for this magnificent revelation of the nature of the universe and my heavenly Dad, and for the wonderful brotherhood of believers—individuals, couples, and families—that I have had the opportunity to become friends with.

LARRY GEIS: High August heat blankets the Southwest desert. The year is 1970. I'm 28 years old and probably the only white, ex-Southern Baptist, agnostic, gay CPA on this planet who's been somewhat psychedelicized. If there are others like me, they're probably in San

Francisco, so that's where I'm headed. A two-week visit the year before has inveigled me into quitting my lucrative job at Arthur Andersen in New Orleans, leaving my French Quarter friends and my spacious Victorian flat.

Three of us guys are on the road in a VW bug with an ice chest and a portable 8-track blaring "It's A Beautiful Day," Crosby, Stills & Nash and, of course, the Beatles' *Abbey Road*. Trading off driving and sleeping, we make Albuquerque, where we crash with some friends. Our goal for the next day is the Grand Canyon, which none of us has ever seen. We opt for a detour to the North Rim, hoping to find some tourist-free solitude.

Arriving about 6 p.m. we find a few vehicles in the parking lot at Point Imperial (elevation 8,803 ft.). A prominent sign says "Danger: Beware of Violent Summer Thunderstorms!" As carefully planned, we ingest some slow-acting, mind-altering substances and prepare to groove on the sunset, spend the night under the stars communing with our inner beings and "come down" just in time to welcome the sunrise.

From where we park it's still a good quarter mile to the rim itself. A nature trail winds through some scrubby, weather-tortured growth that bears witness to fire damage, probably from lightning strikes. We are above the timber line and a few wild rose bushes are in bloom, but mostly there's just lots of barren rock.

Is anyone ever prepared for that first glimpse of the vast majesty of this most awesome natural wonder? Like a big cat, I find a place to perch on a small ledge on the very rim and stare into the nearly limitless space. Vertigo is not in my vocabulary.

Wow! I notice a small plane flying a few thousand feet below me. Then I see a large thunderstorm forming in the distance, as the baking heat from the canyon floor 6,000 feet below rises into the crisp air. It's mind-boggling: the storm is actually inside the canyon, lazily moving in front of me. Now, both my inner and outer perspectives are expanding rapidly, rushing me into a state of blissful, timeless awe.

Suddenly the wind gusts, and a few raindrops begin to fly. The storm, still discretely discernible, seems to be drifting from right to left. I hear the familiar sound of thunder and the strange echo of that sound off the canyon walls—just too fascinating. My friends appear and suggest we head back to the car. "You guys go on," I say. "I don't mind getting a little wet." They leave me to my reverie.

Then—*crack!*—a lightning bolt strikes very near me. Despite my disassociated mental state, I have the good sense to realize I can't stand up and run to the safety of the VW. I would be the tallest thing on that rocky plateau, a perfect lightning rod. (My first twenty-one years on Urantia were spent in Northern Oklahoma's tornado alley.) Climbing down from my little ledge, I assume a fetal position with my face to the ground and turn my back to the storm, just as the psychoactive potentials of those tiny micrograms begin peaking.

Obviously, I have misjudged the path of the storm; it is rapidly growing outward as well as drifting. That roaring maelstrom literally slams into the side of that Biggest Hole on Earth. Clinging to the scrabbly gravel, I struggle to hang on, barely able to breathe. The storm rages on, pinning me to that precipice.

"... *fear can kill*" (p. 971).

The scene shifts inside: This is beyond fear, this is beyond desperation, this is beyond panic. This is final. I feel like a hosed-down fly on a wall, certain to be washed off into the abyss. "OK, God, so this is The End. There's no way out. I give up, I give in, I surrender. Let's get out of here."

If you have read accounts of near-death experiences, or have had one yourself, you know that mere words are insufficient. Here I meet the hellfire-and-damnation God of my religious upbringing. Jealous Jehovah of the volcano. Thor of the thunderbolts. An archetype made painfully real. But wait!—there is something more behind the Wizard's curtain, a vastness of Light and Love.

There are certain images I remember. For a brief moment, I am hanging on the cross with the Master, feeling the inexpressible sorrow (not pain) of benighted rejection. A voice inside me says: "Your life can mean as much. You must go back. There is work to do." You can't mean me. I'm just a nobody.

Who was Jesus, anyway? What about Buddha? The voice says: "Buddha was the most egoless man who ever lived; Jesus was the most perfect ego."

How long all this takes, I do not know. But, still trapped in the roaring rain, trying to keep my mind from completely disassociating, I call out for help. A new calm comes over me. Now, I wonder about my friends: Have they made it to the car? Are they all right? As suddenly as it began, the storm abates. Then, I know it is safe to run back to the VW. How sweet the wild roses smell in the electrified air!

Leaving every stitch of my rain-soaked clothing in a pile outside, I wrap myself in a most welcome blanket and begin to calm down. There is little we can say to each other and my friends eventually go to sleep. I spend the night listening to the thousands of rivulets flowing into the canyon and (I now know in retrospect) my angels whispering in my ear. Alone, at dawn, I behold the sunrise from the very spot of my trauma.

Three days later, while staying with a friend in Southern California before hitchhiking to San Francisco, I meet another guy who is interested in spiritual realities. We discuss some books we have read: *The Doors of Perception*, *The Varieties of Religious Experience*, the novels of Hermann Hesse. "I just passed through Big Sur on my way back here to L.A.," he says. "I stayed with the cook at Nepenthe. His name is Peter Rabbit—really! He showed me this very intriguing, big blue book. I think you might be interested in it."

The next day, my host takes us over to meet someone he knows in the San Fernando Valley who is "into that kind of stuff." His friend isn't home, but his roommate lets us in. Sitting on the coffee table is the Urantia Book. Peter Rabbit's friend says, "Oh, there's that book I was telling you about."

By October of 1970, I was settled in San Francisco's North Beach, rooming with a Tarot card reader, devouring that big blue book as fast as I could. Presumably by chance, I met some more new readers of this revelation. We formed a study group that has met weekly at some place or other to this day.

DAVID BRADLEY: In 1970, I purchased the Urantia Book after my wife had heard that it was a "high" (that's '60s jargon for "mind-expanding") book. At the time my library included books by Carl Jung, John Lilly, Aldous Huxley, Black Elk, Carlos Castaneda, Lynn Andrews, C. S. Lewis, and others. I put the UB on the shelf with my other spiritual adventure books. At this time I did not believe in God, and had had no religious training; but I had experienced good, inexplicable magic in my personal life and I loved synchronicity. I liked to go to rock music bars and power/spirit dance. While dancing, I would sometimes steer myself by imagining that I was moving harmoniously with the presence of Jesus.

At this time I had begun to wonder if Jesus was a *brujo*, like Don Juan or Don Genero of the Castaneda books. I started reading the New Testament with this question in mind, and I found evidence of metaphysical events in Jesus' life, such as his turning water into wine and creating the loaves and fishes. At this time I noticed that the last part of the Urantia Book was also about the life and teachings of Jesus, and I started reading to find out more.

I read only a few pages of Part IV and found them to be intelligently and coherently written. I stopped, went to the front of the book, and began to read there. During that first reading I discovered that God was real and had personal relationship experiences.

I truly thank my guidance for leading me to God, the First Source and Center of that good, inexplicable magic and love. I'm very thankful that the Urantia Book is here. And I still like to dance, albeit more socially most of the time.

DENVER PEARSON: As a child growing up in Santa Fe, I spent many warm summer nights lying under the dark, clear New Mexican skies. I would stare up at the stars and wonder what they were all about and if there was life out there. Something was drawing me to seek for that information.

As a teen I was surrounded by Catholic friends. I had not been raised in any particular faith, and so I was free to think for myself and develop my own philosophy. It became easy to poke holes in my friends' theology. When they couldn't explain something to me, they would say, "It's a mystery." I had a difficult time accepting this answer. Something inside told me there was a real answer somewhere.

Years went by and in 1970, in my early twenties, I found myself working for the National Parks Service at the Grand Canyon. My first summer there, I was in the company of many young people of different faiths—Mormons and evangelical Christians—who were working for the commercial vendors at Desert View, on the South Rim. We all spent many nights in heavy discussions about why one religion might be right and another wrong.

When the summer ended and the others were gone for the season, I was left alone to ponder our discussions. Feeling ignorant and wanting to understand why people believe what they do, I found books on different religions and tried to educate myself. I did a lot of deep thinking that summer. I even came up with my own version of evolution and of the source of life and the human race. My mind was brewing. At night I would lie in bed craving to know what life was all about, sincerely asking for the power to know these things.

One day, near the end of my season, I was at a filling station when a couple drove up in a station wagon. I happened to notice they had two dark-colored Burmese cats, so I struck up a conversation with them, telling them about the black cat I had recently adopted. They invited me to the campground to talk. That evening I went to see them, and later we went back to my place to drink some wine and talk some more. I told them about my search.

As the night wore on the couple revealed that they were from the Chicago area, where a friend of theirs had discovered a mysterious book that had changed his life. They told me that this friend went to inquire about the origin of the book at a place called the Foundation, and that when he knocked on the door a person opened it saying, "We've been waiting for you." That was all it took for me to want to find this book. I asked them the name of the book and they said something like, "You Rancha" but they spelled it "Euranchia."

With the name of the book in hand, I proceeded to the libraries and bookstores in Flagstaff but couldn't find it. Did it really exist? This made me even more curious and determined. Instead I bought some books on astral travel and Buddhism, as well as some by Tuesday Lobsang Rampa. I put the "Euranchia" Book in the back of my mind.

The season finally ended for me, so I took my cat, my books and my quest for truth and went back home to Santa Fe. One day soon after arriving home I was riding in the car with my younger brother, and out of the blue I asked him if he had heard of the "Euranchia" Book. I was surprised when he replied that he had heard of it, and that we had a mutual friend from high school who had a copy of it. This friend was now a dope-smoking hippie, so I wasn't quite sure what kind of book he would be interested in, but I didn't waste any time getting to his house to see this mysterious book for myself. He agree to let me borrow it.

At last I had a copy of this heavy, big blue book with the strange name, *Urantia*. No wonder I hadn't been able to find it. I took the book home and began reading. I couldn't believe my eyes. This was it, the missing puzzle piece that matched perfectly with the pieces in my mind. It was such a strange experience that I became leery. Was this a Communist trick? Was this a deception of the devil? It took me a while to work through my doubts, but finally I had to accept the fact that my deep desires for truth had been satisfied by a revelation from on high. That year I went to France and immersed myself in the book's teachings about Adam and Eve, Thought Adjusters, Jesus, angels and life on other planets. It was such a wonderful experience reading it for the first time.

After years of studying and living this revelation, it has not lost its freshness. The people I have encountered through this book are the most intelligent, alive and fun-loving people I have ever met and I will cherish their friendships forever.

JERRY MCCOLLUM: 1970, Marysville, Washington. I had dropped out of college and was hanging out in a commune made up of drop-outs and unemployed types. Boeing's massive layoffs had impacted everyone in the region.

One night several of us pulled out a Ouija board and began playing with it. It was my first time using one. We tried combinations of partners with not much response. When it was my turn the cursor practically jumped out of my fingers.

Both my partner and I said something like "Whoa!" and proceeded to ask questions. The cursor moved so fast that we had to have one person standing directly over us writing down the letters in sequence. When the cursor stopped we would pause to divide the letters into words. I was startled that all the words were correctly spelled, and that they formed coherent sentences.

An entity named Daljek, who called itself a "Fellowship Guardian," began answering questions. At one point, in response to someone's question, Daljek said, "Ask your Thought Adjuster."

"Thought Adjuster? Thought Adjuster? What the hell is a Thought Adjuster?" We were all looking at each other, wondering, "What is this nonsense?" All of a sudden, a guy who had been sitting nearby on the couch jumped up and said, "Wait, I just read something about that!" He ran upstairs to his bedroom and came back with the Urantia Book which he had bought the day before at the University of Washington bookstore in Seattle.

We put away the Ouija board, waited as he thumbed through the book searching for "Thought Adjusters," and listened as he began to read about them. I remember feeling as if I had tapped into something really significant.

I bought a copy of the UB for myself a month later. I still have it on my bedside stand. The spine has been repaired twice from abusive perusal of spiritual truth.

PHILIP GEIGER: It was 1970. The Vietnam War was raging, Nixon was lying about bombing Cambodia, and the National Guard was killing fellow war protestors at Kent State. I had just graduated from high school and was heading for Alaska to begin my adult life, far from the madding crowd. My first spiritual longings were being fueled by reading D. T. Suzuki and the novels of Hermann Hesse.

I never made it to Alaska, ending up in Hawaii instead. Broke, jobless, and friendless, I took up residence on a boat in noisy Ala Wai harbor in Waikiki. One day my starving stomach got the best of me and I allowed a local squad of Krishna devotees to spirit me away to their temple in the lush Manoa Valley. There they stuffed me full of vegetarian delights and introduced me to a lifestyle of serving and worshipping God. Most of them were recent arrivals from a commune on Molokai and had backgrounds similar to my own. After long hours of conversation, they talked me into joining the temple.

Our daily regime consisted of a 4:30 a.m. wake-up call by a monk shaking our shoulders as we slept on the hardwood floor, saying, "Krishna needs you now." We'd then trudge up a wet hill under the stars to take a cold shower under a garden hose. After dressing in a traditional orange *dhoti*, we'd drag our "skin-encapsulated egos" into the worship room and begin chanting Krishna. After breakfast and chores, we'd head into Waikiki to spread the good word, chanting and praising God for five hours nonstop in our bare feet on the skiddle-hot concrete in the scorching Hawaiian sun.

After three weeks I decided that this wasn't really my path in life. During a worship session in the temple, I remember saying, "God, I don't mind serving you, but get me the hell out of here." I left the next day and accepted an invitation to stay the night at a house on the shores of Waimea Bay. That evening, lost and confused, I headed out to a natural jetty to meditate, to seek some sort of purposeful direction for my life. Armed with a healthy dose of traditional American Indian sacrament, I sat in half-lotus and let the universe know in no uncertain terms I wasn't budging until I got some answers. Hours passed and absolutely nothing in the way of answers emerged. On an impulse, I got up and returned to the house. A young woman asked whether I was aware that it had been raining for the last couple of hours. I absently responded no, and headed over to the bookcase. The first book I put my hand on was Big Blue. Opening it up at random, my eyes alighted on the beginning of

"Energy—Mind and Matter." I was enthralled. I turned back to the table of contents and read as much as I could of the dancing, rainbow-enshrouded letters. But it was enough to convince me that my prayer had been answered.

I rushed back outside, resumed my meditative position, and thanked the universe profusely. I had one further request: a place to read the book, hopefully uninterrupted. Suddenly a single word entered my consciousness: "Makenna." All attempts to elicit further information were fruitless. The next morning, I casually asked the other members of the household if they knew who or what Makenna was. Someone responded that he knew of a beach on Maui by that name, and that it was occupied by a loose community of a hundred or so hippies living naked in the kiawi trees. I thrilled to this information and, counting up my remaining funds, determined that I had just enough for a one-way ticket to Maui. I left the next day.

Having settled into a comfortable camp between two gorgeous beaches in southwest Maui, I began a daily regime of meditation, yoga, and reading. I read *The Zen of Suzuki, Hui Hai* and Alan Watts, perfect accompaniments to my simple lifestyle. A gem of a book written in the first person, *The Impersonal Life*, introduced me to the idea of an interactive God within.

Finally, after a couple of months my mother sent me $20 for my birthday, and I bought the only Urantia Book available on the island. I began reading it sequentially every day over the next three months. More than anything at the time, the book introduced me to my real spiritual family, my real place in the universe.

BILL SPANG: Although I grew up in many areas of the West Coast, I call Seattle home, as it is here that I have most of my adolescent and early adult memories. I started running away from home at 13. My friends were all older than I and having much more fun. The rock festivals of the era were in full bloom and I wasn't interested in getting an education at school, much to the dismay of my folks. It was more fun to travel. I was lost in my adolescent confusion and had nobody to turn to. I remember one night when I found myself alone in the rain, crying and praying. My life was soon to change.

In Seattle, as a 16-year-old in 1970, I first came in contact with the Urantia Book. I had attended a music festival and was staying with friends at the New Age Foundation in Eatonville, Washington. Our host, Wayne Aho, talked about the Urantia Book, among other things. From there I traveled to Montrose, Colorado, where I met a woman who also had this book. It seemed that everywhere I went people were reading this big blue book.

After hitchhiking to New York and back twice I found myself living in a commune on The Hill in Seattle. There I became close friends with a guy named Woody, who also had the book and would often quote from it. As time went on I asked to borrow it from him. The following year we went to Wenatchee to pick apples, and there I met someone who sold me my copy of the Urantia Book. Although it was expensive for me at the time, it was the best $20 I've ever spent in my life.

I have since read the entire book, but have referred to "The Life and Teachings of Jesus" most. Although I strayed quite a bit from religion for about twenty years, I continued throughout to read Part IV and tried to hold on to my faith. Through many life challenges, our Father has always been patient with me. It is never too late to change one's path in life, and Jesus is ever ready to accept us back into his spiritual arms.

SCOTT BROOKS: It was the fourth of July, 1970, when I reached my bottom. My drug-filled life had brought me to my confused state of despair, but it would be a few more years before I realized that. I threw myself to the ground and pounded the earth. I considered suicide for a moment and the shock of even considering such an action made me realize I had to find a new way.

A friend of a friend was reading a big blue book which had impressed my friend. I thought I might visit this fellow, Ralph Smith, and ask him about God. When I told Ralph how troubled I had become he suggested I go to a mountaintop and meditate on some aspect of God.

I drove up the coast to Ventura County and headed for the mountains. I spent the day hiking and, at the summit, meditated on the triune God concept that Ralph had described from the Urantia Book. It was a wonderful day, but as I drove back down the coast highway for my home in Topanga, I realized nothing had changed. I was about to return to my same ragged life.

The next day I had an amazing experience. In the middle of a conversation with a friend, I suddenly announced, "I know what I'll do!" and proceeded to describe a short-term plan of action that would get me out of my bind. The amazing thing was that even as I spoke the words, I did not know where the ideas behind them were coming from. I was actually listening to the words as they poured out of my mouth. It was a fairly elaborate plan, yet during the minute or so that I spoke I was completely aware that I was not speaking these words in any normal way.

The plan that came forth was a good one, so I proceeded to act on it. I believed then that this experience was somehow related to my earnest prayers of the day before and perhaps was designed to show me the reality of God. This religious experience truly lifted me and propelled me towards recovery. The experience was then, and remains today, a mystery and one that has never occurred again.

I began reading the Urantia Book along with other texts on God, from St. Thomas Aquinas to the *Bhagavad Gita*. I was open-minded but skeptical of the Urantia Book for many years. I suspected that someday I would discover it to be a work of fiction or fantasy.

After years of intense scrutiny, I began to relax my defenses and allow it to work in my life.

JIM DOWNS: I first came into contact with the Urantia Book in November, 1970, when I was 21 years old and living in a little town near Vail, Colorado. I had recently befriended a local grade-school teacher. One day he told me he was going to Colorado Springs to visit his family and pick up a book that had been described to him as "amazing." Other than this vague but enthusiastic recommendation, he knew nothing about the book. I gave him $15 and asked him to buy a copy for me, too. To this day I do not know why I did that. He and I weren't close buddies, and I had no particular reason to trust his taste in literature.

But in light of what happened next, I wonder if some unseen helper influenced me to reach for my wallet. I got the book and began reading it. I was not the kind of person to read big books, but I was not put off by this one. Since it was obvious that the first part of the book was well over my head, I did as many others have done—I read the book backwards, Part IV first and Part I last.

I was an eager reader and was more than halfway through the Urantia Book when, in January of 1971, disaster struck. Jenny, the woman I was living with in common-law marriage, died in a freak accident. I was devastated. When such a crisis occurs, all but the core of one's essence is stripped away. I had to examine my reality in its purest state. (I had felt this before when I was 13 and almost died in a ditch. I had grabbed a live wire, was severely shocked, then passed out face down in shallow water and almost drowned.)

As I had just begun reading the Urantia Book, not as many of its teachings had been integrated into my universe as they now are. Yet, I did have an interesting experience. On the night of Jenny's death, as I grieved and prayed, thrown into a trance by the emotional crisis, I found myself in a void. There was no light or dark, no matter or substance. Whether it was purely mental, or whether I was being spiritually influenced, I do not know.

I asked (or, more accurately, I felt), "How can this be?" My plea was for answers from the foundation of primal reality; it spanned the complete void as well as total existence, including all of life and death. The answer came back from within and without: "Because I Am." It was then that I knew I would be fine. I knew that I would grow to understand, accept, and eventually deal with Jenny's death, and everything else for that matter, sooner or later.

Since then I have tried to live the teachings of the Urantia Book, to grow and become more than I am. I realized then, as I do now, that there is a future self that I will become. One can attach the mind to that more complete ideal of one's self which will, by one's choices and experiences, draw oneself forward to that new state of existence. That future self is, of course, the Thought Adjuster, as well as all of one's intermediate selves that occur before fusion.

The teachings of the Urantia Book, and my ever-expanding appreciation of beauty, understanding of truth, and living of goodness, are my religion.

GEORGE COUTIS: I was born and raised in a small Wyoming farm town at the foot of the magnificent Big Horn mountains. My parents came from Greek and English backgrounds. A rather shy, Catholic boy, I was definitely being groomed for the priesthood as I performed my altar-boy duties.

Right from the get-go I felt a deep personal relationship with Jesus. But by age 15, having endured much family turmoil and dysfunction, I said goodbye to Catholicism and began my search for personal identity and truth. I could not buy into that particular brand of religion, because I knew somehow, somewhere deep in my soul, that there was more to it than "We're the best and the one and only true religion." Besides, my nuclear family began to disintegrate and I became very confused. How could God allow so much pain in my life and in the lives of those I loved?

From the beginning my quest involved complete separation from the society that I had known up to that point. By 1970, having transferred to Idaho State University in Pocatello, I began taking drugs to get high. I was full of questions: Who am I? Where am I going? What is my purpose? My intellect was always at work questioning, but no answers quite "got it" for me.

One evening I was directed to someone's house to buy pot. I had no idea who this person was but I went with the flow. As we became acquainted and transacted our business, there was something about him, something in the steady gaze of his eyes, that attracted me. I went back to his place unannounced a few days later. We talked for a long time about life and what we thought we were looking for. As I prepared to leave, he handed me this big blue book, saying, "Here. Read this and come back and tell me what you think of it."

As I carried it home, the Urantia Book seemed to have a radiance of its own—it *pulsated*—and I knew, before I'd even opened the cover, that I had something very good in my 19-year-old hands.

I got home, climbed into bed, and excitedly opened the book. Although the names and terminology were foreign to me, as I skimmed through the pages, mini-lights went off in my head. It all simply and immediately rang true within my being. I *knew* I had a major tool to help answer those questions of identity and purpose. What relief I felt! What inner peace!

Now, thirty years later, I admit that I still have ups and downs as I captain my ship through both the calm and choppy waters of mortal life. But I have a wonderful pilot by my side; I am never alone. The UB is always close by to offer new insights, even from the same page or sentence that I may have read fifty times previously. And all I can say from my tippy-tippy toes to the toppy-top of my now nearly hairless head is: Thank you! Thank you! Thank you!

MARTY GREENHUT: I began searching for a revelation of God in my childhood, after finding out that the world was not exactly as it was presented in the *Dick and Jane* readers or in Sunday school lessons. I was very unhappy with the hypocrisy and jungle-like, survival-of-the-fittest society in which I found myself growing up during World

War II and the subsequent Cold War years.

I went to high school and college at Yeshiva University where I also attended the Hebrew Teachers Institute for six years as a practicing and believing Orthodox Jew. By the time I got out of Yeshiva I was ready to spread my wings and try to change the world. I became a teacher, hoping to nurture the younger generations in brotherhood and love. This ended when I discovered that schools were forbidden to do anything but prepare the next generation for the workplace—for competition. The marketplace with its profit motive was in control and there was nothing I could do about it.

In the mid-'60s I became dedicated to the civil rights struggle and the peace movement. It was through the teachings of Martin Luther King that I became interested in non-violence, and it was in the Black churches that I was introduced to Jesus. Though I had been an activist against the war in Vietnam, part of me leaned in the other direction, toward the belief that violent revolution was the only option. When the moment of decision came—whether to follow the path of violence or non-violence—I had my first real contact with Jesus. When I decided to go his way, I found him by my side and pledged to follow him in my search for truth.

In 1970, while living in northern New Mexico as a hippie, I met someone who, after getting to know me, said, "Marty, you should read the Urantia Book." The book was not available in that isolated place, but one arrived with a person who was visiting our little village from San Francisco for a week and he loaned it to me. My wife Gloria and I spent the entire week reading aloud to each other. I knew that I had received the information that I'd been searching for.

I was given five full years to devote to its study and to work out the questions I had about revolutionizing the world. I found myself understanding Jesus in a certain way because his childhood culture was so much like mine. His education and parenting were things that I understood firsthand. I feel as though I met Jesus in Capernaum on the shores of Galilee and not at all through the introduction of Paul. I still relate to Jesus as a Jew and find my background to be a real advantage in understanding him.

I have been paid in excess for my labors and have since entered the kingdom and been enlisted in the Urantia corps of agondonters. It is the greatest privilege I can imagine to be in the receivership of the fifth epochal revelation for our world, and meeting my Urantia friends has been an unspeakable joy.

JOHN ROPER: My family was not the kind that openly talked about religion. We went to church on Sunday, but not much was said after that. It was expected that you believed in God, so no discussion was necessary. When I was about seven years old we moved from Portsmouth, Virginia, to Richmond, Virginia, and with the connections to our church gone, we were free to find a new church association. I began going to Sunday school at a little Episcopal church with my best friend. Eventually all the family, my parents and brother, went there.

This was the first place I remember hearing about Jesus. I was sitting around one of those very low children's tables with little chairs. The teacher was reading to us out of a book similar to *Fun with Dick and Jane,* but it was about Jesus. I felt a surge in my little heart unlike anything I had ever experienced. I couldn't explain it and it frightened me. I seemed to have a small understanding about God, but who was this Jesus person, and why did I feel so funny learning about him?

I continued going to the Episcopal church, was confirmed, and served in church services. But the story of Jesus' life as presented in the Bible, and the doctrines taught about him in church, just didn't seem right. I could never reconcile the death of Jesus as an act to save us from our sins. It just wasn't logical.

As I grew older, I moved away from organized religion. Science fiction became my source of universe philosophy. Heinlein, Asimov, Bradbury, Smith, Herbert, and Clarke all expanded my perception of reality and allowed me to consider existence beyond the boundaries of this planet.

College and my first marriage came along. I was still in a fog about Jesus, but at the same time God was still there. My wife and I looked into Eastern religions and astrology—the '60s kind of things—but nothing lit my fire like science fiction. Life on this planet seemed to be changing rapidly and there was excitement about the future—I just didn't know what that future was.

In 1970 we were living in the little town of Keego Harbor, Michigan. In September of that year I flew to San Francisco for a job interview. When I returned, my wife and a stranger named George Sammis picked me up at the airport. George was the friend of a neighbor in the apartment complex where we lived, and he was nice enough to drive my wife down to the airport. On the way home, George told me about a new book he had just gotten from his mother. The words he used to describe it were, "... and it is supposed to be written by people from outer space!" Whoa! The magic words: "outer space." I was hooked.

That evening George came over and opened the box containing a brand-new copy of the Urantia Book, and we began reading, the first time for us all. We started with the first Adam and Eve paper, and by the time we finished it I knew that this book was *the* book with *the* answers. The next morning George returned home to Clear Lake, Iowa. The book went with him. No bookstores in our area carried the Urantia Book and we couldn't find it in the library. I had no desire to read any of the four or five unread science fiction books sitting on my shelf. Then January came and George surprised us with a return visit *and* our very own copy of the Urantia Book. What an incredible gift!

My marriage was floundering and I thought a change of venue would help, so off to Colorado we went. The book came along, but other events in my life were taking precedence: The birth of a son, anti-war demonstrations at Colorado University in Boulder, difficulty keeping a job and rocky roads with my wife all led eventually to divorce and a return home to Michigan. My wife kept our original copy of the Urantia Book and I got my own. I read it nightly, keeping it on my night table, where coincidentally, Jane, my true love, first saw it.

Of all the times I have read the book, the most special was with Jane and our three children on our great 1976 odyssey to Alaska where we read it through together for the first time. Driving up the Alaskan Highway, listening to Beethoven, watching the unbelievable scenery and reading the Urantia Book—what an awesome way to finally find out about the matchless nature of our Creator Son/brother Michael! I am forever changed.

THEA HARDY: My earliest memories are of lights moving across the ceiling of my room at night as I lay in my crib under the window. They were only passing cars, but they were magical to me. When I found out about stars, I knew I wanted to be an astronomer. I didn't realize I was looking for God. I grew up mainstream Methodist, but the ideas of God and Jesus promoted by my family and church, while warm and fuzzy, didn't make a huge impression. To me, the feeling of God was mostly found singing Bach in the church choir, with the huge pipe organ thundering joy, and light streaming through the tall stained-glass windows. I ran for sheer joy on the hillsides above Boise, drinking in the sun and sky, but I didn't know that I knew God.

By high school, disgusted with the hypocrisy I saw around me, I was a defiant atheist. I enjoyed tearing down religion. But after a few years in college, I began studying philosophy and even tried inventing a world religion as a class project. I became aware that I was searching for meaning.

In the late '60s I moved to Berkeley and continued my pursuit of enhanced consciousness in the manner of the times. Initially, I was overjoyed by the celebration of diversity that I had never seen before. I felt that I had found my place at last. But over time, as happens in movements, codification and polarization changed things. Diversity shrank until there was a semi-uniform code even amongst the supposedly free. Peace and love were preached, but up close they were still not practiced. Disillusionment only spurred my pursuit. I moved out of the city and into the country.

In 1970, near where I lived in Sonoma, California, I encountered an unusual group of people who invited me to a study group where they read a big blue book. I went because I was attracted to the young man who asked me. At first, I was outraged. These people were obviously intelligent, but they believed such crazy stuff. The young man suggested I treat the book as science fiction. This let me suspend my disbelief enough to start reading. Within a few months, we studied Paper 100. The story of enlarging the picture on the snarling filthy hulk facing the saber-toothed tiger made a tremendous impression on me. The entire paper opened up my heart. Suddenly I knew something very important had happened to me and I had to have my own copy of this book.

I got my first (and still most beloved) copy that summer in Sausalito, and began to devour the incredible quantity of truth, beauty and goodness it contained. In short order, I attempted communication with my Adjuster, something I have continued to seek all these years. My search was being rewarded, and the real adventure began. Learning to understand more about God, the universe, people and myself started to satisfy the hunger for meaning that had been growing in me throughout my life. And yet it left me with a yearning for more. At last I had found the light my child-mind had been drawn to all those years ago.

My personal culture has undergone many changes over the years, but the basic values of the UB have only grown more deeply rooted, deeply felt, and more fully understood as time has passed and I have continued my study. The more I read the book, the more truth it seems to contain, and the more fascinating it becomes. Things I could not begin to understand in the beginning have become clearer and clearer, but more wonderful mysteries to solve always present themselves. In recent years, I have had the opportunity to begin more fully to live what the book has taught me, and that experience of attempting to live the truth is the supreme thrill of all. The book has been friend, companion, and counselor in both good and terrible times. It remains my touchstone for truth and reality. The adventure continues.

ED OWEN: I was born in 1934, in Spokane, Washington. Raised Catholic, I early learned the value of prayer and used it to my advantage to get what I needed to survive a less-than-average childhood. In 1952 I joined the army. From 1952 to 1955 I was stationed in Germany where I encountered the aftermath of World War II. I then bounced around the planet, experiencing various addictions, divorce, and other assorted failures. To be fair I must also admit that I usually carried a joyful outlook on life in general.

In 1970, I was going through some big changes in my life, having quit my job and being more or less homeless, searching for something but not really knowing what it was. I was reading many books on different religions and philosophies, but the only one that really held my attention was the New Testament. There was something magnetic about Jesus' steady sayings: "Consider the lilies," "planting the seeds," "the lost sheep," and many others.

About this time I was hit by a car and thought I was surely going to die. While lying there waiting for the lights to go out, I asked God to forgive me for wasting my life. But I survived, and about six weeks later, while I was healing in shared living quarters, I met someone who was always reading a big book in the corner of our little one-room haven. One day I asked, "W.L., what are you reading?" He replied that it was quite an interesting book, and placed it on my bed so I could look at while he went out for a while.

I opened the book to page 1096, and the first thing I read was, *"The goal of human self-realization should be spiritual, not material."* I closed it, my thumb marking the page, so I could keep reading right there. My thought was, "If it says that much in one sentence, what does the rest of this book have to say? I was fascinated. I couldn't read fast enough. Within a few hours I had visited the mansion worlds, the Garden of Eden, a neighboring planet—just to name a few first-day highlights. I had been given The Revelation.

I looked for a place to live where I could spend some time reading, and moved to Bisbee, Arizona. I realized God was giving me a vacation from all duties so I could align my priorities. I recall reading at the time how Jesus mingled with many different people, and I felt honored to do likewise, attending Urantia conferences in Colorado, Washington, Idaho, Illinois, Wisconsin, and California.

I now live in Sacramento and do volunteer work. I also play and teach the physics of the golf stroke. I look forward to meeting more travelers on our way to the outer space regions. Come and visit—we can talk about God 'n' golf!

RUSS GUSTAFSON: Raised a Catholic, I went to Catholic grammar school and Catholic high school. I took to heart the idea that God loves everyone, and freely questioned whatever teachings did not fit within that concept.

In 1965 I went off to college at UC Santa Barbara. My grandmother said I shouldn't go there because it was full of Communists who didn't believe in God. I was looking forward to college where I would see all points of view and judge for myself. I majored in biology, switched to philosophy and finally graduated in 1970 from UC Berkeley with a degree in bacteriology. The thing I learned was that nobody knew anything.

After college, without a job, I lived with my parents for a short time. My father handed me a big blue book that he had bought at the urging of an airline pilot friend. I glanced at a few pages and fell in love with the long sentences that flowed like poetry. For three months I read the book full time. It became the basis of my life. Thank you, Father!

BOB HUNT: In the spring of 1970 I was living near Monterey, California, and teaching mathematics at the U.S. Naval Postgraduate School. My brother Pat, a professor of speech communications at San Francisco State University, had recently given a hitchhiker a ride across the Golden Gate Bridge. In expressing his appreciation for the ride, the hitchhiker, a young man described as having very peaceful, clear blue eyes, spoke of a book that he said was written by supermortal celestial beings. Knowing of my interest in such matters, Pat told me of the unusual encounter but confessed that he could not recall the name of the book, only that it sounded like "tarantula."

Curious about the story and the book, I began searching with the limited information that my brother had provided. At the renowned City Lights bookstore in the North Beach section of San Francisco, I inquired about "a book whose title sounded like 'tarantula' and was written by beings from other worlds." The clerk, without batting an eye, told me he didn't know whether they had such a book, but that I should search in their "extra-terrestrial section." Having no success, I proceeded to another well-known bookstore, The Tides, in Sausalito, a popular waterfront town in Marin County across the Golden Gate Bridge from San Francisco. There, the clerk replied that I must be looking for the Urantia Book, which they *did* have in the store.

Upon viewing the large book in a pale blue dust jacket and priced at $15, I was immediately struck by the opening words of the Foreword: "*In the minds of the mortals of Urantia—that being the name of your world—there exists great confusion respecting the meaning of such terms as God, divinity, and deity.*" These words rang true and affirmed aspects of my lifelong spiritual search, beginning with positive experiences in the Methodist Church during my youth and continuing with my ongoing interest in world religions and philosophy.

So I purchased the book. It proved to be incredibly consistent with my faith and beliefs, as well as a fulfillment of my lifelong search for truth, beauty, and goodness.

I immediately shared my discovery with my friend and colleague, Phil Calabrese, with whom I was already having discussions about science, philosophy, and religion along lines strikingly similar to what this wonderful book was offering. Within the next two years, I read and studied the book and shared it with other close friends, including Dick and Cheryl Prince in San Diego. In 1972, Phil and I taught an experimental college course on the Urantia Book in Bakersfield, California, and became acquainted with Julia Fenderson, who was at the time the West Coast Field Representative of the Urantia Brotherhood. Julia had been a friend of Dr. William Sadler and a member of the group known as the Forum, who first viewed and read the Urantia Papers prior to their publication. Julia, often accompanied by members of the First Urantia Society of Los Angeles (FUSLA), attended every session of our course in Bakersfield.

In subsequent years, I attended FUSLA meetings and gatherings in Los Angeles, including the first West Coast Conference, which featured a memorable concert by Buffy Sainte-Marie, a long-time Urantia Book reader. I met many wonderful people, including Vincent Ventola, a visionary artist of the "spiritual renaissance," as he called it. By invitation, I introduced the book to a gathering of the World Future Society in Los Angeles in 1974, in a talk called "The Urantia Book—A Guide to the Future and Beyond." In 1981 I gave a talk on "Spiritual Mind Receptivity" at the Urantia Brotherhood's General Conference in Snowmass, Colorado; and another on "Time and Space" in 1988, at the first Scientific Symposium in Nashville, Tennessee.

I remain a dedicated and committed student of the Urantia Book, and I offer praise and gratitude for its appearance on our world at this time in our journey through time and space.

PHIL CALABRESE: Raised Roman Catholic and called "The Pope" by my fellow dorm residents in college, I realized at around age 23 that there is no certainty in Catholic dogma. The principle of papal infallibility was an error. Putting aside the regular practice of Roman Catholicism without losing sight of God, I decided to think about it all after some time had passed.

Six years later, married and finished with graduate school, I resumed my questioning. In college and after I had asked myself and others, "What is my connection to God? Is it the Church? the Pope? the Bible? tradition?" I returned to this question as a mathematician, but was willing to read anything that might be helpful. I thought I should read what Jesus, presumably a master of religious knowledge, had said about this question.

This led me to read the four Gospels, skipping over any words not uttered by Jesus. I soon realized that Jesus was always talking about "the kingdom of God," and I determined to understand what he meant by this phrase. After several sessions of reading, I reached the Gospel of Luke where Jesus answers that "the kingdom of God is within you." It dawned on me that the certainty I was seeking about God could never come from outside my own mind; it had to be like an insight, like a mathematical theorem. It could not be through some outer confirmation; that could always be a magician's trick.

As soon as I had this realization I became aware of another mind in the room with me. I turned around in my seat but there was no one there. Although I could see no one, I was aware of a very strong feeling of being loved. My question had been, "What is my connection to God?" and here was more than an answer. It was a demonstration. After several minutes of this, my mind wandered onto some ideas related to the experience, and I momentarily forgot the smiling presence in the room. When I came back from my daydream I was a bit alarmed to realize that the experience was still happening. I thought, "How long am I going to be this way?" Back came the answer into my mind, "As long as you require it." So after several more moments basking in this presence, after there was no doubt whatsoever about what was happening, I thought, "Okay, now I can practice being as I was." Within ten or fifteen seconds I felt the mind move closer and then coalesce with my own mind, and I was back to normal.

For years I told no one about this experience, but soon I was talking about time and eternity, truth, justice, and other absolutes. One day I was discussing these concepts with Pat Hunt, a professor friend, when he said, "You are reminding me of a book I heard about from a hitchhiker. The name sounds like 'tarantula.'" Pat's brother Bob later found it—the Urantia Book—in a metaphysical bookstore. Bob told me that he'd decided to buy the book after thinking of me.

When Bob put it into my lap it was love at first sight. I devoured the book in four-plus months, beginning with thematic readings laid out in Clyde Bedell's *Concordex*, and then doing a complete sequential reading, including two readings of the Jesus papers.

I've been an enthusiastic reader and student of the revelation ever since. But I've never allowed the written word to supersede the living Spirit that we all carry as our personal connection to God.

Addendum: I heard recently from long-time reader Char Sneve that Sam, a guitarist for Janis Joplin, had hitchhiked up and down California in the late '60s with the purpose of telling people about the Urantia Book. Could it be . . . ?

LYN DAVIS LEAR: After graduating from college, I got married, found a job, and the realities of life set in. I worked long days, and my husband and I had almost no social life. It was at the end of the '60s and we were all caught up in the spirit of the times.

All my life I had been searching, but filling out my silhouette of God now became an all-consuming obsession. For two years I read everything I could find on religion, the occult, New Age and Eastern philosophies. I read Edgar Cayce at lunch and Teilhard de Chardin after dinner. Eventually I had pieced together a meaningful, somewhat coherent world view, but something was missing.

I had been brought up in an extended fundamentalist Presbyterian family. I remember arguing with the counselors and ministers about the poor children in India going to hell because they didn't believe in Jesus. I could not accept that kind of a God in my heart. Eventually I got kicked out of camp for questioning too much. But I always believed in some kind of loving God, and would have long discussions with my younger siblings about infinity and eternity. The philosophical and metaphysical world always fascinated me, but a real understanding of Jesus eluded me.

One day I was in a shopping mall during my lunch hour, exploring a bookstore I had been in a hundred times before. I had been praying to get to know Jesus better, to rid myself of any negative associations I might have had about him, when I looked up and saw the Urantia Book. I couldn't understand why I had never seen it before. I read the front and back flaps and started to cry. I just knew this book had the answers I had been searching for. I had to open a charge account because I couldn't afford the $25 it cost.

I read it every day for several months and strangely, every bit of it made sense, although I hardly understood it all. Eventually I moved to Los Angeles and met Julia Fenderson, became involved in FUSLA [the First Urantia Society of Los Angeles], and have been in and around the Urantia movement ever since.

Discovering the Urantia Book and its teachings has, without a doubt, been the single most important event in my life.

DENIE SCHACH: I was raised in a very Catholic Dutch family that immigrated to the United States when I was six. We were sponsored by Saint Peter's Catholic Church in Fort Wayne, Indiana. My father loved religious philosophy and we would often discuss religion at length.

In 1968 my husband, John Schach, took a philosophy class at Indiana Tech from Dr. Meredith Sprunger. Dr. Sprunger often used the Urantia Book in his courses. John brought the book home and, although he never developed an interest in it himself, he left it out in plain view.

In January 1971 I was living in Jersey City, New Jersey. It was the time of the Vietnam War, and John had left to go into the National Guard. His parents, who had been living with us, were also gone; his mother had died the previous year and his father had taken a job in Canada. I was alone in the house, four months pregnant, and right in front of me was the Urantia Book. Once I began to read it, I couldn't put it down and it became my friend. It answered, and continues to answer, so many of my questions.

I kept on reading the book for twenty-five years without knowing that there were other readers like me out there. Then, in 1999, I gave the book to an acquaintance who looked it up on the Internet. There, to our surprise, we discovered a whole world of Urantia Book readers. Six months later I attended my first Urantia conference, in Vancouver, and was amazed by all the Urantia people there. I was going through a very difficult period in my life at that time, but I was strengthened by finding my Urantia family.

The Urantia Book has provided soil for growth as well as validation that there is an eternal adventure. It would take a book in itself to explain how my life has been affected by the Urantia teachings.

JAMAIL MCKINNEY: I was living in San Francisco in 1957 and a passing tourist was visiting a friend of mine. Over dinner, the visitor talked about the Urantia Book and I, as a compulsive reader of anything, asked to borrow it. I took it up to Kings Canyon National Park for a quiet weekend and only got as far as "The Seven Superuniverses" when I had to return the book. Hungry for more, I searched for another copy. For several years in my quest, I inquired at many bookstores for a book called *Arancha*. I never found it.

Then one day in 1971, while living in a commune in Portland, I found the Urantia Book in a small bookstore for $15. I bought it using money granted me by this communal group, although we were barely surviving at the time. In 1972 we moved to land in Aeneas Valley in Washington and there I finally finished reading it. Inspired, I began a campaign trail of hitchhiking and talking about the book all around America.

That spring, through an ad, I found another reader. Zabriel was the second person I'd met who had ever heard of the book. He came up to our land and we had many talks in my tipi. Together we spent the fall picking apples in nearby Okanogan County. That winter I met Burt King and Doris George of Urantian Research in Los Angeles. A communion of spirits ensued and they opened many doors for me. By then I was well into my third reading of the book.

In the spring of 1973, up on my land, I began teaching a class on the book with seven close friends as students. Deciding to have a larger group,

I left for another tour of America and invited any and all to visit us the following July. That class—a group of seventeen—lasted for ten days and culminated in a fire-walking party. From it an enthusiastic group emerged to travel the national parks all summer spreading the word of the Urantia Book, love and peace. We wore white and conducted daily classes as we hitchhiked from park to park, having fun every step of the way.

In October eleven of us made our way from Washington to Yosemite to the Grand Canyon to Ocala National Forest in Florida. In Titusville we were joined by a turbaned person, and as twelve we moved up to Madison, Wisconsin, for the wedding of two of our number during the Christmas holidays. When we left there, we were eighteen in number and holding daily readings of the book.

In Salt Lake City, staying with the brother of a member of our group, we reached out to Mormons and hippies. Soon the people in the house next door joined with us. When both houses were sold we left Salt Lake twenty-four in number, and bought a large parcel of land in Southern Oregon which we called Ascendington. We spent the spring organizing and cleaning up the land and giving short teacher classes. That June I returned to Aeneas to hold a ten-day class for sixty. That class, and a few more that we conducted that fall and spring, flourished. However, problems eventually arose and the group scattered just before Thanksgiving Day.

I returned to Portland to seek guidance with other groups from Colorado and British Columbia. In the process I learned that to properly lead, you must first walk in the steps as a follower and wait upon God's timetable.

The good seeds were planted; they sprouted, emerged, and slowly grew and began to thrive. Now, many years and many life experiences later, many of us are still connected and we continue to enjoy prosperity, peace and a family of good-seeking friends. Today we hold reunions, parties and gatherings and a few funerals. Living the faith of Jesus in this world, as it is, does make the difference.

JEFFREY WATTLES: When people become receptive to the Urantia Book, they are sometimes prompted to ask a special question. To respond adequately to this question, the person answering must introduce them to the Urantia Book. I asked such a question and received the answer I needed in 1971.

I was living just north of Chicago, finishing graduate study at Northwestern University. Since abandoning the Christianity of my youth, my spiritual quest had turned to Greek and German philosophy. I had recently begun Transcendental Meditation when I got a chance to discuss Hinduism with a visiting meditation teacher. In the course of the conversation I asked how the things we were discussing related to the teachings of Jesus. That was the question that triggered the mention of the Urantia Book.

He told me almost nothing of the book but said that his main reason for coming to the Chicago area was to visit the Urantia Foundation. He invited me to go with him, but I declined. My curiosity persisted, though, and a couple of days later I made the trip to the Foundation myself. Arriving just before the office was to close at five o'clock, I had time only to peruse the titles of the papers. I was not yet ready to buy the book, and returned home. That night, however, as I lay in bed, an odd vision of those titles floated into mind as I drifted off to sleep, and I determined to buy the book the next morning.

Once I got the book back home, I sat down, opened to page 21, Paper 1, and read, *"The Universal Father is the God of all creation, the First Source and Center of all things and beings."* Immediately I knew what I had in my hands.

I will not attempt to describe the wonders of the growing spiritual experience stimulated by the study of the Papers. I read the book in three months, began attending a study group, and have been as active as possible with the teachings ever since.

When I read the outlines on page 43 of "the new philosophy of living," I realized that I would have to begin constructing my philosophy all over again. Worship eventually replaced Transcendental Meditation. In 1973, I began a year of seminar study, intending to go on to some sort of missionary work. The following year I moved to Berkeley, California, to join a volunteer evangelistic organization proclaiming the revealed gospel. In 1986 I moved to Boulder, Colorado, to be director of a school for students of the Urantia Book. In 1988 I attended the University of Toronto for two years of study and teaching, mostly in religion. In 1990 I moved to Kent State University and published *The Golden Rule*, showing how spiritual teachings emerge in cultural history.

I am blessed with my God-knowing wife Hagiko and our son Ben, who completed his first reading of Part IV with me in 1997. Every day I experience joy in our Father and joy serving in the universal family. I am grateful to all who cooperated to bring this revelation to light, all who cooperate to promote the wise propagation of this book and its teachings, and all who help us live in spiritual unity.

STACEY HARLAN: It was 1971 and I was 18 years old. My spiritual search had already been going on for years. It started in childhood with an intriguing book called *The Mind of India*, and continued with the study of works by such luminaries as Alan Watts, Krishnamurti, and Gurdjieff. I had experienced little affinity with the cultural-religion of my childhood, Judaism. Despite this interest in metaphysics, my spiritual development was hardly advanced, as evidenced by my initial contact with a young spiritual teacher named Bill whom I had met through a mutual friend. Bill had come over to my house; already present was a female acquaintance I was interested in.

Bill patiently endured my antics intended to impress this young woman, all the while inserting Truth into my psyche. At one point in the evening, somehow, someway I suddenly awoke to the fact that I was in the presence of a real spiritual teacher. Shortly after this fateful evening, while over at Bill's house, I noticed a large blue book on his coffee table.

"What's that?" I asked Bill. Without saying a word, he shrugged his shoulders and shoved the book toward me.

Leafing through it, I sensed almost immediately that this was, as I put it to myself at the time, "something from the Absolute." I was tremendously impressed by the clarity of the text and the amazing range of subject matter ostensibly dealt with. Even a brief perusal suggested the text was a masterful example of organizational genius and coherency. More than its content, the aspect of the Urantia Book that initially attracted me and got me hooked was its style of expression. I borrowed the book from Bill and, of course, soon bought my own copy.

At one point in the Urantia Book Rodan is quoted as saying about Jesus: *"He is either what he professes to be, or else is the greatest hypocrite and fraud the world has ever seen."* I believe that literate readers must come to the conclusion that the Urantia Book is indeed what it professes to be, or else is the greatest and most astonishing example of literary/artistic fraud and hypocrisy the world has ever seen.

The Urantia Book continues to provide a "universe framework" and inspirational guiding star, reminding me that there are worlds beyond this world.

KELLY ELSTROTT: I was living in a college dorm. It was a Saturday morning, and there was no weekend cafeteria service. My brother had invited me to his house for a breakfast of apple pancakes. His girlfriend's big blue book was lying on the coffee table. I opened it and fell right in. It is now more than thirty years later and I am still exploring the universe of facts, ideas, and challenges presented in the Urantia Book.

The girlfriend cooking the apple cakes was Patti, now my sister-in-law—Patti the artist and truth seeker, painter of grand alien landscapes and mosaics of organic cellular wonderlands. She told me to take the book home.

For months I jumped about in the blue book. In school I was studying comparative religions, and the Urantia Book helped me piece together all the myths and ancient history, serving as an all-purpose *Cliff's Notes* for any test the teacher could dream up.

I was captivated by the sweeping story of man's attempts to build a civilization—the incredible 200,000-year struggle of Van the Steadfast to keep the idea of the one God alive, he alone pitted against a rebellion of powerful angels; Adam and Eve's disillusionment when faced with the primitive warring tribes; the steady hand of Machiventa Melchizedek to bring earth back into the fold; the succession of prophets and Pharaohs each pushing the envelope out further to evolve the concept of God from wrathful to forgiving to loving and eternal. I was mystified by this book and wondered what man or men could have dreamed up this wonderful saga.

I distinctly remember the day it dawned on me that this book was truth. Patti was painting and I was reading the paper on "The Resurrection of Lazarus" aloud to her as she worked. It was cool, the windows were open to a bright afternoon. The smell of herbal tea and honey filled the room. There was another guy there and we took turns reading. I felt a warmth sweep over me. This was really Jesus talking! This was what really happened two thousand years ago!

From then on the blue book changed from being just a history book to being a spiritual touchstone. I then discovered the papers on the Thought Adjuster. I read and reread them, savoring the idea that we each had a piece of God within us. But along with the sudden liberation from all the Catholic guilt came the realization that it was my responsibility alone to discern the Father's will.

A few weeks later I was lying down on a huge open field that the Louisiana State University Tigers band used for practice. It was after midnight. The only sound that could be heard was the distant *whump whump* of an industrial-size cooling fan. I lay there flat on my back, my arms stretched out, looking up for shooting stars. I began to imagine that I could feel the earth swiftly turning below me and I was holding on for dear life. The sound of that far-off machine was really the big engine underground thumping away to keep the earth in motion. I felt as if I were on a planet hurtling headlong through space. I then realized I really was a part of it *now*. I would never be alone anymore. My spirit was with me and we were traveling through the universe, through time. I had arrived.

LES TIBBALS: When I was young, people considered me a street-wise incorrigible, but there was a side of me that my dad and the other authorities didn't know or care about. Trying to be independent of my severely alcoholic dad, I left home at 15 and hitchhiked to Chicago with my girlfriend Luanna, a Menomonee Indian girl I'd met in Wisconsin. The year was 1968—a rough time. The experience taught me that I could survive on my own. I had learned how to weave between the police, the riots, and the perverts who prey on young boys and girls. During this time I was also an avid reader of religious material, especially anything about Jesus, all the while dabbling in yoga and meditation. But none of this satisfied me.

At 18 I started out on a spiritual quest. I remember thinking that if God wanted me to find something—whatever it was—I was open to it. And so began the hitchhiking experience that culminated in my finding the fifth epochal revelation.

In 1971 a girl named Sandy and I were headed for Oregon from Oklahoma City. Our plan was to meet some friends at their grandmother's farm in Salem. At Grand Island, Nebraska, where hitchhiking was against the law, we were picked up by a highway patrolman. Unable to pay the fine, we spent six days in jail. There were no facilities for women, so Sandy was taken to the next county. It meant that when I got out of the pokey I had to hitchhike over to the next county to find her, all the while hoping I wouldn't get picked up and land in jail again.

While still in Nebraska, Sandy and I were waiting for a ride at an exit when I wandered away briefly from the road and found myself standing in a field of marijuana plants ten feet high. Excitedly I ran back to the roadside, shifted my clothes around, and stuffed my duffel bag full of big, bushy tops.

We scored a ride with some folks, and I let them try some of the smoke. After much thought, I said, "If we can ride with you all the way to the coast, you can have the whole duffel bag full." They accepted. We made it as far as Nevada when the car overheated and the engine blew up somewhere in the desert. The guy volunteered to leave his wife and all their belongings on the side of the road with us while he hitched a ride to California to borrow another car. We were camped in the sun next to that car for several days—hot, hungry and thirsty. He finally showed up and we headed for the California coast. Seeing the ocean and the giant redwoods for the first time was a religious experience in itself.

When eventually we made it to our Oregon destination, our friends had already left. After a couple days of home cooking and wonderful hospitality, Grandma drove us into the beautiful Cascades where we found our friends living in a commune of hardcore hippies. Feeling awkward, I sat myself down in the living room and decided to bury myself in a good book—or any book for that matter. On a shelf I noticed a big book with a white cover and letters that said "The Life and Teachings of Jesus." Although I was only 18, I'd read plenty on Jesus, none of it exceptionally informative or terribly inspiring, so with a cynical attitude I thought to myself, "I wonder what *they* have to say about Jesus."

Reading the introduction to Part IV, written by the midwayer who was onetime assigned to the watchcare of the apostle Andrew, the authoritative tone struck a positive chord in me. And when I read about Jesus coming into the world like any other human—no immaculate conception—I was hooked. I headed for the barn and didn't stop reading for six hours. I remember saying to myself, "This is real; this is what it claims to be."

When I returned to the house I was on fire. I asked everyone, "Have you read this book? Do you know where it came from?" Nobody knew or was interested. I was disillusioned.

I hitchhiked back to Oklahoma alone without a penny in my pocket, eating out of orchards and vineyards through California. Back in Oklahoma I found the Urantia Book in a bookstore right off, but I had no money so I worked for a month until I could pay for it. In the phone book, under "Urantia," I found Berkeley Elliott and joined a study group, turned my future wife on to the UB and raised both my kids with the UB experience. My daughter has gone on to the mansion worlds and my son is still an avid reader.

I rambled my way across the States to find God and the UB, yet the book was right in my own back yard and God was inside me the whole time! I guess the angels thought I needed a little more seasoning before handing this revelation to me. My sincere thanks to our unseen friends for their consideration, protection and the continuing adventure.

STEPHEN ZENDT: The fact is, the Urantia Book found me. I was fortunate to be working as a volunteer on a small monthly journal called *The Organic Morning Glory*, whose editor, Larry Geis, was a new and enthusiastic reader of the revelation. My expressed need to tie together my convictions about Jesus and the universe, and for something that fused reality with religion, gave Larry the clue that I would be an appropriate candidate for introduction to the book. He simply went out to his car during a lengthy after-dinner discussion and brought the UB into my apartment, dropping it into my lap. I opened it to the first page of the Foreword, read to the end of the page, and simply knew that this book was what I had been searching for all these years.

Larry also introduced me to the local study group at the same time that he "hooked" me on the book. I've been involved in Urantia study groups for thirty years now, as a result of this double intro.

That took place in 1971, with all the frills of hippie culture and chemical intake that were so much a part of life in San Francisco. My friends in the local Urantia groups became my surrogate family. I was able to overcome many personal problems and dispense with a number of unnecessary habits thanks to my acquaintance with these people who were growing and showing forth the fruits of the spirit in their lives.

While nothing has moved and shaped me more than the influence of my parents (my father was the pastor of several Christian church congregations while I was growing up), the Urantia Book was the key to gathering all the scattered pieces of my life together into something sensible, and to my making responsible relationships with God and with Jesus. These relationships have held me up through my greatest trials, inspired me to grow in love and grace, and literally saved me at a time when I most needed to be saved.

JANELLE BALNICKE: It was 1971 and I was in my last year of high school. I was sitting, as I often did, on my family's front steps in Denver, Colorado, watching the sun set over the Rocky Mountains. I had lost my real father to cancer while I was still an infant, and I never knew him. For as long as I could remember, I had been praying to know what was really on the other side. That night, in a state of sadness and frustration, I declared in my heart that it seemed truly unfair for God to put us here and leave us without a clue. Why couldn't there be a user's guide to help us? After all, a lot of trouble had gone into creating the world... a little help would go a long way, especially for those of us mustering along with just one parent.

The answer to my prayer came within six months, when a high school buddy handed me the Urantia Book. I had always wanted to know the story behind the story, and I could see that the Urantia Book was leaving no stone unturned, from creation to Jesus. But the thing that truly "hooked" me was the statement that a loving God would never demand the sacrificial death of a son he loved. And although, as a Christian, I'd never stopped to consider how odd the belief in the crucifixion really was, the Urantia Book's firm negation of its necessity lifted a veil I hadn't even known was there. Suddenly, I was given permission to see and believe in a new way.

I bought my first Urantia Book with the money my grandfather—my father's father—had sent me as a graduation present. I believe I willed that Urantia Book into my hands, but I like to think it materialized in such a timely fashion thanks to some help from all my loving fathers—my living grandfather, my deceased father and my heavenly Father—who wanted to give me that user's guide I had asked for as I graduated into my adult life—the first of many gifts and many graduations to come.

NORMAN INGRAM: In 1971 the big change came into my life. I'd had several years of success as a sales mechanical engineer for a company that owned five of the thirteen working sugar plantations in Hawaii in those days. Flying was my hobby, and I owned an aircraft dealership/flight school at the Honolulu International Airport.

My new wife Lyn and I were expecting our first child. We were living in a big, old, beautiful two-story lava stone house on the beach in Waiminloa. It had a circular driveway and was surrounded by many coconut and ironwood trees. Inasmuch as we had a big house on the beach we never lacked houseguests, and this was fine with us because we liked their company. If you stayed up to two weeks, you were considered a guest; if you stayed longer, you were a housemouse.

One such housemouse was a young fellow named David Diggs. He had been staying with us for about four months when he came into my study one day and began to tell me about a book. "Knowing you," he said, "I know you will be interested in this." I asked him what the book was about. "Science and philosophy," was his answer.

He then handed me a big, stately, impressive-looking blue book. I began by carefully scrutinizing the table of contents. I could not believe what I was reading. I was amazed at the range of subject matter covered in this book. I got through the Foreword and was totally blown away. I lost track of time, reading day and night, not conscious of anything going on around me. After about four days, on a Sunday morning around ten o'clock, I flipped to the front of the book to see if there was any information about someone I could talk to about this marvelous revelation.

In fine print I found mention of the Urantia Foundation at 533 Diversey Parkway in Chicago. I called directory assistance, got their number, and made the call.

A sweet voice answered, "This is Christy."

I told her that I had received the Urantia Book three or four days earlier and that I had gone into a time warp, so fascinated was I by the truths I was finding in this book. She laughed and offered to send me some literature about the Foundation and the Brotherhood. Before we hung up I asked her if she knew of any other Urantia Book readers in Hawaii. Christy then told me about her friend Le'Ruth Ward Tyau, a Mormon and a mother with many children, who wrote children's books using UB concepts.

As soon as I finished talking with Christy, I called Le'Ruth in Honolulu and arranged to have lunch with her the next day. I had to meet her to give her a pinch to see if she was real. How could anyone read these truths, know the concepts of this revelation, and still exist on this planet? She was a real and a pleasant delight. As we parted I asked her if she knew of anyone else on the island who was reading the book, and she told me that there were about half a dozen women who regularly got together for a study group.

I raised my hand and volunteered our home for these studies. It was great meeting all the other people in the group. Not long after that, we opened a booth at Diamond Head Crater where we sold organic juices poured over shaved ice at rock concerts. With the profits we bought Urantia Books and donated them to local libraries in Hawaii. In those days Big Blue cost only $12.50. Occasionally we would check back with the libraries, and if a copy was missing we would replace it. Later I arranged for the Foundation to ship ten used Urantia Books to supply the prisons. Over the years I have bought at least twenty books a year to give away to those truth-seeking mortals whom our Father has brought across my path.

The Urantia Book has answered all the fundamental questions I've ever had and it has raised twice as many more. It has inspired me to spread its truths to the nations of our lonely planet, and I will continue to do so as long as God gives me the strength, the faith, and the courage to do his will. Such a life on such a planet!

GERALD HARRISON: Prior to finding the Urantia Book, I would describe myself as an agnostic whenever I was asked about my beliefs. Since the time I was bar- and bat-mitzvahed with my twin sister at 13, I had been totally uninvolved with my family's practice of Judaism.

In late 1970, when I was 25, a friend I had met through Peace Movement activities mentioned that he had been reading a big book with a more complete and modern portrayal of Jesus' life and teachings than he had found elsewhere. We didn't pursue the subject further at that time.

A few months later, in early 1971, my sister-in-law and the fellow she was dating came to visit. In the course of a wonderful conversation we were having, her friend (who had no connection to my other friend) brought out this big blue book and showed me page 1429—Jesus' answer regarding free will and the reason for allowing both good and evil to co-exist. I've been reading the book ever since.

I'm still in touch with both of these dear friends who independently and almost simultaneously introduced me to the Urantia Book.

I had been reading the Urantia Book less than a year when, one afternoon as I was waiting for a subway here in Philadelphia in a very busy underground station, a young man sat down next to me. As he arranged his packages, I saw that he held in his lap a brand-new copy of—guess what?—the Urantia Book! We struck up a conversation and he invited me to come along with him to the next meeting of the study group he was attending. To this day I still see some of the folks I met at that meeting.

CHERYL ASHIQA ZENTS: As a young wife and mother-to-be, I left the University of California at Santa Barbara and, together with my husband Richard and all our belongings in a pickup truck, we headed for Denver, Colorado, where Richard had grown up. We rented a small apartment in Northglen, Richard took a job at a grocery store, and we settled in to prepare for family life. In January 1971 the first of our three children was born, and with not much money, we frequented the public libraries for entertainment.

I had spent my high-school days enthralled by astrology, witchcraft, mediums, psychic phenomena, prophecy, and paganism. In college I believed that everything was relative and that there was no God. Then during my pregnancy my mother-in-law lent me *Except for Thee and Me* by Jessamyn West, and I was so intrigued by this story about Quaker life and their socially active yet peace-abiding ways that I began attending a Quaker "silent service." About this time I also started to wonder about Jesus, and bought *Jesus, Son of Man*, by Kahlil Gibran.

One day late in 1971 I was in the library browsing the titles in the Occult/Religion/Philosophy section when I noticed a very large book that I had never seen before. I opened it to page 167, which lists the number of superuniverses, constellations and local universes in the cosmos, and somewhat indignantly thought to myself, "By what authority do they number the universes? Oh well, I'll just take it home for a good laugh."

A few days later, I began to read about Adam and Eve in the Garden of Eden. I always knew there must be more to the story than the snake and the apple, and even though the book seemed kind of strange, here was an account that made sense. The more I read, the more I was intrigued, and somewhat grudgingly I became convinced that it was all true . . . that this book really was the revelation that it purported to be. This all happened within a matter of days, and I began to skip around in the book as my interest led me. By this technique, it took me quite a while to piece together what a Thought Adjuster was, but I was thrilled and amazed to find that the beloved Jesus of my childhood was the actual creator and ruler of our local universe. I used my birthday money to order my own precious copy of the third edition in early 1972. At that time, $15 was a lot to pay for a book.

I tried to interest my husband and in-laws in the book but had no success whatsoever. We moved to Southern California, and after studying alone for two or three years, I finally wrote a dramatic letter to the Urantia Foundation in Chicago: "My family scorns me, my friends ridicule me. Is there anyone else in the world who reads this book besides me?" I got a very understanding and informative letter back from Christy, telling me all about the Foundation and the Urantia Brotherhood, and referring me to Julia Fenderson, who was the West Coast Field Representative. Through Julia I became active in the Urantia Society in Los Angeles and attended wonderful study groups.

The Urantia Book is a profound gift, but I have learned that a gift can only be given where it can be truly received; not everyone is ready or willing to receive a revelation of God's love in this form. I also enjoy *A Course in Miracles* and *The Dances of Universal Peace*, which I've been able to share with others, some of whom are also open to the Urantia Book.

I feel that the book has provided a firm foundation for growth in all areas of my life, and I will always be grateful for the light that it has shed upon my path.

DOUG PARKER: The year was 1971. I had returned to Oregon State University to complete my undergraduate schooling which had been interrupted with a draft notice three years earlier. After my tour in Vietnam life held new meaning, and for the first time I found myself seriously thinking about the meaning of life and death. One evening as graduation approached my housemates asked if I would like to accompany them to a talk given by Baba Ram Dass. I passed.

Upon their return both carried a book titled *Be Here Now*, which I began to peruse in idle moments. From this initial reading I was filled with newfound hunger to read many more books and to eventually seek out a guru of my own. I left Oregon and headed south to California, my native state. I knew there were numerous places in the world to seek enlightenment but California was close, familiar, and had most everything imaginable happening either in San Francisco or in Los Angeles. My quest was to find personal guidance in some form, to experience God connectedness. How this would happen I had no clue, but the search was on.

I hitchhiked to Los Angeles, where I encountered a group of devotees of a 13-year-old Indian guru named Guru Mahara Ji. Within days I was sitting at the feet of a Mahatma seeking to become a devotee and to receive the young master's "knowledge" (secret methods of meditation). The desire for this knowledge led me to San Francisco, London, and back to San Francisco, where I joined nine other devotees known as "premees." Now that we had received "knowledge" we wanted to do something with it.

The majority of our group were formerly from the Northern California area near Chico, so that became our destination. As a group we returned to Chico as "blissed-out," drug-free premees, rented an old three-story fraternity house and opened a premee-style ashram. By day we hawked our organization's magazine *And It Is Divine* door-to-door and sold flowers on the college campus, while at night we held Satsang (holy discourse) about the wonders of Guru Mahara Ji and his special "knowledge." All went well for several months as we were on a communal high of living, speaking and doing God's—the Guru's—work.

In the big house we formed a makeshift library. Devotees brought books accumulated along their spiritual paths and lined the shelves of what was formerly the fraternity house library. One day, while browsing this spiritual smorgasbord I spotted a large blue book high on the top shelf and inquired of someone standing nearby, "What is that big blue book up there?" He replied, "Oh, Kevin took that book as collateral on a hundred hits of acid from some guy up in Paradise, and the guy never came back."

I was intrigued by the size of the book and also because Paradise, California, was the town I had grown up in. I took the book to my bedroll and skimmed the table of contents, then read the Foreword. From the first page of the Foreword I was mesmerized. Here at last was what I had been searching for, *real* information about God. For days, then weeks, I holed up in my room doing little other than read and eat. Nightly Satsang soon lost its luster for me, and people began checking in on me to see if I was all right.

I can clearly remember the day I asked myself, "Do I really believe this book?" I answered, "Yes, I do believe this is a revelation just as it says it is." From that moment on it was clear I had to leave the house. But what of the Guru? Could I follow both, and did I truly want to? To find the answer I hitchhiked that January to Denver, Colorado, to the headquarters of the Divine Light Mission and put the leaders to the test. Three days later I was on a bus heading back to Oregon, reading my Urantia Book. I finished the book and started it again. The rest has truly been divine.

Part IV

1972-1973

DUANE FAW: In August of 1965 I was flying from Portland to Dallas by way of Denver. As we neared Denver the woman sitting next to me asked me about the book I was reading. I told her it was about Edgar Cayce and reincarnation. She asked why I was reading it. I told her the study of religion was my hobby. We briefly discussed reincarnation and life after death.

She asked if I had ever heard of a planet called Urantia. I had not. She said she belonged to a group who believe we live on a planet called Urantia, and that when we die we simply go to another planet for a while, then another, and another, etc. She said she knew exactly where she was going when she died. She'd gotten her information from a book called the Urantia Book, and said I would never know all there was to know about religion until I'd found—and read—the Urantia Book.

In the Denver airport I was waiting in the boarding area for my connecting flight when I felt a tap on my shoulder. It was the lady from the airplane. She had with her a man and two women whom she wanted me to meet. She said to them, "This is the man I told you about meeting on the airplane. He wants to read the Urantia Book." The man said, in effect, that if I were seriously interested in discovering man's role in the universe and his relationship to God I *must* read the Urantia Book.

I met up with my wife Lucile in Dallas and we stayed a few days with her sister before flying home to Arlington, Virginia. One day, left alone while they went shopping, I decided to find a copy of the Urantia Book. I looked in the Yellow Pages and telephoned every new and used book store in the Dallas directory. Each conversation went something like this:

"Do you have a copy of the Urantia Book?"
"The what?"

"The Urantia Book."
"How do you spell it?"
"I don't know—E-U-R? U-R?—phonetically it is Urantia."
"Who wrote it?"
"I don't know."
"Who published it?"
"I don't know."
"Sorry, but we don't have it and need more information to order it."

Back home in Virginia I called all the bookstores in the Washington, D.C., metropolitan area with the same results. I went to the Library of Congress and looked for it under Religion. (I missed it because, as I found out later, it was catalogued under Occult.) Finding the Urantia Book became an obsession with me. I asked for it every place I saw a bookstore.

In the fall of 1971 I retired from the military and we moved to California where I taught law. I kept up my quest for the book. One day in early 1972 I was looking for a particular part for an unusual lamp base. I had a list of six shops. I did not find it in the first five I visited, but as I left the fifth shop I saw a used book store. As was my custom, I asked if the store had a copy of the Urantia Book.

A man on a ladder said "Do I have a what?"

"Forget it," I replied.

"Hey, wait a minute," he said, "I did *not* say I *didn't* have one. I've worked in this bookstore for many years and no one has ever asked for a Urantia Book. I'd never heard of the book until yesterday. I got in an estate of books, and last night I was sorting them. The only book of any interest to me was the Urantia Book. I put it on my desk to read, but if you want to buy it you may."

I gave him $10 for the book.

When I got home and looked at the titles and authors of the papers I became very angry. I had been searching all that time for what turned out to be an occult book, and I was not into the occult! I threw the book, open and face down, into a trash can.

My background was Bible-centered Christianity. My grandfather was a circuit-riding Cumberland Presbyterian preacher, ultimately elected to the church's highest office, moderator of the General Assembly. My father, ordained in the same denomination, organized churches. Everyone wanted me to become a preacher, but I did not feel the call. I did, however, love the Bible and everywhere we went with the service I organized Bible classes. I was not ready for an occult book. The next few days I forgot completely about the Urantia Book. My mind had been cleared of any thought of reading it—not even out of curiosity.

A week or so later, reaching for the *Reader's Digest* on my nightstand to read myself to sleep, I discovered it was not there. Lucile said she had left it at the bowling alley. At that moment I received a very strong impression in my mind. I heard no voices, and saw no writing, but the intensity of the impression startled me. It was this: "If that book you found had been written by John Jones or Joe Smith you would have read it. Never judge a book by its authors." On the off chance that the trash had not yet been emptied, I got out of bed, wandered down the hall to my office and felt in the basket. In the bottom—face down and dog-eared—I found the Urantia Book.

Returning to bed I opened the book at the front. It still looked bad with all those weird authors. I saw, however, that the last part of the book was about the life of Jesus. Now, I had read some crazy stuff about Jesus without it corrupting my thinking, so I decided to start reading there. What I found completely fascinated me. Instead of putting me to sleep, it kept me awake. About 2:30 a.m. Lucile said, "Turn out the light! I need my sleep."

I found in the Jesus papers the most beautiful, loving, lovable Jesus I had ever met. Yet I needed to read the first three parts of the book to understand the words in Part IV. In so doing I learned who God is, who I am, what God wishes of me, my ultimate destination, and much, much more. In the process the Urantia Book did not displace the Bible in my view. I still love the Bible, now more than ever, since I know what it is—and is not.

MARK FREEMAN: As a non-denominational Christian minister I was searching for a more complete definition of spirit that would be helpful to myself and others. The doctrine I had been taught was that spirit is simply an activating force; but I was aware that the original Greek and Hebrew words had meanings that also included qualities of mind.

In the La Jolla, California, public library I picked up a copy of the Urantia Book and, flipping haphazardly through the pages, noticed a number of papers defining the Father's spirit as a fragment of himself that indwells our mind and "adjusts" our thoughts.

After taking the book home and scanning the 65-page table of contents, my doctrinal prejudice against the words "trinity" and "evolution" almost caused me to put the book down without reading further. But my brief glimpse of the Thought Adjuster section roused my curiosity enough to consider what the book's author—a Catholic, I supposed—had to say about it. I felt that I should at least be familiar with his viewpoint.

My second impression, after noticing the names of some of the purported authors—Divine Counselor, Universal Censor, Mighty Messenger—was that perhaps the book was a Rosicrucian publication since Rosicrucian authors had similarly high-sounding titles.

I decided to read further regardless of the source of the information. As I began studying the Thought Adjuster papers I became more and more impressed by the friendly yet unquestionably authoritative tone of the writing. I found the material so believable that I decided to read what the book had to say about the Trinity, to see whether it defined "trinity" in the standard Trinitarian way.

The book confirmed my belief that Jesus was not the second person of the Trinity. But I learned that the Father, Son, and Spirit can truly function as a trinity just as many religionists believe.

Similarly the new revelation corroborated my belief in the direct creation of Adam and Eve while enlightening me on man's evolutionary beginnings on this planet. Opposing views of science and religion were both shown to be partially correct. The book's explanation that man was the final result of a series of sudden mutations which "Life Carriers," in cooperation with divine spirit, had designed as part of the unfolding of the original life implantations, thoroughly satisfied my theological logic.

The enlightenment I had received so far from the Urantia Book was sufficient to overcome my initial resistance to reading the entire book, with its unfamiliar terminology and extensive discussions of science. I decided to start at the beginning and read it at least as far as it would continue to hold my interest.

I began reading on March 16, 1972, and took copious notes as I went along. By the time I'd reached page 651, my notes had become so lengthy that I considered buying my own copy at a used book store. I was surprised to learn that used Urantia Books sold quickly and that many used-book dealers were acquainted with the book, whereas most clerks in religious bookstores had never heard of it. About this time I also discovered the *Concordex*, which not only contained exhaustive reference material but had it indexed for fast retrieval. After all the writing I had been doing this would have been a real bargain for me at double the cost. I bought the *Concordex* as an aid to revive my memory of the passages I had read whether or not I ever finally did get a personal copy of the Urantia Book. I just didn't believe that the book would continue to sustain my interest over an additional 1400 pages.

As I continued reading, I noticed personal differences in writing style from paper to paper but no inconsistencies; minor differences of speculative opinion but no contradictions. I was also impressed by the lack of typographical errors in such a large volume. The book seemed almost *too* perfect. I felt sure I'd find some parts of it disappointing before I reached the last page. At the same time I found my interest intensifying. I even began praying at the end of each day that nothing unforeseen would happen to me to prevent me from reading the book through at least once.

Often I would read a statement that sounded so complex that I was sure it was beyond my understanding. Yet, invariably, the succeeding paragraph would clarify the concept at least somewhat for me.

After 407 hours I completed the first reading on June 18, averaging slightly more than eleven and a half minutes per page, although I remember spending more than an hour per page in some sections.

With the exception of a few book dealers and librarians, no one I spoke to knew about the Urantia Book and no one I met had read the book beyond a few pages. I searched in vain for book reviews and magazine articles about it. As a minister who had discussed many of the subjects contained in the book with thousands of individuals and hundreds of congregations over a period of more than twenty years, I'd never heard anyone mention the Urantia Book. The thought suggested itself to me that I might be the only person on earth who had read it. Yet I couldn't believe that there wasn't a group of Urantia Book readers somewhere who got together to talk about what they had read and how they could best put the information to use.

Alvin Kulieke, then president of the Urantia Brotherhood, was the first to reply to my inquiries. The next letter was from Clyde Bedell who told me about the Los Angeles Society; through them my name was given to Captain Bill Hazzard in San Diego who invited me to the meetings at his home, where in turn I met Betty Tackett—one of the group who had had the privilege of reading the Urantia Papers before they were published, and the individual who had donated the book that I had discovered in the La Jolla Public Library. In discussing how I found the book, none of us felt that my experience had been just a chance occurrence.

JAMES WOODWARD: It was 1972 and I had quit college to travel, play music and search for a larger glimpse of the big picture. I was visiting a high school friend named David who was attending a university in the Northwest. David had this big blue book sitting on a hall stand and I asked him, "What's this? What's in here?" His answer caught me off guard: "Everything, man." We had never discussed the book before; he told me his mother was into it more than he was.

From the moment I began reading there were inner clues that told me I had found something very different from the metaphysical, occult and spiritual books that had held my interest for several years. After finishing the book in 1974 I made a pilgrimage to 533 in Chicago and more inner clues assured me of the book's authenticity.

There have been times since then when I was not reading regularly and was living a largely material existence. I made some poor decisions along the way which offered good lessons but served to delay my spiritual growth.

The greatest step forward in my life came indirectly from the Urantia Book, as a personal awakening to the necessity of living in the truth. This in turn led to an ethical imperative to serve. The book can teach us many wonderful things, but it cannot make our choices. It does, however, contain an inspired recipe for the transformation of a human being. It's right in there between pages 1 and 2097.

FORREST ADKINS: I was born far back in the Ozark Mountains of Arkansas, so far back that even the hillbillies made fun of our county by nicknaming it "Booger County." There were no doctors in Madison County, and when I was born my mother, wishing to be modern, refused the midwife services of my great-grandmother and sent for the veterinarian. So much for my humble beginnings story.

The real beginning occurred with what I believe to be the gift of my Thought Adjuster. I had wandered to the top of a hill where I encountered another little girl. She told me her name and I told her mine. She said she was four and I said, "I'm four and a half." I have oft times wondered if befriending a stranger was in this situation a moral act, because at that moment the horizon expanded and life seemed adventurous and very, very valuable.

My first conscious reaction to this experience occurred some days later as I was trying to dance a dance that I thought had eternal meaning as a movement language. Years later I recognized how similar the dance was to the dance of Lord Shiva practiced in Hindu ritual. My grandmother used to tell me stories about how, in the early 1900s, we hill folk had hung folks for being hermits, Catholic, or anything besides a bush-shaking Protestant. Luckily I wasn't born in my grandmother's day—a little hillbilly girl attempting to dance a Shiva-like dance would surely have raised a hangman's eyebrow. As it was, I just grew up like so many of us with an "alien complex."

My second reaction was the awareness of an unseen art teacher outside my body but inside my mind currents. There were no pictures on our walls, just an old calendar with a photograph of a white chicken. I used to stare at it and marvel as I studied it. With this as my cultural inheritance, at age five I was being taught *chiaroscuro* by my unseen art teacher.

My third reaction was to become a church-hopper. The Pentecostals were sincere and trusted everything to the Father, but I couldn't stand the hellfire they mixed in. Soon we moved to the nearest city where I could church-hop longer and in many more directions. But compared to my personal religious life, the church experience made me feel "unclean." At 12 I was dreaming of becoming involved with a "new religion." In high school I was one of the first members of the Ethical Culture Society in St. Louis, Missouri. I was more determined than ever to "leave no stone unturned" in my search.

In college I found I could church-hop across oceans of time and space by studying world religions. But after a quick scan of the beliefs and sacred writings of non-Christian religions, I ran into a problem. My hopper legs were broken by the *Bhagavad Gita*. Here I had a belief system I could neither reject nor accept; I was stuck for eight long years reading and rereading the first chapter of this book.

One day, in my sixth year of rereading this first chapter, my husband and I were traveling in our car when he suddenly slammed on the brakes. By the side of the road was a hitchhiker. I happened to be carrying a copy of Geoffrey Hodson's *Kingdom of the Gods*, a book that for many years I had considered a treasure. I was thinking of a way to give it to the hitchhiker when I noticed that he was carrying a blue book. I thought it would be a good trick to offer to exchange books. As it turned out, he was just as anxious as I was; if any words were spoken, I don't think either of us heard them. It seemed we instantly switched books. I opened it up to where it talks about the six Sangik races of Urantia. I could feel truth vibrating from the pages with a strength I had never felt before. My immediate exultation wrought extreme jealousy in my husband and he refused to let me read the book.

Two years later I was in my eighth year of rereading the first chapter of the *Bhagavad Gita*. As I read once again the words, "Arjuna, I will tell you again," a soft, angelic voice accompanied my silent reading. I looked around to see who was speaking but there was nobody there. I few seconds later, my husband popped though the door and called to me, "Let's go buy a Urantia Book!"

We found a copy in a used bookstore for only $4. After my honeymoon with the book, during which my husband and I read about Andon and Fonta, I began to become critical over tiny details. But after another twelve years of discovering over and over again that I was wrong and the book was right, I grew weary of wasting my time and re-embraced the book. As a friend of mine once said, "After a while it becomes illogical to desire anything but the Father's will."

PEGGY M. JOHNSON: The time was June 1972. My world was closing in on me. I was grasping to hang on to life, but I didn't know why. I was emotionally, mentally and spiritually bankrupt. I contemplated murder, but ruled that out as I would probably get caught. I then contemplated suicide, and after some thinking ruled that out as I might be missing something really beautiful that life had to offer.

You see, I had become an alcoholic—me, the perfect mother, wife, and hostess. At least, I had *tried* to be all these things, but I couldn't, so I drank. My husband Dick had sought help for me through Alanon in February of 1971. At their instruction he had ceased to talk to me or take me anywhere. He was constantly gone. I felt as though I had been abandoned. We had five children who were left to grow up on their own as I certainly was in no condition to be of any help to them.

From the time Dick went into Alanon, I became very resentful of AA and Alanon and blamed them for what had happened to my family. I wanted to get sober, but I didn't want to go to the program. I thought there must be some other way, so I started seeking answers to my problems by reading any book I could get my hands on, from self-help to the occult to the Bible to some of the well-known philosophers. I liked what I read, but that was all it was—interesting reading. I took no action on any knowledge that I acquired from these writings.

Finally, on June 26, 1972, I reluctantly went to an AA meeting with an uncle. I thought just going would get everyone off my back, but it didn't and I didn't stay sober.

A short time after I had begun attending AA, Dick called to read some stories from a book he had found at a local bookstore. It was the Urantia Book. Everything he read to me rang true. He finally brought the book home. When I saw the size of it, I thought I could never wade through such a monstrous thing and urged him to audiotape it so I could listen to it while doing my wifely and motherly chores.

He started taping and I listened to the tapes just as fast as he could tape them. When he had finished I felt confident that I could tackle reading it, so I went out and bought myself a book. For the next few years, it was difficult to get my head out of it. I never left the house without it and many times I sat in a coffee shop after an AA meeting until the wee hours of the morning, reading until Dick picked me up. The Urantia Book became my text, and the *Twelve Steps* became my tools. I took my last and final drink on October 5, 1972.

I have been studying the contents of the book ever since. I owe my life to my God, the Urantia Book, and the AA way of life. I shall be eternally grateful for all that has happened to me, for without those experiences I would not be where I am today, and the chances are very good that I would never have found what I had been unconsciously seeking all my life.

JIM HARRIS: In 1972 I was traveling in Western Australia when I visited, on invitation, a community called Shalam, near Perth. It sat on only a few acres, but operated in a back-to-the-land mode, supplying most of its own needs and attracting truth seekers like myself.

After making myself useful there for a couple of weeks, and reading books by Edgar Cayce and part of *OAHSPE*, I offered to go as part of a foursome of travelers about 250 miles north, well into the outback, to an associate community named Carranya. Having split up to hitchhike rides with the frequent truck traffic, we all arrived at our destination about the same time, after dark, and were warmly received with a hot meal in the kitchen.

Next day, at the evening meal one of the members sat and read aloud from a book which the group had recently become interested in, called the Urantia Book. They were at a point in the reading which told about the war in heaven.

I reacted with excitement at that, saying that I had always wanted to learn more about the war in heaven, as what I had read in the Bible left me with several questions. Immediately, I volunteered to read while everyone else enjoyed the meal. My progress was punctuated by exclamations, or impromptu comments such as "hmmm," and "Isn't that interesting!"

I borrowed their copy of the book whenever I could and read more, and noted the address of the publisher in Chicago. After a week I decided to continue my journey, as there were several other places I wanted to visit before returning to North America.

In 1974, when I'd finally made it home after many adventures in Asia, I went immediately to a bookshop I knew in Toronto and purchased a copy of the Urantia Book. While there, I read a note posted on a message board which connected me with the first study group to form in Toronto, and possibly the first in Canada.

I recall reading somewhere, perhaps in the Urantia Book, that we are challenged to greater knowledge according to our ability. I often reflect on that, and think of how our unseen brothers must have had a great time leading me to the polar opposite side of the planet to find the Urantia Book on a remote outback station in Western Australia!

MICHAEL PITZEL: When I was about 21 I was attending Michigan State University and working various jobs to pay for my studies. One of my jobs was head chef and manager of a vegetarian restaurant called A Small Planet. The job was so time-consuming that I advertised for help in the local paper.

I'd already interviewed and dismissed several undistinguished applicants when a fellow came into the kitchen who looked as if he had just climbed a mountain to get to me. He was dressed like a traveling yogi in colorful, loose-fitting clothes that spoke of other lands. He sported a full beard, and his long, reddish-brown hair was tied in a ponytail which hung down well over the rucksack that he wore high upon his back. His name was Michael.

His cooking background came, literally, from all over the world. He'd had formal training, as had I, at some fine multi-starred restaurants, and he'd attended cooking schools. He was perfect for the job, so I hired him. We quickly became friends. (He was a great chef and continued to run A Small Planet successfully after I left.)

One day, while telling me of his fascinating travel experiences, Michael mentioned the Urantia Book. He soon exhausted all superlatives in describing it. Then he told me that he had a copy of it at home. My curiosity was immediately aroused, for although I had read many spiritual books, done many spiritual things, and often felt spiritually elevated, I had not heard of this book before.

We rode our bicycles to his home which, being located in the flood plains of Lansing, had recently been damaged by water and was without electricity during the remodeling. Since it was dark when we arrived, I thought there would be no chance of much reading. But Michael showed me the Urantia Book by candlelight. In reading just a few small selections I became convinced this book held immense merit. It actually seemed to glow—those remarkably thin pages seemed to light up from within!

I pleaded with Michael to lend me the book for a while, and finally he agreed. One reason for his hesitation was that he himself had borrowed the book, and he knew he'd eventually have to return it to its owners. Thus I found myself with a copy of the Urantia Book, lent to me by a person named Michael, while we both ran A Small Planet. Interesting coincidence, eh? Three Michaels, so to speak. I carried the book wherever I went so I could read it every free moment.

A few weeks later, at a party given by some vegetarians I'd met through the restaurant, I dragged the book out. To my surprise, I found that the hosts not only had heard of the book, but they actually owned not *one* copy, but *two*! They'd recently loaned one to a friend. Upon further inquiries, we discovered that the book I was carrying was actually the one they had loaned to Michael, who had loaned it to me!

The very next day I ordered my own Urantia Book from a local bookstore. Thereafter, the book became a major part of my spiritual and intellectual property, and it continues to assist me in my pursuit of educational and intellectual accomplishments.

One of the more amazing things about the book, for me, is its description of the ultimaton. This description helped me develop an appropriate topological model of this ultimate particle. I made this patentable discovery about the time I was first reading the book's passages on the ultimaton, while taking an advanced mathematics class on topology. Needless to say, besides the Urantia Book's insights into spiritual values, its science intrigues me greatly.

Since I'm a Michael from Nebraska, and since I found the book about Michael of Nebadon through yet another Michael, for a while I was fairly convinced that few, if any, other persons had actually read the Urantia Book cover to cover as I had. I was amazed to find out that people all over the world get together routinely to read it. Live and learn.

AL LOCKETT: For as long as I can remember I have been spiritually curious. I used to listen to Bible stories, wondering what was behind them and what they meant. Growing up I questioned things that did not make sense to me. I would pray for hours at a time, asking God for answers.

As I got older I began to study other beliefs, although I never officially joined any organization. I was always interested in different religious practices, and I began creating my own religious viewpoint. I did not think my spiritual longings strange, however, until I recalled a story told to me by my great aunt Lula and my mother.

The story goes like this: Aunt Lula's husband, Rev. Calhoun, was the pastor of Lizzy Chapel Church in Macon, Georgia. He died a couple of months before I was born. My mother and her sister, both of whom lived with Aunt Lula, were pregnant at the same time and both delivered boys in February of that year. One night Aunt Lula had a vision: Her husband came into the room where the two infants were sleeping and placed a crown at the foot of the bed of one of the boys. He then turned to Lula and said, "This one will be special."

Later, they told me I was that special child. When something like this happens, it is expected that the child will grow up to become a great preacher. There was no doubt in anyone's mind that this was my destiny, until my cousin and I both left college the same year—he to become a preacher, and I to join a band. On the surface this would seem to contradict the dream, except that my spiritual experience is still evolving and maturing. I've always felt that my life was being lived in preparation for something special.

The band I joined was called Psalms. We were devoted to playing music with a positive, and sometimes spiritual, message. Then in 1971 a guitar player joined our band and everything changed. His name was Eugene Patricella, and he had just returned from Hawaii where he'd found the Urantia Book on a table at the house of some friends.

One evening we were sitting around playing some music, engaged in a conversation about spiritual matters, when he handed me a big blue book, simply saying, "Check this out." My first impression was sheer amazement. I said, "Wow! This is what I've been waiting for!" Some time prior to this I'd had a vision wherein I was told, essentially, that I would receive a special book. It was unbelievable to me that the truth was now right here in my hands.

For days I read constantly. The material was so intellectually pure, so absolute. I would read, fall asleep, awaken, and read some more. It was as if I had to sleep so that my Thought Adjuster could present images and meanings to me of the sometimes dense material. For weeks I glowed with excitement. Everything was new, as if I had been reborn. Every aspect of my life seemed perfectly relevant, leading me to the precise moment. I had always believed in God, but now I knew with assurance. I attempted to tell everyone the good news but I quickly found that that wasn't the prudent thing to do. Friends, associates, and family members (except my brother and father) all backed away from me. Some even thought I had totally lost it. I realized that not everyone was ready for truth on that level.

I thank God for this gift—an answer to prayer. I continue to actively disseminate the teachings of the Urantia Book, but I now find that people are drawn to me who are ready for the good news.

GARD JAMESON: I found the Urantia Book in the spring of 1972 at a remarkable bookstore in Palo Alto called The Plowshare. I would often spend time there perusing the Religion and Philosophy section.

That day I was reading a book on Ouspensky in a wonderfully comfortable chair, and overhearing a conversation about the life of Jesus. What I was hearing sounded novel and very interesting—stories about Jesus' childhood that I knew were not in the Gospels. When these people left I located the book they were discussing, the Urantia Book. I looked it over and knew that this was a book deserving of some attention. I bought it and returned to campus.

A few weeks later, a close friend, Brian Cox, came to my room, hearing that I was interested in spiritual things. He described a deep spiritual experience that he had had; I recommended the Urantia Book as something that might provide an explanation of his experience. He returned after a few days, exclaiming, "Do you know what you have here?—a revelation!"

I have been attending study groups and enjoying fellowship with other students of the Urantia Book ever since those life-transforming days.

K. BRENDI POPPEL: I began reading the Urantia Book in March of 1972, on the island of Jamaica. I had gone there after my husband's suicide. I was 23 at the time.

My husband and I had first seen the book in September of 1971. We had traveled to Colorado with a group of friends, all recent graduates of Cornell University. Our lifestyle was typical of the times—we were hippies and political activists. We found ourselves living in the Colorado mountains in a large trailer with nine people and five dogs. One individual, Ron, who had been living in the trailer before we arrived, had the Urantia Book and would often read passages aloud. We all congregated around a large cable-spool kitchen table, and were generally stoned. At the time, I didn't understand what Ron was reading, but I had this strange and unusual notion that the Urantia Book was a holy book, and that Ron and his girlfriend, Sheri, could help me. This is, in fact, what happened.

Our Colorado commune was short-lived. After six weeks or so, many of us decided to go back to Ithaca, New York. Instead of driving back in a caravan as we had done when we originally drove out, we went in separate directions. Ron and Sheri arranged to come with us. By December of 1971, six of us (three couples) found ourselves living in a comfortable house in upstate New York. This too was short-lived. On January 3, 1972, Allen, my husband of less than five months, killed himself by jumping off the suspension bridge at Cornell University. (Sadly, this is not an uncommon phenomenon). As you may imagine, I was in total shock. I felt utterly lost. My whole life was disintegrating.

Two months later, I went to Jamaica with Ron and Sheri. We planned to stay there forever. We went to a non-tourist part of the island where Peace Corps workers lived. Ron resumed reading from the Urantia Book. This time he was reading about Thought Adjusters, and what he read went straight to the core of my consciousness, resonating truth to my soul. I immediately usurped Ron's book and was soon reading it voraciously.

Not long—maybe a few weeks—after starting to read the book, I had an experience with Jesus. My background is Jewish. I knew absolutely nothing about Jesus. I was with my two friends on the beach and felt I had to kill myself—drown myself—in retribution for Allen's death, yet I wanted to live. Tears streamed down my face and I felt the presence of Jesus come to me. I felt him say that he didn't want me to die. I was cradled in his comforting presence. I believe I was truly reborn there.

Shortly after this, I received a telegram that my father had suffered a severe heart attack. My mother had been stricken with a debilitating stroke not long before, so I left Jamaica after being there about six weeks and stayed with my parents until October of 1972. I had no siblings. Everyone close to me was dead or dying. However, I felt very strong. I was empowered by God. I had never known God before. My reality was completely transformed.

I finished reading the Urantia Book that October. Ron and Sheri stayed with me and my parents for a while, then went to live on a commune in upstate New York. I never heard from them again. The Urantia Book completely changed my life. But that's another story.

SONNY SCHNEIDER: My friend and I knew we would be snowed in for months as we prepared to do the winter on Salt Springs Island, British Columbia in 1972. So I gave him all the money I had for supplies and he headed for Vancouver to buy the season's goods. He came back with some food, a guitar and a Urantia Book. He decided to play the guitar, so I ended up with the Urantia Book.

The first night I started reading the book, I knew I had received a gift from a friendly universe, a gift I had been asking for for several years. And what good timing, as I was to spend the next five months snowed in! It sure did help to pass those long Canadian nights.

TAMMY HORTON: In 1972, looking for a back-to-the-land place to live, my then-husband and I were traveling to Arkansas, where friends suggested we go. We stopped on the Missouri border at a small town called Seligman. This quaint town must have had a population of about 150, but it had a bookstore and a small general store.

My husband went into the bookstore. While I stood outside taking in the local scenery, a young man walked up to me and we started talking. He said he lived in a cabin in the woods and had just come to town for supplies. He told me about the area and how he loved living in Arkansas.

Our conversation led to the cosmos and spirituality, and he asked if I had ever read the Urantia Book. I said no. He proceeded to tell me about the book and how it had affected his life. When my husband came out of the bookstore he joined in the conversation. My husband's fundamentalist background—his parents were "holiness ministers"—had turned him off from religion of any sort, but the conversation piqued even *his* curiosity.

We went back into the bookstore. They did not carry the Urantia Book but said they would be happy to order it. We lived 250 miles from there and decided that that would give us a good excuse to return to the area. We paid for the book and two weeks later we came back. We tried to find the young man who had turned us on to the book, but nobody knew anything about him.

We eventually moved to Arkansas. During that time we met many folks who read the book in the area and a study group was formed of five couples. We had some really great times when the Urantia group from Oklahoma City, headed by Berkeley Elliott, came and stayed at our friend's trout fishing resort on several occasions to hold meetings there. We had wonderful gatherings out on a point with a bonfire at night on the White River. I realize now what a special time that was.

I have been reading the book ever since. I wish I could thank that young man for giving us something that changed our lives. The lesson learned is that you never know what enlightenment a stranger may have to offer.

DAVID GLASS: I graduated from Florida Presbyterian College in St. Petersburg in 1971 with a B.A. in world literature—a preparation, I think, for appreciating the exalted prose of the revelation. I loved school and was sad to leave it. Of course, now I know that the whole universe is a school, and I'm already enrolled! In college and afterwards, I had read a lot of existentialist philosophy and was consequently depressed and without faith that anyone would survive death, myself included.

But somehow there seemed something poignant about just being alive. Who had set up this universe? I started reading history and science and, later, religious and spiritual books in an attempt to answer this question, but the answer eluded me.

Then I met a college friend who introduced me to *The Autobiography of a Yogi*, by Paramahansa Yogananda. I was hooked. I began meditating and practicing Hatha Yoga, and felt I was getting in touch with something real. I joined The Self-Realization Fellowship.

Later, in June of 1972, some friends and I went to Colorado to attend the summer meeting of the "Rainbow Tribe," a group which prophesied that great American Indian chiefs were reincarnating to lift the world to a spiritual level. In Granby we hiked to a high plateau and camped there for four days. There was no program, just fellowship and free discussions of our interests, which ranged from astrology to the Divine Light Mission. Afterward we all descended into the town of Granby where we filled up all the motels. In my room there were eighteen of us, many sleeping on the floor in sleeping bags. As I was nodding off, I heard Stephen Zendt say, "Well, the best book I've found so far is the Urantia Book." I made a mental note of the title. I didn't know Stephen at that point.

We all went on to San Francisco. The first day there I found the Urantia Book in a huge metaphysical bookstore. The cashier said, "This book is the handbook for the New Age." That sounded good to me at the time and I had the requisite $20, so I bought it and decided to read two papers a day. I went back home to Florida and read the book for six months straight, doing little else but eat and sleep. I am so thankful that my parents allowed me to do this rather than hurry me off into job-hunting without my values and principles intact.

When I finished the book, I went to Chicago and met Emma (Christy) Christensen and James Mills, then president of Urantia Brotherhood. I was so eager to volunteer my services that I offered to work for the Brotherhood for free and get a paying job somewhere else in Chicago.

I am now on my ninth reading. I have written articles for more than ten Urantia Book-related newsletters, and I published my own newsletter for about four years. I've attended just about every summer conference since 1973 and have prepared talks or workshops for most of them.

ARDELL FAUL: Born in 1947, I grew up in a Mennonite Brethren Church environment in North Dakota. When I was around seven years old, my older brother Edward and I were playing with our toy trucks one day when Edward asked me if I was "saved." I didn't know what he was talking about. He told me that when it was time to go to bed that night, I should tell Mom and Dad that I wanted to be saved.

That night, as I was crawling into my bunk bed, I remembered what he had said. So I went into my parents' bedroom and stated: "I want to be saved." We all got on our knees by the bedside and prayed. I don't remember who said what, but I saw the most beautiful, bright-white apparition imaginable. He didn't say anything to me, but his presence was overwhelming and the encounter changed me forever. At that point I knew beyond a doubt that other unseen realities existed.

The power of that experience was enough to carry me through my youth until I was 15, when scientific curiosity and a belief that the world was understandable soon put me at odds with the creation story of the Bible. I took many wrong turns on my way back home—the major one was turning to alcohol for relief.

I discovered the Urantia Book in 1972 and read it alone for many years. But I never felt my childhood connection with God again, and couldn't understand why. I used to tell people, "They put me here on the planet and didn't give me any instructions!"

It wasn't until 1995, when I ran out of self-will and went to a meeting of Alcoholics Anonymous, that I finally reconnected with my God. The Urantia Book immediately became my Big Book, and now I know I'm right where I'm supposed to be. I have finally gotten over my desire to die and enter eternity, and understand that I'm already living in eternity—right now!

BUCK AND ARLENE WEIMER: Arlene and I got married twice. The first time was in June of 1970, in a hippie wedding in California with most of our friends; the second time in September of 1970, in a Jewish wedding in New York for most of our family. My wife is a Brooklyn Jew and I'm from a Protestant background, but at the time we were both avowed agnostics.

Shortly thereafter, we jumped on a freighter headed for Greece. After two months there, we took another boat to Israel. We were without a travel itinerary, but soon we found ourselves in Bethlehem witnessing the traditional celebration of Jesus' birthday, which we thought was "cute." From there we moved on to Turkey for the long journey overland to India. India was, at first, very exciting, especially because of the many Hindu temples and ashrams. But before long we fled northward to Nepal and Katmandu, the capital. And again, as fate would have it, we observed a huge celebration of Buddha's birthday. These events made us begin to question our spirituality.

After visiting Burma and Southeast Asia, we arrived on the Indonesian island of Bali where we were confronted with a big decision: Do we continue eastward across the South Pacific, or accept the invitation to crew on a 40-foot, yawl-rigged yacht going west for 3600 miles, across the Indian Ocean to the Seychelles Islands? While in deep meditation, a clear voice said to me: "A man must do everything." And, though not hearing it quite as clearly, my wife had a similar experience. We chose the westward journey, which turned out to be fraught with danger. We even had a near-death experience. As a result of this episode we gained an acceptance of death and a sense that "everything is going to be okay."

After nine months in the Seychelles, we went to Pakistan and traveled westward to Europe and Amsterdam, eventually getting a flight from England to the States, where we arrived too poor for subway fare.

Arlene, who had received a Ph.D. at the University of Southern California at the time we got married, landed a job teaching at a small college in Orlando, Florida. One of the courses she taught was on personality. One of her students, a "wigged-out" Vietnam vet, showed her the Urantia Book one day after class and said that if she was really interested in learning about personality, she should read it. (He later acknowledged not having read much of the book himself.)

Arlene felt that she had read enough books for a lifetime while getting her education, so she asked me, since I was not working at that time, to look into this very large book. I started reading and recognized immediately that this book was "different," but I remained skeptical and felt the need to read it from cover to cover.

In the meantime we decided on more travels. Together with five others, we converted a school bus into a camper, wrote GOD IS LOVE in bold letters across the side, and proceeded to drive to Costa Rica, where we lived in tents on a mountain. I finished reading the Urantia Book there, and by then had made such character transformations that Arlene was inspired to delve into the book herself. And her experience was similar to mine.

After ten or eleven months, with the tents beginning to rot, we sat on a log on the mountaintop and made the decision to return to America and raise a family. We settled in Pueblo, Colorado, had three sons, careers in psychotherapy, and became active members of a study group.

Although it is only ink on paper, the Urantia Book has been our guide, a guide for loving God better while striving to become like him, and for serving our brothers and sisters while learning cosmic citizenship.

DON TYLER: I have my older brother Larry to thank for getting me interested in the Urantia Book. In the early '70s I was visiting him during a break from college when he shoved this large tome at me. I've never forgotten his intense look and the tone of voice in which he commanded, "You've *got* to read this book! It has the one and only true story of Jesus Christ!"

"Sure, sure," I thought. "If it makes you act like that, I want no part of it." Larry has always been intense. He and I laugh, today, that I came to the book *despite* him.

I started thumbing through it as I would approach any volume so large, skipping about and looking at the table of contents. "No! no! no!" he said, and turned to page one of the Foreword. "You have to start reading *here*." I began. I woke up to find that I had been nose-down asleep on the book at page three.

I was in college sometime later when I first got a taste of the revelation's cosmology. Several of us had been indulging in a long (and chemically-assisted) intellectual inquiry into the Big Bang, the Big Collapse, and other current theories of cosmology, when I found some written passages about the structure of the universe which Larry had copied from the Urantia Book. At this point several items clicked into place for me to fill some of those "missing links" in known theory.

Despite sibling-induced resistance, one day I started reading the book on my own in my own way. I finally found a toehold in the evolution papers in Part III. The description of the later evolution of humans especially intrigued me. I ended up reading from that point to the end of the book. I got my own copy and read it through again, from the beginning. The answers it gave on theological issues which I had previously considered unanswerable, and the correlation it drew between supreme and absolute concepts which I had thought irreconcilable, put this book forever on a level above anything else I had ever read. But by far the most convincing facet of the revelation, for me, was Part IV, the Jesus papers.

A few years earlier I had experienced a spiritual rebirth, sparked primarily by reading the four Gospels and rediscovering the Jesus I had known and loved since childhood. But the Gospel of John had left me hungry for more, leaving so many questions unanswered. I had read other "revelations" and "lost gospels," but none had the truth-feel of the Gospels until I read the Urantia Papers. There I found that same superb and sterling Son of God who had intrigued and inspired me in the Gospels. The gospel material which the UB expanded upon, that which they ignored, together with new and revealed information, all coordinated perfectly with my highest understanding of Jesus.

The next year, a friend from college, Mary Jo Clark, came to visit me in Oklahoma. I had written to her about this unusual book I'd been reading, and the first thing we did was to sit down and read the revelation through together. Her college anthropology background caused her to take an interest in it at about the same point in the narrative that I did, at the hominid evolution descriptions. Her visit led to a lasting marriage and produced three children, all "raised in the Father."

DANIEL RAPHAEL: In 1972 I was a counselor at the Oregon State Penitentiary in Salem. My office was on the third tier of E-Block, which housed four hundred prisoners. One day, outside my office, I was talking with an inmate who was in my caseload. We were discussing science fiction, talking about the great sci-fi authors and the classics of the genre. Another inmate, a friend of my fellow sci-fi enthusiast, stopped to overhear what we were talking about.

As do many who live behind those walls, this inmate decided to play the one-upmanship game. When a break came in our conversation he mentioned that he'd been reading the most incredible science fiction book he had ever run across. The book he described was prodigious: over two thousand pages long, not written by humans, and describing universes upon universes like so many grains of sand on the beach.

I was pretty flabbergasted by his claims, so I asked him for the title and publisher of the book. After the yard line had been called and the work line had been called and all the prisoners were celled in, I went to the library, found the publisher's address in the card catalogue, and wrote to the Foundation in Chicago to find out the price and shipping costs. In a couple of weeks the answer arrived and I sent in my $27 for my own copy. Now that I think of it, it was rather amazing that I ordered it: I hadn't seen the book, hadn't read a review of it, hadn't ever heard of the publisher, and hadn't ever paid $27 for a science fiction book!

When my big book arrived, I began with the Foreword. After going through it rather slowly, not understanding much of what it was saying, I read Paper 1.

Almost thirty later, I am here to tell you sweet people that although I was disappointed that it wasn't really a science fiction book, Paper 1 provided me with the most enjoyable, heartwarming description of God that I had ever read. I went on to finish the book in eighteen months, having to get up an hour earlier every morning to do so. The Urantia Book has given me a more interesting description of the universe and its inhabitants than I could have ever imagined. And that's how the Urantia Book found me.

CLAUDIA AYERS: Religion was not a big part of my life when I was a child because my parents were not churchgoers and did not seem to have religious beliefs. As a sixth-grader, I was captivated by the lunchtime arguments that took place between the religionists and the atheists. I soon found myself siding with the atheists. In 1961, the atheists were vastly outnumbered by the Protestants in my community.

During many a starry night when my friends and I gathered for campouts or sleepovers, discussions of cosmology were inevitable. I rather enjoyed poking holes in biblical versions of reality. I'm sad to say that I may actually have contributed to the eventual "undoing" of faith for a small number of people. I had learned enough about other religions on this planet to conclude that they were remarkably similar. They all seemed to have the same take on the goodness and oneness of God. But I felt they were all a crutch for people who couldn't face the fact that evolution accounts for life. I admire those few friends and acquaintances who could hold up their faith even in the face of contradictions and confusion.

By the time I was a sophomore in college, however, it seemed as if every thinking person I knew was a non-religious humanist. A close friend and classmate, whom I respected tremendously for the wholeness of his personality, ventured that there may actually be something to the theory of God. He wasn't like other engineers I knew; he had read widely in non-conventional religious books. But I was shocked at his suggestion. I figured a few evenings of my pointing out the inconsistent arguments of the various theologies would help to educate this otherwise brilliant and sensitive person. Unfortunately, he was electrocuted before such discussions could occur. It was hard for me to face his demise, even as the stoic I felt myself to be.

When I was 23, in the first months of 1973, I was reading Bertrand Russell's *Why I Am Not a Christian* at my parents' place in Sonoma, California, while recovering from having my wisdom teeth extracted. I was well into Russell's anti-Christian arguments when my brother happened by for a visit. I hadn't seen him for almost a year because he'd been spending time in a variety of hippie communes in California, Hawaii, and British Columbia.

My high school drop-out brother joined me on the sun deck with a big blue book and was soon quite immersed in it. I had never known him to read books by choice, so this was an unusual thing to behold. My brother's name is also Russell. In no time I was hearing another Russell's arguments, this time *for* religion. Instead of "God," he referred to "our Father" and "the First Source and Center." It all sounded so hippie to me. I figured he'd smoked one "doobie" too many and had "wigged out" in some fundamentalist commune. I thumbed through his book and found it completely "bogus."

It was as much a surprise to my mother as it was to me to see Russell so devoted to reading. She figured she had nothing more important to do than try to understand him, so she took a more serious look at his book. A few months later she suggested that I also take another look, for she had never seen anything like the philosophic writing it contained. Of course, I felt challenged to prove it wrong. Over several months, I tried to find a lie or some lack of continuity in this remarkable book. Suddenly, one day, a dramatic realization literally shook me: The book was true!

I once was blind, but now I see. It has been an eventful quarter century!

ROB CRICKETT: In Melbourne, Australia, during the early '70s, a young lady I knew took me to meet a fellow who had a copy of the Urantia Papers, a chap by the name of Keith Bacon. I chanced to notice a phrase in the text which read: *"The mission of the Thought Adjusters to the human races is to represent, to be, the Universal Father to the mortal creatures of time and space"* (p. 1185). Some months later I was preparing for a period of religious retreat and that phrase was sufficient to inspire me to buy a copy of the Papers to take along as my companion.

Throughout the years, the Papers have challenged all things very dear to me, and have brought me to the precious presence of God. In the pursuit of the realness of that phrase concerning our Father, I have been amply blessed. The Papers helped to bring me into living contact with Michael, Mother Spirit, Father indwelling, and previously undreamed-of optimism and opportunity. The Papers also ushered me securely through many dry and barren times in search of the factual truth of Jesus' gospel; but, true as that gospel is, the Father-child relationship has proved to be the foundation of eternal life and righteousness. I have been tremendously privileged to share that truth with hurting people all over the world, through the Church of Christ Michael, prison and drug treatment ministry, and spiritual outreach. Jesus and his gospel have never failed me and have only given me increase from which to share his riches.

To the best of my knowledge, the Papers were carried to Australia in 1955 by two individuals, Keith Luckett and Tom Reynolds. At the time these men would have both been in their late twenties or early thirties. They had been in the United States on separate business with no knowledge of each other. They still live in Melbourne and are active readers of the Papers.

Over the years, numerous people spearheaded an assortment of group, social and apostolic activities in Australia. In the '60s and '70s a Urantia community existed south of Perth, Western Australia. One extraordinary couple bicycled around the continent, evangelizing the Papers. Several national and international newsletters were sources of fellowship and news. Libraries were given hundreds of copies of the Papers and, whilst some were returned, most remain in place. Church services, spiritual retreats and spiritual growth workshops began in the mid-'80s and continue to this day. Study groups, fellowship feasts, home church, interfaith contact, facilitation and representation at national and international Urantia conferences—all this and more has been the fruitful impact of the Urantia Papers in Australia, to the glory of God and the praise of this most precious revelation and its production team.

STELLA RELIGA: Coming from an atheistic/agnostic background, with no religious instruction from my parents, I nevertheless was a lifetime searcher for spiritual truths. Even as a child it would turn me off when I'd hear preachers on the radio saying I was a sinner. I hadn't had a chance to sin or even to know what sinning was. Jesus died for me? That was a foolish thing to do, according to my childish mind. Who and what was he anyway? Had he even existed? But with all these questions I somehow knew that something greater must have created this awesome world and cosmos.

My search took many paths and byways until one incredible day—I didn't know it was incredible then—my son Robert gave me a magnificent gift, the Urantia Book. He had picked it up from a study group led by Pat McNelly at the University of California at Fullerton.

The Urantia Book provided answers to every question I'd ever had, whether it was about God, Jesus, the universe, archeology, anthropology or philosophy. This was a four-year college course crammed into one 2,097-page blue treasure.

The book has inspired me to find the strength and even the wisdom to do things I didn't know I could. One example was founding a shelter for victims of domestic violence. And now I've published a book, *The Secret Revelation*, that dares to decode the Book of Revelation.

Who knows what the eternal journey will bring? Isn't it exciting to live in this eventful age when new but old spiritual truths are being beamed to Urantia? How privileged we are to have a blueprint for living in the greatest book on this planet, the Urantia Book.

EMY HOY: It was an autumn weekend in 1973 when I dropped by to visit my friend Stella Religa for a few minutes. I liked to hear her political viewpoints and see how she was coming along with her latest home decorating projects, as these were some of the same hobbies I was involved with at the time. I found Stella and her son Robert at home. Robert showed us some books he had just come by. He made a few enthusiastic comments about a thick, blue book entitled the Urantia Book, saying it was a religious book and that I could buy a copy from him if I wished.

After examining the impressive chapter titles of Part I, "The Central and Superuniverses," and getting a small glimpse of where I might be in this great universe, I was awed with what these papers offered.

I immediately admired how well organized the material in the book seemed to be. The cover, a beautiful blue, was well designed, with the name "The Urantia Book" across its face. The pages were thin and strong as in a costlier Bible, and the print was easy to read. I loved the book before I'd even read a paragraph. After browsing through it for ten or fifteen minutes, I was absolutely amazed by its contents. This was a religious book I must own and I wanted it immediately.

Then and there I purchased my first copy and took it home, excitedly wondering what I would learn from its many pages. I vowed to myself that I would read every word. I immediately began with the Foreword, and then read continuously through. In the midst of a busy work and school schedule, I completed the book in almost a year. I can remember reading the last page and thinking how fortunate I was to have had this book pass into my hands. I thanked our heavenly Father and promised to keep the Urantia Book in my home and refer to it often.

GLENN BELL: I was a devout follower of the Bible, convinced that it was the inspired Word of God, when a friend, Early Spires, began telling me things about Adam and Eve that were not in the Bible. After he had said enough to show me he didn't know what he was talking about, I asked him where he was getting his information. He said it came from the Urantia Book, which was written by angelic hosts to reveal God to man.

I knew from this that Early was as cuckoo as a March hare. I loved Early and thought I could read the book to point out its inconsistencies and maybe save his mind as well as his soul. Well, I read the book from cover to cover and found it to contain nothing but the truth. This was 1973. I became convinced it was a true revelation of God to man and have been devoted to it ever since.

ANGUS BOWEN: I was led to the Urantia Book in 1973 by a comment from my cousin. I was living in Wichita, he in Los Angeles. My cousin and I had shared many religious experiences since our days in grade school. He and I would get together, draw pictures and talk about God from the time we were about seven until we graduated from high school.

In 1958, in my sophomore year in high school, I became a born-again Christian. My born-again experience happened in this way: I was scheduled to see the minister in order to "get saved." That date was days away and I was concerned that something might happen to me—I might get run over by a truck, for instance—before I actually got saved. I was lying in bed discussing this problem with myself—and with God, if he was listening—and I remember saying, "If I can be saved, right here, by myself, instead of waiting for my appointment with the minister, I want to be saved right now."

I was immediately flooded with a vibrant rush that swept through my entire body. I was startled. I did not know what it meant, since I had no reason to believe, at that time, that I could make such a momentous decision by myself. When I went through the ritual of getting saved with my minister a few days later, it was anti-climactic. I *knew* that I had been saved that night, by myself, alone with God.

After graduating from high school, I went on to a Bible school with plans to enter the ministry. But after two years at the Bible institute, I had to drop out and enlist in the U.S. Air Force because my parents divorced and I had no financial backing to continue school. In the Air Force I became a chaplain's assistant. I worked with chaplains of all faiths and learned that, although they didn't seem to know it, their beliefs were all basically alike. It was a great lesson to learn.

Following military service, I spent the next ten years searching—for what, I wasn't certain. There was a vacuum in my soul, caused by the unanswered questions left by the Church. My search included just about any spiritually oriented belief or mind-expanding practice I came upon. I found no single answer. Then my cousin, who had gone through a lot of the searching with me, happened to mention the Urantia Book.

I was immediately impressed with the thoroughness and exacting detail of the UB. It was the opposite of the Bible in that respect. But the section that really hooked me was the Jesus papers. Jesus had been the focal point of my prior "pure" religious experience, and I knew he was the avenue to real spiritual growth and understanding. The UB told me of the Jesus I knew in my heart. It was a more complete Jesus than the Church had presented. The UB didn't refute the Bible; it augmented it. It brought the Bible to life. It brought Jesus to life.

Although I immediately accepted the UB as authoritative, I didn't accept everything. Some of what it had to say made me angry. At times it seemed cold and almost *too* objective, almost merciless in its descriptions and judgments of the human condition. But each of those "anger" sessions—after which I would close the book with a sense of "no way can that be the way it is"—led me to further understanding. Those contentious points worked within me and eventually I would come to realize the truth in them.

For the next twenty-four years it was just the UB and me. I had no other readers to relate to. It was the best thing that could have happened because I developed my own sense of what the book was saying and was able to see how it worked in the real world. I held every new idea or philosophy or scientific discovery against what the UB had to say. I began to recognize things in books and movies that had a "UB-like" quality to them.

Today I have no doubt as to my eternal destiny or the existence of God. These are no longer pie-in-the-sky beliefs. The aspect of blind faith has moved its parameters much deeper into the universe. I would be more shocked if I *didn't* survive death than if I did. I am looking forward to the experience, but not as anxiously as I used to. At one time I wanted to be *there*—on the other side, free of human bondage. Now I know that I *am* there, and that *there* is *here*.

I'm so thankful for the UB. It has replaced the incredible with the incredibly logical. It has helped me substitute a true sense of responsibility for a sense of guilt. It has given me a certainty of the future without an escapist attitude, a sense of my place in the eternal process, and the instructions on how to navigate the eternal journey successfully. And to think that the journey has only just begun!

MARTHA GROH: My father was an avid reader, a self-taught man, and a seeker of truth. I don't think he believed in a personal God, but my mother was Catholic and raised us as such. The Catholic Church meant little to me other than rituals and dangerous nuns, and after twelve years I decided that I never really believed in God at all. My father had always been interested in science, ancient pyramids, and UFOs, and in my later years these interests became a common bond between us. I read many books on those subjects and was convinced of the existence of extra-terrestrial life.

In 1970 I was still in school and working during vacations. My best friend had moved to Oregon after high school to live in a commune. She was a poet, a young mother, and a follower of the Guru Mahara Ji. She told me she had come across a book that I might like, though she herself could not understand it. She claimed it was written by extra-terrestrials and had been dropped off on earth. Something inside me knew that was true and I wrote down the name of the book. I told my dad about it, and since it was close to my birthday, he said he would give it to me as a present. Together we went to a bookstore in the Coventry area of Cleveland, a hip community from the '60s, and ordered the Urantia Book.

When I finally got it, I was shocked by its size and complexity, and intrigued by the table of contents. I started at the beginning, but the enlarged concept of God had no meaning for me since I was still an unbeliever. I stopped after three pages, but I must have at least glanced at the Jesus section, because I recall telling friends that "when certain planets are in trouble, a Jesus is sent to straighten things out." I wrote to the Foundation asking for more information, but I stopped reading the book.

Years later, Walter Dychko, a Urantian from the west side of Cleveland, called one day to try to organize a study group. I thought it would help me to understand the book if I could study it with other readers. We corresponded for over a year without getting a group together. Something always got in the way.

I had been working as a medical secretary in a hospital for three years, and a nurse friend of mine phoned me from Atlanta where she had moved the year before. She had been quite wild, and I was shocked to find out that she and her new husband had become Jehovah's Witnesses. She spent a long time telling me about her new beliefs and the prophecies of the Bible (which I had never even looked at in my twelve years of Catholic schooling). The prophecies were interesting, but my main thought was that she had been duped by those Jehovah's Witnesses. I felt sorry for her.

The phone call had come early in the morning so I went back to bed but couldn't sleep. I found myself thinking about God and what little time I had given to learning about him. Suddenly, the room was filled with a warm and glowing light. I felt so strange, as if I had received the gift of faith right at that moment, as if I had been "born again." I couldn't get back to sleep and had an irresistible urge to be out in the summer morning. Taking my dog with me, I went outside and was amazed at how clear and bright everything looked, like I was wearing a new pair of glasses!

I came home and had such tremendous urges—to read the Bible, to join a church, to learn everything I could. I called different churches at random, went to the library, and got some books on Edgar Cayce, the Dead Sea Scrolls, world religions, the Koran, even the Talmud.

That same day I called Mr. Dychko and told him how I felt. He suggested I read the Urantia Book but to start with the Jesus section this time. I read for about five hours without stopping and my Thought Adjuster must have responded because I knew that every word I was reading was the truth. It was exciting to finally believe in something, to have faith in God! I kept reading and studying the UB together with the Bible and my other library books, and was amazed at how they interconnected.

My family knew of this experience I was having and encouraged me to go to the Midwest Urantia conference in Michigan. There I met some great people, including my future husband, Richard. Richard had found the book on a friend's coffee table in Hawaii while stationed there in the Navy. We discovered that we lived in the same area, and decided to try to get a study group together. We met with Mr. Dychko a few times, but his wife, being Catholic, refused to let us meet there anymore. So Richard and I studied together, fell in love, got married, and had a beautiful baby daughter.

LEE ARMSTRONG: My father being a military man, I was raised in military chapel. My idea of religion was "God bless Lyndon Johnson and the Vietnam War." But personally I decided that I believed in God because I *needed* to, although I was certain that much of what I was hearing in church was not really related to the God I felt inside. So one afternoon, as a junior in high school, while considering all of this, I prayed, "Father, I don't really know what is true. But I don't care how far I have to go or what I have to do, I want to find what is true. Please help me."

Four years later, a guy named Terry Kruger and I became good friends when we both took a theater class at Illinois State University in the early '70s. He and I shared a deep personal interest in things spiritual, discussing many philosophies. Terry would say things like, "Reincarnation, Lee, I think that's *really real*." He would be so certain, but I knew that if I waited several weeks he would come back equally as adamant: "Reincarnation? That's for the birds. How could anyone possibly believe that?"

So when Terry returned from a trip to New Mexico and I heard about his latest "ism," the Urantia Book, I took it with a grain of salt. Strangely enough, however, this one didn't pass with the weeks. In fact, Terry's attachment to it grew stronger. Finally, after two or three months—a long time in my experience at that point in life—Terry put his foot down: "Lee," he stated, "You have *got* to buy this book!"

Well, if he felt *that* strongly about it, okay. There were no Urantia Books to be found in Normal, Illinois, so when I took the trip up to my parents' home in Chicago I was delighted to find the book in a bookstore. I put down my $20, and in February of 1973 (I wrote the date in my book) I began reading the Urantia Book.

Terry told me that the best way to read the book was from the front to the back. He told me that I might not understand much of the Foreword, but not to get discouraged and to keep pushing on. At the time I was playing Marcellus in *Hamlet*, and while waiting to go onstage I sat in tights and armor reading the Foreword to the Urantia Book. Terry was right. I didn't understand much of it, but I had a *feel* for it.

As the weeks passed, I would rush through my studies so I could get to those precious hours before bed and read the book. I'd put on Tim Weisberg's flute album, *Hurtwood Edge*, and read. (Those early emotions associated with my first reading come back to me when I listen to this music again.) I remember reading a sentence with my eyes wandering off into space as I thought about it for fifteen minutes. Questions would flood my mind; the answers would be in the next paragraph. I felt my mind opening, my soul exploding. I had never read anything like this.

Terry would ask me, "But when did you *know*, Lee?" I'd look at him blankly and say, "Know what, Terry?" Quite frankly, I had no idea what he was talking about, but I tried to be polite. I continued reading on through the book. Finally, I finished Part III, "The History of Urantia." *Blam!* Bells rang, lights went on—I *knew!* What Terry had been trying to get me to tell him was, when did I know that this was an epochal revelation of God to our planet? I *knew* in my experience that this book was true and that it was what it claimed to be.

I had found the truth. I had asked for it. I got it. The truth had set me free. So one night when Terry dropped me off at my apartment I looked over at him and said, "Do you remember those times when you asked me if I knew? I *know* now." He looked at me in agreement, and that bond of solidarity is one we will carry into eternity.

Having absorbed the first three parts of the book, I then began Part IV. All of the concepts and descriptions of the nature of God given in the previous sections were now personally demonstrated by this man, Jesus, who humanized these values by living them. "The Life and Teachings of Jesus" is a handbook that demonstrates how to incorporate the teachings into your life and actually *do* them. And at the center of it is Jesus. Now I know him as Michael of Nebadon. He is superb. He is *real*.

As the years have passed, my focus has changed from encountering and trying to understand the teachings to trying to live them. It has become less important to me how many times I can claim to have read the book, and more important how well I can live as a son of God. While I have had my successes and my failures, I can honestly say that the Urantia Book has changed and enlightened my entire adult life experience on this planet.

JESS HANSEN: Back in 1973, I was allowed to examine the contents of a flight bag and a suitcase that had belonged to the late guitar maestro, Jimi Hendrix. That was where I first laid eyes upon the Urantia Book. Jimi possessed a well-worn copy that featured notes in the margins made in his own distinctive handwriting. At that time, I made note of the title and publisher of the book. Shortly thereafter, I met a personal friend of Jimi's, and during the course of our initial conversation I mentioned the Urantia Book. Jimi's friend confirmed for me that yes, Jimi had been very familiar with the book and its teachings. I then tracked down a copy for myself, and the book and I have been together ever since.

JANET QUINN NILSEN: In the early '70s I was a young mother with two small sons. My husband and I were building our own home in a tiny, rural neighborhood, with very little experience or money. Times were often challenging, and I found myself in dire need of some sort of spiritual transfusion plus straight information on how best to deal with the difficulties of life.

Around this time a nice young man who was interested in UFOs was staying with a neighbor. This fellow mentioned to me that his sister had told him about a book written by aliens—that it was very thick and had little, teeny printing. I am a reading addict who loves thick books, and I remember thinking, "Hmmm.... Maybe that would be something I could really sink my teeth into—a fat book by aliens! How interesting!" and I put the thought in the back of my mind.

During the next few months I investigated some of the current spiritual trends: TM, yoga, mysticism. I dusted off my old Sunday school Bible, read it, and once again came to the conclusion that the Old Testament was profound but barbarous. I felt deeply that I loved Jesus but that he had been grossly misrepresented by the men who wrote the Gospels. I needed to know about the *real* Jesus.

Shortly thereafter a new couple moved into the neighborhood. I was slightly acquainted with the woman, and so I helped them move boxes from the van to the house. I picked up a box of books—the fellow's small but varied library of spiritual books—and on top of the stack was a beautiful, big blue book. I knew in a flash that this was the book by the aliens! My hunch was confirmed when I flipped it open and saw the list of titles and authors—Lanonandeks, Vorondadeks—yep, this was indeed the book! I borrowed it and started reading it that day. I gobbled it up the next month or so, starting with the life of Jesus, and anything in the front sections that caught my fancy. After I finished the Jesus papers, I started at the Foreword for a proper front-to-back reading, the first of many.

As I was reading the Urantia Book, I also had a chance to peruse the rest of my neighbor's collection of spiritual books. All were interesting, some perhaps inspired, but none were revelations, and all suffered in comparison with the big blue marvel—in scope, language, and in direct spiritual helpfulness. I was thrilled by this book and thought everyone should read it. I scraped together $20 and bought my own copy at an esoteric bookstore. It seemed to me that any literate and somewhat spiritual person should want to read this book—should be thrilled to know more about Jesus, God, and the universe.

I was disturbed that so few people who I thought would want to read the book, actually did. The fellow who had first told me of the book didn't want to read so thick a book. The neighbor whose book I first read was convinced that Guru Mahara Ji was the latest incarnation of Michael of Nebadon. The esoteric bookseller stopped carrying the Urantia Book in his store when he realized it denounced astrology as a superstition.

"What is it with these people?" I wondered in frustration. But I soon came to realize my own arrogance in introducing the book to those folks I thought needed to read it. My irritating zealousness subsided as I began to absorb the gospel of Jesus and incorporate it into my life. When I am tempted to say, "The Urantia Book says . . . ," I try to share my version of the gospel instead, that we are loving children of a loving God and cherished members of a universe family. I have not met one person who is offended by those words.

My hope for all future readers and disseminators of the Urantia Book is that they have as wonderful an introduction to it as I did, and that they take the teachings deeply to heart. Most important, in response to Jesus' request, I hope that they become ardent proclaimers of his gospel: the Fatherhood of God and the brotherhood of man.

DONNA OLIVER: I grew up in Ft. Lauderdale, Florida, with my mother and two sisters. I was the sister in the middle. My mom was a wonderfully humorous and upright woman whom I greatly admired, but she did little to nurture her spirituality or that of her children. I had never gone to church, nor had I read the Bible or had a religion. Even so, as a young child I felt God's presence hovering nearby, and wherever I went I knew he followed. I came to depend on his watchcare, his guidance and training, his patience and sense of humor. We developed an unceasing, informal dialogue.

In my early teen years I began searching to know more about this God of mine. I visited churches of various denominations, not knowing what I was looking for but confident that I would know it if I found it. I read parts of the Bible before turning to Indian and Eastern philosophy. I visited the world of Carlos Castaneda. I meditated, prayed, became a minimalist and a vegetarian; I did whatever I thought it took to enhance myself spiritually.

At 16 I found a job in a vintage clothing store. The owner and I would launch into lengthy discussions about people, the world, the universe, and the purpose of life. Sometimes I would find him sitting at his desk reading a big blue book. I looked over his shoulder at words that seemed complicated and foreign. In response to my inquiries, my boss/friend told me the book had been written by various celestial beings. I knew I had to know more about this book that dared to make such a claim. He soon found *me* sitting at his desk reading his big blue book. I would scold him whenever he'd take it home and forget to bring it back the next day.

Soon after, I found myself in possession of my own Urantia Book, gold-stamped with the initials DLB. I took it with me wherever I went. I was inspired to read "The Life and Teachings of Jesus" first, which gave me the foundation for appreciating the other sections of the book. I learned much, which only added to a stirring within.

By the time I was 20 I was living in California where I married and became a mother—or was it the other way around? Oh, well . . . I had now read and reread the entire book multiple times, understanding more and more as God spoke to me through every page.

There was one day in particular, as my new baby lay in his crib nearby, that I refused to go on feeling that God was near me but not a *part* of me. I fell to the floor and cried out from the depths of my heart, "God, where *are* you?" It was then that I was filled with an overwhelming feeling of love as I awakened to Michael's beautiful gift, the Spirit of Truth.

I have since made an irrevocable choice to be life partners with God as I move ever closer towards fusion with my Thought Adjuster and towards my destiny as a finaliter in the universes yet to come.

SUSAN HEMMINGSEN: I was living in Sydney, Australia, during the time of the Vietnam War when U.S. troops would come there for r & r. One day I ran into a poor, shell-shocked young American soldier whose money had been stolen, and I offered him a place to stay. While I was at work, he went into a bookshop to purchase paper and a pen with the only money he had left so that he could copy the poem "Desiderata" for me. The shop assistant, seeing how much he obviously wanted that poem, gave it to him, and later on the soldier gave it to me as a gift for my hospitality. He went back to Vietnam a couple of days later and I never heard from him again.

But "Desiderata" rang a bell within me, making me once again consider the possibility that there could be a personal God. Up to that time I had been agnostic. I had explored other religions, particularly the Eastern ones that were trendy back then, but I didn't like the idea of merging into the One after death; I wanted to stay *me*. I had discarded the personal-God concept when I was about 18, perhaps after objecting to the injustice implicit in the idea of Jesus' having to die on the cross to "save us from our sins."

During those years I had many unanswered questions. For example, if Adam and Eve were the first humans on earth, how could Cain go out into the land of Nod and take himself a wife? Where did she come from? I also believed in evolution and was unable to reconcile this belief with the creation story in the Book of Genesis.

A year later, my partner Dick and I were writing a science fiction novel about a world on the brink of disaster. In our book, special people in some countries could stop time to communicate telepathically with each other when disaster was imminent and act to divert the impending catastrophe, after which time would move forward again and the population would be none the wiser. Imagining such a scenario opened my mind to the possibility that, unknown to us, other universe personalities could be living in our midst. I actually began to sense their real existence, although I had no idea who they could be. (The major characters we conceived for our science fiction story, I later realized, had characteristics similar to those of the members of the reserve corps of destiny, as described in the Urantia Book!)

About this same time, I happened to read an Australian-authored book which suggested that we were allowing the inferior to breed at a faster rate than the superior, and that the intelligence quota in the world was declining accordingly. I later found these ideas amplified in the Urantia Book.

I was just finishing the outline and beginning the first chapter of the novel when a friend showed us the Urantia Papers. I read the cover flap, *"There is in the mind of God a plan . . ."* (p. 365), then went to the Foreword, *"Your world, Urantia, is one of many similar inhabited planets. . ."* and continued with, *"You humans have begun an endless unfolding of an almost infinite panorama, a limitless expanding of never-ending, ever-widening spheres of opportunity for exhilarating service, matchless adventure, sublime uncertainty and boundless attainment. . . ."* (p. 1194).

That was it for me! Bells went off and I knew I had found what I had been searching for. I immediately embraced God as a personal being and went on to read the entire book in three months.

KRIS REINECKE: A serious seeker of truth since childhood, I early on rejected the atonement doctrine of Christianity because I found it inconsistent with the Christians' own concept of God. As a 13-year-old, at the request of a middle-aged lady who had no children of her own and had taken an interest in me, I took a correspondence course on the Catholic religion. Upon finishing the course, I politely turned down the offer to become a Catholic because I was unable to accept all the dogma required of a believing Catholic.

In 1962 at age 21 I joined the Masonic order, partly because I believed that there I would, eventually, learn all of the secrets of the universe. Although I went all the way through the Masons, ending up as a Shriner, I kept on waiting for the light bulb to go on above my head. It didn't. I then joined the Rosicrucians in 1969 while in Vietnam; I found their beliefs satisfying and was comfortable with their doctrine of reincarnation. What was not apparent to me at the time, but what I believe now, is that I was being set up by my Thought Adjuster for my introduction to the Urantia Book.

In the autumn of 1973, when I was 31, my wife and I were visiting her friend Carol, who was attending the University of Oklahoma at Norman. While the two were chatting in the kitchen, I wandered into Carol's living room/study and began to browse the titles of the books she had accumulated during her education. About halfway up the shelves I saw the Urantia Book in its white dust cover. After I finished scanning the rest of her library, my eyes immediately snapped back to the big white book. I had to move a hassock close to the bookcase and stand on it to reach the book.

When I opened to the table of contents I was instantly intimidated by the book's complexity and put it back. But something told me to give it another chance. So, using a technique I had learned earlier in life—just stick your finger somewhere into a book and start reading—I opened it randomly to the first page of Part III, "The History of Urantia." Halfway down the page I read, "*Urantia is of origin in your sun...*" Wait a minute, I thought, the author of this book is not from the planet Earth, because he/she said *your* sun.

I slammed the book shut and put it down on the hassock, baffled by the statement. I then thought, either this book is the truth or it is a great science fiction novel. I walked out into the kitchen and asked Carol if she had read it. She said no, and told me one of her friends at the university had given it to her. I asked her if I could borrow it, and the rest is history.

LARRY PAWLITSKY: In 1953, when I was seven, my parents where swayed from their Catholic religion by some new friends of my dad. All of a sudden, I was a Jehovah's Witness and I soon found that I was very interested in learning more about God and his plans for me and this world. I became a devout Bible student and indicated my dedication to serving God by being baptized when I was 14. I attended Bible and book studies, went out on service, and as my knowledge grew, many questions came to my mind.

By the time I was in the eleventh grade, I was asking questions that neither my parents nor any of the elders could answer to my satisfaction. I was also beginning to rebel against the strict rules of the organization. Slowly but surely I drifted away from the religion of my youth. Soon after graduating from high school in 1964, I moved away from my family's home and started working full time. I also stopped attending any Witness meetings. I hadn't given up on the idea of God; I was just looking for a different approach. I was raised in a religion of fear and I just couldn't believe in the concept of God that the Witnesses preached, a God so cruel as to heap all these punishments on us.

I married a non-Witness woman in 1966 and we had a few good years together. All that time, I was searching for something that would relieve my fears and give purpose and meaning to my life. Then the Summer of Love and Woodstock came along and I wholeheartedly embraced the hippie lifestyle. For the first time in my life I felt freedom, and I started exploring other religions and other paths to God. Still, a part of me was keeping a fearful eye on the approaching 1975. As a Jehovah's Witness, I had been led to believe that the great battle of Armageddon was going to take place that year, and that all non-believers would be destroyed.

In the spring of 1973, my wife and I parted ways and the pain and sorrow of the breakup intensified my search for enlightenment. My path led me to explore many Eastern religions and New Age philosophies. Here I was, a small-town mountain boy getting into some heady stuff, and although I was finding some truth, something was missing. And then I came across a book which had a huge impact on me, *Be Here Now*, by Baba Ram Dass, which filled my mind with visions of oneness with the universe.

One day in October of 1973 I stopped by a friend's house for a minute to pick up something. He had out-of-town guests who were just leaving. On their way out, one of the guys, Art, said to me, "What do you think of this?" and handed me a brand-new Urantia Book. I only had time to read the dust jacket and skim through the table of contents but what I read in that short time sent a tingle throughout my body and made my hair stand on end. This happened on a Sunday, and I could hardly wait until Monday morning to phone the bookstore in a city 300 miles away, where Art had bought his copy. I received my book the next day C.O.D. I've been reading and believing the Urantia Book and trying to live the teachings ever since.

Within a month of getting the book, I met Nancy, the love of my life, and she readily accepted the fifth epochal revelation. We were married in the spring of 1974. Ever since finding the Urantia Book I no longer worry that our loving Father could get so angry with us that he would hurt or punish us. I'm free—and I've found truth and love!

I still keep in touch with Art although we live in different towns. He tells me that one of these days he is going to dust off his Urantia Book and read it.

LYNN GOODWIN: Ever since I was a little child I realized that truth was slippery, that it meant different things to different people. An event in kindergarten Catechism stands out to this day as a turning point in my life. The good sister was teaching us about Jesus and she said that people living in deepest, darkest Africa wouldn't go to heaven if they didn't know about Jesus. This was very alarming to my child mind because I already knew that our heavenly Father would not punish us for our ignorance. I sensed that the nuns were trying to tell me something really important, but that they had somehow gotten it wrong.

As I grew up I suspected that the Bible contained more than the truth. The idea that the heavenly Father would require his Son to die on the cross for our sins was an insult to the Father himself, and evidence to me that the Bible had been rewritten too many times. While I did not throw the baby out with the bathwater I began to take my Catholic education with a grain of salt.

Throughout my angst-ridden teenage years, I sought answers from many sources. I read voraciously, sampling from the world's religions, psychology, philosophy, and parapsychology. I was aflame with questions. I wrote poetry, did LSD, received a mantra, and was rolfed and rebirthed. I checked out the Buddhists, the Rosicrucians and Esalen Institute. I looked for goodness and nobility and graciousness in the world and found little. I looked inside and found a lower and a higher self and recognized that I needed Jesus in order to master myself.

In the winter of 1973 I was living in a log cabin on the beach in Lincoln City, Oregon, experiencing the mystic, hippie dream. I still had many questions and some sorrows but I also had the solace of the sea and the beauty of nature. Into my life came four musicians from Chicago: Billy, Al, Jim and Brian. They were members of a jazz band on a road trip out West. They turned me on to jazz, and after those boys expanded my musical palette they changed my life by introducing me to the Urantia Book. They said they had been studying the book with a Dr. Brown and his wife at their summer place somewhere in Illinois.

The Urantia Book had come to me after an extensive search, and I devoured it. In page after page, it provided answers, insights, and affirmations that I had been seeking for years. It gave me the perspective of cosmic citizenship. As others have reported, I knew immediately what it was and I was overwhelmed by the importance of such a document. I felt honored and humbled and deeply grateful for receiving such a gift.

Most dear to me is Part IV, "The Life and Teachings of Jesus"; I never tire of studying the Master's life. It so beautifully fleshes out the biblical account, filling in the holes and correcting mistakes by relating the rest of the story.

My entire life has been tremendously blessed and uplifted by the Urantia Book. I am able to look at the world and see meaning in the struggle, see my fellows as beloved children of the divine Father, and visualize the outworking of the divine plan. I look forward to the ongoing ascension adventure in service and in love.

DARLENE SHEATZ CRINER: My early twenties were spent looking for answers, not about God necessarily, but about the world and beyond. I studied various philosophies and religions, only to hit the wall fairly quickly.

In 1973 I moved to California from Colorado, having spent two years studying yoga and Tai Chi, which I now feel prepared me in many ways for the discovery of truth.

The very month I arrived in California I met a great lady. She wasn't a Urantia Book reader but she led me straight to the book. While visiting her home I noticed her husband was always reading a blue book. His reluctance to talk about it intrigued me even more. It so happened that on the same block lived a number of wonderful folks who were also Urantia Book readers. My first loaner book was given to me by a reader named Jim McNelly.

As I began to browse the book, my reaction was, What is this stuff? Nebadon? Andon and Fonta? Now, really! It took some doing for me to get over the table of contents.

I must admit that the cosmic information was most interesting to me in the beginning. What really took me in was the information on the Solitary Messengers. I found myself also going to the Thought Adjuster papers over and over, fascinated by the connection between all that was out there and all that was within me. It was a long time before I ventured into the Jesus papers, but when I did, the meanings and values became real to me. I no longer thought it was corny to believe in Jesus, as I had felt when growing up.

Now, over thirty years later, I feel my life has been tremendously enriched by the discovery of the Urantia Book. But it took me a long time to integrate what I was reading with what I was doing in my life. I'm still trying.

MICHAEL MANN: When I was 13 I got through my Bar Mitzvah by faking it. I had been thrown out of Sunday school when I was 11 for asking questions like, "Wasn't John the Baptist Jewish? Wasn't Jesus Jewish?" Even my Reform temple couldn't handle that. So, in order to make my parents happy, I took a crash course in Hebrew phonetics, to learn my Haftorah and the song I had to sing. When the big day finally came, I didn't understand a word of the Hebrew I was reciting. I felt nothing inside. I was hungry, maybe, but otherwise, zippo.

From that day until several years later, I considered myself an agnostic, leaning heavily towards atheism. I was part of the great hippie generation, graduating high school as a clean-cut kid in 1968, only to become a draft-card-burning demonstrator in the streets less than a year later. My road took me to California where I met some hippie friends who were true believers in Dr. Tim and who had a line on pure doses of LSD-25, then known as "Orange Sunshine." My acid experiments were many, and from the start I felt that I was being led back to the true God, the One God. An acid experience in the Nevada desert in 1972 caused me to understand fully that We are One, and that God was the One. I was already headlong into this adventure of personal religious experience a full year before I ever saw a Urantia Book.

In September 1973 I was back in New York, married to a girl I had met in California. A very good friend of mine, an electric guitar player, showed me the Urantia Book in his apartment in Westchester. It floored me. I couldn't believe it existed and the more I looked at it and read the author's names and the names of the papers, I knew I had to get this book. It seemed to provide a complete explanation of the very simple concept, We are One. It gave names to things and beings that I had already suspected existed.

My new wife and I immediately bought two copies of the book from the Foundation's offices in Chicago. I remember sitting in the front room of the building at 533 W. Diversey, filling out forms while we waited for them to bring us our books.

I began reading. I tried to start from the beginning but couldn't help jumping around. I loved a lot of what I was finding in Part III, but I was still having trouble with the whole Jesus thing in Part IV. I admired much of what Jesus says in the Bible, but could not accept what the organized religions had to say about him. Finally, I read the last paper of Part III, so I would understand about bestowal missions, and then I began Part IV. I was immediately drawn into the story but a creeping thought lay at the back of my mind, that I was a trained, professional journalist falling for what had to be one of two things: either the most elaborate literary fraud in history (which would make it a good story!) or the truth. It took me about thirty pages before I surrendered my doubts. I continued to read Part IV and began to accept this new Jesus into my heart.

Shortly afterwards my wife and I returned to California where we met a whole group of people who were reading the book and trying to live the teachings. A lot of socializing and music took place at these meetings. I studied the book with a man who was like a Zen master of the Papers, just because he was so good at reducing it all to a simple way of life.

The book has remained with me all these years, though at times it got dusty sitting on the shelf. When my marriage came apart, I became addicted to dangerous drugs to relieve the pain. In rehab, ready for some answers, I opened the book again and began reading the Jesus papers once more. I became a leader in the 12-step programs, and for years I was a speaker and musical performer at their meetings and conventions. I kept working the real Urantia messages in, even though I never mentioned the source. Just recently, the book has helped me enter a new phase of my life, spreading the good news about Jesus through my music. My songs are not directly about Jesus, but his message is always there.

As the book says, "*It is literally true: if a man has Christ Jesus within him, he is a brand new creature, old things are passing away, all things become new.*" And it has happened like that for me, exactly as Jesus promised.

DELORES DINSMORE: The sun! When I was very small I wondered why something so important could be dangerous to look at. Angels! My father read the Bible out loud to us. I was amazed by the story of the angels in the fire, preventing Shadrach, Meshach and Abednego from burning up. Death! Gramma died of a heart attack when I was ten. My mom reported that at the end Gramma opened her eyes and smiled, saying, "I'm coming, Jesus!"

Such thoughts comprised my childhood spirituality questions. It may seem funny, but I never questioned the reality of Jesus. He was always a very real, living presence to me.

At 18 my spiritual quest began in earnest when I left home to go to college. It was 1968. Campuses in were turmoil, the revolution was in full force—the Vietnam War, riots, draft-card burning, tear gas, civil rights, environmentalism, Women's Lib, hippies, drugs, and free love. Where did I fit in?

My life was changed by a near-death experience. My heart had stopped. I floated away from my body and out of the room until I found myself hanging onto a huge golden grid somewhere in space. Beings appeared and led me back to my body. "But I don't want to go back!" I begged. "Please, can't I stay with you?" "No, Delores," they answered, "you don't know enough about the world yet." A dog barked loudly and it seemed to start my heart. I believed I had almost died, but after that I also believed there were helpers out there.

The Great Tao, where we melt into an energy field and lose all our friendships and relationships? I couldn't buy it. Jesus didn't lose his identity when he rose from the dead.

The great wheel of reincarnation? In that case, shouldn't Jesus have been reborn as a gnat or a dog or a sacred blue cow? No, he came back as himself.

Or you die and there is a big black emptiness of nothing? Why would God bother with all this amazing detail if that were the case? Sorry, that was not for me.

Transcendental Meditation—what? I need to pay money for a secret mantra for enlightenment? But I loved Yogananda's poetry and the way he kept saying to keep going, beyond all the psychic phenomena, beyond the out-of-body experiences, beyond the tricks of energy manipulation, until we find the true connection to God.

And why did the churches mostly leave Jesus hanging on the cross, glorifying the sacrifice rather than the promise of a loving, abundant life-everlasting? I could never reconcile the idea of a Father God doing that to the beloved Son. Something was wrong there. Drink the blood? Eat the body? Did the churches know how barbaric that sounded? What could these things really mean?

I liked the idea that I could take pieces and leave the rest, so I began to build my own cosmology.

In early 1973 I was in Bethlehem, Pennsylvania, working at a movie theater selling tickets. Some Jesus freaks working the streets handed me the Bible and told me it was a "good book," so I decided it was time to read it to see what all the fuss was about. I loved Isaiah and the Psalms, but the Bible did not have good enough answers to many of my questions.

That summer, just when I'd gotten into the New Testament chapters, my older brother, Doug, sent me the Urantia Book. Doug had received Big Blue in 1972 from Norm Du Val, his mailman in Missoula, Montana, who had struck up a friendship with him. Having just injured his back, Doug had spent the next few weeks reading the book intensely cover to cover. He then passed it on to me, saying, "This book answers all your spiritual questions, but remember, you can't read your way into heaven."

How wonderful to receive this Urantia Book while I was studying the Bible! I began to see that the Bible was the barest outline of a much more elaborate and elegant story presented in the Urantia Book. For a while I tried to share this great revelation with my Christian friends. I brandished the big blue book like a mighty enlightener, trying to enlarge their beliefs. However, I soon realized that I was alienating myself from the churchgoers. Most were appalled that I did not accept every word in the Holy Bible as sacred and true. How could I say there was no hell? How could I add anything to the Scriptures? They believed the devil most certainly was alive and well, and his best ruse of all was to convince fools like me that he did not exist! One day I stopped in weariness from fighting against these limiting beliefs. I asked Michael, "What should I do now?" I heard him quietly reply, "Please, quit scaring my sheep."

I realized that I needed to embrace the concept of "wise as serpents, harmless as doves," so I gave up my Urantia Book evangelism. When I returned home to Helena, Montana, I joined my mom and some others who had been receptive to the revelation and started a Urantia Book study group for those who needed deeper answers to their spiritual questions.

Part V

1974-1976

JOY BRANDT: I was on vacation out West, traveling and camping with two girlfriends from Michigan. One day we picked up three hitchhikers who, it turned out, belonged to a group of hippies who called themselves The Traveling Light Circus. Their "guru" was a cocky gay guy named Jamail McKinney who had read the Urantia Book seven times and was now claiming to have fused with his Thought Adjuster. I must admit that it wasn't the message of God's love they shared as much as the fact that there were so many men in the group, which first interested Karen, Peggy and me.

At that time, in 1974, I considered myself to be agnostic, having tossed out belief in God when I rejected the fundamental Christianity of my upbringing. But I'd been jolted into a philosophical search for life's meaning when my parents both died a couple of years earlier. This group was the "highest" bunch of people I'd ever met. I decided to travel with them later, and made plans to join them after finishing our vacation. When I got back home, I purchased the Urantia Book, since Jamail had made it required reading for everyone who wished to travel with his group.

Months later, I'd been hitchhiking with The Traveling Light Circus and had read about a quarter of the Urantia Papers but still didn't believe in God. I was being stubborn. I didn't want to believe in a God just because it made everything seem nicer. I wanted to know the *truth* about God. If there *was* a God, I wanted to know it; but if there *wasn't*, I wanted to know that, too. I didn't want to be swayed by the obvious psychological benefits that my fellow travelers seemed to be experiencing due to their faith. I wanted to know what was real, but was in a quandary as to how to go about it.

One night our large group of hitchhikers rendezvoused at the house of a man named Joe Zabriel who also read the Urantia Book. I was reading quietly to myself in a corner when I overheard Zabriel talking to someone from our group about Jesus' twofold purpose in coming to this planet. Suddenly, like a long line of dominos falling down with one small push, everything fell together. Things Zabriel was saying started fitting in with what I'd heard from my Christian schooling. Thoughts I'd had, subjects I'd studied, experiences in my life, plus ideas I'd recently read in the Urantia Book, all fell into place in my mind.

All at once it was like I was standing at a major fork in the road. I looked up the "high road" and down the "low road," seeing with a clarity I'd never had before. One road was the choice of God, and it included an eternal life where beauty always outshines ugliness, where truth never fails to conquer error, where goodness always wins against evil, and where there is endless love and joy in the eternal adventure of serving with my brothers and sisters in God's divine family. The other road was one of selfishness, darkness, loneliness and eventual death; there was no God; all one could do was try to find happiness in material possessions, snatching everything for oneself, because we were all pitted against each other in the struggle for a life which was altogether too short.

A moment earlier I could not have made the choice. But now, as I stood at this fork in the road of my life, the decision was easy. I realized God's existence could never be proven or disproven, that faith was a choice—and the time had come for me to decide.

I stated to myself and to God, "I choose faith in God!" And immediately I experienced a thought that was so distinct and clear that it seemed like another's voice spoken aloud, although inside my head. This thought-voice said, "Of course you know there's a God! And you knew it all the time, didn't you?" In a rush my mind was flooded with memories of relating to God as a child. All of a sudden I realized that, yes, indeed, it seemed I had known all along that there was a God! It was as if those years of agnosticism had been merely a mental exercise, but deeper down I'd always known God!

From that day on, when my faith sometimes falters, I look back and remember that fork in the road. I've made my choice. This is the road I choose to walk, the one of faith and love as a child in God's universal family. Thank you, Father!

RICHARD OMURA: It was 1974. I was 23 and living in Hawaii in a small, rundown house with two other potheads in a little two-store town called Honouliuli, about fifteen miles west of Honolulu. I suppose you could describe my lifestyle as counterculture. I was basically a hippie with a small pot farm, living an idyllic life. I tended my plants, went surfing, and partied a lot.

Nearby lived a buddy named Fred. He was the unofficial leader of our tiny cadre of pot farmers and surfers. One night, after visiting Fred, I was walking home down a dirt road looking up at the bright panorama of stars. A few days earlier I had seen the movie *The Exorcist* and it had left me feeling confused and uncertain about God, the devil, Jesus, heaven, hell, and religion in general. I may even have been a little scared. So I gazed up at the stars and spoke out to whatever was up there. I said, "I'm really fed up with this lack of information. If there is a God, why can't you just tell me everything I need to know in a logical, straightforward way without all the myths, dogma and inconsistencies I find in all the religions? Just give it to me straight and I'll believe it."

It was not too long afterwards that I went over to Fred's house and found a big blue book on his desk. I read the Foreword and knew right away that this was an extraordinary book. I couldn't believe it was for real. The effect it had on me was not only mental but physical. My head rang as if I were on a drug. As I leafed through it, I became convinced that I must read the entire book. I asked Fred where he'd gotten it.

"Oh, that book?" he said off-handedly. "Bob So-and-so didn't have twenty bucks for a 'lid' so I took the book instead. He says it's worth more."

Little did Fred realize what it was *really* worth. The Urantia Book in exchange for twenty dollars' worth of marijuana was probably the best deal he'd ever gotten.

After reading the Foreword I turned to "The Lucifer Rebellion." Having just seen *The Exorcist*, I wanted to know what the devil was all about. The UB's explanation cleared away all the fear and confusion I'd had regarding that topic.

It took me a while before I bought a book for myself. And even after I got the book, I didn't read it from cover to cover immediately like so many other readers have. I only opened it and read it when I had the inclination, which was sporadically and periodically.

I was not changed by the book in a noticeable way until I'd had it for about ten years, and had decided—and become determined—to practice its concepts and values. Since I knew no one who had read the book or had even heard about it, I entertained for a split second the fantastic notion that I was the only person on earth who had discovered the book and was therefore chosen by God to deliver the message to the world. But since the book had a publisher, that idea was immediately seen for the grandiose concoction that it was.

After having had the book for about five years and with no one to discuss it with, I decided to contact the publisher, the Urantia Foundation. I was overjoyed at last to talk to someone else who knew of the existence of the book. The woman on the phone gave me some study group phone numbers but the groups were either in the continental United States or on another island, and I was still living near Honolulu. When I finally had a chance to go to Los Angeles I attended my first study group, at Dick McDonald's house in Van Nuys. There were about ten readers and I still have fond memories of that time.

For the first twenty-three years I was envious of my fellow UB readers who had successfully turned others on to the book, because it seemed I was unable do so myself. Then in 1996 a producer from the *Strange Universe* program invited me to speak about the book on TV. I initially had qualms about it but decided to go ahead, with assistance from my friends Don Roark, Norman Ingram and Andrea Barnes. Many, many new readers were introduced to the book as a result of the show. This made me realize that we do not need to be envious of anybody. We just need to have faith that everything comes in good time—because it does!

BYRON BELITSOS: My junior year at the University of Chicago ('73-'74) was an exciting but confusing period of questioning and discovery for me. The unrest of the '60s was coming to an end—a bitter end, in my estimation—and a wave of new spiritual teachings and teachers was beginning to sweep through college campuses. Eastern literature in particular was flooding in. Self-styled gurus like Ram Dass were in vogue, as well as "genuine" Eastern gurus such as the Maharishi Mahesh Yogi, Sri Chinmoy, and Chogyam Trungpa. I was attracted to them all, and so were my friends, all of us being Humanities and English Lit types. Here was a striking solution, I felt, to the problems of a sick and violent society, a solution far superior to that offered by the left-wing politics I had espoused as an outspoken high school and campus radical.

For a few months that spring, my friends and I lived in a haze of spiritual books, drugs, jazz, and late-night rap sessions. We felt justified in mixing spiritual teachings with psychedelics; after all, hadn't Ram Dass, a college professor at Harvard, found God, or Brahman, or atman—or whatever he called it—through the same experimenting?

From observing myself in these ecstatic states of consciousness, I came to the overriding conclusion that something grand—perhaps something infinite and ineffable—lived within my own mind. Despite a few incidents of getting hopelessly lost at rock concerts, this chemically induced gnosis was incontrovertible: God or spirit lived within, and the Eastern teachers were right.

But what about the transcendent God, the Jesus I had grown up with as a socially active Greek Orthodox Christian in Ohio? What about that garish icon on my mother's dresser? Were those gorgeous liturgies—with the chanting, the robes, the choral singing, the clouds of incense—only for raising church dues? What was behind all the rich mysticism that was hinted at in the church rites? These questions fueled my search for the transcendent One, in every form I could find him.

By the end of the semester the number of friends who were still seeking with me had dwindled down to three. We read every esoteric book we could lay our hands on—on UFOs, out-of-body experiences, flying gurus, kundalini yoga, Vishnu and Krishna, shamans, altered states of consciousness—you name it, we read it.

Now the school year was over and I was spending an uneventful summer at home in Cincinnati, living in my parents' basement and working as a waiter. One night I was up smoking joints and talking with my younger brother, feeling excited, confused, and happy all at once. He eventually fell asleep, but I stayed up listening to an all-night, anything-goes college radio station broadcasting from Miami, Ohio. At 2:45 a.m. a man with a very pleasant and confident voice called in to the station, saying, "Everybody out there should know about this amazing book I am studying, called the Urantia Book. It was handed to a bunch of people in Chicago, right out of a flying saucer! If you read one paragraph, it will make you high, with a profound buzz, for an entire day. You've just got to read it—it is totally wild and totally from God."

I wrote down the name, fumbling excitedly for my pencil. The caller mentioned that he was a go-cart racer, and that he would be racing the next morning—a Sunday—in a large parking lot at a local college. The next day I found him there by asking around. I don't remember his name, but he was about 30, handsome and dignified, and very kind to me. He seemed to be the leader of a go-cart group of about fifty people.

This gracious man then told me to go a bookstore in downtown Cincinnati where I would be sure to find the flying saucer revelation. I immediately headed over, and there it was, the big blue book, on a shelf at about eye level. I grabbed it, flung it open, and began reading in the section, "The Modern Problem," on page 2075. Something in me knew I had found what I'd been looking for—it all just clicked in a huge intellectual and emotional catharsis. I was stunned for a few minutes, then began to skim excitedly. After an hour of reading, sitting oblivious on the floor in the bookstore aisle, I bought it, looking forward to finding my answers, never suspecting that after this my *real* problems in life would begin!

Today I thank God, the angels, and this unknown man in Cincinnati for giving me one of the greatest gifts any of us can ever receive.

ESTHER WOOD: I have loved God all my life. When I was a young girl I went to church every Sunday and to Bible school every summer. I loved the stories about Jesus. Then one summer, when I was around eight or nine, my grandma took me to an evangelical revival where the preacher gave one of those hellfire-and-brimstone sermons, and it scared the hell right out of me. When they called for those wanting to be saved to come up, I went up the altar and gave my life to Jesus that day. I was as sincere as I could be, considering what I could understand at the time.

For a while after that I was "on fire for the Lord," but the way the "good Christians" in my life acted—gossiping about their neighbors, treating each other with disrespect, their lack of honesty—left me feeling disenchanted. I withdrew from the church and my family—but not from God. Somehow, I still knew that he was the true righteousness. I looked for Him in a lot of unconventional places (my grandmother would shudder if she knew all the places I looked!). The amazing thing was that no matter where I looked, I could see God. That was my first clue that God was bigger than any man-made religion. He did not forsake me, even though I'd gone to some God-forsaken places.

In the early '70s, after two years of college and a lot of partying in Michigan, I moved to Portland, Oregon. I still read the Bible, as well as many other books about different religions, mysticism, the occult, psychology, sociology, and philosophy. I was spiritually hungry and actively looking for truth. In 1974 I met the man who is now my husband. We talked a lot about life, God, those "interesting coincidences," and anything else anybody brought up in our search for truth. We invited everyone we knew to join us in our quest.

One day, our neighbor brought over a big blue book and handed it to us, saying, "I think you are ready for this." He left it with us for two weeks. We looked through it, read portions here and there, discussed it, and read some more. I remember the first time I read pages 1007-8, where the revelators tell us about the five epochal revelations given to our planet. The fourth had been Jesus' life on earth and the fifth was the Urantia Papers, *"of which this is one . . ."* Those words hit me with a feeling of profound discovery: If this is true, this is a big deal; if not, it is a big deception.

I laid the book down for a moment and prayed about it. I decided to go back to the Bible. The Bible fell open at 2nd John 4: 1-6. "Believe not every spirit, but test the spirits, whether they are of God . . . . You know the spirit is of God if it confesses that Jesus is the Son of God." The whole Urantia Book confesses that. We bought a book of our own soon after that.

In 1975 we moved about forty miles south of Portland, to Molalla, where we started our family and our study group. It has been a long process of growing up in the kingdom of heaven, but our Father has been with us through all of our trials, tribulations and joys. I feel very lucky that we found the Urantia Book.

SUE SMITH: Having been in the Church most of my life since childhood, for several years I was inspired to search religious bookstores, attend church groups, study, and talk with church people concerning the Spirit in our lives. In September of 1974, while living in Hawaii, I was somehow directed to the Religion section of a Honolulu bookstore. There I found a very large book with a white cover next to the Bible. Curious, I took it down and read the dust jacket. Slamming it shut, I said to myself, "It is humanly impossible to know this kind of information, therefore it is a sacrilege to place this stuff next to the Bible—God's Word."

No one was at the check-out counter at that time except the store manager. I decided to go over and tell him off for placing such a book next to the Bible, but by the time I had crossed the store to the counter, a line of people had formed waiting to check out. I gave up on the idea, and as I headed for the exit door I suddenly heard a voice that seemed to be in front and above me, saying, "Leave it alone. I will take care of it." Stunned, I went home.

In December of 1974 I found that same large book on my coffee table in my living room. None of my family would own up to having put it there.

December was always a busy time, so it was not until January 1975 that I began reading the Urantia Book. After a while, I concluded that the midwayers must have placed the book in my home. It was months before my oldest son confessed that a high school teacher—a Urantia Book reader—had encouraged him to buy the book. My son was not ready for this information and thought it would be a challenge to tease Mom. Little did he know that Mom was ready for this book—I fell for it hook, line and sinker.

Reading, researching, cross referencing with the Bible and jumping from one subject to another, I had to decide for myself if this book really was all that it claimed to be.

Soon I was invited by my Urantia Book mentor, Eva Sepp, to attend a gathering of Urantia Book readers to meet a representative from the Urantia Foundation, Paul Snider. This was my first experience with other readers, and I was delighted to meet such a dear, kind, and loving person.

Later, our business took us to Chicago, where I spent a full day at 533 Diversey Parkway talking with Emma ("Christy") Christensen and Meredith Sprunger, then president of the Brotherhood. Meredith suggested rather emphatically that I read the Urantia Book from cover to cover, beginning to end, from the Alpha to the Omega. By doing this, the revelations fell into place in a chronological order. My soul was satisfied that this book was genuine. Now after years of study, it all seems so simplified.

I began to host my own study group in January 1976. Though we eventually moved to Arizona after fourteen years in Hawaii, the study group I started has continued meeting almost every week since that time.

I know the book is true because it has brought me that glorious spiritual peace of mind that is beyond all understanding. May God bless the teachings of the Urantia Book, and guide us all in the way he would have us go.

JANE A. ROPER: The year was 1969 and my first husband and I had just graduated from college in Iowa. We had both been accepted to law school in San Francisco, so together with our two-year-old daughter, Samantha, we moved to that glorious city the day after graduation. The Summer of Love, Haight-Ashbury, hippies, and anti-war sentiments were all very appealing after living in the Midwest. We rented an apartment in Sausalito and eventually became resident-managers of a magnificent Victorian mansion that had been converted into apartments. As managers it was our responsibility to screen tenants and rent out the apartments.

One apartment we rented was to a very nice interracial couple, a Black man, Johnny, and his Caucasian wife, Pam. We were told that Pam worked nights at a nursing home, and we accepted the information without question.

We became friends with Johnny and Pam. One day I was downstairs in their apartment, looking at their bookshelf. Sitting there was a copy of the Urantia Book. I had never seen it before. Being an inquisitive soul I picked it up and leafed through it—strange names, very big, kind of spooky, but then Johnny was into stuff like that, and had been lecturing us about the revolution to come.

"Hey, Johnny," I asked him, "What is this book? What's it about?"

"Well, Miss Jane," he answered playfully, "I haven't really read much of it, but from what I can tell, it is a book about everything!"

Later, my husband and I learned from Pam that she was actually a prostitute and that Johnny was her pimp and not her husband at all. Eventually they moved out. My marriage later broke up, and I returned to my parents' home in Michigan with my daughter. I became a charismatic Episcopalian with a vibrant, daily, loving relationship with Jesus.

Eventually I met John Roper, who would become my husband. The next time I saw the Urantia Book was at John's home in Bloomfield Hills, a wealthy suburb of Detroit. Needless to say, I was a bit freaked out to see the book again in the possession of such a different sort of person than the "first" Johnny, and it took quite a while for me to get over my resistance to it. John Roper had been reading seriously for some time and our first dates consisted of talking about "life and stuff," with him reading me large chunks of the UB and me thinking, "I am getting to know a lot about this book, but not much about this interesting man!" Finally I decided that I could not criticize the book without reading it myself.

I did start reading, and of course you won't be surprised by the rest of the story. The truth contained in the book spoke deeply to me, enlarged my existing relationship with Jesus and our Father, and affirmed long-held philosophical concepts. I felt, "Yes, that's the way I've always thought that this whole life experience, and God, and everything, should be." It spoke to my heart and mind, and filled in all the missing gaps left by Christianity. I was able to affirm that indeed, I had found the fifth epochal revelation to our world—the Urantia Book.

MIKE KUBIK: I first had an opportunity to discover the Urantia Book in 1966. I was working in the warehouse of a department store while going to college. Working with me was a peculiar, introverted guy, a Urantia Book reader named Mike. After listening to him talk about Adam and Eve being "purple giants," I more or less tuned him out from then on. Now I'm sorry that I didn't get to know him better and pay more attention to what he was saying. Shortly after that I joined the Navy. I would have looked at the historical places I visited with a keener eye if I had been reading the Urantia Book back then.

It wasn't until 1973 or 1974, in Houston, that I came across the book again. It was given to me by a mechanic who took my old, broken-down Karmann-Ghia in exchange for an equally old, broken-down Volvo. He was a recovering drug addict and thought I might be interested in the book. When I asked him what it was about, he replied, "It's kind of science fiction." Right!

I struggled through the book for several days, maybe weeks, wondering where all of it was leading. It told an incredibly detailed story. I speculated a little bit about the authorship, but did not bother to glance ahead to the Jesus papers. I didn't even know they were there.

One night at a meeting with some people who could best be described as early New Agers, I happened to mention the book to a woman who was a friend of my ex-wife. She said she read the Urantia Book all the time to see how Jesus would handle things.

"Jesus? Is he in the book, too?" I asked.

"Of course," she replied, "that's what it's all about!"

I had been trying to discipline myself to read the book from front to back, suffering through some of the more complicated papers, building images in my brain of the panorama of other worlds and creatures it revealed, when suddenly I learned that the book also contained the *real* story of Jesus as recorded by midwayers who were there when it happened. I went home and skipped ahead to the rest of the story. That was when the power of the book suddenly hit me. I have never been lonely since then, and I live with the assurance that I have an eternal future in the service of my Father and his children.

While sometimes I regret not having found the book earlier in my life, I know that through my struggling and ignorance I learned how to determine right from wrong. Failure usually followed error, and pain usually accompanied failure. My Adjuster managed to lead me through literature, relationships, vocations, war, and even peace, and still always pointed me toward something better. I wanted the magic of the spirit. I wanted the power that the sure knowledge of eternal life offers. I wanted to know the love of God.

Of course I didn't know that's what I wanted. I only know that in retrospect. As Jerry Garcia of the Grateful Dead said, "What a long, strange trip it's been!"

MICHELLE KLIMESH: When I was 12 I began to believe that the Holy Roman Catholic Church was not telling me the real truth. I started browsing through the Bible, skeptically, intending to prove to myself that God was some bogus myth. Most of the Bible seemed like mumbo jumbo to me, but I was attracted to the "red words," the words of Jesus. I decided to find out if he was telling the truth by testing his advice in the real world. The first thing I tested was: "The Spirit of Truth dwells within you, and the Spirit will lead you to all truth, and the truth will set you free." That sounded pretty weird to me, that some spirit was living inside of me.

But after about five years I had enough evidence to admit that maybe there was some inner source of wisdom that I could tap into besides my own brain. So I chalked one point up for Jesus, and went back to the Bible to pick out some more red words. I chose "love your enemy." This was clearly illogical, and I was sure I could refute it. But in the real world, in actual practice, it worked brilliantly. Two points for Jesus now. I started to think Jesus was pretty smart, maybe even a genius.

It was 1974. I was 19. I signed up for a piano class at the local junior college. After class, the guy I shared a piano with and I would talk about things like, "Who is God?" and "What happens when we die?" I told him that I thought there was no such thing as hell. He agreed. I told him that I didn't think it was God's sick idea to torture and murder Jesus. He said that's what *he* thought, too.

I started to think he was just agreeing with everything I said, so I pulled out my really big theory, the best thing I had ever come up with while hanging out with the Spirit of Truth all those years. I told him I thought that human beings were just embryos. Of course, he said that he thought that, too. So I told him that he couldn't possibly have thought that, because I had made it up myself. He said, "Oh yeah?" and, opening his backpack, pulled out a big blue book. He started flipping through the pages, showing me the section on the atonement, and the part where the soul is the embryo made by the human mind and the divine spirit.

I was dumbfounded that someone had swiped my own ideas and put them in a book. I asked to borrow his book, but he said, "No. Go get your own." I ordered one from B. Dalton.

When the semester ended I lost touch with the guy in the piano class. I kept reading the book, wondering about each paragraph: What does this mean? Is it true? It took me seventeen years to get through the whole book, because I had to stop and think about each new thing, and there sure were a lot of new things. I decided there were three parts of the book: the parts I couldn't understand (such as absonite reality), the parts I couldn't verify (such as how fast a Solitary Messenger travels), and the deepest, purest truth I'd ever met. I let the things I didn't understand go by for a while; I find that the older I get, the more I understand.

Epilogue: Seventeen years later, when my daughters were five and nine, I wanted to give them some religious bearings. I couldn't figure out how to break the Urantia teachings into child-size bites, so I went looking for other UBers. After several months of dead ends, I found a study group meeting at Sara and Bob Blackstock's house. Guess who showed up? The boy in the piano class, Mark Turrin. We fell in love. Isn't that a fun ending?

ROGER J. ABDO: Finding the Urantia Book was the culmination of forty years of searching for truth, reality and God. During those years, as I read hundreds of books on various philosophies and religions, I kept an open mind and stayed true to my focus. But I still had many questions about Jesus and the Trinity doctrine.

I found Clyde Bedell's *Concordex* first. Fascinated by the leading questions about life, God and the universe on the dust jacket, I bought the book right on the spot. After four days of intensive search I finally found the Urantia Book at a bookstore.

The Urantia Book opened a clear path for me to follow, and gave me a renewed surge of assurance that what I was searching for was within my grasp. When I first found the book I knew no other readers, but I have since come into contact with a wonderful group of Urantians who have blessed me with their friendship and feedback. I feel very fortunate to be able to share my discovery with others.

TERRY GALVIN: I was raised in the Irish Catholic tradition. Good, loving parents nestled us, their seven kids, close to the Church and Roman Catholic values. I attended Catholic schools right through college. I was devout and active in the Church and even had thoughts of becoming a priest—until love for a pretty girl and the '60s got hold of me.

One night in 1974 a bunch of us mellow hippie types were gathered in E.K. and Beth's apartment. E.K. was a house painter and Beth an elementary school teacher. She was also a serious astrologer and had many New Age books on her shelves. We were playing guitars and singing soft harmonies, drinking beer and wine and passing joints, talking about Man, God and the Law. While I was playing guitar, I kept staring at a big blue book on one of the bookshelves. During a break in the music I went over and got it down and opened it. I'd never seen or heard the word "Urantia" before. I sat on the floor and perused the table of contents.

As I began to recognize names like Melchizedek and Adam and Eve and Gabriel and saw how the book was divided into four astonishing parts, my eyes got bigger and low whistles puckered my lips. For a few years I'd been investigating things like Buddhist chanting (*nam yoho renge kyo*); the Divine Light Mission of Guru Mahara Ji; the doors of perception (with the aid of LSD); mystical poetry and all kinds of etceteras. I had studied Teilhard de Chardin's *The Phenomenon of Man* at the Jesuit college I'd attended, but when I tossed the Church out of my life at age 20, I tossed Teilhard out, too. (Later, parts of the Urantia Book would remind me of his writings.) But this blue book thoroughly intrigued me. I asked Beth if I could borrow it. She said sure. She had glimpsed through it but hadn't been grabbed by it.

I took it home and gradually, attentively, struggled through large, difficult chunks of it. I found myself astonished and more astonished, and astonished that I comprehended what was astonishing me. It took me five years to finally believe that it was an actual revelation, but suddenly, with a liquid clarity and overflow of joy, I did.

One of the ways the Urantia Book has helped me in my growing of a soul is that it inspired me to go to Alcoholics Anonymous to confront the disease that has plagued me since a teenager. I find many parallels between the teachings of the big blue UBook and the big blue book of AA.

I'm grateful that the Urantia Book came to me, and gratefully enjoying the journey of inward ascension it so exquisitely describes and explains. The book has banished lonesomeness from my life forever.

SIOUX HARVEY: Ever since I was a child I can recall a feeling that is difficult to put into words, but can be described as a need to feel closer to God. Many of my school friends had the same feeling. We attended different church services in our home town of San Diego but had never joined a particular congregation.

In high school in 1974, in eleventh-grade English class, we were each asked to interview a classmate, then give an oral presentation about that person. When my interviewer, a male classmate, asked me what my life goals were, I said, "To grow spiritually as much as possible." I was the only person in my class to say this, and it was the first time I had ever expressed this need out loud in front of anyone.

Two weeks later, I was attending an auction together with my mom and a friend. The auction featured American Indian rugs and jewelry, and my mom purchased a rug. Afterwards, a man approached us and asked my mom if he could buy the rug from her. This man, whose name was John, and I got to talking and we exchanged phone numbers.

Although my mom kept the rug, John and I became friends. He traveled frequently and I would house-sit for him. He lived in a fantastic, modern house perched on a hill, a true James Bond-type bachelor pad—at least that is how my high-school friends and I saw it. I loved it when John went out of town, when my girlfriends and I would stay in his beautiful home on the weekends and feel like adults.

The very first time I entered his house I walked in and saw two things on his coffee table: a note that said *"Mi casa es su casa,"* and the Urantia

Book. I still remember picking up the book (it had no dust jacket) and wondering what the heck it was. I opened it, read the first paragraph, and got goosebumps. I knew I had found what I had been searching for.

Though John was a Urantia Book reader, he did not attend a study group. We discussed the book but read independently of one another. I asked for my own copy for my next birthday and my parents bought me one. I read off and on for the next twenty years. In 1990 I devoted myself anew to the revelation and began to attend a study group. My life has forever been enriched and blessed by these amazing teachings.

ROBERT BURNS: Raised in a Catholic family, the oldest of six children and the first-born grandchild on both sides, I learned about responsibility and duty at a young age. I went to Catholic schools, served as an altar boy, and faithfully attended church. I believed in God and prayed the Lord's Prayer and Hail Marys as I had been taught. I studied catechism and wondered about things like Abraham's willingness to kill his son for God (and even more, God's desire to test Abraham that way); the great flood and the ark; people turning to salt due to God's anger; plus many other things about God's nature and the universe. Oddly, I never questioned Jesus' dying for our sins or God's reason for requiring him to do so.

In Catholic high school I became an advocate of science. Here were explanations and descriptions of how things worked. Biology, chemistry, and astronomy provoked my curiosity and a growing desire for answers. I began questioning, asking things that could not or would not be answered by the priests, brothers, and nuns, and in return I received only platitudes.

By age 17, I had stopped praying and going to church, and I questioned the concept of religious belief. I saw the horrors of life. People were starving and being massacred needlessly. God—if he *did* exist— seemed to allow this, was uncaring and unfeeling. I increasingly could not believe in such a God. I had lost the magic of belief. I was no longer in Disneyland. No more Santa, no more Easter bunny, no more tooth fairy, no more guardian angels, no more God.

Various tragedies befell my family, and at 19 I left home. I promptly fell in love with an almost-18-year-old Jewish girl, Cindy Hirsh, and moved in with her. A year later we were married. Cindy introduced me to a new world, one of Jews, atheists, hippies, leftist politics (my family was heavily into the John Birch Society), and futurists. There was no more Catholic dogma, just other forms of dogma. I was stimulated by so many avenues of thought but still felt a void.

I discussed various ideas with people, including my brother-in-law, Gary Mathews. I admired this long-haired, bearded ex-Marine for his good sense and his thoughts unifying politics, religion, philosophy, and science. He had been through hell in Vietnam, losing his best friend and seeing and participating in unspeakable horror, yet he still believed in a God who was infinitely good, just and fair.

He still believed in God! We debated and discussed his belief in God over many a night and he told me things I had never heard before. He described the universe, a variety of beings, the purpose of man, the vision of God. I kept coming back with more questions, wanting more answers, until one day he said, "I think you are ready for a book I have. I will lend it to you, but I want it back!" He gave me the Urantia Book.

I purchased my own copy within the week. I was hesitant at first. My old fear of the devil resurfaced. If God was real, then maybe the devil was also, and this could be the devil's work. I read various papers and was always enthralled, but also always leery. It wasn't until reading the story about Adam and Eve that I became filled with emotion, and I again began to talk with my Eternal Father. I spoke to him not with the formal prayers I had learned as a youth, but instead just shared my thoughts with him. As I prayed, I reflected on what Adam and Eve had gone through for us; that even though they had failed, they had shown such devotion to each other and to him, our heavenly Father. It was then, with tears running down my face in a comforted joy, that I believed in the book, in God, and in my destiny.

I tried locating other readers by calling information, and that's how I was eventually steered to Julia Fenderson. I talked to Julia on the phone for about an hour that first time. She asked me many questions and seemed genuinely interested in my thoughts. Just before ending our talk, she referred me to a lively study group in nearby Anaheim, hosted by devoted readers Marlene and Pierre Chicoine. She said that Pierre and I shared an interest in science and predicted that the two of us would become best of friends.

Hanging up, I thought Julia was a very nice, strange lady. She had never met me, yet she could state with certainty that Pierre and I would become best friends. And sure enough, when I got together with the

Chicoines we became best friends instantly, just as Julia had foretold. When later I met Julia at the Chicoines' I fell in love with her also. She spoke to me about the importance of study groups and "the need for thousands of study groups" every time I saw her.

The Urantia Book brought me back to the Father, to loving Jesus with the utmost faith, to understanding mankind, to gaining a perspective on evil, and to comprehending my origin, appreciating my status, and longing for my destiny.

MARIO CAOILE: The Philippines is where I was born and Paradise is where I am bound—that is, if I remember to do God's will. I have all the time and opportunity to say No to life eternal, but how can I possibly reject this potential future after catching a glimpse of it, the grandeur and adventure of it all, in the Urantia Book? Just say Yes. I want to see the great, infinite face of eternity.

A few years before moving to the United States, the curiosity bug caught me. Next to movie theaters, bookstores were my favorite hangouts in Manila. I was especially drawn to the Alternative Religions, Philosophy, and Psychology sections. I skipped classes and spent countless hours keeping a low profile at the library of the University of the Philippines.

Years later, in the '70s, in a bookstore in Yakima, Washington, a big blue book with a strange title caught my eye. I flipped it open: Melchizedek . . . Superuniverses . . . Supernaphim. . . . I checked the Foreword. Nothing doing. I replaced the book on the shelf—too heavy a fare. I needed something else in the shopping mall and the parking meter was running out.

Months passed. In between art classes one afternoon, at the Central Washington University library, my wandering feet led me to . . . that book again. What the heck is it all about? Paradise? Sure. Adam and Eve? Hmmm. What and who else are in here? The first human beings? What? I rifled through the table of contents and moved to various chapters. I read and read, on and on. That must have been a sight to the angel watching me, my gobbling up pages right and left! I was hooked.

The next day I drove down to Yakima and invested $20 on Big Blue. Quite a return on this, the best investment I have ever made. The Urantia teachings have changed my outlook on life. This is an understatement. I cannot imagine what I might have turned into had I not come across it. It is the one pearl of great price.

RUTH L. STEACH: I was a preacher's kid and grew up with an inner knowing that the Bible wasn't the whole story. My dad urged me to read and search, but I was too busy with the other parts of my life to do so. Then, in 1962, at age 39, I joined a group of women searching for more. We read and pondered over everything from the Bible to ghosts. Nowhere could we find the "missing link"—the answers to our questions.

Then, in 1974, one of our sons brought the Urantia Book home from college and told his mom, "This was meant for you." At first we were skeptical, and approached it as we had every other book to which we had been led. But this one answered all of our questions. It filled in the blank places.

One of our group could not accept it and dropped out. It became the main study for the rest of the group. We bought Urantia Books and placed them in libraries. We loaned books to anyone interested. Some became readers, some joined our group, others rejected it.

I now belong to two Urantia Book study groups: One is the initial group which meets during the day, of which I am the only original member remaining—my friends have either moved away or graduated to the mansion worlds; the other is an evening group meeting at my house, and it is slowly growing.

Due to my long search, during which I continued to study the Bible in depth, I am considered a Bible expert by some ministers in the area. I teach Bible with a UB twist to two groups at the retirement complex where I live. (I helped to build The Village and now serve as president of the Board.) If anyone asks where I get all of my knowledge, I introduce them to the book.

BETH BARTLEY: It all began one day, three years earlier, when I came to the realization that the void I had been feeling in my life was the lack of God. I didn't know how or when my path had strayed from God's, for our relationship had started when I was a young child. I have always known that God came into my life between the ages of five and six. Now, however, there was an inner hunger, an emptiness within me, and I was at a loss as to how to find God again. My prayer that day was simple: "Father, if you are still there, please help me find you." I presume it was my Thought Adjuster that had been causing this inner hunger, and my prayer testified that communication still existed.

The answer to my prayer was instantaneous; I was enveloped in ecstasy, in a wonderful cocoon of love. I immediately knew the Father was still there as he welcomed me home and held me in his loving embrace.

I was then led through a three-year educational process that opened my mind to a wider concept of God. The books I read in this course of study were found in strange and varied places, yet each one held something special that helped me open my mind and let God out of the covers of the Bible. After eighteen months of this process I even commented to my husband that God was educating me for something. The education continued for another eighteen months, and then the goal was brought within my grasp.

It was May 11, 1974. We were at a church retreat. At the end of the day one of the other participants said to me, "I have a book you *have* to read; it is called the Urantia Book." I immediately realized that this was the object I had been working towards for the previous three years. This friend agreed to lend me her personal copy, and as she handed it to me she commented that she didn't understand why she was doing it because she wouldn't even let her own family members borrow her book. I was lost to my family for the following four months as I read voraciously from the title page through to the end.

The Foreword to the Urantia Book was quite challenging and I wondered if the whole book was going to be the same. But when I got to Paper 5, "God's Relation to the Individual," I wept. Here, finally, was the God of my childhood, the God who loves his children beyond our ability to comprehend; the God who expands our concept of unconditional love. At last I had a God who answered all my needs—spiritually, emotionally, intellectually and psychologically. This was a God I could believe in wholly. At last I was at home.

LORRIE SHAPIRO KRASNY: It was 1975. I was 23 years old and just out of UCLA. I had spent the previous five years as an activist in the anti-war movement and the women's movement. I truly believed in the brotherhood of man. And my political struggles had just been vindicated. The war I had fought so strongly against was almost over. The President I despised was also almost out of office. I was an activist without a cause.

I found myself working to pay off years of college debt in the front office of Erewhon, a natural-foods distribution and retail business. A lot of young people worked there. Some were into EST and some were into the 15-year-old "perfect Master," a chubby Indian boy with some serious lineage. I was into neither. I got the job because the manager thought my astrological sign, Aries, would be good for the place. I thought the people around me were well-meaning but deluded beyond belief.

One of the millers from the grain department and I began a romantic relationship. Of course, he was *really* a rock musician with a day job. Steve was a spiritual kind of guy, and my first non-political boyfriend. A great love developed. He spoke to me of spiritual matters, and I was responding like crazy. I had never even heard these things talked about before. My higher mind was opening for the first time.

Six months into our relationship, we went on an overnight camping trip in his VW van (what else?). He said he had something special to give me, that he had been waiting for the right moment, that it would change my life. I couldn't imagine what it was. We had done a lot of mind-expanding drugs together. Was there something new on the market? I was filled with anticipation.

We parked the van in a cow pasture by Lake Piru outside of Los Angeles. Night fell, and we talked by flashlight. Finally, he reached behind the driver's seat and pulled out a large blue book. The hairs on my arms stood straight up. The base of my neck tingled. Somehow, I knew this was the *thing*! I reached for the book. "Wait," he said. He turned to page 1118 and began to read aloud the preamble to Paper 102:

"To the unbelieving materialist, man is simply an evolutionary accident. His hopes of survival are strung on a figment of mortal imagination; his fears, loves, longings, and beliefs are but the reaction of the incidental juxtaposition of certain lifeless atoms of matter. No display of energy nor expression of trust can carry him beyond the grave."

As Steve read on through those first three paragraphs, a membrane burst in my mind. I *saw* for the first time.

". . . Each day of life slowly and surely tightens the grasp of a pitiless doom which a hostile and relentless universe of matter has decreed shall be the crowning insult to everything in human desire which is beautiful, noble, lofty and good."

"No!" my mind screamed in despair. "This cannot be true!"

"But such is not man's end and eternal destiny; such a vision is but the cry of despair uttered by some wandering soul who has become lost in spiritual darkness, and who bravely struggles on in the face of the mechanistic sophistries

of a materialistic philosophy, blinded by the confusion and distortion of a complex learning."

"That's me!"

". . . And all this doom of darkness, and all this destiny of despair are forever dispelled by one brave stretch of faith on the part of the most humble and unlearned of God's children on earth."

That was it! One brave stretch of faith was all it took. I stretched in that moment, and have never looked back.

I spent the next eight hours wearing out the flashlight battery as I pored over this amazing book. I understood it totally. There was nothing I read that night that sounded new to me. It was as if I already knew everything in it, but was relearning it by reading it.

And thus it has been ever since.

Four years later, my relationship with the rock-and-roll miller ended. My life has taken many turns throughout the years since that fateful night, but the one constant, the one undeniable and unwavering truth about me that has remained is that I believe in the fifth epochal revelation. As the preamble to Paper 102 concludes:

"This saving faith has its birth in the human heart when the moral consciousness of man realizes that human values may be translated in mortal experience from the material to the spiritual, from the human to the divine, from time to eternity."

I had been born in faith that night—July 4, 1975. And today, as in every day since, I thank the Father for this great gift.

ROSEY LIESKE: The Urantia Book came to me directly as a result of a prayer. In my mid-twenties I was going through a lot of trial and tribulation (of my own making) and in the midst of it searching hard for the real meaning of life. I'd always been a spiritual person but had become increasingly disenchanted with my search through religious philosophies, both Eastern and Western. It dawned on me, one day in the shower, that I could simply choose *not* to believe in God at all. Somehow that thought had never occurred to me. As I had the thought, I mused aloud, "Why believe in God, anyway?" and a voice clear as a bell, from inside my head, said a single word in reply: Survival.

I'd never had anything like that happen before. It shook me up and I began searching again, only now through books on physics, on the philosophy of mathematics, on Copernicus, Newton, Einstein—piles of books, searching and searching.

Finally, still frustrated, I prayed. I hadn't prayed since I was a child. Sitting on the bed, addressing this prayer to "Uh . . . dear God or anybody else out there," expressed how frustrating it was not to be able to find any intelligent data on either God or the meaning of life.

A few weeks later, strolling past a neighbor's house on the way to the woods, I was invited in for tea. There was a big blue book on the coffee table. Having befriended many books in recent months, I was astounded by the odd feeling that this one was somehow alive, like an organic entity of some kind, vibrating. I commented on it to my neighbor and he encouraged me to look through it.

It was the claim that many of the papers were written by angels that caught my eye. I'd believed in angels from childhood. Yet, the book seemed strange. From then on my neighbor would let me come over and read it whenever I wanted. Finally, I asked him if I could take it home and make up my mind about its being real or not. Three weeks of reading passed—till critical mass was reached. "I want to understand this. No, I want to *master* this." Ah, the ego of youth!

Now, many years later, I want it to master me.

JIM LEE: I was raised in a kind and loving home, the youngest of four children. Our religion was a rather strict brand of Lutheran Protestantism, and it was relentlessly followed. It had been handed down to us from my mother's father who spoke German in his home and was renowned for his complete collection of Luther's sermons.

I attended a one-room parochial school in northern California. Our daily class routine began with Bible study—the King James Version—and I would often ponder the apparent inconsistencies. For example, to the dying thief on the cross, Jesus said, "Today thou shalt be with me in paradise," yet according to the Apostles' Creed "he [Jesus] descended into hell and rose again on the third day." This quiet inquiry continued into high school, and was often intensified by seeing church leaders say one thing and then do the opposite. This led me to seek truth in many different avenues—Eastern writings, ascetic mysteries, and astrology, to name a few. All seemed to have fragments of truth here and there.

In the late summer of 1975 I began to attend monthly presentations hosted by guest speakers at our local library. At one of these evening studies a Rosicrucian was delving into the mystery of Adam and Eve. He said that the serpent in the tree of life symbolized evil because it rotated in a counterclockwise fashion. Since it made seven complete revolutions around the trunk it meant there were seven planes transcending the earth plane; and on and on. Following the meeting, an old man in the back of the room stood up and mentioned that he had just read in the Urantia Book that Adam and Eve arrived on this planet 37,848 years ago, that they came to biologically uplift the evolutionary races of this world, and that our world is one of trillions of other inhabited worlds in this vast, grand universe. Wow! Where did this come from? I could hardly wait to hear more!

The old man, Walter Seavey, and I became good friends. Through him I had my first study group experience and met many wonderful people associated with this epochal revelation. I often wonder if it was a chance occurrence or the intervention of our unseen friends that coordinated events in such a way that I was led into the fruitful and life-enriching joy which only the Urantia Book can provide.

JJ JOHNSON: I was born in Kentucky. My grandparents had a tabernacle with a crackerjack stand in front on their farm. A preacher would visit once a week to give a sermon. Looking back, they all must have been holy rollers, since they spoke in tongues. When I was five, during one of these scary, and to me meaningless, worship services, I ran out into a huge empty field, looked up into the sky and, addressing myself in silence, affirmed, "I can't believe in God! If this is what God is all about, I don't want any part of it!" I was prepared to get hit by a bolt of lightning.

For the next seventeen years I was an agnostic—who was I to say there was no God? I knew that if there *was* a God he would know that I was sincere and he would somehow give me proof of his existence.

In 1969, in my early twenties, I was attending a business seminar in Chicago. The attendees had broken up into small discussion groups. Suddenly, from out of nowhere a warm, loving presence manifested itself and everything around me lit up. This loving presence communicated to me—not in words but in "feelings that lie too deep for words"—that there was a loving heavenly Father. This experience, so personal and so sublime—which I had no doubt had been caused by something other than my own mind—was the turning point in my faith journey. This was my spiritual birthday and it transformed my life.

Prior to this experience I could not make spiritual decisions. I could see other people being motivated by living faith, but in myself there seemed to be a spiritual void. The experience gave me the ability to discern spiritual truths for myself and act on them. I also felt very comfortable perusing any book to perceive for myself the truths revealed inside and discard anything that wasn't in harmony with what I knew to be true.

I was in Hawaii in February 1975 when I received a letter from a man named Bill Ibarra, whom I'd gotten to know when we worked together on Kwajalein in the Marshall Islands. Bill mentioned the Urantia Book. As soon as I saw its name, I had a compelling urge to rush out and get my hands on the book, even before finishing Bill's letter. I realized how strange my reaction was, since Bill hadn't really described what the book was about.

After calling around I found a copy in a downtown Honolulu bookstore. Starting from the front, I enjoyed and was fascinated by the Foreword, but it took me until page 24 to recognize that no human could have revealed such knowledge. The UB is the only text I have found that I can wholeheartedly embrace.

Faith to me means experiencing the tranquility of supreme and unquestioned trust in God and feeling the tremendous thrill of living, by faith, in the very presence of the heavenly Father—the new and higher type of living so magnificently and humanly demonstrated by Jesus. My favorite line in the Urantia Book is: *"Love is the desire to do good to others."*

JOE FELLER: I came home from Vietnam in 1970 feeling like little more than a wild animal. Addicted to heroin and with no direction in life, I didn't even have a clue what the questions were. I had been raised in Seattle, and when I got home, Boeing was laying off five thousand workers per week, people with Ph.D.'s were pumping gas, and the job market was virtually nonexistent.

I kicked the heroin, but not drugs entirely. Later that year, while under a massive dose of LSD in Long Beach, California, I was approached on the street by a man named Brother Jack, who looked me right in the eyes and said, "Jesus loves you." I immediately knew this to be unequivocally true. Nothing inside of me had any argument. Several days later, I looked this man up and my spiritual journey began.

Jack was from a strongly Pentecostal background and had been through much of what I'd been through, but he was older and had been forgiven much. The love he had for his brothers and sisters was palpable and made a lasting impression on me. My life began to change, and I found myself going to a Bible college in Costa Mesa. At first all was well, but I had questions as I studied the Bible that no one at the college could answer; they told me I was flirting with Satan by asking those sorts of questions. They were afraid, and yet I kept reading Jesus' watchword, "Fear not."

So I left the school and moved north to Sonoma, where my cousin's ex-wife, Patricia, was caretaker of the Religion of Jesus Church. The first evening my cousin took me over there, Patricia called me into a little side room and said she had a book that she was certain would interest me. She opened the Urantia Book to page 21, said "Start here," and left the room. When I saw the title of the page, "The Universal Father," I prayed for God to keep me from harm, and began reading. By the time I'd finished the page, I could hardly see through the tears that were falling. Thus began my relationship with this marvelous book.

That was in 1975, and though I was to go through a whole lot of self-induced misery and addiction for another sixteen years, God never left me. And, except for having my Urantia Book stolen once in 1980, I have always had a copy in my living room. Best of all, I had the privilege of introducing it to my wife when we started dating, and she is still reading it. The book has served to enhance my personal relationship with God, and I do not entertain the slightest doubt that it is exactly what it says it is.

LARRY WATKINS: Most people will never hear the word "Urantia" at any time during their life. I heard it twice. The second time changed my life forever.

I grew up in the 1950s in Coos Bay, on the Oregon coast. After a year of college I left Oregon and moved to Los Gatos, California, with my parents. Because of a chance encounter at a metaphysical bookstore I found myself sitting in on channeling sessions with a man who claimed to be in psychic contact with UFOs, which he said were prevalent in the area. (Neither I nor anyone but him ever saw them). He'd go into a deep trance, his voice and features would change, sometimes he'd speak in a galactic language, and he'd transmit important messages and predictions from outer space visitors (none of which came true as far as I can remember, but it was exciting nonetheless). I transcribed the sessions and even participated with him in a stage play about UFOs at a community theater in San Jose.

In 1961 I saw a big blue book on his coffee table. He told me it was a book given to us by our cosmic friends. I picked it up, thumbed through it and lighted on descriptions of angels. Angels weren't a big item in my life then and I told him the book seemed too Catholic for my taste. I wouldn't meet the book again for another fourteen years.

In 1975 I was living in Jericho, Vermont, and attending a graduate course in Silva Mind Control—a technique for improving one's psychic sensitivity—when I came into contact with the Urantia Book a second time. Although I was comfortable with my New Age beliefs and thought I pretty well knew all the answers to life's spiritual and religious problems, I still felt a deep-down restlessness.

During a break, an encounter with another course attendee led me to mention that I still didn't feel that I knew Jesus as well as I wanted to. She said, "I've been reading a book that I take everywhere with me. In fact, I'm on my third copy of it because I wear it out and write so much in it. If you really want to know Jesus then you have to read the Urantia Book." I said I'd seen the book long ago but hadn't been interested in it. She said that maybe now was the time for me to begin to read it. I took her home to have lunch with my family, and even photographed her with my children, but I never heard from this red-haired angel again.

I studied the Urantia Book for nearly ten years on my own, reading it through several times, much of it out loud to my family, and talked about it to anyone who'd listen and to a lot who wouldn't. Afraid of being disappointed by other Urantia Book readers, I hesitated to reach out to them, but I eventually did attend my first study group.

I believe the book itself is the revelation. You have to read the book yourself in order to feel the revelation's true power. In a similar way, during the times of Jesus, hearing rumors and stories about him was no substitute for sitting with him and learning firsthand. We may wish for our lives to inspire and transform others because of our association with this revelation, but to my way of thinking, the revelation is personal; it is transmitted through the interaction between the words on the printed page and the reader's inquiring mind.

The Urantia Book: you have to read it to believe it!

LAURENCE R. WHELAN: In the summer of 1975 I was in a bookstore in Ventura, California, checking to see if there were any new Edgar Cayce books. Nearby was the Religion section, where I noticed a large book with a white cover on the top shelf. I had to stand on my tiptoes to reach it.

At this time in my life I had collected just about all the Edgar Cayce books that were in print; I was a member of the Association for Research and Enlightenment and I attended a weekly Edgar Cayce study group. About a year earlier my mother had told me about a book, written by angels, that a study group in Oxnard was reading, but she did not know the name of the book or exactly where the group met.

As I took the large volume down from the top shelf, I felt that I had found the book my mother had been talking about. Opening the Urantia Book for the first time, I checked out the table of contents and saw it contained a 774-page section entitled, "Part IV, The Life and Teachings of Jesus, the story of the Son of God and the Son of Man." I believed the words spoken by Jesus in John 14:6: "I am the way, the truth and the life." After perusing the list of papers for another fifteen minutes I reluctantly returned the book to the top shelf, not having the $20 to buy it. I wandered around the bookstore for another fifteen minutes or so until I finally decided that I *had* to have that book and bought it with my Visa card.

Once I got home I could not put the book down. I completed my first reading in fifty-six days. I knew the part about Jesus was true, but what about the rest of the book? I started over from the beginning, and after reading it a second time I still had questions. I shared parts of it with my then-wife, a Jehovah's Witness. She declared that it was the work of the devil. I read it again to see if she was right. She was not. I am now on my fourteenth reading and I know in my heart and soul that the Urantia Book is the fifth epochal revelation of truth to our world.

SHERYL BELLMAN: I was born in New York into a very Jewish family, and accordingly I started my spiritual search with traditional Jewish teachings. In the early '70s my husband and I were hippies living in the East Village in New York. In our search for truth we had both turned to Buddhism. In 1972 we bought land in a small town in Maine and prepared to do the country thing.

In 1975 an old hippie friend from New York visited us, carrying a bunch of books. He showed my husband Chuck a big blue book and said, "You must get this book." Chuck sent away for it, spending an enormous amount of money—$20. When the book arrived he was not interested in it. I thought that since he had spent so much money on this thing someone should read it! I opened to Paper 1 and was blown away—I had never read anything like that about God before! Within a few pages I realized that I had something from heaven in my hands.

In 1999 I went back to the East Village and saw—for the first time in twenty-four years—the friend who had introduced us to the Urantia Book. He had never become a reader himself—he didn't even know what the book was about!

Finding the Urantia Book has been one of the greatest blessings in my life. I will always be grateful to that old friend for being the channel that brought it into my life.

KAREN FARRINGTON DANIELS: In the early '70s I moved from Connecticut to Key West, Florida, with my husband and two daughters, to join my parents in an art gallery and framing business. I had majored in art at college, and in 1975 I decided to continue my studies at Florida Keys Community College, which boasted the only floating art department in the United States. Classes were held in a two-story houseboat, with wonderful sea breezes and sunset views from the doors and windows.

During one of my figure-drawing classes, I overheard my teacher discussing something with two of the other students. Many of the words he used were unknown to me and I heard the word "Urantia" for the first time. Later, I asked him what he'd been talking about. He smiled at me and said, "When the student is ready, the teacher will appear." In other words, when I was ready to find the Urantia Book, a copy would show up. I was not satisfied with his answer. "I'm ready now," I thought, and went hunting for a copy.

In the neighborhood was a health-food store/hippie hangout called The Herb Garden. I rummaged around their bookshelves in the back and found a dusty copy of the Urantia Book on the bottom shelf. I brought it to the cashier without even opening it.

"Thirty-five dollars?" I said in amazement. But I paid for it anyway and walked slowly home. Inside, I sat down in a comfortable chair and opened the book for the first time. I couldn't believe my eyes. What was all this? A hierarchy of deities? Universes? The life and teachings of Jesus?

It sounded too much like a religion to me, and I was beyond all that. I had been brought up as a Roman Catholic and had divorced my religion at 15. I believed in God, but my beliefs were closer to Buddhism and Hinduism than to Christianity.

Overwhelmed and disappointed, I muttered, "You've got to be kidding!" and I put the book on the shelf next to my set of *Great Books of the Western World*, which were also unread.

A few months later, a lawyer friend of mine came to visit and we sat talking in the shade on my front porch. He announced that he had found Jesus and was giving up the practice of law. He had joined a Christian ministry group and was heading down to South America for four years of missionary work.

Out of the blue, he asked me if I had ever heard of the Urantia Book. Someone had told him that he should read it. He said that he had been looking for a copy to take with him to South America and could not find one. I told him to wait on the porch. I went inside and pulled my copy off the bookshelf. "Here you go," I said, handing him the book. "You can return it to me when you get back in four years. Maybe by then I'll be able to read it."

Four years went by, during which time I studied and practiced Transcendental Meditation and read all kinds of New Age books, including the *Seth* books by Jane Roberts. I felt pretty "hip" and reckoned my consciousness had been expanded quite a bit.

One day in 1979 I heard through the coconut telegraph that my friend had returned from South America and was back in Key West. A few weeks passed and I hadn't seen him around, but I was curious to find out what he thought of the book. Remembering that he had promised to return it to me, I drove over to his house and rang the doorbell. A strange person opened the door and I inquired about my friend.

"He died last week of a heart attack, just after returning from South America," was the reply. I was stunned. He was only 45 years old. I was told that all his personal effects had been sent to his parents' home in Tallahassee. Not wanting to bother his family in their time of grief, I walked back to my car.

Driving home I saw a yard sale. As usual, I could not resist stopping. As I walked into the yard, I noticed a copy of the Urantia Book sitting on the corner of an old red card table. It appeared to be brand new, but the price was $1. I slowly picked it up, held it against my chest and said quietly to myself, "Well, I guess this must be *my* copy!"

In 1986 I purchased a beachfront cottage in Jamaica and moved all my books and art supplies down there. There, in the quiet, balmy days on the beach, I began again to read my Urantia Book, to paint and to write. My new boyfriend, a Swiss chef, was quite intrigued with the book. Each morning at breakfast we had a reading session. His English was limited, so I would read out loud. At the end of each paragraph he would ask me to explain what it meant. Most of the time I couldn't.

My life has taken many turns since then. I still have a long way to go, but I know that the Urantia Book has the answers to all my questions. I will never give up my connection to it. My friend Leonard Ablieter (his story is also included in this book) trusted my judgment when I told him to buy the Urantia Book. When I became frustrated with my inability to understand it all, I trusted Leonard when he said: "Just read it. The understanding will come in time."

DOLORES NICE: I found the Urantia Book in 1975 in the public library. Although I was raised Catholic and attended Catholic schools for sixteen years, I was searching for "more." I wasn't sure what that "more" was, but I started researching parapsychology and other esoteric practices such as astrology and numerology. It was in the section of the library dealing with these subjects that I found the Urantia Book. As I flipped through the pages, I was particularly drawn to the papers on life after death and the Jesus papers.

My mother had died in 1970 and I was still grieving. We had been very close and her death was very hard on me. My two sisters and I were too young to lose our beloved mother. Even though I'd believed in life after death before finding the Urantia Book, reading about the mansion worlds was a great comfort to me and helped me with the healing process.

The Jesus papers—how can I possibly express what reading them meant to me? I already had, since my early childhood, a deep love for Jesus. I remember stopping at the parish church on my way home from school to "visit him." Receiving holy communion was special to me, and I greatly enjoyed all the religious events both at school and at church. Being able to read his whole life story fulfilled a deep yearning to know more about Jesus.

Finding the Urantia Book has been a blessing over and beyond what I could have ever hoped for. I am most grateful not only for the extraordinary teachings, but also for the wonderful community of believers and friends I have found in my study group, Society and in the greater readership.

God has answered my prayers; I have found the "more." Like Ganid, I too can say: *"I will every day thank God for his unspeakable gifts; I will praise him for his wonderful works to the children of men. To me he is ... my spirit Father, and as his earth child I am sometime going forth to see him"* (p. 1454).

CHRISSY PALATUCCI SMITH: One autumn in the early '70s, living in the town of Westhampton Beach, New York, I was one of a group of many friends who were enjoying the return of the town to its quiet post-season status. We were having a potluck when a friend began to tell me about a book his ex-girlfriend had loaned him called the Urantia Book, that it was in four parts and really cosmic. We even went over to his room where he showed it to me. It was big. We talked a bit—he hadn't really read much of it himself—but after a few minutes I was anxious to get back to the party.

The next day, my boyfriend and I were in the town of Southampton where we stopped in at a small bookstore called Keene's. I, being a seeker, went over to the Occult section. There on the shelf was the Urantia Book. I took it down, opened it to the first page of the Foreword, read down to "The Eternal Isle of Paradise" and stopped. In five years, I thought to myself, I'll be ready for this. I put the book back.

A few years later, at the wedding of my best friend Elaine in New Hampshire, I was having a conversation with a small group of people on things cosmic. One guy asked if anyone had ever seen the Urantia Book. He told us a story he had heard about it, that it had been found in a garbage can with $10,000 and a note attached that read, "Print me!" As he talked a recognition seed was planted in my mind.

In 1975 I found myself driving to California with my friend Aubrea, who was planning to attend her high school reunion. I had always wanted to see California, and as I made preparations I had a vision flash that I was to meet a "spiritual man with a golden glow."

Traveling up the California coast, we visited different towns, including Capitola-by-the-Sea, where my sister-in-law's parents lived. Stopping for directions to their house, we turned a corner and up on the right was a shimmering gold sign that read The Pyramid Works. I remarked to Aubrea that we *had* to visit this store—I had recently finished reading a fascinating book that talked about pyramid power, *Psychic Discoveries Behind the Iron Curtain*, and was excited to see a place selling pyramids.

Later that day our host Peggy took us on a walk into town. While Peg stopped to buy some cards, Aubs and I went into The Pyramid Works. There we found all manner of pyramid-related articles, books, candles, and clothes, as well as a delightful salesman (with lots-of-time-on-the-beach golden hair) named Lee. Never having met anyone from New York before, and certainly not two women travelers, he found us intriguing. He invited us back to the store on Thursday night to attend a presentation on pyramid power. I almost missed what has now become my life as I was tired that night and didn't really want to go. Luckily, Aubs was in a better mood and talked me into it.

By the time we arrived, the demonstration was over and people were milling around getting ready to leave. Lee was happy to see us, and after he closed up shop the three of us got together. The night continued with much sharing and good conversation, and ended up with all of us going dancing.

Lee had invited us to visit him the following Saturday. On the property where he lived was a tree house and I mentioned that I wanted to climb up there. I was starting to feel very attracted to Lee and wanted some time alone with him. As we sat in the tree house facing each other cross-legged, what I remember most is the incredible energy that flowed out of my eyes and into his as I declared my love for God. I know he received it because the look on his face was unmistakable. It was, as I have come to recognize it now, a Spirit of Truth moment. The energy flowing from me to him felt like a circuitry coming through me rather than from me. My intention was that Lee should understand the meaning God had in my life—I only had a moment and the Spirit did it for me!

When it was time to leave, I decided to stay an extra week with Lee and meet up with my traveling companions later. One day, when Lee and I were working in the pyramid shop, I saw a notice on the bulletin board that read, "Anyone interested in reading the Urantia Book talk to Lee." I was amazed! I felt that my spiritual journey was about to take a major leap. Excitedly I shared with Lee the Keene's bookstore event, my declaration of five years earlier, and that he, Lee, was the "spiritual man with the golden glow."

Lee and I started a Urantia Book study group in 1975 and it still meets in our home. We were married one year later and the rest, as they say, is destiny!

KAREN JEPPESON: I grew up in the Lutheran Church. I was a "Jesus freak" for a time, but never intensely—it was just fun. I asked a lot of questions. The answers went round in circles after a while, so I quit asking. As a senior in high school, I was clued in by a gifted teacher to the truth of myth and the falsehood of what we often consider fact. He then taught our class Eastern religions from the inside. I did an independent study of religion for an advanced seminar. Though I didn't realize it at the time, my teacher was leading me to the understanding that there are many facets of personal religious experience, that each person interprets his or her religious longings and experience in the light of his or her cultural beliefs. This meant there was a truth in religions, that there was one thing that linked all religions together, making them more than a giant psychological delusion.

What was this truth? It had to be experienced.

I became interested in Gestalt psychology, then drugs, then mysticism. Just as I was starting to get in over my head, a friend said, "I know a book you might be interested in. It's the history of earth, written by beings beyond time and space."

I sensed this fantastic statement might be true, for by now I had seen that while all religions had truth, some contained more truth than others. In my mind there was a triangle of truth; some religions were closer to the top, others near the bottom, but none at the peak. I thought maybe the truth was beyond what we might know on earth, so my intellect and my soul were prepared for a revelation from beyond this world.

A couple of days later I went to the bookstore where I had been told I could find this Urantia (Earth) Book. As I was paging through the table of contents, another woman came in to look at the book. Excited to meet another Urantia Book reader, I began asking her questions such as how she had come to find the book. Her brief and meaningful replies astounded me and made me even more curious. She said she would be having a meeting of Iowa City Urantians in two weeks' time and that the area representative would be there.

After such a meaningful coincidence I bought the book. I remember vividly walking into the Urantia gathering two weeks later. The atmosphere was so high I felt like I was walking two feet off the ground. At first I was very suspicious. Will they be like Scientologists and ask for money? Will they warp my mind, like the pseudo-sciences I had studied? None of this happened.

I read the book that summer. Every day more doubts and fears fall to the truths of living as revealed in the Urantia Book.

SHARON ZIGLAR: In the early '70s I was actively seeking God in my life. I tried out a variety of churches and bought any book I could get my hands on which might help me to grow as an individual. I still have quite a large library of books dating from that time: *I'm OK, You're OK*; *Your Erroneous Zones*; *Mindstyles, Lifestyles*; etc.

In 1975 I started attending a fundamentalist church. It had a large congregation and quite a community feeling. While attending this church I met my future husband, Wally Ziglar, in the church parking lot. We started dating and shared a lot of wonderful philosophical discussions. In our marathon telephone conversations he would occasionally read me something interesting that he had "found." Everything he read rang a bell in my soul as being true, and I was awed by the possibility that answers to some of my questions, and confirmations of my inner beliefs, were in writing. I asked Wally where he'd come upon the portions that he was reading to me and he usually said, "It's out of some Christian history book I've come across." These exchanges went on for at least a year.

We were also attending a Bible study class connected with this church. At times I would feel very uncomfortable with what was being said. I would comment on this to Wally and he usually responded by quoting something he had "read someplace." One night there was a discussion about demon possession. I could tell that Wally was really keen on this topic; he told me he had something at home that he wanted to read to me. When we got to his house he pulled out a big blue book and read me a passage about demon possession not existing since the time of Pentecost. This didn't mean anything to me, as it was just something he was reading out of some book.

At this point he said, "Some day I want to share this book with you, but not right now." Well, that was the wrong thing to say to someone who had been buying up bookstores looking for answers. I practically broke my neck trying to get a look at the title. The next day I went down to B. Dalton Booksellers and lifted a copy of the Urantia Book off the shelf. I looked at the front cover and almost fell over. What is this? "The

Central and Superuniverses"? "The Local Universe"? "The History of Urantia"? ("The Life and Teachings of Jesus" I could handle.) I took a deep breath. I knew how important God was to Wally and that there had to be something to this book. I began reading the inside dust jacket and by the time I had finished ". . . *the greatest truths mortal man can ever hear—the living gospel of the Fatherhood of God and the brotherhood of man*" p. 2086), I knew that I had come home and that this book was the answer to my quest for truth and knowledge. Needless to say, I bought it.

It took me three months to complete my first reading—living and breathing the book. Since then, I have read it at least three additional times. I love going to it for answers or to search for something I remember reading before. During the raising of our children I must admit that I have not always taken time to keep up my reading, but the truths exist in my heart and in my life and I know that the book is there whenever I need a "refresher course."

TOMMY OUTERBRIDGE: I was searching for the Truth, to find out why the Biblical story was okay for Christians but not for me. The Spirit urged me to study theology at university. My teachers were surprised. My father was aghast. I was supposed to become a lawyer not a preacher. Just before I started at Exeter University in 1976, an old friend of my dad, Alaine, thrust the Urantia Book into my hands and said, "Read this." To this day Alaine still has no interest in the fifth epochal revelation.

My interest in Spirit dates back as far as I can remember, but the defining moment came in 1968, when I was "saved" in Harrington Sound, a landlocked body of bright blue sea water in Bermuda. An old black fisherman who was harvesting mussels off the shallow bottom using a long pole and a glass through which he peered at the water's surface, hailed me over. After I tied my new 11-foot fiberglass boat alongside his old 14-foot cedar fishing boat, he inquired, "Have you been saved?"

But my boat was not sinking. Saved? Saved from what? "Saved from the Devil," he intoned earnestly. Was I assured of Jesus coming into my life and of my going to heaven? I should hereby confess my sins, accept forgiveness and be saved. Well, in the unfolding of my young life—I was 11—this seemed a logical next step. Solemnly I bowed my head, closed my eyes, formally repented and was thereby saved. From that day on the quest was on to connect with the Urantia Book.

Come September I returned to boarding school, whose grounds

bordered on a railway track so you could hear the sound of passing trains quite clearly. One night I had a tremendously vivid nightmare in which I dropped off a cliff and landed on my back with a *bang*. I startled awake only to hear the loud and distinct clickety-clack of a speeding train, a real train. A strong impression was forged but in the following years the episode was naturally forgotten.

Fifteen years later, on Father's Day, whilst trying to build a nest for Bermuda's indigenous sea bird, the longtail, I was atop a 100-foot cliff near my home when the ledge collapsed and I plummeted to the beach below. I broke my neck, my back and my left arm. Upon surfacing from a coma three days later, I was a C5 quadriplegic strapped to a Stryker frame and wearing a halo brace. After a period of auditory and visual hallucinations accompanied by delirium, lucidity returned but my memory was shot, vaguely hovering at about age seven, with the rest of my life a zero. Physically crippled with flailing spasms and mentally handicapped by amnesia, my mind and body were seriously challenged. I was not abandoned, however. "Footprints" says it in a nutshell: "God carries you when you can no longer walk." And when Jesus taught that the good shepherd actively searches for his lost sheep, he wasn't joking.

Two years after my fall and firmly entrenched in hospital, my memory was still blank. My Adjuster must have been working overtime, because I recalled and mentioned the UB fairly often in those dim days of rehabilitation. Eventually I had the hospital bursar prepare a draft to send to the Urantia Foundation in Chicago, asking for the UB to be sent to the library at my old school. Soon after that, I had the same dream. I fell off a cliff, felt myself falling and crash landed—*bang!*—onto my back to awake with a startling jolt, only to hear the loud and distinct clatter of a train outside my window. It faded eerily into the distance, same as I'd heard somewhere before . . . but where? Slowly, over a long period of months, it came back to me.

"To God there is no past, present or future; all time is present at any given moment" (p. 34).

The task of rebuilding my life and recalling my past has been a wonderful if grueling ordeal, a superb challenge. To look over the ongoing scenario and see the Father's helping hand along the path has been a unique education, and I feel very grateful to be alive to praise Him. Indeed I feel fortunate to have been afforded this unique opportunity to appreciate Him, the Master, and life on Earth.

My human guardian angel is my wife Angela, whom I met when she was my physiotherapist in hospital. Our son, Robert, was born in 1992. I now join the actor Christopher Reeve in a quest to be healed and independent. However, rather than simply anticipating a "cure" through medical research, I concentrate on prayer, meditation, visualization, affirmations, positive thinking and faith.

JULIANNE CLERGET: Returning from a camping trip in the mountains in 1975, my friend Lauretta Blackburn proceeded to tell me about her experiences: The happy campers had been sitting around the campfire after their evening meal, discussing why we are here, what religion is, and the meaning of the word God, when from far below they heard the unmistakable sound of an approaching vehicle echoing off the hillsides. It took a long time for it to attain the crest, but finally a pickup truck became visible.

The driver stopped, parked, and got out. He had long hair, a beard, and a twinkle in his eye. He approached the group's primitive hearth and soon joined in the conversation. He talked about the teachings in the Urantia Book, keeping Lauretta and her friends spellbound until dawn. Before this mountain man departed, he turned to Lauretta and gave her a Urantia Book.

Lauretta only had time to tell me of this little adventure before moving several hundred miles away. Her story interested me so much that I wanted to read the book myself, but I couldn't find a copy at any local bookstore. Nobody had heard of it.

Several days after Lauretta moved away, a mutual friend of ours, Ron Worthington, arrived at my door. I told Ron about Lauretta's odd camping adventure, and that I was dying to read this Urantia Book. Ron was a seeker after truth, had studied many of the world's religions, and he was as intrigued as I was.

Some months later, Ron visited me again. This time he announced happily that he had found out there were copies of the Urantia Book in Wenatchee, approximately four hours east of my home in western Washington. They were $20 each. Ron offered to pick up a copy for me, too, but I was currency-deficient at that time, and could only plead, "Could I read *your* book sometimes?" Ron agreed, then departed on his adventure.

During the four days of Ron's absence, much occurred. The house my family and I had built with our own hands burned to the ground and we lost all our possessions. Curiously, two years earlier the same thing had happened to us. Once again we rallied together, trying to survive and make the best of the situation. My youngest son Scott seemed undaunted and immediately asked, "What kind of house will we build this time?"

Lauretta, who had recently moved back to our area, had been living with us at the time. For the next few days we salvaged clothing, bedding, and other necessities; we burned the remains, since the fire from the house was still smoldering. We also pulled all the burnt metal out of the ruins and piled it in the driveway. At night we stayed with friends, and went back to the "job from hell" during the day.

By day four of this, with all of us covered with soot and looking rather comical, we piled into Lauretta's car and were driving to a friend's home to shower when we passed Ron on the road, heading in the opposite direction. We looked at one another and in unison cried, "My God, that's Ron! He doesn't know about the fire!"

Lauretta screeched on the brakes, turned around and drove back to our driveway. There was Ron, standing on what used to be the porch, looking very upset. I got out of the car and ran up to him, saying, "Ron, it's just the material world. We may not have any possessions but now we don't have any possessions to worry about, either. We're all okay. We are alive."

Ron replied, "But . . . you *do* have a possession. I've brought you a Urantia Book."

That was September 27, 1976. Now, many years later, my children are grown and my entire life is devoted to understanding and disseminating the teachings of the Urantia Book. I thank God every day for the knowledge, hope, and faith inspired by this wonderful revelation.

Lauretta has often wondered, who was the gentleman with the long hair and the twinkle in his eye? She'd love to contact him some day, and I'd also like to give him a big hug.

MATTHEW BLOCK: I first came across the Urantia Book in early 1976, while sitting in on a metaphysical class my mother was taking. My mother actually had little interest in metaphysics; she was more interested in the marketing potentials of pyramid power. I, on the other hand, was obsessed with the esoteric, and as I sat in that class I found myself in my element. At the time, I was a tortured, searching, 18-year-old college dropout (I'd started at 16), on my third psychiatrist, and working as a Boy Friday for a well-known Philadelphia psychic.

I don't remember what the lecturer was talking about, but I recall that at one point he held up a copy of the Urantia Book and invited us to look through it after class. At first sight I was lured by its encyclopedic size. Flipping through the pages, though, I was more repelled than attracted. It seemed to be written too dryly. I was put off by the rosters of superhuman personalities and the neologisms, and cringed at bizarre chapter titles like "Melchizedek Teachings in the Occident." The lecturer noticed my reactions and advised me not to dismiss the book too rashly.

Several weeks later, while haunting the bookstores in a new suburban mall, I found it again and decided to delve into it further. Its analytic style of prose still didn't sit well with me; I'd always supposed that a revelation would read like the *Upanishads* or Kahlil Gibran's *The Prophet*. But certain passages about God and religious experience—written with a unique combination of eloquence, fervor, rational intelligence and authoritativeness—began to appeal to me.

Despite my fascination with the occult, and despite the fact that I'd rejected the Judaism of my childhood when I was 12, I retained a very strong, liberal Judaeo-Christian sensibility. I never gave up craving communion with a personal God. Since childhood I'd felt drawn to Jesus, but was never able to get a good grasp of him from my Catholic relatives or from reading the New Testament. The Urantia Book was one of the very few books I'd come across that seemed to be written in a Judaeo-Christian vein and yet had something urgently new to say. I remember feeling a dim excitement at the prospect that the Urantia Book might help lead me to God and perhaps even to Jesus.

In the weeks that followed I kept going back to that mall, since it was the only place I knew that carried the book. After four or five visits, I finally rushed back to buy a copy after realizing that beneath its stark exterior, the book carried intensely beautiful and inspiring messages about God, life and destiny. The deciding factor, I think, was the "Rodan of Alexandria" paper, one of the few that didn't presuppose familiarity with Urantia terminology. I was inspired by its sound, affirmative, God-centered philosophy, and its message about the precious values of friendship.

Once I'd finally bought it, I felt a tremendous sense of relief. The book seemed to glow as it rested on my desk. But it took several months to integrate the book into my life and thoughts. The pull of astrology and psychic phenomena was still strong; I kept thinking of Jesus as a Leo and had trouble squaring Edgar Cayce's account of Jesus with the Urantia Book's. Nevertheless the Urantia philosophy beamed its way through the occult haze, and I gradually stopped thinking in terms of astrology and reincarnation.

Though I thumbed through the book every day, it took me about a year and a half to actually read it from cover to cover. Ironically, the stumbling block for me was the Jesus papers; while I was intensely interested in Jesus, I simply wasn't ready to follow such a detailed narrative with all its Biblical references. For years my favorite part was Part III; but since 1991, as a result of a quiet, Jesus-centered spiritual experience, Part IV is now my preferred "literary gateway" to God.

In 1977, I decided to return to school, choosing a university in Chicago to be near the Urantia headquarters. Thus began a twenty-plus-year association with the Urantia movement, during which I worked as a volunteer and, later, a paid employee of Urantia Brotherhood (now called The Urantia Book Fellowship). Since 1992 I've been doing research into the sources of the Urantia Book, an endeavor which has immeasurably enriched my understanding of the whole Urantia Book phenomenon. But that's another story.

JEAN ASCHER: I was born in 1945 to a Jewish mother and most likely an Arabic father. I never knew my father. My mother was an attractive woman, concerned mostly with her own life, so most of my basic upbringing came from the streets of the Copenhagen suburb where I grew up.

Since the time I became conscious of the world, I wondered about the questions of life. I asked myself why people seemed to be split into two groups: one group believers of all kinds, and the other all non-believers of one kind. I simply could not accept that there wasn't a universal, cosmic truth which could somehow combine people's views into a harmonious, global whole.

I decided to find out, to begin searching for knowledge, understanding and truth. I started reading all kinds of books—natural science, science fiction, philosophy, theoretical mathematics—and religious works such as the *Kabbalah*, *The Book of Death*, and *Toward the Light*. I read all through my formal education as a chief cook in the Danish merchant fleet.

After five years I returned home and became friends with a young Black musician, Jimmy Moody. We shared the same curiosity about life and interests in books, and soon we were exchanging books. Years later, he left Denmark to live in Ibiza, Spain, which at that time was the place to hang out if you were a hash-smoking, mushroom-eating hippie, which we both were. Occasionally I would go to Ibiza to see my friend, and on one visit he showed me the Urantia Book.

As soon as I got back to Copenhagen, I ordered a book from Chicago. When it arrived a few weeks later, in April of 1976, I began reading. As far as I can recall, I did nothing else for nearly four years. I finished my first reading on February 13, 1980. All my questions about the puzzles of life, love and God were answered. I was transformed into a completely new human being.

The book has changed my life. It has made order out of confusion within my mind. It has turned a young, crazy mortal into a harmonious, simple adult. It has opened my eyes, so that I now can see what is unseen. It has given me the knowledge that no schoolteacher, parent or adult could. It has made me understand what could be understood. It has made me aware of a divine Thought Adjuster within my soul. The Urantia Book has made my mind whole, repaired my intellectual horizon, inspired my creative potentials, and generated in me a craving to be like The Universal One. To the best of my ability I try to live by our Father's commandment, "Be you perfect even as I am perfect."

Since the people here in Denmark to whom I have introduced the book have shown no interest in it, I have started translating the book into Danish, upon the request of my daughter Catjaya. I hope thereby to make the book more accessible to the people of Denmark.

BETTY BRIGHT: I moved from Cincinnati to Los Angeles in 1976 and got a job with an architectural firm on Wilshire Boulevard. I didn't know anyone in Los Angeles except my friend Joyce, who had written me urging me to make a change in my life and join her. Joyce, however, was busy every night with the EST Foundation so I spent my time poring over *The Thomas Guide*, dreaming of new adventures.

I soon met a spiritual woman named Debra who worked in the same building as I. We began to spend time together in the evenings and sometimes I would house-sit for her when she went away to visit her parents. Debra did not own a television set but she had a great library, and every time I went there I would go straight to her bookshelf to see what was new.

One Friday night I let myself into the empty house and headed for the library. There on the shelf was a used blue book that fell out by itself. I picked it up and took it over to the couch with me, and that is where Debra found me on Sunday night when she arrived home. I asked her where she had come across this book and what she thought of it. She told me that she'd discovered it in the Bodhi Tree used book store and that she didn't know why she'd bought it. She said she'd looked through it and didn't think it was for her but that I could have it if I wanted to take it home.

I read the book every day for five years with a dictionary and world atlas spread out on the floor before me. I would ask everyone I knew or met if they had heard of this book. No one had, and I began to think I was the only one in the world that had it. Desperate to talk to someone about it, I finally wrote to the Urantia Foundation and asked them if they could tell me if anyone else was reading this book. They referred me to Polly Friedman. When I arrived at Polly's house and she opened the door I couldn't say a word—I just cried. Just writing this I am crying again, remembering what a life-changing event that day was for me. Polly put me in touch with Hal and Lucille Kettell's study group—about five blocks from where I was living at the time—and the love affair goes on to this day.

PAULA LYNN SUTTON: I was about six years old when I knew for sure that God existed, because that year he answered a prayer of mine immediately. I believe that event is what kept him alive in my heart through my teenage years of doubt and wondering, and even pretended agnosticism. I had doubts because what I believed God to be and what I saw in this world did not fit together. The Bible lessons I'd received during my many years in our town's non-denominational community church only served to raise more questions. So one night when I was about 16, I told God that I was going to quit bothering him with the rote prayer I had been reciting at bedtime for as long as I could remember. I told him the next time he heard from me, I would be sincere and it would come from my heart.

That was when I put God on hold in my life. I didn't begin my search to understand him until I was in my early twenties, at which time I began reading, casually and with no real urgency, about the different religions the world had to offer. Nothing rang true within me. Then one night in 1976, it finally clicked.

I was driving a friend home. I don't recall the circumstances of our being together that evening, or how the conversation turned to spiritual matters. I just remember that she began to talk about a book she was reading, and I had to know more. We sat in her driveway for some time while she told me all about this book. It was getting late, but I didn't want to leave, so she asked me if I wanted to see the book. "Of course!" I said, and she invited me in.

I felt so hungry for the knowledge she was imparting that I stayed until she told me everything she could remember of what she had read so far. Finally, I copied the Chicago address from the book so I could order one, and left her house, on fire and anxious to get my own copy of the Urantia Book. I knew this was what I had been looking for.

How did this book change my life? I was able to relax. I had a better understanding of why this world is so imperfect. I had the assurance of God's unfailing love.

CHRISTOS KONSTAS: This is the story of how my parents, Zachos and Maria Konstas—and I—came to find the Urantia Book. In 1975 they were in Switzerland attending a Krishnamurti convention. There they met a Swiss-German, Theo Schwartz, who gave them a copy of the Urantia Book in English, another one in French, and a *Concordex*. He also told them a story regarding its origin.

According to my parents, Theo Schwartz was a trustworthy and reliable person who had worked on the German translation of the Urantia Book, a fact that has been confirmed by others. Theo was said to have firsthand information about how the Papers came into existence. His source was his close friend, a Frenchman named Jacques Weiss, who (according to Theo) claimed to be an eyewitness to the events that led up to the appearance of the Urantia Papers. Weiss was also known in the Urantia community as having translated the UB into French. (His name appears on the title page of the first French edition.)

This is the story as told to my parents: Around 1910 a French girl confessed to her father that every night for two years she had been writing some strange things. When she handed her father the manuscript, he was surprised to see that it was written in English, a language his daughter did not know. The father, also no expert in English, took the manuscript to a friend of his. According to Theo, this friend could have been Jacques Weiss.

When the friend examined the manuscript closely he soon discovered that it was about the universe and Jesus. He also found that it was written in near-perfect English, with only about twenty errors in spelling and grammar.

The name William Sadler was not mentioned and my parents had never heard it. For twenty years this was the only story about the origins of the Urantia Book with which I was familiar, and we were the only Greek UB readers I knew of. Only recently, when I began to visit UB sites on the Internet, did I find that the rest of the world knew a very different story. On the Internet I tried to confirm what I had heard from my parents but instead I learned about Sadler's role. Since then, I've been trying to connect the loose ends of the two stories.

It is known that between 1910 and 1920 Sadler traveled to Europe at least once. If the version I've told is true, Weiss could have engaged Dr. Sadler to psychiatrically treat the girl as a patient.

I can't say that the Urantia Book changed my religion. But the Urantia teachings fitted nicely into the whole picture. Perhaps I should say the Urantia Book broadened my perspective.

PAULA GARRETT THOMPSON: On Halloween night 1975 my husband was arrested on drug charges. I was 20 years old at the time and our daughter had just turned one. My husband had had several run-ins with the law and this was his third strike. He would end up spending the next seven months in jail. But this was not the worst thing that happened that fall and winter. On the evening of December 22 my best friend and biggest fan, my father, died of heart failure immediately following surgery. He was 59 years old.

My dad was one of those good people who make the lives of others good. No one who knew him could ever imagine life without him. He was devoted, loving, strong, gentle, wise, funny, and my hero. It took two years for me to be able to think of him without crying. To this day I cry to think how much I love him and miss him.

My family went into a tailspin of inexpressible sorrow and grief. Because my husband was in jail, I was living with my parents when my dad died. I have often thought that the angels put me and my beautiful little child there, at just that time, to help keep my mom together. The loss of my dad was simply more than she could endure. It was only the adorable antics of a one-year-old that brought her out of her depression and gave her relief from her crushing agony.

At the time, I felt utterly alone. It was my dad who had helped me see the bright side of things; it was always he who could make me feel better. He was gone, my husband was unavailable, my mom and my siblings were grief-stricken, my baby needed me, and I had nowhere to turn. So I turned to God. I told God that I needed to hear some good news. I wanted to know specifically where my dad was. I thought I could find it in the Bible—where else would it be? I searched through it numerous times and each time became increasingly more disappointed.

One evening in early 1976 I reached the peak of my crisis. I had decided to read the Bible from cover to cover. I reasoned that if I did, surely then I would find the "good news" I was looking for. I read up to the part that explains who begat who begat who. I remember thinking, "So what? Who cares who begat who?" My need to hear the good news was so great that I couldn't bear to read one more page. I threw it down, sobbing to God, "I have to hear the good news now! If I don't hear the good news soon I am going to lose my mind!" I then sobbed myself to sleep.

The next day my husband called me from jail. He asked me to bring $12.50 with me when I came to visit on Saturday. I didn't have much money, so I asked him what he wanted it for. He said it was for a book.

"What kind of book?" I asked.

"A big, spiritual book," he said. "I've been reading it with some friends here and I would like to have my own copy. A guy named Buck is going to bring it to the jail; he will meet you outside the fence in front. Bring the money and he will sell you the book."

"Okay," I said, wondering what kind of spiritual book could grab this man's interest.

That Saturday I went for our weekly visit. There was Buck standing behind his car with the trunk open. Inside he had a box of big blue books. I sheepishly approached him with my $12.50. He said nothing; he just smiled at me broadly and handed me a book. I took it and went inside.

I met my husband at the regular table and after our usual greetings I handed him the book. He pushed it back at me. "Open it," he smirked.

So I did. I opened it to the paper concerning the birth and infancy of Jesus, and began with the section on Mary and Joseph. Reading about these two people, I was struck at once by the richness of detail. I will never forget what went through my mind. My first thought was, "This is not in the Bible." My second thought was, "Who would pretend to know this?" And my third thought was, "If they did pretend to know it, why would they do such a thing?" I looked up from the book and said to my husband, "I need to read this book." "I know," he said. "Take it with you." "But... what will you read?" I pushed the book across the table to him. "I will share a book with someone else. You take this one with you." He firmly pushed it back at me. "Well, all right, if you're sure." I took it with secret delight, knowing full well that this was the answer to my prayer.

I couldn't wait to start reading it. Oh, how delicious it was, how soothing, how sublime! I felt as though I were being tenderly nurtured, fed and watered by a divine hand. I was born again, as a child of a divine creation, and I became a member of a cosmic family. I understood that I was loved by God as much as any man or angel. I came to know the God of my dreams—the God that I could not hesitate to worship. And how could I forget the reality and rapture of Jesus' promise: *"Ask and it shall be given you; seek and you shall find; knock and it shall be opened to you. For every one who asks receives; he who seeks finds; and to him who knocks the door of salvation will be opened"* (p. 1619).

I asked, I sought, I knocked, and all that I wanted was given me in such a measure that I could not have imagined. I was pulled back from the precipice of doubt and despair by the truth in the Urantia Book, and I am eternally grateful.

My husband, Robert, died in 1982 in a car accident. He never read the Urantia Book. He even refused to let me read it to him. I have come to believe that Spirit uses some people as conduits to deliver what needs to be delivered. Often they are not involved and do not necessarily believe what they are compelled to deliver to you.

RON FAULK: I ran across the Urantia Book in January of 1976. I was living in Chicago and attending college there, although my home was in the South. I had taken a part-time teaching job with Project Upward Bound in Evanston, and during one of our team meetings I met a fellow teacher named Mike who subsequently became a good friend. For years

I had been reading anything and everything, and one day I noticed that he had a big blue book under his arm. I asked him what it was, and he replied, "The Urantia Book." This of course meant nothing to me. He explained that it was a strange book about God and the universe. "Here," he offered, "why don't you borrow it?"

After work, I went home and opened it. In our living room we had an old couch covered with a yellow blanket, facing two tall windows with bamboo shades through which the light fell in long white lines. It was a quiet and pleasant place to read. I sat there and began with the Foreword. I could not put it down, and in the next few months I read the book from cover to cover, occasionally at the expense of my academic studies. I well remember the excitement of plowing through the pages as rapidly as I could, never knowing what the next page would bring.

The next time Mike came over he asked if I had gotten to the part about the Thought Adjusters, those spirit fragments of God that indwell us. That part had stuck in his mind as one of the most profound revelations of the book, and I agree with him. In subsequent years we have spent many pleasant hours discussing ideas generated from the Urantia Book.

Across the years and places, I have asked many readers about their initial response to reading the book. The vast majority say they became interested in it gradually. Some have never read it completely or very comprehensively, but get the gist of it by listening to others and participating in study group discussions. A few people, though, are gripped immediately by the text, as I was. In some way the narrative voice speaks very directly to me. While I am not very literal minded, I do believe that the UBook operates in high levels of metaphoric and symbolic truth. It synthesizes a breadth of knowledge, encompassing religion, philosophy, aesthetics, history, science and cosmology, better than any other book I've read; it makes sense of it all, reconciling these concepts into a harmonious whole.

From my perception, the best thing of all about the Urantia Book is that it speaks so directly about God and his manifestations and relationships to persons. Despite the angelic nomenclature and celestial credits, it is essentially a very human book, composed largely of the best that has been thought and written in the history of our world. As such, it is a monument to the best minds and spirits of the world, and something of an example for us to follow through the ages ahead.

DAVE TIBBETS: Raised in a fundamentalist Lutheran environment, I took catechism classes. The ministers' questions and rote answers were supposed to lead to the "inescapable conclusion" that we Lutherans were the truly anointed and enlightened ones. Instead, they had the opposite effect on me and generated questions such as, "How come God plays favorites and picked *me* over the less fortunate?" This line of thinking inevitably caused me to reject virtually everything I'd been told. I became agnostic with atheistic leanings. I joined the Air Force, and flexed my new-found philosophical and religious freedom in a search for bottom-line truth, a search that lasted several years.

On leaving the service in 1974, I was still looking. I joined the Unitarian Universalists; I liked their hands-off approach to the unknowables and their focus, instead, on being good to one another here and now. But still, I felt the drive to find something, somewhere, that had an absolutely, undeniably factual basis. I was starting to lose my mental glue. Reality gets a little shaky if you have nothing to anchor your belief system. That was the low point *and* the starting point for me.

Having come to the conclusion that I knew nothing, I was open to truly learning. That's when it happened. I was sitting at my bench at work, concentrating on wire-wrapping an electronic circuit board, when a billboard-sized announcement flashed inside my head: *"Truth is not fact, but a state of realization."* It nearly knocked me off my stool. My recovery was assured; I now realized that my truth would continuously change and my understanding grow.

At about this time, I was invited to a party after work by a fellow who was a friend of a friend. As the party progressed, I voiced some of my searching questions during a philosophical "bull session." Shortly thereafter, the fellow said, "I've got something I think you'd be interested in." It was, of course, Big Blue! I thumbed through the table of contents and knew I had to have the book. I copied down the Foundation's address and phone number and ordered my book the next day.

When it arrived, I tried in vain to read the Foreword. I saw the Jesus papers in the back of the book, but just set them aside mentally as I was not ready to deal with them; I was still severely rejecting my earlier fundamentalist Christian teachings and had a knee-jerk, negative reaction to anything that had Jesus' name associated with it. It took fourteen years of my occasionally pulling the book off the shelf and putting it back again before my Thought Adjuster was able to drain the poison from me, allowing me to begin reading the story of Adam and Eve. I fell in love. Here, finally, was something that *felt* true.

And I've been making all my friends and relatives a little crazy ever since. My Thought Adjuster is now trying to train me in the art of sharing. You'd think I'd know better than to become a fundamentalist myself, but when you discover the keys to the universe and beyond, it's a little difficult to be self-restrained!

FRED SMITH: I must go back to 1968, to Hiram Johnson High School in Sacramento, California. In the sophomore gym class the teacher required us to stand in line according to the alphabetical order of our last names. That is how I met the incredible guy, Rick Ulvevadet, who would one day introduce me to the Urantia Book. We struck up a close friendship which has lasted to this day.

In 1969 I moved to Modesto, and for a while Rick and I went our separate ways. A few years later I was transferred to Fresno through my work with a restaurant company, and Rick became stationed in Fresno as a fireman with the Department of Forestry. It wasn't long before we contacted each other, and from then on we often got together to share the details of our lives.

During the early '70s I became involved in the Pentecostal experience of speaking in tongues and believing in the fire-and-brimstone message of the end times. After receiving my personal revelation of the Rapture and finding God within me two years later, I moved on from that fundamentalist organization and began searching for the answers to the universe. This led me to several different groups of New Age thinkers and seekers. All the while I was relating my experiences to my friend Rick. New Age beliefs did not sit well with him at the time, as he was still clinging to the traditional Christian doctrine about receiving Christ as your personal savior. Soon thereafter we again went our separate ways when I was transferred to Petaluma to manage a Happy Steak Restaurant and he to work in Columbia, more than 150 miles away.

About two years later, in 1976, I received a call from Rick that transformed my spiritual outlook. Rick had changed. He was telling me about his revelation. It sounded a lot like mine, except that his was much more in-depth about God and the universe. I asked him what had he found to bring about such a profound change in his life and to give him such increased knowledge about the universe. He answered, "I've found a book—the Urantia Book! When I first picked it up it felt like I was being energized!"

"Wow!" I exclaimed. "Where do I get one?"

He said that he had checked it out of a library in Sonora, and that perhaps a bookstore would carry it. From what he told me about it, I knew I *had* to have that book, so I ordered a copy from a bookstore in Petaluma. Twenty-four years later, I still feel that same energy and spiritual inspiration every time I read the Urantia Book.

Since I became a full-time artist in 1987, the Urantia Book has become my sketchbook. I've drawn a great variety of ideas, thoughts, feelings and doodles in it; now I mostly draw animals—hundreds of them—from insects to elephants. My Urantia Book is truly a work of art, a unique, one-of-a-kind UBook. I do, however, keep several extra copies around for reading purposes. Now that I live in Southern California I try to attend as many local study groups as possible. I love sharing my experiences and my drawing-filled UB with other readers.

MARY EBBEN: In 1976 I was living in Fort Lauderdale, Florida, with my first husband. A close friend of ours, George Cheshire, had been to Colombia on business, and while there he met a nice American couple named Archie and Rustie. When this couple needed to come to the United States to get supplies for their ranch, George suggested they stay with us.

Archie and Rustie were wonderful houseguests. They even cleaned my house the first day while I was at work and spent a lot of time visiting with me. I was 25 years old and these were the first people I'd ever had great philosophical discussions with—in fact, they were the *only* people I'd had deep, meaningful talks with up till that time. One night I asked them, "What is that big blue book that you read, that five-pound book that you carry everywhere with you?"

"Why, it's the Urantia Book," they answered, "and we saw one on your bookshelf when we were cleaning!"

My husband claimed that some girl had once given it to him and he had simply stuck it on the shelf. I never saw him read it, and the following year when we divorced I asked him if I could have it. Since the answer was no, I bought my own copy for $26—a lot of money to me at the time.

My second husband would hum the theme song from *The Twilight Zone* every time he saw me reading the Urantia Book, so I didn't pursue it much around him. I didn't mention it to my third husband until I had finished reading at least half the book. Our children were in preschool and I was around 40 by then, living near Boulder, Colorado.

As a child I had disconnected from God and stopped all prayer, although I continued to attend church and go through the motions. After having children I tried harder to feel something but it simply wasn't happening—I didn't know *how* to connect. The Urantia Book is a difficult book to read cover to cover, but something compelled me to finish reading it, if it was the last thing I did! And I was determined to understand the damn thing, too! Along the way I learned to relax and savor it because I realized that I have all of eternity to learn. At some point I gained an awareness of the eternity of my soul; a sense of soul security beyond explanation. I went through my "dark night of the soul"—my spiritual crisis—when I finally asked God to help me tear down my walls and give me the courage to open my heart and allow him back in.

When I finally finished reading the Urantia Book I connected with the Urantia community in Boulder, which was very active, and where I met people who've become precious friends. There I also went to work for the Jesusonian Foundation, which disseminates the Urantia Book and secondary works. One day, while searching through their large mailing list trying to locate an Archie and/or a Rustie (I had never known their last names), I came across an Archie and Rustie Lowe in Steamboat Springs, Colorado. It was them! Although they were actually living in Texas, they owned property in Colorado. They came to our regional Frontier Conference, and after eighteen years I finally had the chance to thank them for being the instruments that got me connected with my Father.

Life has not gotten easier for me; perhaps it is harder than it might have been, but it is definitely not a lonely journey anymore. The Urantia Book was my doorway to re-establishing my personal relationship with God. I feel very fortunate and very blessed that I finally committed myself to reading this life-changing book.

DENNIS NICOMEDE: At age 15 I left the Catholic Church and began my quest for God. For years I looked high and low—in churches, synagogues and temples—for the "golden thread" that binds us all together. Wherever I looked I found those who believed in the Fatherhood of God but failed to accept any brotherhood beyond their own group.

I spent the next two years in the army, where for the first time I lost my faith in God. There was just too much death and destruction over ideology and cultural points of view, not to mention a long string of assassinations ending with the death of Robert Kennedy. At the time it was more than this heart could handle. But thanks to the ever-present spirit, my doubt lasted only a short while and was followed by a beautiful spiritual resurrection. After saying goodbye to Uncle Sam in 1969 I continued my divine search.

Next on the path was starting a small business with my father (it ultimately failed), then marrying my high-school sweetheart in 1971. After doing a short tour through metaphysics and mind-over-matter material, I found a small esoteric manuscript written in the 18th century. It was one of only five known copies. It was hard to decipher and didn't make much sense to me at the time, but it was so rare, I assumed it must be valuable.

One evening in 1976 I was attending a party. It was there, while throwing darts, that I met a young man named Pat McNelly. We talked about religion and philosophy, and this became our common ground. When I told him about my manuscript, he asked to see it. A few days later, Pat stopped by my apartment, picked up the manuscript and off he went. Two days later he returned saying it was an interesting read, but if I wanted to read something *really* worthwhile, why not try this "small, blue book"? He then handed me my first copy of the Urantia Book. Thanks, Pat!

Wow! My first reading was full of *Aha!* moments. I felt I had come home. My heart was filled with peace; my mind knew it had found the "golden thread" it was seeking. The great mystery was now an open secret. The truth I've found in the book and the good spirit I've found within the readership have forever added to my life.

My search was finally over, but the journey has just begun.

DAVID ROBERTSON: Back in 1972 B.C. (before children), my wife and I were involved in a serious auto accident. One of our friends was killed and other friends were injured. We were hit from the rear by a drunk driver who was being pursued by the highway patrol. Estimates were that he was driving in excess of 100 mph.

This experience caused me to realize just how precious and fragile life is. I remember one night asking God for some answers. That night, in a dream, I saw a vision of Jesus. He stood without speaking but I knew who he was. He had an incredible look of peaceful understanding on his face. I was so excited I could hardly contain myself. I tried to speak but could not. Then, as if knowing my thoughts, he simply turned and pointed. This gesture told me without a doubt that my answers were within my grasp. All I had to do was to seek the truth and he would lead me. I woke up, soaked with perspiration. I hadn't cried over anything in years but the emotion of this experience overwhelmed me.

Some time passed without any visible confirmation of my dream. Then, on Christmas Eve, I went to the local mall to do my shopping. I went into a bookstore, although I had no intention of purchasing a book as a gift. There on a table, in the middle of the store, was a large blue book without a cover on it. It was one of about fifty books on the table. I picked it up, opened it, and read only one sentence. To this day, I don't remember which sentence it was, only that it was so profound that I knew I had been led to a source which had the answers to many of my questions. I looked at the price of the book. It was $20. My practical side took over. At that point in my life, $20 was too much to spend on something I really didn't know anything about. I left the store empty-handed.

I finished shopping and returned to my truck parked out on the fringe of the lot. But something would not let me leave. I returned to the store and bought the book with an already overloaded credit card. All the way home I tried to think of how I would explain this purchase to my wife. Finally, it came to me: I'd give it to her for Christmas! The next morning, after opening it, she looked at me as if I were a little crazy but accepted the book graciously. That evening, I confiscated the book and began to devour it. The rest is history. The Spirit of Truth did its job perfectly.

The journey continues!

CHARLIE BEYER: In the beginning weeks of 1976 my friend Joe and I decided to take an extended vacation to Colombia. A few days before we left New Jersey, another friend had given me a copy of *Seth Speaks*, by Jane Roberts. This book claimed to be the true story of Jane Roberts's contact with a spirit being named Seth, who was revealing information about the spirit world through her. Although I was skeptical, I skimmed a few pages. I liked how quickly the dialogue moved along and decided to take the book with me to South America.

We arrived in Colombia on February 4, 1976. Ten days later, while visiting a beautiful town named Silvia some 8,000 feet up in the Andes Mountains, I happened to meet a guy named Fred from Connecticut. When Fred noticed the *Seth Speaks* book hanging out of my knapsack, he commented that he'd heard it was a pretty good book, and added, "It looks like you believe in spirits."

"Well," I told him, "I don't believe in spirits like Seth, but I do believe in God and angels."

At that moment Fred reached into his knapsack and showed me the Urantia Book, which he'd covered in brown paper the way we used to cover our schoolbooks. He said his grandmother had given it to him. As head librarian in Hartford, Connecticut, and extremely interested in learning about God, she had found plenty of time and opportunity to read many religious books. But once she'd found the Urantia Book, she told Fred, her search was over; this was now the only book she needed to read. Fred also informed me that the book was very deep—too deep, in fact, for him; he suggested that we swap books for a while, and I agreed.

The cities in Colombia were pretty wild at that time. Every day and night there were riots, gun shots and killings; the military was everywhere. By contrast, the Colombian countryside was lovely and peaceful, a foretaste of what heaven must be like. Joe and I had rented a beautiful inn outside the city of Popayan, about an hour from Silvia. Each time we'd meet other tourists in town, we'd invite them back to stay with us at our farm. I extended this same offer to Fred, and he readily accepted.

A few days passed and I still hadn't had a chance to check out the Urantia Book. One day when Fred and I were in Popayan he met a beautiful Colombian girl. I considered myself a good judge of people and could tell right away that this girl was a street hustler. I tried to alert Fred but he ignored me, blinded by her beauty. Despite my warnings, Fred decided to stay in town with her that night rather than go back with me.

When I returned to the farm I told Joe about Fred. "Fred is gonna get ripped off by that girl," I said.

Joe said, "Well, I'm going into town tomorrow, so I'll make sure he's all right."

The next day, alone on the farm, I had the perfect opportunity to check out this Urantia Book and see what it was all about. I recalled what one of my English teachers had told me: If you think a book might be too complicated for you, just open it up randomly and start reading; if you can grasp what the book is saying, then you should have no trouble with it. So that is what I did. I opened the Urantia Book and in bold letters I saw the words: "Time-Space Relationships." This topic had always fascinated me, so I proceeded to read. The book explained these concepts to me better than I have ever heard them explained before or since. I actually *grasped* the concept, and at that moment I felt I was in possession of great knowledge.

As soon as I finished this section, I leaned back to contemplate what I had learned, and in my reflective moment I had a vision in which Fred had had everything stolen, including my *Seth Speaks* book. In this same vision I heard Fred say to me, "Listen, Charlie, I need $9 for an exit visa to get out of the country, and since I lost your *Seth Speaks* book I'll sell you the Urantia Book, which costs $20, for only $9."

A few hours later when Joe returned to the farm together with Fred, my vision was right on the money. The girl had slipped something into Fred's drink, then lured him into an alley. There he passed out and she quickly took everything he had. Fred lost his wallet with all his money, his knapsack containing my *Seth Speaks* book, his wristwatch, an emerald ring, a necklace, and even his sneakers. The only thing she didn't get was his passport and his plane ticket home, both of which he had left back at the farm.

Fred then looked at me and said the exact words I had heard him say in my vision. I couldn't believe my ears. It seemed as though I was meant to have this book. I immediately gave Fred the $9.

The next day Fred was on a plane back to Connecticut and I had the Urantia Book. I have been reading it and learning from it ever since. No book has changed my life and enlightened me as much as the Urantia Book has. And ever since that fateful day back in February of 1976 I have been thanking God, his angels, and my Thought Adjuster for leading me to it.

Part VI

1977-1979

CHARLOTTE WELLEN: I made it a habit, throughout my adolescence, to walk around a bookstore or library and wait until I felt an urging to take a particular book from a shelf. Invariably, the book I'd choose would turn out to be important for my spiritual growth.

One evening in 1977, over winter break from college, I was at the wonderful library at the A.R.E. (Association for Research and Enlightenment)—the Edgar Cayce Foundation. I picked a huge blue book off the shelf, took it over to a table, and flipped it open to a section which described, in great detail, the structure of the universe. The narrator's tone, absolutely sure and not at all speculative, filled me with awe. I continued to leaf through the pages. The tone was the same throughout, authoritative and utterly intriguing.

I realized that I would either need to quit school for the upcoming semester to read the book and investigate the truth of it, or put it back on the shelf until some other time. I thought long and hard and then put it back on the shelf.

A few months later, towards the end of my senior year in college, I was listening to a friend talk about his interest in an ancient civilization called Mu, which had supposedly existed on an island in the Pacific Ocean. I told him I hadn't heard anything about it, but then I remembered the big blue book at the A.R.E. I told him that if any book would have that kind of information in it, it would be *that* book. He asked if I'd be willing to go to Virginia Beach with him to check it out.

A week or two later, my friend (soon-to-be-husband) and I journeyed from Williamsburg to Virginia Beach, checked out the UB and took it back to The College of William and Mary with us. We were living in a special-interest dormitory called Asia House and decided to leave the book on a table in the common room. Soon it was the talk of the place. Everyone was browsing through it and discussing what they were reading. The last month of school was filled with debate about who the authors could be.

We wondered if it were possible that some group of the best minds on the planet, versed in religious studies, sociology, economics, archeology, paleontology, biology, human sexuality, mythology, history, etc., had somehow gotten together to create the book. After a while, after we'd read enough, the question of who had written it became ludicrous. No matter who had written it—humans or spiritual beings—it had a great deal to offer.

When my husband and I graduated, we purchased our own copy as a wedding present to ourselves and we've been loyal readers, participators in study groups and online forums ever since. Our marriage and our lives have been enriched beyond imagining. Each of us had gone on spiritual journeys because of our dissatisfaction with the obvious inconsistencies and injustices of the mainstream religions. We had explored Buddhism, Hinduism, Jainism, Taoism, and various sects of Christianity, especially the Society of Friends. Nothing had fit together or felt right or made sense, except in bits and pieces, until we digested the Urantia Book. It answered just the right questions, and left just the right things (like Mu and Atlantis) mysteries, as they should be. It straightened out the mess Christianity has become and it clarified the human relationship with God. For this we will be eternally grateful.

JON DETOY: Early 1977 found me floundering in search of eternal truth. My journey took me down many paths, from Catholic Bible study to Ram Dass. I found company with my friends Howard and Charlotte King, whose house was known as a haven for earnest seekers to discuss theory and philosophy. We would sit around their table exploring our minds while enjoying various gifts of the earth and playing endless games of Risk. I believed that through concentrated thought and worshipful meditation the doors of knowledge and wisdom would be opened. Many times the light would shine through, but mostly it was like digging through a ton of dogma for each pearl of truth.

All that changed in June of 1978. One evening at the Kings' home a young man dropped a large blue book onto the table, saying, "Here. This is a little too heavy for me." He explained that while in Colorado he had run across a wild man collecting herbs up in the mountains who introduced him to this book. Our friend couldn't figure any of it out but felt that with all the discussion we'd had on these strange matters, possibly *we* could. Well, we dove into that book with restless abandon, staying up to the early hours of morning, taking turns reading to each other from wherever we opened the book.

I could not believe what had fallen into my lap. After years of searching, here was the ultimate truth—no more digging, every concept was perfection. This was mental heaven. I wanted to share these truths with everyone.

The peace and joy that comes from knowing the life of Joshua ben Joseph surpasses all other experiences in my life. I have found in the recital of his life experiences inspiration for most of my own life situations. I pray now that all the followers of Christ Michael will show in their lives Jesus living again on Urantia. Amen.

NANCY BROWN: In August of 1977, I found myself facing the hardest decision of my life. Out of the blue, my ex-husband invited my precious eight-year-old son, Christian, to move to Seattle with him and start a new school year there.

Chris's dad and I had been divorced six years. Two years previously he had left our hometown outside of Chicago to take a new job in Washington. Chris hadn't seen his dad since and I knew he wanted to go. After two weeks of prayer, agonizing and talking to a child psychologist, I reluctantly agreed to a trial arrangement for a year. Somewhere in my heart, I knew Chris needed to be with his dad. I will never forget the day I took my little son to the airport and watched him, tears streaming down my face, fly away to his new life.

I immediately fell into a depression after he left. Christian was my only child and I loved him dearly. I loved being his mom and I sorely missed him in my life. At night, I would toss and turn in my bed, unable to sleep. I was plagued with disturbing images of life and wondered what living on earth was all about. I felt nothing but pain and anguish inside of me. I was beginning to see the world as evil, with little patches of light on an otherwise dark and foreboding landscape. I was slowly becoming engulfed by all the bleakness and I would cry out loud to God for help. Where was he in all my pain? Where were the answers I was so desperately seeking?

Shortly after Christian left, I began dating a young man named John.

John appeared suddenly in my life, and disappeared almost as quickly. John was a free spirit who never stayed in one place very long. During our short time together, he and I would have long talks about life. I'm sure that he sensed my confusion and growing negative outlook. Before John left on his next adventure, he bestowed upon me three Carlos Castaneda books and the Urantia Book. I devoured *A Yaqui Way of Knowledge, A Separate Reality* and *Journey to Ixtlan*. These three books began to turn my life around; they taught me that everything in life is one's perception: Change your perception, change your life.

In the meantime, the oversized blue Urantia Book sat on my mantel in the living room where I had set it the day I brought it home months before. One day, I found the flap from the torn-off dust jacket sitting inside the cover of the book and grabbed it to take to work with me. At some point during the day I picked it up and read the most astounding words I had ever seen: *"Your world, Urantia, is one of many similar inhabited planets which comprise the local universe of Nebadon. This universe, together with similar creations, makes up the superuniverse of Orvonton from whose capital, Uversa, our commission hails."* Something stirred inside me as nothing had before. I felt that excitement of discovery that literally quickens the spirit. It was the most feeling I had experienced since my son had left—perhaps since he was born.

That night, at home, I eagerly flipped the book open for the first time and read these words: *"As you view the world, remember that the black patches of evil which you see are shown against a white background of ultimate good. You do not view merely white patches of good which show up miserably against a black background of evil."* I couldn't believe my eyes! The very image that had plagued my mind for months was being addressed in this strange book. I felt that someone or something understood me to the depth of my being.

Christian came home the following summer, and although it had not been an easy year for any of us, he liked his new environment, new school and new friends. Once it was decided that he would go back to Seattle, this became a way of life for our family—the school year with his father, the summer with me.

After Chris went back, I moved to Chicago and found myself living a few blocks from 533 Diversey. I began to attend Sunday study groups at the Foundation headquarters and didn't miss a Sunday for many years. In 1987 I moved to Door County, Wisconsin, and opened a metaphysical bookstore called Star Gazer so that I would have the opportunity to share these teachings with others. I still own this store today.

In 1991, Christian was home with me in Door County before starting his senior year at Washington State University. In the early morning hours of August 14, my precious and most loved son was killed in a car accident. That night, as I stood under a black sky filled with little white specks of starlight, I held the Urantia Book in my hands fully intending to destroy it. Something within stopped me. Instead, I held my book over my heart as tears streamed down my face. I closed my eyes and watched my son fly away to his new life.

SASKIA PRAAMSMA: Religion was an unpleasant topic in my family when I was growing up. My mother regarded all religionists as either hypocrites or fanatics, so when my father joined the Jehovah's Witnesses and began preaching door to door, there was trouble. A truce was called, and from then on my dad rarely mentioned his beliefs. When the taboo topic did crop up once in a while, it would lead to shouting and bitterness.

What I heard about religion and God from my friends sounded like a fantasy. How could anyone worship a phantom God who kept himself hidden? Certainly not I! I automatically dismissed such concepts as the blood of Christ washing away my sins and Jesus dying for me on the cross; I could not fathom anybody falling for such ideas or worshipping a God who was always angry and who showed less tolerance for humanity than an ordinary civilized person would. I reasoned that the Creator should at least be wiser and more mature than his creatures.

And why, if he wanted us to know about him, would he give us only one book that was written thousands of years ago and that I couldn't decipher? And why would he make it a sin to add anything to it? Why wouldn't he give it to us straight? If human beings were capable of making themselves understood, then why did God—who *created* the human beings—insist on talking in riddles?

Religion, I decided, was not for me. I didn't even try searching along those lines. I had rarely attended church, barely skimmed the Bible, knew nothing about God and Jesus, and made fun of people who prayed and turned to God for help. The idea of a God upholding the universe appealed to me, but unless someone who really knew the truth could explain it to me properly, I had nothing to pin my hopes on and would have to remain agnostic.

Like everyone else, I sought happiness. I would set my sights on something, acquire it, then find myself holding a big, empty balloon. I spent a great deal of time shopping, mainly for clothes. I tried to get ahead at work. I changed the color of my hair often. I thought that if I got married I'd be happy. Once married, I realized I needed a divorce to be happy. I had a string of relationships. I moved from country to country. I became more and more frustrated. I was doing everything within my power to be happy and nothing worked. At night I lay awake wondering where it would all lead. Would I simply die one day, and would that be the end of me? Miserable as I was, I still wanted to live forever.

I enjoyed reading and had managed to fill my head with earthly knowledge that represented a giant pile of jigsaw puzzle pieces that didn't fit together. The more I learned, the more confused I became. I had many questions but no answers.

My brother Michael had begun his search a couple of years earlier and in the process had found the Urantia Book. "You would love this book!" he insisted. But when I saw that it talked about God and Jesus I refused to look at it. The last thing I needed was to be converted to some wacky religion.

When yet another relationship ended, I was forced to temporarily move in with Michael. Several times I went along to visit his friends in Topanga Canyon, David and Barbara, who had given him the book. They all radiated a certain peace whereas I usually felt extremely agitated; the contrast was noticeable, even to me.

One evening the book lay open on Michael's dining room table to "Dawn Races of Early Man." Years earlier I had helped my parents put together an educational filmstrip that dealt with this topic, and in our research we found that the available human knowledge was largely conjecture. But the way *this* was written, the authoritative tone in which the subject matter was presented, impressed me and I couldn't stop reading. They—whoever *they* were—were stating facts and clearing things up for me.

When I reached "The Survival of Andon and Fonta" light bulbs exploded in my head. This book is telling me the truth! We will not die! There's a big universe out there that is fully under control, and there *is* a God after all! All the knowledge I had accumulated over the years clicked together, the pieces of the giant jigsaw puzzle forming a coherent picture of the universe that resembled a detailed tapestry. The astounding thing was that I recognized the picture as something familiar, something that deep down I had known all along but couldn't see because it was blocked. Now the veil was lifted. I saw angels going from one planet to another carrying beings around in their arms; everything was connected with ladders and invisible wires, and I was a part of it! This life was not the end at all—it was the beginning! Although I still had two thousand pages to go, I knew that this book would give me it to me straight. That was the happiest day of my life, April 18, 1977. *"You shall know the truth, and the truth shall make you free."* I wept tears of joy and relief.

On that day I turned my life around 180 degrees. All my attitudes and values were changed in one fell swoop. I read the book for three months straight, barely coming up for air. I learned where I came from, where I was going, and why I was here. What I had believed to be important was meaningless, and that's why happiness had eluded me. I discovered that there is no happiness apart from God. The stress and tension dropped away, the furrows in my brow relaxed, and I still hadn't read a word about Jesus—that came much later. In fact, I resisted reading about him until I had exhausted all the other papers. But when I finally did, I was ready to accept him and his teachings wholeheartedly. Since that day I have had peace of mind—the peace which passes all understanding.

M. (SEK) SEKLEMIAN: Those who seek shall find. There are millions who are searching, some desperately, to find meaning in this life, to learn why we are here and where we are going. I was one of those desperate seekers.

When my wife of forty-eight years passed on, I suddenly began to search. What happened to her? Is there a soul or something that lives on? I had given up on standard churches when I was 25. My wife and I had gone happily on, not giving much thought to life and death. Then came the shocking experience—the departure of my loved one into the unknown.

The unknown! It was terribly hard to take. I could not accept death as the end. My science studies had taught me that nothing is destroyed. A lifeless atom endures forever. It may change form but it never ceases to exist. Even a light ray is forever. If a lifeless atom is forever, why must a beautiful personality—a fantastic, living, loving, incredible intelligence—perish? I couldn't accept that. It didn't seem right. Surely this personality was a million times more important in the scheme of things than a lifeless atom or a stray light ray!

My search for truth began. I re-read the Gospels. I examined Gibran, Gurdjieff, the philosophers ancient and modern. I took a flying trip to France to study with the renowned Maharishi Mahesh Yogi. The more I studied, the less sure I was. It was amazing to me how little real information was available about life after death and the survival of the soul.

For five years I lived in torment, hating life and even railing against God. I finally considered suicide as a means of learning the truth about death. At this juncture—it was 1977—I received a note from Clyde Bedell. He'd enclosed a sheet of paper describing the Urantia Book. He said, "Thought you might like to know what I've been working on lately." (Clyde was referring to his recently published *Concordex*.) I immediately wrote a check for both books and sent it to Clyde. I thought, "Who knows? Maybe I should look into this. I've known Clyde for years. If he's involved it can't be all bad."

Clyde promptly sent my check back. He wrote, "I don't want you to pay for these books unless you really want them. Read first, then decide."

One Saturday morning, with a full weekend of work to do, I started reading the book. Sunday evening I put it down. I had not slept a wink or paused to eat. I hadn't done a stitch of work either. That evening I wrote a note: "Dear Clyde, you successfully ruined my weekend."

It's needless for me to tell Urantia Book readers what a thrill it is to open this incredible volume and start reading. All doubts fade away. All questions get answered. And faith is renewed with a bang!

What prompted Clyde to send me the Urantia Book? Even though I had known him as a businessman for many years, we were not particularly close. I had long since lost track of him. He had no idea of my personal loss and desperate search for truth. What persuaded him to suddenly break the silence and send me that first note?

Clyde says that I made the first step. There had been a devastating fire in Santa Barbara and three hundred houses had been destroyed. Among the names of affected homeowners listed in the local newspaper, my eye caught the name of Clyde Bedell. I knew he had been living in Santa Barbara but had no idea that he'd sold his place and moved away. The article had mistakenly listed him as an owner.

Acting on this information, I tried to reach Clyde to offer him my house, to tide him and Florence over in this emergency—a simple, neighborly thing to do. Clyde says that that gesture moved him. We both agree our divine Thought Adjusters got together and decided the time had come for my search to be over. I am forever grateful to Clyde Bedell for his thoughtfulness and, above all, I am eternally grateful to our Father for this fantastic revelation and for the hope and joy it has brought me. I have one mission now—to be ever aware of my Thought Adjuster's leadings and to zero in on others who search.

DANIEL LOVE GLAZER: My parents did not believe in the fatherhood of God, but they ardently believed in the brotherhood of man. They were active in promoting liberal political and social causes. They were the children of Eastern European Jews and reared me with a strong Jewish identity. This identity was primarily ethnic, but they did send me to Hebrew school and a Jewish Sunday school. We never went to a synagogue, not even on the High Holy Days. We did attend Passover Seders at the grandparents' and celebrated Chanukah.

I was a religious boy. I would fast on Yom Kippur—no one else in my family did. I used to pray every night. I was proud to be bar mitzvahed, though I did not know the meaning of the Hebrew scriptures I'd memorized for the occasion.

My religiosity lasted until high school, when I fell under the spell of Bertrand Russell. I read so much Bertrand Russell that my friends called me "Bert." Russell's philosophy, purporting to base everything on logic and nothing on metaphysical assumptions, won me over to agnosticism. As for Jesus, I particularly remember reading Russell's book, *Why I am not a Christian*. Russell asks, if Jesus was as good and as powerful as Christians believe, why did he not banish disease from the face of the earth, rather than just heal a few individuals? To me, that seemed a knockdown argument.

At 17, after participating in Martin Luther King Jr.'s March on Washington, I went off to college, to Columbia in New York. I was experiencing the traumas of adolescence and suffered from an acute inferiority complex. I spent most of my freshman year playing chess and most of my sophomore year hanging around the downtown pool halls. My major reading was Henry Miller. After two years I decided to stop wasting my parents' money and dropped out of school.

Then came grass. Smoking grass changed a miserable life to a pleasant one. One of the first few times I turned on, I went to a lecture at Columbia by Timothy Leary, onetime Harvard psychology professor-become-evangelist of the drug-inspired gospel, "Turn on, Tune in, Drop out." Leary talked about higher consciousness. He told us why Eastern mystics meditate in the lotus position for hours at a time: to get high!

I started doing yoga exercises when turned on, and sure enough, I got higher. I read and reread Paramahansa Yogananda's *Autobiography of a Yogi*.

In November of 1966 I attended a lecture by Swami Satchidananda, an Indian yogi with a long beard and charismatic manner, who had recently come to New York. I became his student and disciple, attending his Integral Yoga Institute in New York each day while working as a mail sorter for the Post Office. Under his influence, I foreswore drugs, meat, caffeine, alcohol, and sex. I covered the walls of my efficiency apartment with pictures of the Swami and converted my walk-in closet into a meditation room. I expected to become a Swami myself, if only I could achieve the elusive samadhi, the state of enlightenment. But after two dedicated years on the yoga path, I continued to experience conflict, confusion, and other distinctly non-enlightenment states of mind.

Eventually I allowed myself to entertain the possibility that something in the yoga path itself, as I had adopted it, might be at the root of my non-enlightenment. I looked deep within and asked for the truth, putting everything on the table. When I did so, it became clear to me that my yoga path had taken on some false and unhealthy aspects. One was the guru trip. I realized that achieving enlightenment could not mean following in someone else's footsteps and obeying his commands. Second was the realization that the drive to transcend my individual personality via absorption in the Absolute was ultimately false and impossible. So I left Satchidananda, initially becoming a Hatha Yoga teacher on my own, and eventually moving to Washington, D. C. and becoming a computer programmer for the Federal government.

For the next five or six years I didn't bother much with ultimate questions. Then I was visited by a friend who had been living in California for six years. He told me that I had been an inspiration to him in his spiritual quest. In the wake of his visit I was reawakened to the realization that there was *something* spiritual going on in the world. I was determined to find out what it was and to avoid the errors I had made on my previous spiritual search.

With all my being I embarked on an intense search for the truth. My constant meditation, day and night, while working, playing chess, square dancing, or listening to jazz, was "What is the truth?" I went to lectures. I frequented Washington's Yes! Bookstore, which housed books from all sorts of spiritual paths. I read widely: zen, Edgar Cayce, Hazrat Inayat Khan, Gregory Bateson, Alice Bailey, the *Seth* material, Krishnamurti, yoga.

The *Seth* books of Jane Roberts made a particular impression on me. Their message that each of us creates his own reality via every belief and thought he entertains was a tempting one. It seemed to me at one point that if I adopted the framework of Buddhism, reality would take on a Buddhist coloration. Likewise a Christian or Krishna Consciousness premise would cause the world to take on the contours prescribed by those worldviews. But I finally concluded: "Reality cannot be something I make up. There must be a true reality underlying all, independent of my beliefs."

My best friend, Arthur, a psychotherapist and onetime yoga student of mine, told me the answer: He forcefully proclaimed that unless I accepted Jesus' sacrifice on the cross as atonement for my sins I was doomed to hell. In my incessant search for truth I prayed, "God, if this is the ultimate truth, let me know and I will accept it, but I must know from *you* that this is it." Meditating on this proposition with my entire being, I got an answer from beyond myself: "No, this atonement doctrine does not express who God is, who you are, or what you must do to be saved. Indeed the only possible requirement for being saved is your wholehearted desire to know the truth and follow it." Along with this realization came the assurance that I would be guided into whatever truth I needed to know.

Three weeks later, in the spring of 1997, I was visiting a good friend of mine, Al, another psychologist. He remarked, "Here's a book someone loaned me that you might be interested in" and handed me *The Urantia Book.* I opened it up and was immediately fascinated. It was inspiring and had the aura of authority. But a major red flag for me was the 700 pages devoted to the life and teachings of Jesus. I had come to *know* that the Christianity of the atonement doctrine was false. Of course, when I had read enough to realize that the Urantia Book's verdict on the atonement doctrine was the same as that provided by my inner guidance, I became open to the whole book, and along with the book, to Jesus, the real and living Jesus. Thanks be to God!

DAVE HOLT: When I moved to Sonoma County, California, to start a new job in 1975, I went to live in a small farm town called Valley Ford, miles from urban society. My first serious relationship had ended and I wanted to try out loneliness. Valley Ford was a very lonely place, and I reveled in the quiet aloneness. I wanted to see if God would speak to me. I thought that if I made everything around me quiet enough, maybe I would be able to hear him. I hung a colorful picture of an Indian Bodhisattva by my morning window. Feeling a deep need for healing and insight into my problems, I was primed for a spiritual revival.

It had been easy for me to regard Jesus as a great human prophet, but in a yoga meditation one day I was suddenly reintroduced to the Master. The eyes of faith were opened and I saw him not as a memory from childhood or from history, but as real and present, a being still living in the same universe I lived in. I had what was in some ways a traditional born-again experience, except that I brought it on with chanting and by meditating on a hilltop overlooking the Pacific Ocean.

A few months after this experience, my friend Eric was involved in a car accident. He'd slipped into a deep coma and hovered near death. As I struggled with the loss, I was also confronted by the now immediately relevant question: What would happen to Eric in the afterlife were he to die? I discussed these topics in my first conversations with a new friend who worked at People's Music, a musicians' meeting place and music store in Sebastopol. We would have our talks between the comings and goings of my friend's customers. I immediately recognized that she had delved deeply into the questions of death and the afterlife, and I often returned to hear more of what she had to say.

When Eric died a few months later I felt that his spirit came to visit me one evening soon afterwards. Whenever I took my experiences to my new musician friend for discussion, she always had a helpful response for me.

In the summer of 1977 she astounded me with a new thought: "We live in a friendly universe." Deep in my soul I wanted it to be true that goodness and friendliness ruled, that the Creator did not have an equally strong desire to destroy his creation. I had struggled with the fatalistic concept of the cyclical creation and destruction of the universe which I'd learned from Eastern philosophy. I was certain that a rule of the good was a logical and therefore possible reality. Jesus' life and words promised it. Now here was a person declaring to me that the universe was created to allow me to achieve all possible good within it. I wanted to know more.

She invited me over to her house in Santa Rosa to read a book that talked about time and space, among other matters. I accepted. On this "first date" (as we referred to it jokingly later on) she introduced me to the Urantia Book, her primary source for the ideas with which she had inspired me. Within a few months of that evening, we fell in love. We were married a couple of years later, had a beautiful daughter, and have made a wonderful family together.

CATHY JONES: As far back as I can remember, up until the time the Urantia Book found me, I was engaged in a relentless, nagging pursuit for the meaning of life and wondered where it was all leading me. I was born in Texas, in the Bible Belt, to a traditional Christian family. I moved to Georgia, married, and bore three sons. I followed accepted religious thinking.

Mormon elders introduced me to *The Book of Mormon* and, after studying privately for six years, my husband, sons and I converted. We never felt closer as a family than we did the day we were all baptized together. I became absorbed in the Mormon teachings: *The Book of Mormon*, *The Pearl of Great Price*, *Marvelous Work* and *A Wonder*, plus volumes of history. I became what some call a "master teacher."

After moving to Illinois from Georgia, certain circumstances in my personal life caused me to question the teachings and the assumed authority of the Mormon leaders. This led to a desire for a more personal relationship with God and a discovery of self-realization. Being a health enthusiast, I had already been certified as a Hatha Yoga teacher. I studied the yogic philosophy for three years before being initiated into Kriya Yoga and becoming a certified Kriyaban Yogi. In spite of the physical, mental and spiritual advantages of yoga, I was unable to refer to the revered teacher as "Master." Due to my early mindset, Jesus was still my master. During this time I explored many New Age leadings, from Tarot to astrology.

I lived and worked in the Chicago area for some years before relocating to California, where all of my sons had moved. One day while driving I inadvertently made an unauthorized turn and received a traffic ticket. The morning I left home to pay the fine is one that is printed in my memory. In my morning prayer I had made an earnest appeal to the Father for guidance, telling him that I had gone as far as I could in my spiritual life, that it was up to him what direction my life should take.

I never dreamed my prayer would be answered immediately. While standing in a long line waiting to pay, I engaged in light conversation with the gentleman behind me. After a few words about how slowly the line was moving, out of the blue he asked me, "Have you ever heard of the Urantia Book?"

"No. What is it?" I asked. I thought I had gone through all the New Age stuff, but I wasn't prepared for his answer. In about three sentences he told me it was a book about our universe, our creation, and who God and Jesus really are. I asked him where the book could be found, and he told me to try the library, which I did. When I opened the book to the table of contents and read the paper titles, I was astounded. In a week I bought my own book. That was in 1978, and from that day to this that feeling of wonderment has never left me.

I will always be grateful to that wonderful stranger—Wally Ziglar—who had the courage to ask me that life-changing question.

IRWIN GINSBURGH: When I was young, I was taught a lot of the Bible and its version of creation. In college and graduate school, I learned about science's version of the creation of man. It is easy to find conflict between these two versions of creation. But if the Bible is telling us what happened, and if scientists understand what happened, there should be no conflict. Both versions of creation should be telling us the same story.

If you compare the two versions of creation, you will find places where they seem to fit together. However, there is a major discrepancy: Science does not have an Adam and Eve. If I could find an Adam and Eve that were acceptable to science, it would be much easier to piece the two versions of creation together. I went back to Genesis to read about Adam and Eve, and tried to understand who they were. Genesis tells us that they lived 900-year life spans and talked directly to God; the Talmudic literature further says that when they died, their bodies did not decay. They were not the same as you and I; they were superpersons of some kind. I could not find any place on the earth where such people could have originated, and ultimately I began to wonder if they had come from another place in the universe.

Following the scientific method, I hypothesized that Adam and Eve were extraterrestrials who had come here to upgrade the human race; that when they arrived they found an indigenous stone-age civilization.

Their offspring then crossbred with stone-age people to create a hybrid, whose descendants we are. This idea became the major concept of a book I wrote entitled *First, Man. Then, Adam!* It was published in 1977.

After your book is published, you receive lots of letters ranging from high praise to vehement condemnation. But several letters told a different story. They said there was another book that claimed Adam and Eve were extraterrestrials: the Urantia Book.

I found a copy in a local library and started to read. A month later I bought my own. The history of man as recorded in the Urantia Book is very similar to the assumption I made in my book. I had felt that it would never be possible for me to prove my hypothesis about Adam and Eve because the available records are not detailed enough. But the existence of the Urantia Book might just offer the opportunity to prove that my theory was correct.

Now I needed to show that the information in the Urantia Book was valid. Because of my science training, I concentrated on the science part of the UB and wrote three analytical papers on the science content of the Urantia Book. One dealt with the scientific predictions; the second with the cosmology or large-scale structure of the universe; the third with the range of energy manifestations described in the UB. The Urantia Book was published in 1955, and some of the science it contains disagreed with our science at that time. Since then our science has revised some of its theories and concepts. In about half a dozen subject areas where science originally disagreed with the Urantia Book, current science now agrees with it. In other words, some of the UB science predictions are coming true. Furthermore, astronomy's very latest discoveries using the most modern telescopes are starting to show a large-scale structure of the universe which may be similar to the structure described in the book.

These apparent scientific validations of the UB have begun to suggest that the rest of the information is valid, and I hope that science will one day prove that the assumption in my book is correct.

DAVID WEBER: I was living in the dormitory at Seton Hall University and spending most of my time hobnobbing with the musicians on campus. It was the early '70s and the scene was quite lively for someone who could sing and play an instrument. One of the people I met was a bass player named John Hynes, who has remained a friend ever since those fragile years. It was from him that I first heard of the Urantia Book. He hadn't read it, but he'd heard about it from a mystical kind of guy and mentioned it to me. It came up in conversation several times during the next few years, but neither of us had a copy and I had no idea where to get one.

In 1978 John and I were in a band that played extensively throughout northern New Jersey, Eastern Pennsylvania and into New York, including New York City. On our days off we often hung out in the bohemian environment of Washington Square Park. I was soon introduced to a bookstore in the area that carried "unusual" books. I don't remember its name, but I recall that it had a huge display of *The Necromonicon* in the window. To my delight it also carried the big blue book. I paid around $21 and clutched my prize all the way back to Greenbrook, New Jersey, where the band had rented a house.

I went crazy for the Urantia Book. My first reading took me a full year wherein I did little else but immerse myself in the book and perform at gigs with my band. I read it in the same order as many others I've talked to: first Part IV, then Part III, Part II and finally Part I. The information I'd been searching for all my life was there: the nature of God, the ascension plan, the Supreme Being, Thought Adjusters, and the unparalleled life of Jesus of Nazareth. Whew! The book made a tremendous impact on me. I couldn't have been happier.

Since then I've read the UB four times through and some portions many more times than that. I was in a bi-weekly study group in Trenton for a few years and we managed to spark remarkable insights from one another. I came to appreciate the multitude of levels on which the UB can be understood. I've turned a few people on to the book over the years and have been hosting a loose but interesting study group in Barnegat Bay, New Jersey, for several years.

DONNA MARIA HANNA: It was a cold and snowy night the day after Christmas 1978, when an old friend dragged me out to go disco dancing. At the time I was working as a courtroom illustrator for a TV station in Pittsburgh, Pennsylvania, and thought I could use the time to sharpen my skills rendering quick studies of bar folks.

Before I knew it, we were hip swirling and arm waving to the disco beats of "YMCA" and "Copacabana." During that time I noticed a gorgeous, dark-haired man with his eye on me. I smiled, and he came over and introduced himself. His name was Michael Hanna. There was an immediate mutual attraction, and though I had no intention of starting a new relationship, I hardly hesitated when he asked me to write my number on his portrait. The next thing I knew he was gone.

The following day he called, and I invited him over to visit. Before long our conversation drifted to things spiritual. When he said: "*Righteousness strikes the harmony chords of truth, and the melody vibrates throughout the cosmos, even to the recognition of the Infinite,*" then and there I wanted to know more about this messenger and his message.

Later that week he introduced me to the Urantia Book. Reading the dust jacket alone, with its mighty quotes, enthralled and awakened my longings to know the truth of the cosmos. Michael and I became inseparable and, all these years and three children later, we still are. Never underestimate the power of those UB zingers!

MARK GREER: For years I felt that my mom's spirit was watching over me. My mom—a very intuitive, artistic woman—had died of stomach cancer when I was ten. Nine years later, my dad—a brilliant, humorous illustrator and ladies man—became very ill with lymphatic cancer. As the only child of two successful New York City artists, I knew my world would change dramatically if I lost my dad. Cannabis opened my teenage mind to possibilities and paths as well as providing relief from the mounting pressures of being an only child caring for an ill father.

In 1978, during my first year of college in West Chester, Pennsylvania, I was on a crusade to find truth—any truth—the deeper the better! I was into astrology, every branch of Christianity and many Eastern religions. I had gone from being a born-again Baptist to a Mormon. I used to jog a mile around my neighborhood late at night and have "conversations" with God. It was then, when I was 19, that I found the Urantia Book.

I had intensely devoured almost half the book when, having no one to validate my interest, I fell prey to the opinions of several Mormon friends. They said the UB was tainted, demonic, not for our eyes. When I joined the Mormon church, I was required to cast aside any books that were not officially sanctioned. Consequently the big blue book went up in smoke in the fireplace, along with a couple of dozen astrology, channeled and psychology-cum-religious-hip-hip-hooray books. My LDS experience ran its eventually disappointing course though two marriages, and two great kids from my first marriage.

At long last, eighteen years after my first encounter, I began to pick up Big Blue again at the Barnes & Noble. I would read it for hours then set it sadly back on the shelf, still locked in the guilt of someone else's dogma. I hoped hard that what I was absorbing wasn't a brilliant hoax. I continued to be open, and the unified, sultry poetry of concise expressions of truth seeped in deeply.

On New Year's Day 1997 I splashed out the $50 to buy my precious Urantia Book again. My suffocated spirit was insisting on room to breathe.

I'm ecstatic to say that today the UB is the most important book in my life. Not until 1998 did I finally break free of the chains of organized religion. I turned off my ego long enough to get to know myself and to learn that the kingdom was not some future reward, but was to be sought and experienced now!

PAUL DEFOURNEAUX: In 1978 I was working as an assistant to a plastic surgeon and had a promising career. We used pharmaceutical cocaine quite often in surgery and it was my responsibility to throw away what was left over because it was no longer sterile and could not be used again. Being raised Jewish, I could not let all of this possible money go down the drain, so I kept it and sold it to friends. Most of them were professional people with much to lose if they acted irresponsibly.

This went on until a friend got into trouble and sold me out to get out of trouble. I ended up doing thirty days on a six-year sentence and losing my license. Because I had money and an influential father, I did very little time in the prison system. Three days before I was to be released I was given a copy of the Urantia Book to read. The person who showed it to me had smuggled it out of the prison library and was going to take it home with him. He told me that this book had all the answers to all the questions about who we are and where we come from.

Once I started reading it I could not put it down. I told all my close friends about it but their reactions were disappointing. The book always stayed in my mind though, and remembering what Jesus said about not casting pearls before swine, it would be many years before I began actively promoting it again.

A few years ago I finally mentioned it to a friend who responded positively. I believe my guardian seraphim put us together, and now we are both active in the Foundation and study groups. I have realized that not everyone is ready for what the book has to offer, but when the time is right, and if I sense the person to be a good risk, I tell them about the book. I believe that soon this life-changing book will become widely known throughout the entire world.

DANIEL MEGOW: At the age of 25, in 1978, I got married. Three days after we returned from our honeymoon, my wife's ex-fiancé came over for dinner. He and I hit it off great. We started discussing science fiction. I was a sci-fi fanatic, reading just about everything in print on the subject. Soon talk turned to alien life, UFOs, angels, and religion. We were having one of those really great conversations when he said to me, "Hey, wow, man! I've got this really cool book I think you'd like."

"Far out, man!" I said, "What's it about?"

"Um . . . well, I don't know," he said. "I've never really read it."

"Uhh . . . then why are you telling me about it?"

"Well," he answered, "whenever I have a question about anything like outer space or angels or stuff, I go through the table of contents until I find something that looks like it might answer my question, and then I go read it, and it's great!"

"Okay," I said. "Who wrote it?"

"Whoa . . . like, these spacemen delivered it and put it in a bus locker in, like, 1935," he replied. "And then, about twenty years later, they busted open the locker, and there it was, man. So they just started publishing it. You gotta read it, really!"

At this point my interest was piqued, so when I asked where I could find one of these Urantia Books, he promised to send me one as a wedding present.

About four months later (two months after I had given up on him), I happened to be in my favorite bookstore looking for some new sci-fi. I was depressed because I'd already read it all. I started to leave, but instead of turning down the aisle towards the exit, I caught myself walking straight past it. I stopped to turn around, and there, on the bottom shelf, stuck in the corner, I saw . . . the Urantia Book!

"Whoa! That's that book by the spacemen!" I thought as I picked it up and opened it to the Foreword. I read the first page. "Hey, I like this!" I said to myself. "This might be fun!" Glancing through the table of contents, I spotted "Government on a Neighboring Planet" and quickly turned to read about the planet of the spacemen. It wasn't about the spacemen but it was kind of interesting, anyway. Finishing that paper, and still standing in the aisle, I wanted to see what the spacemen had to say about the Garden of Eden, so I began reading the next paper.

I stood in the aisle for the next three and a half hours reading all of the Adam and Eve papers. By the end of that time I began to doubt the spaceman theory and had an urgent need to know where this book had really come from. Not having the $28 to buy it, I snatched the white pamphlet from the inside cover to write to the Urantia Foundation to find out more about it.

I sent a letter off to them immediately, asking, "Where in the heck did this book come from, anyway?" The next day found me reading in the aisle of that bookstore for another four hours. (I replaced the pamphlet, by the way.) Every day I returned to read for hours at a time. When I finally went to the main library seeking the book, although there were twelve copies at that branch, I was dismayed to learn that all had been checked out. And while all of the other library branches carried Urantia Books, every single copy except one was checked out. I raced to that branch library like a madman and there it was! But when I carried that precious book to the check-out counter, I was told I could only keep it for one month, and then I'd have to wait for someone else to check it out before I could borrow it again.

"Double damn!" I didn't want to go through this again. "All right, I'm gonna read this thing in a month! Period!"

I became a man on a mission. Nothing was going to stop me from finishing that book. While some days I only spent eight hours reading (I had to take time out for work and sleep), often I would read for sixteen hours a day. I couldn't stop. I was addicted. My friends thought I had gone over the edge. Why would they think that? I'd found the answers to all of life's questions, for God's sake!

About three weeks later, I got a letter from the Urantia Foundation giving me the name of another reader in my area, Dick Prince. I called him immediately and found out about a Tuesday study group. It was Wednesday. I had until Monday to get the book back to the library. I calculated that if I only slept three or four hours a night I could finish it in time. Monday at 1 p.m. I finished the last page. I did it! I had conquered the world!

The next night's study group at the Princes' home was wonderful. Dick had a new UB I could buy for $13, and he said I could make payments on it. We read the beloved book and discussed it for two hours. I was home! I started reading my own Urantia Book from the beginning the next day. But this time I decided to take my time with it—at least six months or so. It took me five, but I was much more relaxed about it the second time around.

KATHLEEN VINSON: In the late '70s I was a manager for Pizza Hut. The area office secretary, a woman named Paula, was reading the Urantia Book on her lunch break one day when I came into the office to turn in some reports. I have always been an omnivorous reader, and always ask people what they're reading. When she said it was a book about God and spiritual things I became really interested.

"Who's it by?" I asked her.

"Uh . . . uh . . . angels, sort of," she stammered.

By now I was even more intrigued, and asked if I could borrow it. As I recall, she was able to lend it to me just long enough for me to read enough to convince me I had to get my own copy. I did so immediately, and the course of my life began to change.

From the time I was very small, I remember being convinced of God's love for me and the essential goodness and friendliness of the universe. My poor family was a mess; we were dysfunctional before it was "in" and before it was so named. Some horrible things happened to me as a child, but somehow I always knew that wasn't the way it was supposed to be.

One of my earliest spiritual memories is of roller-skating around my block at dusk and watching the stars come out, speculating whether somewhere among the stars there was another little girl looking out at me and pondering the same things. I would talk to God and wonder if I would ever know why I was created and what my true destiny, my purpose for being, was. Conventional religion never satisfied me. Years later, when I found the Urantia Book, not only did it confirm what I had always known about our heavenly Father, but it eventually supplied the answers to all of my questions.

PAUL HALL: It was 1978. My friend Doug's brother, who was going to the University of California at Berkeley at the time, gave Doug a book that he had been reading with others in the San Francisco Bay area. One night Doug introduced this book to my friend Bruce and me. The three of us—Doug, Bruce and I—had rented a motel room where we spent three days, armed with our UB, *The Egyptian Book of the Dead*, a Bible, Clyde Bedell's *Concordex*, and enough crank to keep us from falling asleep, trying to find in the Urantia Book where God lived.

At first I had a strong feeling that this book was authored by the devil, but it had so many answers to questions that I've always wondered about, that after three days I decided that this was not the work of the devil and it was not the work of any man.

Not knowing anything but what was written on the inside cover of the Urantia Book, I was off to the largest used book store to find a copy. I saw a new one behind the counter for $45. Too much for me. I searched from 8 a.m. when it opened until 5 p.m. when it closed, but I didn't find a used copy of the book. As I was leaving by the back door, a young woman with a large pile of books was struggling to get in. I helped her with the door, and as she passed I couldn't help but see this big blue book. She was arranging the books on the counter when I approached and asked her if that was a Urantia Book. She said yes, and sold it to me for $5.

It's really amazing that I still have that book today. One day it was sitting together with a *Concordex* in the back of a van, when we turned a corner too fast. Five gallons of paint went everywhere. The *Concordex* was a total loss, but the UB didn't have a drop of paint on it, although the two books were sitting one on top of the other in the back of the van. Just another miracle.

For a long time I was an isolated reader. It was a rewarding experience to find the book on my own, and then to come to believe by faith that it was what it claimed to be. But it's always nice to find other readers—I've met a few over the years.

BRUCE CARRIKER: In 1978 I was recovering from open-heart surgery that had been performed about three months earlier and I was back on speed, which is what had caused my heart problem in the first place. I was on a spiritual search, reading anything I could get my hands on. Tarot cards started to scare me because the death card kept reappearing. The *I Ching* was kind of cool because it sort of talked to me, but I started to get frightening readings from that oracle also. Theosophy seemed pretty interesting but I didn't seem to have the patience to meditate and see the astral realms.

This was my situation when I sat up all night one night rapping with my friends Paul Hall and Dougy. We had been talking about history and checking out the Bible, but somehow it seemed lacking. Then Dougy suddenly pulled out this big blue book that he'd had buried among his "tweeks."

He said his brother had given it to him and that it contained some weird history. Opening the book, I read the part about Paradise being the geographical center of infinity and the only stationary place in the universe. The hair on the back of my head stood up and I got kind of paranoid, but I was hooked. It took a while for it to change my life around, but the book finally won.

JOHN DUPREE: My father died unexpectedly when I was 13. I still remember him watching an obscure program on TV every Sunday morning. It featured a man talking about God and our relationship to him. Later, my brothers became involved with this man, who was training a group of people to prepare for the second coming of Christ. The group held many meetings and even used biofeedback to achieve a better communion with their indwelling spirit.

I recall my brother Pat mentioning that he'd perceived "another presence" at a meeting one time, but astonishingly he was told to ignore it by the teacher. This group was to become glorified upon Christ's return and help to establish a spiritual kingdom here on earth. Their beliefs about life after death—that we would all be together again with our earthly father in glorified bodies—gave me the strength to endure my father's death and to regard it as just a vacation he was on for a while.

Although I wasn't a member of this group, I desired to find my own way to prepare myself and others for this great impending event. Then, when I was 18, the Urantia Papers were introduced to me by my drawing instructor, Richard Hill, at the Atlanta College of Art. I readily accepted the truths from the beginning; the book helped to unify my understanding of the world of ideas presented in my classes, and to awaken me to my own spirituality.

That first year in art school stands out as one of the most memorable periods of my life. As I was being born intellectually and spiritually, this blue bible found its way into my hands almost every day. Many of the questions I had built up for years were answered in its pages. For instance, I was thankful to find out that there was no hell; having been raised a Catholic, hell was a constant fear of mine, and I could never really reconcile it with a loving God.

After many years as a lone reader, in 1997 I searched "Urantia" on the Web, and among over three hundred entries up popped www.urantia.org. That's where I found a listing for Hal and Lucille Kettell's Arcadia study group. Being with this group has changed my life, and has made me wonder why I waited so long to reach out to such a truth-loving fellowship.

I pray to find the way to God, to gain the courage and discipline to seek with a whole heart, and to be of loving service to other truth seekers or any being who needs me.

LAURENCE GWYNN: I was standing on the pier on St. Simons Island off the coast of Georgia, gazing at the lights dancing on the choppy ocean waters. I was alone and depressed—no, desperate. I was broke mentally and financially, my brain bleeding from self-castigation. I had searched for many years through the mystic strains of every major religion, searching—for what? Nothing made sense. I had spent sixteen years as a journalist, raising two daughters together with my wife. That was now shattered. After twenty years of marriage I was divorced and separated from my family. I had no job and no prospects. I had to begin all over again. I didn't think I could do it. At 42, my life was without worth.

The lights danced. Then the lights moved towards me. Through teary eyes I watched as the lights came before me. Then the lights moved into me. Yep. Right inside. I was enthralled. All my molecules were rearranged. That night, standing in the mist at the end of the pier, what looked like an upright white halo the size of a man appeared in front of me out over the water. An undeniable thought surged through me: "This is a promise that in time all will become clear. You do not need to understand it all at once."

Leaving the pier, I stopped at a Kentucky Fried Chicken place on the mainland to dodge the rain. Looking out from the portico towards the island, I saw a rainbow begin to form, framing the island. Then a double rainbow. Then large green and red bands between the rainbows. Then . . . edges of the rainbow on the right began creeping down through the trees, the telephone lines, the asphalt street. I noted the left edge was also moving down, until they linked and formed a perfect circle at my feet. I was transfixed. My thought was: "Oh, so *that's* where the pot of gold is!"

These phenomena can be explained scientifically. What was remarkable was their timing and the feelings I attached to them.

The next morning I found work on the back deck of a wooden shrimp boat that was leaving for the Tortugas, off Key West. That first night on the boat, far off the coast in the Gulf, I was trying to get used to the rigors of wet, rock 'n' roll, physically dangerous work. In the galley, an old, high-spirited guy with strange eyes and a thick Swedish accent pulled a big blue book out of his duffel bag. I glanced over his shoulder, reached over and took the book. He smiled at me curiously, as if he knew something I didn't. I looked at the titles. He never got the book back. I was home.

LIZ ENGSTROM CRATTY: Searching, searching, searching. I'd done the EST training, taken classes in witchcraft, gone to a wide variety of churches, participated in religious drug rituals, been rebirthed, listened to gurus, read books by the Enlightened Ones, had my Tarot cards read, my astrological chart done, the runes thrown, and still nothing clicked. I was living on Maui, in the middle of New Age crystalline weirdness, trying to find out my purpose in life and my location in the universe. There was only one thing of which I was absolutely certain, and that was that God existed. I had no model or concrete idea about that concept, but one look around me told me that my physical body, this society, this planet, certainly had an architect. This was no accident.

I went to work for an advertising agency as head copywriter in 1978. Tonia Baney was the art director. One day she breezed by my desk and dropped a copy of the Urantia Brotherhood's journal, *The Urantian*, on my desk. "Take a look at that when you have time," she said. I had time. Right then I had time. I can't remember what I read, but I do remember the feeling of excitement that grew in me as I read. Ten minutes later, I invited her to lunch and I said, "What is this?"

"Have you ever thought about the personality of God?" she asked.

I was floored. Personality of God?

"If he created it in us, then he must have one of his own, don't you think?" she said. "What do you imagine his personality attributes are?"

"Duh-h-h," I said.

"When you think of spiritual growth, you must think of growing more Godlike," she went on. "Who is your role model? Where is your destination?"

"Ahh, well . . ." I said, trying to look intelligent, and failing. I had no response. I'd never considered these questions. I'd always wanted to be a "better" person, but better than what? Where was my ideal, anyway?

On the way back to the office, we stopped by the local bookstore. I bought a copy of the Urantia Book, Tonia bought me a *Concordex* as a gift, and I have been a rabid reader ever since. I read randomly, haphazardly, for about a month, trying to get a handle, an overview of it. As I recall, I was a nightly imposition at the Baney kitchen table, enthusiastically discussing it with whoever happened to be in the room long before I had any idea what I was diving into. Eventually I started at the beginning and read the whole book on my own.

We began holding weekly study group meetings in Tonia's home. At first it was just Tonia, her husband Steve, and me, until the word got out and closet readers ventured forth to join us in worship and study. We experimented with a variety of meeting formats, then eventually read the entire book from beginning to end. It took us thirteen years, including a hiatus now and then, plus those nights when we would barely read a paragraph before engaging in spirited conversation that lasted the whole session. Sometimes one discussion would last two or three consecutive weeks.

I'll never be able to pay Tonia back for listening to her inner leading and placing that journal on my desk. But I can follow her example by consistently and lovingly placing spiritual concepts before my brothers and sisters. Now that I have an ideal, a destination, a goal, a vision of the ideal spiritual life—one of love, mercy and ministry—I have a true plan for living.

BRAD WORTENDYKE: In 1977 I was living in Bend, Oregon. I was in my twenties and had moved there from Portland. On the day I left Portland to move east, I ran into a severe snowstorm as I was approaching the Mt. Hood wilderness area. Driving was hazardous and, since I was in no hurry, I pulled off the main highway and stopped at a small grocery store. Inside I struck up a conversation with a young man named Brian, about my age, who was also moving to Bend. When he invited me to spend the night at his family's cabin to wait out the storm, I politely declined—wanting to, but somewhat suspicious of his friendly and hospitable demeanor. We exchanged pleasantries and said that we'd probably run into each other again. Brian was moving to Bend to attend community college, but was also an avid skier and intended to frequent Mt. Bachelor, the local ski area.

We became friends. Brian was a character who made strong and lasting impressions upon people—though not always positive ones. He was handsome, intelligent, and had long blonde hair down to the small of his back. In those days Bend was rather a redneck place, and a longhair could easily find himself harassed. Brian, however, didn't seem to be bothered or intimidated by anyone or anything.

Brian and I started skiing together. He drove an old pickup painted John Deere green and would swing by and pick me up en route to Mt. Bachelor. One day as we were riding along he handed me a large book and said, "You might like this." His copy showed signs of use and wear. This was my first encounter with the Urantia Book, riding shotgun with a friend between Bend and Mt. Bachelor, having a few minutes to kill before we set out on our skis.

On a number of subsequent rides, I looked through the book and was repeatedly awestruck. As soon as Brian realized the depth of my interest, he offered me a copy—his own second copy, virtually brand new. I accepted his generous gift with considerable appreciation.

What never ceases to amaze me is the impact and "staying power" the Urantia Book has had in my life. I consider myself a late bloomer in terms of learning to live responsibly. There were long stretches of time when I didn't pay heed to the teachings in the book. But in my late thirties I began to settle down and make some positive life changes. The book quickly became an integral part of my life, shaping and influencing every aspect of my being. The Urantia Book is truly a treasure, and I'm very grateful to have been blessed with the opportunity to benefit from it.

JOAN BATSON MULLINS: In 1977 I was living in upstate New York. I had been brought up as a Catholic, and had examined various other religious persuasions. Feeling a deep hunger for something more, I began to pray for a teacher. But I did not trust "gurus," nor did I wish to be associated with a cult. So I prayed for a teacher in the form of a book. I began searching libraries and bookstores. On occasion I would borrow a car and drive to different towns to visit bookstores, hoping I would somehow be led to the book I was praying to find. I bought mainly metaphysical books, but they were all disappointing to me.

One afternoon a friend dropped by to invite me to a party a few blocks from my apartment. I declined, but she persuaded me by saying,

"Joan, I know you are looking for a book. You should come to this party because the guy who's throwing it is an intellectual and has a huge personal library." As we walked I could feel my anticipation growing. We arrived at the party, and everyone was gathered in the kitchen. I immediately spotted the library just beyond, and barely paused to say hello as I made my way over to it. As I entered the first of two rooms of floor-to-ceiling books, my eye was drawn to a single volume across the room. I walked over, reached up, and took it off the shelf. It was the Urantia Book. As I sat down in a rocking chair and started skimming the contents pages, I stopped at the words "Thought Adjuster." I remember thinking, "My thoughts need adjusting." So I turned to that section and started reading.

Time seemed to stand still. I was so engrossed, I did not notice the host of the party was squatting beside me until he spoke. "That's an unusual book." I was so excited by what I was reading I blurted out, "Who wrote this book?" He referred me back to the table of contents and showed me the names of some of the authors of the various papers. He went on to explain that he was a scientist—a geologist—and that he had been given the Urantia Book by a hitchhiker he had picked up. He was astonished by the scientific content of the book, especially the geological content. He said the continental drift theory was especially advanced, and he could hardly believe someone had so clearly postulated the phenomenon of plate tectonics in 1955.

He told me that while on a trip to Chicago he decided to look up the "scientist who had written the book." At 533 Diversey Parkway he was surprised to find only "two old ladies" who told him there was no scientist, and no human author to meet. They said the names of the spiritual authors are in the contents pages of the book. They added that the book "speaks for itself."

"You mean there is no guru? No church?"

"No," he assured me, "just the book."

That was what I needed to know in order to openly explore it. As I looked at his earnest face, I was moved to ask: "Did you find answers about God in this book?"

He seemed startled. "Oh, no. I am an atheist. I keep the book because it is a phenomenon. You are welcome to borrow it if you wish."

Borrow it I did. After a few days of intense reading, I knew this was the book I'd been searching for.

LAMAR ZABIELSKI: Raised Catholic, I went through the hoops and was confirmed at age 14, in 1964. When I was 16 I volunteered at a hospital as a weekend aid to patients in the Candy Striper program. When I got in the van to go there, I discovered that all the other volunteers were girls. The coordinators didn't know what to do with a boy in the program because Candy Stripers wore dresses striped like a candy cane, so they gave me gray garb and called me a "Gray." Doing this work was fun, and it gave me an excuse to quit going to church.

While in the army in 1972, I had my dog tags changed to "no preference" as to religion. By then I considered myself an atheist. But EST ads got me looking for other ways to make sense of our antlike existence. I got involved in New Age studies, old-cult studies, numerology, astrology, and so on. But it wasn't until I learned to appreciate a flower and began to consider the wonders of nature that I switched from atheist to agnostic. Paths are many, but God is one.

Around 1977 I was sharing life with a dear woman in a Chicago suburb when she pointed to a big blue book in her library and said, "You should read that book." I looked at it and said to myself, "Yeah, sure—like I'm gonna read a book that big!"

A few months after that, I was visiting my older sister in Lexington, Kentucky. My brother Steve happened to be there at the same time, fresh from life in California and eager to share what he'd learned from the *Don Juan* books. One day he and I were in a bookstore when I noticed the big blue book sitting on the shelves. I pointed to it and said to Steve, "You should read that book." He looked at it and said, "Wow! This is the same book I saw on a ride while hitchhiking Highway 1 along the coast!" He bought it and really got into it. Over the next year his enthusiasm induced me, another brother, and our mother to read it.

I still remember the moment I accepted Jesus, as I was driving down a road at midnight on December 1, 1978, with dark softball fields on the right and houses on the left. Since then I have taken on life with the peace of one who knows the big picture.

KAREN PIKE: When I was a little girl I would have high fevers accompanied by a fantastic dream. The dream was always the same: I would find myself high above the planet looking out into space, knowing that there was an abundance of life out there and that even if life ended on the planet below me, life would still go on. I was supported from behind, being held high above the earth by a strong, light force. I never saw the face of the being who held me up there, but she emanated a powerful feeling of peace.

Looking down at the earth so far below and seeing myself hanging out in the middle of space, separated from my body, I would begin to feel anxious. The one holding me assured me that I was fine and that I could choose either to go out into the fullness of space or to return to earth. But the instant the anxiousness entered I was back in my bed, slammed back into my body with a tremendous force that left me disoriented, doubting the experience and wishing I was back in the embrace of my angel. This happened to me several times before I was five or six.

So many thoughts and feelings went through my mind during and after these episodes: confusion, regret, fear, uncertainty, doubt, longing, wishing—wishing from the moment I chose to return to earth that I had chosen to go on instead, yet feeling afraid to leave, feeling obligated to stay here.

The last time my angel came, she communicated to me that it was time to decide which way to go. I could go out into the stars or stay and live this life. I admit that fear was part of what made me stay. I was just a little kid and didn't quite trust what was happening to me. How could it be that I was floating above the earth? It couldn't be real, could it? So I chose to stay, and my search for God on earth began.

While growing up I was sort of a closet seeker. Not wanting to be led by the personal charisma of others, I read lots of religious books on my own. I picked out the parts that rang true to me and left the rest behind. I had many, many questions and found a few answers, just enough to keep me looking for more.

When I was 21 a friend and I were talking about the meaning of life. He told me about a book—I had never heard of it before—called the Urantia Book. I bought that big blue book and brought it home. I knew immediately that it was something different. I read the Foreword, looked over the table of contents, opened the book randomly, and read. I knew that once I started to study it my life would change in a big way, so I held off at first. I still had some issues to resolve in my life. For about six months I let the book gather dust under my bed. But through the mattress I felt the book drawing me, whispering to me.

Once I began reading it, the book became my constant companion. I would carry it with me to work, read it on the bus, study it at night, turn to it in times of despair, and come to love the truth it held. The gaps were closed, my questions were answered, my heart was filled, and the harmony chord of truth rang in my soul.

I studied the book on my own for nine years before I contacted any other students or attended my first study group. I wasn't sure what kind of nuts would be reading a book like this, but they turned out to be nuts like me and I felt at home with these people.

I like the idea of starting at the very bottom, as we do here on Urantia. We have more challenges, more chances to learn, more obstacles to overcome, and consequently a greater feeling of accomplishment when we succeed. I thank God that I've been given the revelation contained in the Urantia Book and I am honored to be a native of the "world of the cross."

KATHRYN PIKE: As far back as I can remember, I have always loved God—but on my own, not because I was taken to church and told to love God or else. My parents had already given up attending church long before I came along, but I heard vague things about God and Jesus and religion from other people and was left to draw my own conclusions. When I did go to church, I felt stifled by the routines and rules, and was filled with questions. As soon as I learned to read at age six, I devoured everything I could get my hands on, both at home and at the library. By the time the Urantia Book came into my life I had searched through many books in vain looking for a reason for being here on earth.

In the late '70s my daughter Karen heard about the Urantia Book and one day she brought it home. I read the list of chapter titles and authors, and when I saw that it contained a section on the life of Jesus, I realized almost at once that this was what I had been looking for. I didn't know what it could tell me about Jesus that I had not already read, but I was eager to find out.

The Urantia Book showed me Jesus in his wholeness. My heart broke with happiness to know that Jesus was real, alive, and always here—yesterday, today and tomorrow. The fact that he is so much a part of our universe, our world, our lives, and our future is sometimes more than I can bear to contemplate, but the book has made it all real for me.

I read my daughter's book whenever I could, but when she began carrying it with her all the time, I bought my own copy.

For almost twenty years I read the book alone, on an occasional basis. Only recently have I gotten in touch with local study groups. But the book has always been there for me when I've needed it. If you need the book, it will find you.

SANDOR SZABADOS: Jesus said: "Seek and you shall find." In 1973 I left the University of Colorado, where I had been working on my Ph.D. in philosophy. Although I had learned much, I found myself with many pieces of information that did not add up to a coherent and complete philosophical model. I believed in the existence of a God but I also believed in evolution, and during all the years in school I had found nothing that would tie the two together. Thirsting for answers, I left academia.

After a couple of years in Vail, Colorado, where I worked as a ski instructor, I went to Seattle and resumed my search. Shortly after my arrival, away from the plastic environment of the mountain resort I had named "The Disneyland of the Rockies," I began to think about Jesus. His simple, straightforward yet profound pronouncements in the New Testament began to appeal to me. But what really affected me was the way he had been put to death. As I visualized myself nailed to a cross, with large nails piercing my hands and feet, a terrible anguish would come over me. I would cry for long periods, unable to stop.

Moved by a tremendous compassion and love for this good and beautiful man whose life had been so cruelly ended, I began to attend Sunday functions in the churches of different Christian denominations, looking for ways to share what I felt inside for him. For three long years I joined in the singing and listened to the sermons with those attending, but to my great disappointment I did not find and could not share his spirit. This produced in me a deep feeling of sadness and loneliness.

In June of 1978, looking through the Yellow Pages, I called a non-denominational church and was told that they were reading from different religious books, at that time the Urantia Book. When I arrived the next Sunday morning, the congregation was beginning to read the section on page 192 titled "Morals, Virtue, and Personality." The initial words hit me like a bolt of lightning: *"Intelligence alone cannot explain the moral nature. Morality, virtue, is indigenous to human personality. Moral intuition, the realization of duty, is a component of human mind endowment and is associated with the other inalienables of human nature: scientific curiosity and spiritual insight."* I knew instantly that here was what I had been looking for and had finally found—or better yet, that had found me.

LUANN HARNEY: In 1977, at the age of 23, I was working for the government, going to the university in Lincoln, Nebraska, attending my favorite church, and hanging with all of my Christian buddies in my spare time. Prior to this, at the age of 17, I had attended Nebraska Christian College. My goal was to be a missionary, but I realized after a year and a half of Bible college that the only degree most women sought there was the MRS degree—to become the *wife* of a minister or missionary!

In February of 1977 I had a sudden attack of "I have to get out of Nebraska!" One of my friends suggested I move to Boulder, Colorado, where there was a university and an affiliate of my church to help me get settled. That still small voice inside kept repeating "Boulder," so there was my decision.

Driving through a blinding snowstorm on March 1, I found the youth hostel in Boulder. After registering, I walked outside to see the majestic Flatirons through the parting clouds. The sight of the snow-covered mountains sent my heart soaring, and I thought, "I am home."

I soon found a place to live and gained a new family of brothers and sisters in the Boulder Valley Christian Church. There I met a vivacious and outgoing woman and we became great friends. When she left for Boston a year and a half later, I was devastated. It was at her going-away party that I met the man who would replace her friendship and be the one to introduce me to the Urantia Book.

By that time I had somewhat forsaken the church. I still attended occasionally, but partying had become much more important to me. Besides, after being church janitor, secretary, youth group leader, and a member of the choir, I felt I deserved a break. I grew discouraged thinking that so many let so few do the work of the Lord. The man whom I'd met at the farewell party heard me talking of these things and said, "You ought to check out this book."

As I was skeptical of anything other than the Bible, time passed before I actually began reading the Urantia Book. In the meantime, this man became my boyfriend. A friend of his knew all about the Urantia Book, and I began asking him questions I had been piling up for years, which I'd been afraid to ask in church. I asked: Is there really a hell? What happens to all the people who don't believe in Jesus? What about Adam and Eve—is the Bible's account true? Our discussions would last for hours at a time. I finally decided that just reading this book would not be harmful to me.

I began with "The Life and Teachings of Jesus," and quickly read to where Jesus had reached the age of 23. I was blown away. I had never heard of the things I was reading; I didn't even know that Jesus had brothers and sisters. I already knew and loved the divine Jesus, the Son of God, but through the Urantia Book I began to fall in love with the human Jesus, the Son of Man. Still, I was not convinced that the Urantia Book was really true; I fought with my old mental tapes regarding the infallibility of the Bible—"Thou shalt not add to . . . ," etc. My old beliefs were being challenged.

I put the Urantia Book down for several months, and then a devastating thing happened. My father died in a truck/train accident on May 1, 1980. After the initial shock and grief, I was angry that God would take my father at this time of his life; he hadn't even been able to retire! Then I started reading the mansion world papers. The peace I felt after reading them convinced me that the teachings in the book were genuine. They were too beautiful to be anything else.

Since then I have grown enough in understanding to realize that God does not take our loved ones, that the accidents of time just happen. I know that my earthly father's soul had plenty of "mercy credits." I need not worry about his salvation. Most comforting of all, I believe that as soon as I get to the mansion worlds I shall see my father in person.

So many wonderful visions and insights have been mine since reading the Urantia Book. And the changes in my life! My dream of being a missionary is being fulfilled in a far different manner from what I had imagined. I'm now a missionary of the fifth epochal revelation, dedicated to spreading these incredible teachings. I never dreamed at age 17 that my life would be centered around a new revelation, nor that my missionary work would be to those living in the United States! May I always be available for the spirits to use, just as they used my good friend who had a going-away party.

BRUCE WHITE: As a child of ten I was involved in an accident during which I watched my life pass before me twice. The first presentation was choppy and partial, as though the reel hadn't been fully rewound and synchronized with the sound. The second showing was full, continuous and rapid.

Soon after this, my search for truth began. I could not find answers in the world's conventional religions.

Then one day, at a Spiritualist church, a friend who knew of my interests asked me to read the Urantia Book and give her my opinion. I said, "Sure." My quest was over in 1978. My experience exemplifies the promise: "Seek and you shall find."

SHARON SADLER: I wanted to believe in God, but could find no proof to support such a belief. After having read every book on religion and metaphysics that I could get my hands on, there I was, 33 years old, not really believing anything. My husband Barrie mentioned a book that a friend of his, Pat, had encouraged him to read. Barrie didn't like reading, so Pat suggested that I might like to read it. But I didn't want to read any more books—I'd had enough! One day, Barrie came home with Pat's Urantia Book. He set it down on the kitchen table and left it there. It sat there for days and days before I finally looked through it. Then I began to read little bits, and then more, and more. I've been enthralled ever since.

It is interesting how the book came into Pat's hands, in the remote, rural interior of British Columbia. Pat was a carpenter, and he frequently worked with Larry, another carpenter. Larry had been working in another valley, about thirty miles from ours, clearing a burned-out homestead in order to begin building another house. In the ruins of this house he found the Urantia Book, completely unharmed by the fire. After reading it and finding it to be an incredible revelation, he eventually gave the book to Pat.

It seems that the old homestead had been populated by Americans who had fled to Canada to avoid being drafted during the Vietnam War. Many of these people simply squatted on the land and later returned to the United States, so we assumed that they had brought the Urantia Book with them.

It is amazing that this book did not burn up in the fire. To me, it is just as incredible that it came to be in my hands. I had been searching for many years, and can only believe that these events are absolute proof of the work of our unseen friends doing the Father's will.

CRAIG ROHRSEN: In 1978 I was living in the San Francisco Bay Area and working for the Bay Area Rapid Transit District (BART) as a repair technician. At a wedding I met a woman named Debbie, a widow with a three-year-old son. We started dating. One evening, looking through her scrapbook, I found a photo of a flying saucer with a U.S. insignia on it. This prompted many questions, the first being, who took the picture?

Debbie told me that her father-in-law worked for NASA at Moffett Field in Mountain View, California. He worked in their prototype machine shop developing specialized parts. He was an avid photographer and always carried a camera with him. One day he went into a hangar, uncovered the saucer, and took the photo. Up to this point I hadn't paid much attention to flying saucer stuff, but now I had to find out what this was all about.

Next I talked to her father-in-law. He told me that the saucer was something the government had built as an experimental aircraft. I asked him if there were any other interesting things he had come in contact with. He proceeded to fascinate me with a story about a piece of material that he had been given to analyze. He knew nothing about the origin of the material, and after analyzing it, he found that it could not be cut, drilled or welded. It defied his analysis. Several years later he found out it was from a crashed UFO. Now my interest was piqued. I went out and bought several books on UFOs and began to ask people if they'd had any experiences with this phenomenon.

One day at work, a call came in from a train operator requesting a technician to troubleshoot a problem. So down I went, ready to provide assistance. I met the commuter train as it pulled into the station. I went up to the cab, a closed-off area in the front of the train where the operator sits and controls the train. The operator was someone I had talked to casually before. When I asked what the problem was he stated that there was no problem and that he just wanted someone to talk to.

We began to talk about UFOs. He smiled, his eyes got bright, and he started to tell me about an experience he'd had in Alaska: He and a buddy were at a party. They walked out onto the deck and looked into the sky. What they saw was a glowing disk about the size of the moon, almost directly overhead. It started moving so they jumped into a car and followed the UFO for several miles until it hovered over a large canyon. After a few minutes the UFO disappeared. The next day articles appeared in the local paper; thousands of people had seen the object, and the Air Force had detected it on radar. I asked him if that had been his only experience with UFO phenomena.

He thought for a minute, then stated that he was reading a really strange book that talked about life on other planets, alien contact, and lots of other weird stuff. He offered to lend it to me but advised me to read the introductory chapters on the Urantia Book found in its companion volume, the *Concordex of The Urantia Book*, first. I stopped by his house and picked up both books. I had plenty of time at work while waiting for trains to break down. So I started to read. Since then the Urantia Book has transformed my life.

KITTY AND TIM TRAYLOR: In the fall of 1978 my husband Tim and I were living in Arkansas in a town called Russellville, near the foot of the Ozark Mountains. Tim was working in construction. He and his friend Tony had formed a partnership in a business called The Wood Shed. I had chosen to be a stay-at-home mom for our two beautiful little daughters. We were on a tight budget.

Around October, we noticed that our water supply was getting low. We hired a well driller to drill a deeper well, but it was to no avail. We were charged $800 for a dry well. We had just enough water to flush the toilet occasionally and take a fast shower. For a long time, I hauled in water for drinking and flushing. It looked as though we would have to abandon the beautiful house that Tim had built for us. My state of mind at that time was sheer depression and worry.

I was an avid reader, always searching. I studied Edgar Cayce, Swedenborg, metaphysics, science fiction, Eastern and alternative religions. I had become disillusioned with the Baptist religion I had grown up with because I could not understand its dogmas, especially the doctrine of punishment in hell. How could a God of love subject his children to a torturous hell for eternity? I used to bug my Sunday school teacher with questions she could not answer. For example, where did Cain get his wife if Adam and Eve were the only two human beings?

One day I got to thinking about the books I'd been reading lately. I was upset that none of them were really satisfying. Tony had come over, and I said in a frustrated voice, "I just wish someone would write a book that would give me some answers!"

"I've heard of a book that might do that," he said. "I don't know anything about it, but I used to know some people in Montana who sat around under trees reading it. They said they had gotten a lot of answers from it." He gave me a haphazard spelling of the name of the book, and I was able to find it listed in *Books in Print* in my county library. The library did not have a copy, but said they would try to order it from the state library in Little Rock. In a few days they called to say that they had found one.

I was so excited, I went right away to pick it up. The size of the book was overwhelming, but I could hardly wait to start reading it. I keyed in on the chapters on Adam and Eve first, since this story had so fascinated me in my childhood. Then I hit the pages on life after death. I kept finding more and more good things. At the end of a month, I decided not to finish it, because if I did I might not buy it, so I returned it to the library.

In January 1979 I started working part time cleaning houses. With the extra money I'd earned, I went down to the only bookstore in Russellville and placed an order for a Urantia Book. When it finally arrived I became fully absorbed in it. It was speaking to my mind and my heart. Something within me told me that it was true. It made sense and gave some real answers. It made me realize that my life had meaning and purpose. The hunger in me was being satisfied.

I talked about this book continuously to Tim for about six months. He always listened but never once made a comment. One Sunday morning, to my surprise, I saw him reading it. What had I said to make him start reading? I realized it must have been my comment, "It makes science fiction seem real." Though not as much of a reader as I was, Tim enjoyed the occasional science fiction novel. He became so engrossed in the Urantia Book that he was keeping *me* from reading it. Eventually he bought his own copy.

The lack of water forced us to relocate. The episode with the well turned out to be a blessing in disguise. In 1980 we moved to Austin, Texas. The Urantia Foundation in Chicago referred us to other readers in our area, one of whom was teaching a class on the Urantia Book at a Unity church. We made that next Sunday service, and became regulars at study group meetings in Austin.

The book has been the best thing that has happened to us. We thank those who told Tony about the book and the person who was responsible for placing the book in the Little Rock library. You may not have thought, at the time, that your actions would make a difference, but your ripples have had far-reaching effects.

MIKE RAYL: Born and raised in Catholicism, by the age of seven, at the time of my first communion, I had already begun to doubt Catholicism's validity.

Several years later, in 1979, I was studying with the Ancient Mystical Order of Rosicrucians (AMORC) and living in the town of Lahaina on the island of Maui, when a friend, Linda Gray, started telling me about the Urantia Book. I was always a seeker of truth and I began to read it. For several years thereafter I also studied Unity and Science of Mind. I even converted to Mormonism in 1981, and after the Mormons confiscated my Urantia Book, I bought another one.

For a while I tried to incorporate into my philosophy a little from each of the different teachings. But as I continued to read the Urantia Book, more and more I realized that, for me, this was as close to the truth as anything I had ever studied. Being a mystic, this realization was not easy for me to accept. My greatest battle was in letting go of the concept of reincarnation, in which the Rosicrucians strongly believed. For years I struggled with this. I really loved the AMORC as it had taught me to be open to the truth. I had even moved to San Jose to be closer to the Order, and I studied at the Rosicrucian University.

But finally I arrived at an unswerving belief in the teachings of the Urantia Book. The book always spoke to my heart and it continues to do so.

Once, just for fun, I took a calculator and the calendar and checked the accuracy of the days and dates mentioned in Part IV. They all proved to be correct. That did it for me. Now the Urantia Book is the foundation for my beliefs. Even after having read it several times, the book is always fresh, new, alive, and awe-inspiring.

GREGORY MCCORMACK: I first read the Urantia Book in 1979. A friend had it sitting on his coffee table, the only book he owned. He suggested I read the Foreword, which I did.

I immediately realized the importance of the Urantia Book, if the claims in the Foreword—that the book was a revelation authored by divine beings—were true. Who would have had the audacity to write a 2,097-page book on the origins of everything? This question rang in my ears as I read the paper titles. I began to spot-read in various papers. Soon I didn't want to miss a thing, so I started from the beginning and proceeded to finish my first reading of the book.

I had to find out how this revelation had been produced and published. At the time I was living in Florida, but a training seminar took me to Chicago. What had been impossible to imagine six months earlier was now going to happen—I could finally visit the Urantia headquarters. I took advantage of an afternoon break to make the visit, feeling as though I were on a mission. The staff were friendly and willing to help me find answers to my questions. I do not recall the name of the gentleman I spoke to but I do remember and appreciate his patience and understanding. Today we are blessed with the Internet. I have found explanations for the origins of the Urantia Book on the Web consistent with my memories of that meeting.

STEVE SHINALL: One night, back in the late '70s, I found myself at a party surrounded by swirling smoke and the din of loud music, laughter and voices. Not really knowing anyone except the person I had come with, and being somewhat shy in those days, I eventually found myself sitting alone on a couch. As I sat there my eye was drawn to a big blue book resting on the middle of the coffee table. I reached over, picked it up, opened it at random, read a couple of paragraphs, and then put the book back. I remember thinking, "What did that book just say? 'Thought Adjusters'?" So I picked it back up, read a little more and put it back down. "Is this supposed to be a novel?" I wondered.

Although I'd always been an avid reader, I usually didn't read in the midst of a roaring party. But I kept being drawn back to the book. This process of reading for longer and longer periods of time continued until it was time to go home. My date was not amused that I had spent the evening reading while everyone else socialized.

About a week after coming into contact with the book I had a vivid dream in which I found myself in an old-fashioned sleeping shirt, down on my hands and knees clinging to a homemade raft, the kind you would see in Tom Sawyer movies—logs lashed together with rope. I was surrounded by fog and pelted by a hard rain. Thunder and lightning crashed all around and waves threatened to capsize me at any moment. I'd never been a good swimmer, so this dream had all the makings of an old-fashioned nightmare, except that it wasn't—I was smiling! Everything in the dream was in black and white—the fog, the water, the clothes, the sky, the lightning—everything, that is, except this blue book that I was carrying in one hand.

When I awoke the next morning I recalled riding out the tempest on the flimsy raft and how that blue book had stood out so vibrantly against the varying shades of gray. Even more memorable was the fact that I had not been afraid. Hell, I'd been exhilarated!

Within a day or so of having the dream I happened to have a conversation with a guy named David. Although David and I are now close friends, back then we knew each other only because of my friendship with his brother. David was not one to whom I would normally have related my dream life, but for some reason, on this particular day I began to tell him about my vivid dream and how I had felt so safe with this Urantia Book under my arm. He listened patiently and then replied with a smile, "Yeah, that's a really strange book. I have a copy if you'd like to borrow it."

When he said that I felt as if electricity rushed through me. I still wonder, what were the odds of running into someone whom I would tell about my dream, who also happened to have a copy of the Urantia Book to lend me? I took him up on his offer.

Soon I recognized that what I had been looking for all my life, I had found. I literally wept with joy. The book struck a chord that resonated deep within my soul. Since then I've come to realize how blessed this world is and how blessed we, as individuals, are. Progress is the watchword of the universe. From those of us to whom more has been given, more is expected. I've even learned how to swim.

Part VII

1980-1986

BARBARA JO HOWELL: God killed his own son? Even as a young child I couldn't believe that. When I was about 16, my best friend Shelly and I would walk aimlessly around Julia Davis Park in Boise, Idaho, where Jesus freaks with their happy faces would approach us.

"Have you been saved?" they'd ask us.

"Huh? Does it look like we need to be saved?" we'd reply. "Do you see us hanging off the side of a cliff by our fingernails? No? Then I guess we don't need to be saved."

"Jesus loves you!" they'd call after us.

"Yeah, right."

But at home I'd secretly open my Bible, searching in vain for something to make me feel better. Those awful years from the seventh to the twelfth grade were the worst time of my life.

At 18 I moved up to the Idaho mountains, got married, and soon after had two children. But not having had a lick of guidance or discipline as a child left me totally unprepared and inept. The marriage didn't last long.

In the summer of 1980 I was a 26-year-old, long-haired, country-hippie girl, divorced a year and living in the midst of wheat and hay fields with my children. The nearest town, with a population of only five hundred, was about thirty miles from our little old house. I was moody and spiritually restless. I also had a habit of smoking homegrown pot first thing in the morning and drinking beer as the day wore on. We were surrounded by the incredible beauty of the mountains, and I remember many times thinking, "The world is such a beautiful place—but what's the point?"

I'd been fighting insecurity and depression ever since I was a young teen and had finally reached the end of my rope. I realized that because I was a mother I could no longer afford to be depressed. My children were two and four, and I could not stand the thought of their being raised by a miserable wretch. For their sake, something had to change.

And so, one sunny afternoon when the kids were taking a nap, I went out in the yard with my Bible and tried again to find something within its pages that would help the world make sense. I opened it randomly and read what basically said, "God loves *us*, but he doesn't love *them*. He told me to go kill them. So I did. In fact, I wiped out the whole village, including the children. Now God is pleased and I am blessed."

"This is it?!" I wailed. With hope dashed to pieces I closed the Bible and started crying. "Now what?" It was then that I had my first real talk with Jesus. I remember it well. Sitting there in the grass with tears streaming down my face, I looked up to the sky and pleaded:

"Jesus, are you real? Please be real, because I don't know what I'll do if you're not! I kind of think you might be real because people still talk about you after all these years. Please—if you *are* real—I need help. I need answers. Can you give me something that makes sense? This Bible just doesn't cut it for me."

The next day, out of the blue, my ex-husband Craig came by and said he would take the kids for the weekend. This was unusual because for the past year he had been a very busy boy—busy partying and dating, that is, trying to fill the emptiness in his own life. Not often had he given up a weekend to relieve me of child duty.

So, whoopee! It was my turn to kick up my heels! I could hardly wait to get to town and dance my frustrations away. I prettied myself up, threw a six pack of beer in the car, and headed for The Ace Saloon. On the way there I guzzled at least three of them beers to give me the confidence I needed to walk through the door.

Back then The Ace Saloon was a happening place—noisy, stinky, smoky, and with a whole lot of slurring, stumbling drunks whooping it up. I made my way past gangs of cowboys and loggers and found a place at the bar. There I downed another beer or two and soon found myself engaged in conversation with a woman who seemed ill at ease and out of place.

Did I say "engaged in conversation"? Actually, we were yelling into each other's ears trying to be heard over the barroom din. She turned out to be a proper Nazarene who, on the street in broad daylight, probably wouldn't have bothered speaking to a heathen wench like me. I doubt I would have spoken to her either, had I not had a belly full of beer. I surmised that her only reason for being there was to keep the hussies from pawing her handsome husband, the singer in the band.

She didn't know it, but she was instrumental in changing my whole life. With the band playing loudly and the crowd babbling uproariously in the background, this woman for some reason blurted out an invitation to a "Urantia study meeting" at her home the next evening. She quickly added that she had nothing to do with it—it was her husband's deal.

I couldn't have cared less whose deal it was because I didn't know what the heck she was talking about. I remember making a smart-aleck remark about the name Urantia. "U-a-*rancha*? I thought y'all were farmers! Ha!" Then I was off to the dance floor to stomp and wiggle with the rest of the inebriated natives.

I probably slept most of the next day, but with the kids still at their dad's house I had one more evening of freedom, and no way was I going to waste it. So I showed up at the Nazarene's home for the "ranchers" meeting, not having a clue as to what it was about, just wanting to fill what would otherwise be a boring and lonely evening.

I think there were about five people plus me. The woman who had invited me stayed in another room the whole time. She meant what she'd said the night before about it being her husband's deal. She obviously wanted no part of it. Her husband began to read from either "Religion in Human Experience" or "The Real Nature of Religion."

All it took was one paragraph and I felt tears come into my eyes and my heart beat faster. I probably had a stunned and stupid look on my face, too. As he continued to read I became completely overwhelmed. It was all I could do to keep from dropping to the floor in front of these people and crying out loud to God. I sat with my hands in my lap, not uttering a word—but inside I was a blubbering mess. "This is the truth! You've answered me! You're real!"

The next day when Craig brought the children back to me I piled them into my orange Toyota Corolla and drove the hundred and fifty miles to Boise so I could find a Urantia Book. I didn't care how much it cost. I would have sold the car to pay for it. I found it in the second bookstore I checked, then drove right back home and began devouring it as if I'd been starved.

God became a reality and life finally made sense. I could begin to understand what it was all about and where I fit in. I had answers and no longer needed pot and beer. The world became enchantingly new again, just like it was when first discovering it as a child. Yes, I finally understood what those crazy Jesus freaks meant when they said "born again." I was one of them.

And that's how my new life began. I'm grateful to the angels who've guided my footsteps. Over the years I continue to say "thank you" for this gift of revelation.

ROB ESTRADA: My mother was a devout Catholic and I was an altar boy and even worked as a receptionist in the rectory. I began to question my conventional Catholic beliefs when I was about 13. I remember becoming skeptical about what I had been taught about God, the devil, heaven and hell. Quite frankly I just didn't buy it, and thus searched for more. At about this time my father gave me a book by Erich Von Däniken, *Chariots of The Gods*. His theory about aliens visiting this planet really made sense to me.

I couldn't get these new concepts out of my mind. I just wished that I could find some source that would answer all of my questions and put my doubts about Deity to rest. Then one summer afternoon, at the age of 15, I fell into a deep sleep. In my dream I was confronted by a being of light. This being was feminine and I could communicate with her through instant thoughts. I asked her why I was here and what this was all about. She asked me if I was ready to know these things, and in my naiveté I said yes. In an instant I was transported at tremendous speed, passing countless celestial spheres and bombarded with more knowledge than I could comprehend. At that point I woke up drenched in sweat.

Soon after having this dream I went to a party with my older sister, who was in college at the time. There I met a graduate student, Dave Vaccaro. Dave and I got into a deep discussion about spirituality, religion and the universe. This guy couldn't believe he was having this conversation with a 15-year-old. Before leaving the party, Dave recommended I read the Urantia Book. The next week I went straight to B. Dalton and ordered a copy, even though it was quite a financial sacrifice.

When I got the book I first had to read the section on the Lucifer rebellion. These papers answered so many questions for me, I knew I had found the truth. Throughout my late teens and early twenties the Urantia Book acted as a moral and spiritual reference guide in my life, though for about ten years afterward it mainly sat on shelves or in boxes and collected dust.

Then in 1998 I went through some rather dramatic life changes and once again sought out the solace of Urantia truths. Since then the Urantia Book has reaffirmed my belief in Jesus and has helped bring a general peace into my life.

CHRISTILYN BIEK: I grew up in Ghana, West Africa, the daughter of medical missionaries. While my mother had wanted to be a nurse and a missionary since she was a child, my father was motivated—following an epiphany he'd had during college—to become a doctor and serve in developing countries. Though he was a passionate truth seeker, he was not particularly sold on Christianity. He had problems with Christian theology, including the concepts of the Trinity and the atonement doctrine. He was a troublesome missionary and was frequently at odds with the rest of the mission community.

I was around six years old when, on furlough in the United States, my dad gave a talk at Rev. Meredith Sprunger's church in Indiana. That night, Dad and Meredith stayed up into the wee hours of the morning discussing religious issues. My father was surprised to find Meredith so supportive of his questioning; rather than debating him on many points, Meredith was agreeing with him. At some point after midnight, he gave my dad a copy of the Urantia Book to take with him. Dad devoured it in about a month, barely taking time out to eat or sleep.

My mother began reading it after my dad started; she was impressed but a bit skeptical, being a Christian missionary who did not have problems with the theology. Then, after returning to the States, she attended her first Urantia conference. There she encountered hundreds of intelligent, well-educated people who all believed this strange stuff. Perhaps this book really *was* what it claimed to be. She has continued reading and studying it to this day.

I was first exposed to the teachings after the death of my baby brother. When we asked our parents about death and what happened after, my brother and I were given answers from the Urantia Book. They were very satisfying answers. The mansion worlds sounded like paradise to me. I wanted to go right away, but Dad explained that there was nothing more important than growing where we were right now. Everything had its time. As long as we really wanted to live on and know God, we would—it was assured. The decision was ours. Nothing bad could ever befall us, in the eternal sense, as long as we had faith in God.

I will forever be grateful to my biological father and my Father in heaven for the dual blessings of growing up without fear of God and without fear of dying. What a gift! If that were all I got from the Urantia Book, it would have been a great gift, but there has been so much more. I've had the good fortune of being part of a family that can discuss and share the book's teachings. Even when things are tense, we know there is a higher way and can call upon our spiritual resources to help us resolve our conflicts.

When my family left Africa, my father left some Urantia Books behind. Imagine our surprise twenty-five years later on our return to Ghana to find such a large readership there and such enthusiasm! My dad was disappointed that the other Western missionaries we encountered in Ghana were not interested in the book; he he never expected that the Ghanaians would be the ones to become so enamored of it.

A little side note: One day my folks ran into some former missionary friends, Betty and Ralph Zehr, at a Urantia conference. "Oh, my!" my parents exclaimed, "What are you guys doing here? Where in the world did you hear about the Urantia Book?" "From you guys," the Zehrs responded. "We were warned about you and that big blue book when we first arrived in Ghana. It wasn't until years later, after we had been reading the book for quite a while, that we realized they must have been referring to the Urantia Book."

After I finished college, where I studied comparative religion and art, I decided to read the book for myself. Because I had been raised on the teachings, I never had that *aha!* experience that others talk about. I guess I took the book for granted because it had always been part of my life. I moved to Boulder to attend the Urantia school and to become involved with a community of Urantia Book readers. One by one my family members joined me here and we now enjoy a wonderful extended family and community.

In 1999 I attended the Parliament of the World Religions in South Africa and that is where I met the man who would become my husband. He was one of two listeners critiquing my "Introduction to the Urantia Book" before I presented it to a group in Cape Town. In a challenging question-and-answer session, he forced me to dig deep for personal answers. That same night he asked me to marry him. It was partly our Urantia discussion that made me decide to give the relationship a chance. To my surprise, he then read the book in about six weeks. I now look forward to having a family of my own and hopefully adding to the roster of third-generation readers.

LUC LACHANCE: Three times in my early life I was confronted with the terrible reality of death. From the ages of 15 to 50, I searched everywhere for an explanation for life, suffering, and death. I read a huge number of books and essays by the great writers of the world. I came to believe that of all the literature I'd read regarding life, love and society, the most important were the four Gospels.

Then, in 1980, on a friend's recommendation, I read the Urantia Book. I was amazed. No book up to that time had been able to answer so many of my questions. No book was as universally complete and logical, as instructive, as well-written, as precise, as exciting, as exalting, as motivating, as stimulating, as galvanizing, as inflaming, and, most of all, as full of love and hope and fundamental truths as the Urantia Book. I found to my astonishment that the book was revealing the sublime plan of the Father—*my* Father—concerning all of mankind and the whole universe. And the Urantia Book did not contradict the four Gospels in any way; on the contrary, it clarified, simplified and reinforced their sublime teachings. From now on, life made sense, suffering could be explained, and death itself was no longer senseless.

I read the Urantia Book a second time, a third time, and a fourth, always with an ever-growing passion. Save the four Gospels, I had never been able to read the same book so many times with the same electrified zeal. For me there was only one explanation for this incomprehensible phenomenon: I had in hand the greatest revelation that had been given to mankind since Jesus! I will never cease reading and learning from this great book.

PIERRE GIRARD: It was February, 1980. My father had died a few weeks earlier and I was recovering from a traumatic separation from a sect I'd been involved with. The guru believed himself to be the most powerful spiritual ruler on the planet, an incarnation of Satan, and claimed to head a corps of forty other physical beings.

Searching for some spiritual help and support, I decided to buy a Bible. In a bookstore on St. Denis Street in downtown Montreal, I found the Bible I wanted. At this same bookstore, I also saw a photocopy of *La Cosmogonie d'Urantia*, the name given to the first French translation of the Urantia Book. Due to litigation over that version, the Urantia Foundation had retired it from the market, and to satisfy the demands of French-speaking truth seekers, a Urantia Book lover had made photocopies of the French version and was selling them. When I remembered that this guru had told his followers not to read the Urantia Book, I decided to buy the photocopy of the book as well as the Bible. I paid $75 for it, but didn't consider that expensive because I'd heard that some copies were going for $200 or more.

At home, I started to read the Adam and Eve papers. This was the beginning of my love affair with the book during this difficult and painful period in my life. I was 31 years old and had already come to realize on my own some of the book's important teachings. For me the Urantia Book was a response. It supported my own personal faith, belief, and experiences.

I believe the Urantia Book will become the most important book of spirituality on earth once we finally understand the lesson it has given us regarding personal free will—a gift from God to all of his children. May we live and grow under the reign of love and truth.

MICHAEL MARK: The Urantia Book found me in April of 1980, in Southwest Oregon. Unlike many other readers, I had not been a spiritual seeker. In fact, I had never even looked at a book about spirituality. If anything, I was a seeker of pleasure and ease, self-centered and self-willed, and moving in a downward spiral in many ways. It seemed to me at age 27 that I was a cosmic orphan, just trying to muddle through life with no particular connection to God and no thought that there might be any spiritual source of help or guidance.

For about ten years, whenever I visited the home of my friend Chris, I saw a copy of the Urantia Book on the coffee table. The book was bound in deerskin with a homemade, Indian-style beadwork design on the cover. For some reason, it never occurred to me to look through the book, and Chris never mentioned a word about it—or God or Jesus—in all that time. But I had always admired Chris. He often taught me things by his observations or by asking me questions. Looking back, I believe it was his worshipful approach to problem-solving that most attracted my attention, but at the time I only vaguely sensed that he might possess some wisdom that I didn't.

Finally, one day and apparently out of the blue, I asked Chris if I could borrow the spare copy of the Urantia Book on his bookshelf. I was at a low point in my life emotionally, but I don't really know why I asked to see it then. He still had never said a word about it! Several weeks later, while the two of us were hiking in the woods, he asked me, "Michael, have you been reading the Urantia Book?" I jokingly replied that I believed my Thought Adjuster had been very busy lately.

On May 18, 1980, it suddenly dawned on me what I'd been reading. It was the exquisite beauty of the language as much as the content that appealed to me at the time. Later that day, the nearby Mt. St. Helens volcano erupted. The birth of religion in my soul had been a turbulent one, and I quickly assigned my spiritual rebirth as the probable cause of the volcano! Later I came to my senses. Anyway it was a good metaphor for the cataclysmic upheaval taking place in my life. It took me about seven months to read the book cover to cover.

Finding the Urantia Book has put me at the end of many of my old problems, but at the beginning of many new and challenging ones. It has caused me to spend the past twenty years striving to reorder my thinking, reassess my values, and re-establish my priorities, in the hope that I can be a benefit to others the way my friend Chris was to me.

HELEN MARKELLOS: The Urantia Book came to me in answer to a prayer I had made twenty years before. It hadn't come earlier as I probably wasn't ready for it.

I had grown up in an orphanage in England. By 1960, when I was 20, I was living alone in London in a bed-sitter flat. It was Christmas day and people all around me were celebrating. As I lay alone in my cheap room, feeling very sorry for myself, I began to pray. "Why am I alone? Why don't I have a family like other people? Give me someone to love me, please, because I am so lonely!"

After my crying stopped, I sat there listening to the people downstairs laughing and happy. I called out to God, "Do you exist? Why are you so cruel? What did I do? You don't love me! I don't even believe you are hearing me! It's all a pack of lies!" When I calmed down, I said in a small voice, "If you exist, then move something in this room. Show me you hear me." Suddenly I felt a hand on my head, stroking it slowly. I jumped up and looked around but there was only the wall behind me. The stroking continued for a few seconds, then I felt a warmth inside of me. I knew somebody or something was near me in that room. I fell asleep.

Many years later, in 1980, I was married with four children and living in Greece, in the town of Corinth. It was summer. One day my English friend Pat, who also lived in Corinth, brought an American friend of hers around. Her name was Saskia. They had recently met on a three-day bus trip from London to Athens, and Saskia was now staying with Pat for a while. We all became friends. One evening Saskia began telling my Greek husband George the history of the Greeks, where they came from and who they were.

"Where did you get that information?" he asked, as he had never heard it before.

"From a book that I read," she replied. "I'll let you borrow it."

And so she gave us the Urantia Book. That first night I sat up all night reading about Jesus. I was shocked, as it was just what I wanted and needed. From the minute I started reading I couldn't put the book down. It took me three months the first time. I couldn't wait for the children to leave for school in the morning so I could read it during the day when I should have been doing my housework. I'd go to bed at nine o'clock just so I could read it, and I'd still be reading at three in the morning. I could hardly grasp my good fortune. It was too good to be true. There it was, all my questions about life answered in one book!

Every day I would put the baby in her stroller and walk down to visit Saskia so we could discuss what I'd read the night before. We'd take long walks around the town, talking about midwayers, Solitary Messengers, angels and Jesus. I will always be thankful to Saskia for being my messenger and bringing such joy to me, for delivering the good news all the way from America right into my own home in Greece.

It is now twenty years since I got the book, and even on my fourteenth reading of it, it is just like reading it for the first time. It has given me hope and comfort through this life. Now I know that I *do* have a family—the whole heavenly host! I belong at last!

I have tried to tell my friends about it, but they are either too busy or not ready for the great news. I have given one to each of my children, as it is worth more than all the treasures on earth. The Urantia Book tells us why we are here and where we are going. What more can we ask?

ED HEALY: I was living in Venice Beach, California, in 1981, when I received a call from a female friend in Northern California. She told me I needed to read the Urantia Book.

I had recently helped my neighbor Isaiah Compton move. In his late nineties, Compton was a psychologist who had worked with the famous Viennese psychiatrist, Alfred Adler. I knew Compton had a lot of books, since I had recently packed and unpacked them for him. He was a wise man, wiser than the dopers I usually talked to. I asked Compton, "Do you have the Urantia Book?"

He pointed to the walls that were full of shelving and replied, "It's up there somewhere."

I looked and noticed the *OAHSPE* book. I took it down and we started to read it. It seemed quite remarkable. After some time I found the Urantia Book. I opened it and turned to Compton, saying, "It's got Jesus in it!"

He said, "Yeah, that's why I've never read it."

Compton had been born of Jewish parents on a ship from Amsterdam; and while he did not consider himself religious, he was a spiritual man. I was born Irish Catholic. The last thing I wanted to hear about was virgin births, atonement doctrines, and so forth.

Nevertheless, I read Compton one paper a night until we finished the book. I could hardly believe my ears, so fantastic did I think the whole book was. Compton died within five years, but before he died he said to me, "You don't know how painful it is to me about my people, but I completely believe that book."

We never finished reading *OAHSPE*. The Urantia Book was the entire focus of our meetings after that momentous initial reading.

ENNO BENJAMINS: Early in 1982, during a phone call with a guy named Frank who had placed an ad for musicians which I was answering, I first heard those memorable words: "Have you ever heard of the Urantia Book?"

"The what?"

From that moment on, my life has been ignited by something so powerful to me, yet so frustratingly unrecognized by others. It would be many years before I would have the experience of passing this "gift of gifts" to someone else. And then, to my surprise, it would be to the people nearest and dearest to me, but that's another story.

Before this blessed event occurred in my life, I had been searching for several years for an explanation for my misery. You see, from my youth I had been imbued with the idea that I was to be great. I was going to ROCK this world. I was good at school, earned top grades, and performed well in athletic endeavors. I also found that I could play the hell out of most musical instruments. And when I entered high school, I couldn't help but notice that girls paid an unusual amount of attention to me. Oh, what a life it was going to be!

Well, here's what happened: Three months after graduation, my girlfriend became pregnant. One month later we were married. Although this was far from disappointing—even at the time I considered it a blessing—I couldn't let go of the feeling that *I* hadn't made the decision to marry—*Beelzebub* had! I still needed to find a way to flex my world-rocking muscles, so off I went on my search for rock 'n' roll superstardom, which led to that fateful telephone call.

Frank (I don't know what became of him) started telling me that this book explained that our planet was known in the universe as Urantia, that it was part of a system of worlds, that this system was part of a bla-bla and this bla-bla was part of a bla-bla-bla and all of these bla-blas were part of an even greater bla-bla-bla.

"Hold it! Hold it!" I interrupted him. "Who wrote this book?"

He skirted the question, then continued with the bla-blas.

Now my heart was pounding. "So, do you mean this book is from aliens who are going to land on earth and solve all our problems?"

"Well . . . ," he responded vaguely.

Now I had to see this book. We agreed to an audition, and I was sure I had finally found the rock band of my dreams. It wouldn't be long before the world knew how great a musician I was.

I had already come to accept "salvation through the blood of Christ," but it took no great intellect to see that a lot was left wanting in that concept. I often wondered, where is the rest of the story? In a moment of true meekness I might have thought to myself, "If God is truly all-knowing and all-powerful, he ought to be able to find a way to get the *real* information to us!"

After my audition, I asked Frank if I could see "that book." He acted surprised and handed me his extremely weathered copy, with the front cover and several of the title pages missing. I started thumbing through it: "The Central and Superuniverses," "The Local Universe," "The

History of Urantia," "The Life and Teachings of Jesus." *"The Life and Teachings of Jesus"*? My eyes nearly fell out of my face. I began to scan the Jesus papers and to my delight and astonishment there it was: his childhood. And it was presented authoritatively, in plain English—no mumbo jumbo—with dates, times, and places. The pit of my stomach started to burn. I was as "high" as I could be.

Strangely, six months passed before I went in search of my own copy. But those six months were spent with my feet gliding along as though suspended above the ground. I wanted to savor the moment—a real miracle in my life. An all-knowing and all-powerful God *had* found a way to get this information to me; I'd prayed for it and he'd answered me.

When I could hold out no longer, I began calling used bookstores to see if they had a copy. I assumed it could only be found in a used bookstore because Frank had bought his at a local swap meet. A few days later I located a copy, a first edition in fair shape. Whoever had it before me had marked it up with red ink. It cost $15. I've since bought many other new Urantia Books, but that first book is special to me. I feel genuinely honored to have it in my life.

See you all sooner or later on the way to the super stars!

ROBERT O'GUIN: During my youth I was wild, daring God (if there was one) to show himself to me. And if there were a God, I could not understand how he could allow the oppressive conditions existing on this planet. In my mid-twenties life brought me to Catalina Island, twenty-six miles off the coast of Southern California. There I met a woman, got married and had children. But I decided I needed more answers to life.

I studied various religions, became a vegetarian, chanted, meditated, practiced yoga, and became a Christian. I studied the Bible voraciously; it answered many of the questions I had at the time. I knew Jesus was the answer, but I sensed there was more. I wanted to know as much as there was to know. I wanted the truth. About that time a thought came repeatedly to me: "You shall know the truth and the truth shall make you free." I did not know then that this expression was from the Bible, but it stuck in my mind. Eventually I became a deacon, an elder, and then a minister in the church. Ah! Things were good then—a happy marriage, children, a good job, and the church.

We were the ideal American dream family—or so I thought.

Then my wife tired of marriage, said *sayonara*, and left me with the kids. Arrrrgh! At that point I needed the truth, *all* the truth, more than what was in the Bible. But where was this truth?

Around 1981 I found myself in an old, rundown bookstore in Santa Monica. I was browsing the shelves when an older, bearded gentleman jumped down from the loft and said, "I have what you want." I just looked at him. He led me to the rear of the store, pulled a book from the shelf, and handed it to me. I opened it, read four or five sentences, and said to myself, "Yes!" The book cost about $20, which seemed expensive, but I bought it. I was on autopilot.

When I first began reading the Urantia Book I could handle only one or two pages at a time before needing to sit and contemplate what I had just read. I thought, "Wow! This is either the greatest book ever written or the biggest fraud perpetrated on man." The first months of reading were exhilarating. I was several feet off the ground most of the time. All the answers I had sought were there. I loved this book.

In 1982 there were no study groups on Catalina Island. I often telephoned Julia Fenderson in Culver City on the mainland. She was my link to other readers. A few years later, I returned to Santa Monica searching for the old bookstore. Alas, it was no longer there, nor could anyone in the area remember it or the bearded man who introduced the book to me.

AL ALDO: In 1982 I was interviewing for a job. The interviewer remarked that I was "a very spiritual person" and began telling me about strange beings such as secondary Lanonandek Sons and this unusual book called the Urantia Book. He further claimed to be able to dematerialize and re-materialize in crowds for the purpose of finding people. I wasn't sure what to make of this man, but I needed this job—for which I was uniquely qualified—and went back to his office with him after the interview.

Left alone in his office for a while, I couldn't help noticing a large blue book sitting on the table in front of me and, sure enough, it was the Urantia Book. I picked it up and flipped it open to page 891. At the top of this page it read: *"Presently the Sicilian land bridge submerged, creating one sea of the Mediterranean and connecting it with the Atlantic Ocean.*

This cataclysm of nature flooded scores of human settlements and occasioned the greatest loss of life by flood in all the world's history." I was astounded by this casual statement about major events of which I had never heard before.

Seeking to learn the date of this amazing geographic event, I read page 890 as well, but found no information. So, I began backtracking, finding the first date reference on page 887. I skipped around in the book and read a variety of different papers. By then, I was hooked on the Urantia Book, considering it a work of history.

In October 1982 I attended a mini-conference of Urantia readers in Fishkill, New York. At that time I still thought of the Ubook as a history book. Soon after the conference I bought two copies and gave one to a close friend. For the next six months, we each searched—unsuccessfully—for errors and contradictions, sharing our epiphanies along the way. Eventually I came to the realization that I had found a higher source of truth than the standard of my upbringing, the Christian Bible.

In my late teens I had been a truth seeker, but was turned off by the claims of each of the world's major religions to be the only way. That attitude clashed with my concept of God. I even told God one time that if he could show me a spiritual path that did not force me to deny my sense of logic, I would probably be one of his greatest supporters. I believe the Urantia Book was an answer to that prayer.

STEPHEN THORBURN: One day at work, after a discussion of UFOs and the possibilities of extraterrestrial life, my co-worker suggested that I read the Urantia Book, saying I would find it "interesting." I bought a copy, opened it and read just a little. My eyes grew big and my brain caught fire, and I couldn't put it down until I had read the whole thing.

About a year later, I was listening to my favorite radio talk show about UFOs and the like, and a caller mentioned the Urantia Book. The host inquired, "Have you read the whole thing?" When the caller said, "No, I haven't," the host put out the question, "If there is anybody out there who has read the whole thing, please give me a call."

I called, thinking myself to be probably the only other person in the world who knew anything about it. I was invited to be a guest on his show and fielded questions from callers for about three hours, only to discover that there were other readers and study groups. That was in 1983.

I still read the book daily and go to the study groups. The Urantia Book has changed my life in ways I never could have imagined. Thank you, Father!

HENRY ZERINGUE: I first saw the Urantia Book back in 1978 at the home of an acquaintance in Santa Barbara, California. I was impressed by the words "Melchizedek" and "archangel" in the contents section, and I read a page from "Energy—Mind and Matter." I wanted to borrow it but was told that would be impossible because it belonged to someone else. I looked for it (thinking it was called the Avanti Book) but couldn't find it nor did I meet anyone who had heard of it until five years later.

In 1983 I survived a near-fatal motorcycle accident and was laid up with both legs in casts. One day I received a conference announcement in the mail, addressed to someone who no longer lived at the address where I was then living. I was ready to throw it away when the picture on the back took me by surprise. It was an aerial shot of the University of California at Santa Barbara, with the Santa Ynez mountains in the background—a stunning photo of my alma mater. I went through the mailer again and saw the faces of Sek Seklemian, Barrie Bedell, and Asana Oliver Duex. Then I noticed the name "Urantia," which began to sound familiar. It hit me that that was the name of that book I'd been interested in. I immediately wrote to the organization that was sponsoring the conference, CUBS (Center for Urantia Book Synergy), and was given a Urantia Book within a couple of weeks.

I had already become aware of a spiritual rebirth taking place in me, brought on by the accident and the recovery process. I was lucky to have the opportunity to peruse the Urantia Book during those months of disability.

I was to learn later, when I started attending the CUBS meetings, that Asana had had to use Joel Andrews' computer to do the labels for the mailing announcing their Summer 1983 Urantia Conference. Joel had insisted that Asana also use the *Course in Miracles* mailing list, but Asana adamantly refused, and tried to segregate the database. But all his efforts to do so failed. In the end there was no way around it: he *had* to use the ACIM list. Since I was the only person who had responded from that list, he realized that the angels had seen to it that he use it, even against his better judgment. He learned an important lesson from this experience. I got to see the angels at work many more times during my involvement with the CUBS organization. I am thankful to have been part of that wonderful and vital group while it existed.

So the Urantia Book had found me. I was inducted into the corps of the many diverse and stimulating readers whose lives have been forever changed through the reading and sharing of this book. I feel that I am in good company.

STEVEN MCWHORTER: Let me take you back to the days of the early '70s and through my three marriages into the '80s. I was raised a Southern Baptist. My first marriage, in 1970, was to a Methodist woman from Alabama with whom I lived in the San Francisco Bay area and had two great kids. My wife wanted us both to become Presbyterians, and divorced me in 1974 after I espoused the Mormon faith. Next I married a Mormon woman whose family lived in Orem, Utah, and we had two wonderful children, a boy and a girl. This Mormon marriage, performed in a Mormon temple for all time and eternity, lasted just five earth years.

And now we come to my third ex-wife. We were living in an apartment in Macon, Georgia. Right before our son was born in June, 1983, I noticed a big blue book sitting on the end table next to the sofa. For weeks I had been using the book as a coaster, then one day I opened it and was blown away by the first few pages listing the authors of the papers contained therein. I began to read.

As I became more excited about the contents of this big blue book, I asked around to find the book's owner. Where had it come from? No one knew. I have come to the only conclusion that makes any sense: a midwayer dropped that book off, knowing I was ready for it.

My wife got so upset with my reading it all the time, that one rainy night in Georgia she took it for a ride and threw it out the window of her car into some bushes beside the road. The next day she decided to retrieve it, now a little weatherbeaten. I read that book several times through, highlighting many sentences and making dozens of notes in the margins.

In November of '94 I spent a night in a hotel in Jakarta, Indonesia. In the hotel bar I met a man of Chinese ancestry, and our conversation turned to religion. I ended up offering him my book, worn as it was, and he seemed overjoyed with the gift. I look forward to meeting him again in the morontia life to see what impact that book had on his mortal life.

Not long after I returned from Indonesia, I met a lovely lady in Destin, Florida, and soon our conversations included the Urantia Book. I ordered a copy for her and at the same time ordered one for my 18-year-old daughter in Utah. That daughter, Martha Kelen, was killed in February 1997 in an auto accident on I-15 south of Salt Lake City. I couldn't have come through that mortal experience as well as I did had I not been grounded in the teachings of the fifth epochal revelation, thus knowing full well where she was headed. The support from unseen Urantia Book readers was unbelievable—from Hawaii to New York to Florida to Colorado—as word of this tragic event went out over the readership email lists.

Martha's brother, Gordon, wrote me after he got hold of the book to say that it was "of the devil." I often wonder where that one copy will wind up. Some midwayer will probably place it on an end table somewhere in Utah. It will not go unused.

MICHAEL HAYES: In a mid-sized town in Indiana I was raised Roman Catholic, the youngest of four children. My brothers and sisters were teenagers by the time I was born, so I grew up sort of an only child. I went to Catholic grade school and Catholic high school, was an altar boy and orthodox in my beliefs, but deep down I sensed there was more. My father was an alcoholic, but had begun to go to AA meetings by the time I came around. Although there were hard times that I remember well, my parents were always there to show me love and support. This unconditional love and perhaps the timing of my birth are what I credit for any successes in my life.

Back in the early '80s, fresh out of undergraduate school at the University of Wisconsin, I got a summer internship with a small architectural firm in South Bend, my home town. One of my colleagues, Bob, whom I had worked with before and who was seven or eight years my senior, began suddenly one day to read a large blue book at lunch time. The book had been given to him by a friend in Mishawaka.

Because I trusted Bob, I felt no apprehension in asking probing and sometimes skeptical questions about some of the verbiage he began spouting when he described the contents of the book. I was immediately intrigued by the breadth and scope of the book. It answered questions I had long wondered about. More than that, it made connections between otherwise unrelated areas of study which had always interested me:

philosophy and science, evolution and religion, astronomy and particle physics. In all these disciplines, I was not an expert and only knew enough to whet my appetite.

In high school I had taken a course in comparative religion, which opened my eyes to the idea that people could love God, do good, and not necessarily be Catholic. The lunchtime dialogues with my friend Bob were enough for me to really feel the pull of the fifth epochal revelation, but because of my analytical and somewhat skeptical nature, my reaction was more a recognition of truth than a wholehearted acceptance. The latter came after a long, slow, incremental progression punctuated by incredible glimmers of insight which gave me great hope.

I would often ask Bob, "What is the origin of the book? Who wrote it?" He would only answer, "Don't worry; it doesn't matter. That can come later." He was right. I was learning to judge things on the merits of their content without bringing to the table too many preconceptions based on questions of origin.

I soon left that job and my friend Bob to move with my new wife and soul mate Cynthia to Chicago, where I began a new job as a project manager for a construction company. Tucked into my briefcase were still some well-worn photocopies of several of the Urantia papers I'd taken from Bob's book, as well as a pamphlet of quotations from the Urantia Foundation. The book's $55 price tag seemed like a lot of money at the time, but part of my hesitancy was my skeptical nature: "Who's going to make the money on this? I'm no sucker!" In my mind, true salvation was supposed to be free.

One sunny day, riding my bike near Lincoln Park, I stopped abruptly on Diversey Parkway to admire an unusual and extraordinary edifice with fancily carved limestone ornamentation. But there was something else. My eyes widened as I examined the facade and saw the sign near the door with the now-familiar concentric-circles symbol. I recognized the circles from the back of the quotes brochure in my briefcase as being those of the Urantia Foundation. Given all the places I could have moved to in the world, here I was only blocks from the Urantia Book headquarters. This, I felt, was significant. I thought, "Well, I'd better buy the book now."

Over the next ten years I mostly read alone. I also read other books on science, religion and philosophy that discussed state-of-the-art ideas and concepts. To my continuing delight, a book that had a copyright of

1955 said exactly the same things that the experts in the fields of astronomy, evolutionary biology, archeology and particle physics were just proving in the late '80s.

I bought more books and gave them to my friends. To my dismay, few believed the big blue book as I did. But I figure the books will continue to sit on their bookshelves, just waiting for a particular person to come into their house and say, "Hey, what's this big blue book about?"

VIRGINIA BROWN: The universe has a way of providing what we really need, and I needed the Urantia Book. I was stuck in a morass of trying to be good, especially good enough for God, but not feeling good inside. One of my daughters had gone to live with her dad in a distant state, so to prove I was still a good parent I decided to take care of foster children in my home. At work I was busy trying to prove that I was a good employee. In our church I was trying to prove I was a good Christian. To prove I was a good wife, I was taking care of my husband's needs. To prove I was a good daughter and daughter-in-law—well, you get the picture.

Then one day everything came crashing down around my ears. After a misunderstanding with another employee at work, I started crying and couldn't stop. My employer had a free Employee Assistance Program, and I was referred to a counselor. She saw me for a few weeks and then gave me the names of two psychologists. I was to choose one and start therapy.

So I did. I'll never know what would have happened if I had chosen the other therapist, but the one I chose led me to the Urantia Book. After he found out how much I liked to read, he started recommending books for me. One book just happened to be the Urantia Book. I checked it out from the library and started reading the section on the birth of Jesus; it was close to Christmas and I wondered what the book had to say about it.

Even though I could only understand about every third word, I was fascinated with the book. It's the only book I've ever been tempted to steal—I just didn't want to let go of it! But Doug, my therapist, offered to order me one for $23, so I was a good girl and took the copy back to the library.

Then Doug broke all the rules of therapists and invited me to join his Urantia Book study group which met in his home, and in Bob Bruyn's home on alternate weeks. In my mind's eye I can still go around the room and see the people sitting there at that very first meeting. We took turns reading and discussing the book and I was hooked. The only problem was my fear that they would throw me out if they found out who I really was, so I didn't volunteer any opinions or comments for at least six months.

The first teaching in the book to grab hold of me was the concept of God as a loving Father rather than as a difficult and demanding parent waiting to punish me for doing something wrong. When I read of the Father's love, it resonated within me. Even though I hadn't experienced much love from my parents, I knew how much I loved my children. I reasoned that if God was infinitely good, he must love me more than I am capable of loving my children. I knew that nothing my children could do would make me stop loving them, therefore God must love me, no matter what my transgressions.

The second thing that drew me was pure snob appeal. The readers were almost a secret society. The people who attended the study group were professionals and they accepted me, a housewife and clerk who hadn't even graduated from college. And the difficulty of the book's language challenged and inspired me. Eventually I got to know these people as friends, but I will always be in awe of their intelligence, kindness, and generosity. And now that I am on the Internet I'm meeting another group of readers to add to my family. I am richly blessed.

PETER HAYMAN: In the San Francisco of the late '70s my friends Lowry and Linda McFerrin and I used to listen to John Lawrence preach at his church. John was a devotee of Yogananda, and like Yogananda he was an apostle of love—always encouraging, engaging, looking to help others, uninterested in the barriers of creed. John was elderly then, but he may still be living today amidst his beautiful collection of Eastern art treasures. Part of my attraction to John was his ability to read auras. John once described Lowry and myself as the "blue boys" because he saw that our auras were shot through with blue. He said it indicated a spiritual bent.

I liked Yogananda's autobiography for its many accounts of purported supernatural experiences. Carlos Castaneda's books were particularly fascinating to me because they had an internal consistency which was even more alluring than their stories of the unknown and unknowable.

In the early '80s I was living on Nob Hill, kitty-corner from Grace Cathedral. The McFerrins and I often had dinner together. One evening, with the cable cars loudly making the final spurt before Jones Street, with candles glimmering, with the fog swirling madly under the arching streetlamps, with the homey smells of basil and oregano wafting up from my steaming zucchini casserole, with the wine poured and my grandmother's emerald green water goblets gracing my humble table, Lowry said, "Did you know that Rick has this big book with the life of Jesus in it?"

"Really?" said I, a veteran of Castaneda, Leadbeater, T. Lobsang Rampa, Edgar Cayce and Jane Roberts. "What's it like?"

Lowry shrugged. "Oh, it has all these orders of angels and stuff like that. It goes on and on."

"What do you think of it?" I asked Linda. She was as unimpressed as her husband.

But the seed was sown. Thereafter I kept reminding Lowry to bring the book when he came over, and finally one day he showed up with it. I read it non-stop. It is peerless. I am deeply thankful for its message that God is our heavenly Father.

GINNY MCCARTY: Raised in a small town by loving parents, I spent the first thirty years of my life as a member of a Baptist church. After becoming disillusioned by the authoritarian approach to theology, I began searching for a broader, more open approach to religion. A friend gave me a book by Leslie Weatherhead (a liberal's liberal), who had written a number of books—mostly after retiring from the Methodist ministry in England—which questioned traditional Christian beliefs. Many of his questions were ones that had plagued me. I read everything of his I could find. His most affirming book for me was *The Christian Agnostic*. I am convinced his thinking opened my mind to the Urantia Book.

I was introduced to the book by a new-found friend in mid-Missouri. She mentioned a study group that she attended; when I asked her more about it she was vague, so I did not bring it up again. But around a year later she started telling me about the Urantia Book, adding that she did not want me to think she was weird.

She must have decided *I* was weird because she gave me a copy of the book! I began reading the Jesus papers and could not put it down. It spoke to so many of the questions that I had been struggling with, on such issues as the virgin birth, the atonement, the inspiration of Jesus versus the example of Jesus, and the smallness of God in traditional theology. I was intrigued by the vastness of God and his domain as depicted in the big blue book. Immediately I knew it held what I needed.

We moved away from the area shortly after I found the book and I have been devouring it ever since. My husband and one daughter have also become readers. I am now in my seventies and thoroughly enjoy the empowerment I feel from the study group I attend in Kansas City. My life has been expanded, enriched and enhanced by the teachings, and by the lives that have touched me in association with other readers.

FRED BECKNER: I was brought up a Southern Baptist, and my education was in physics and mathematics. I have worked all my adult life in research and development, in both university and private enterprise environments. From my early teens till my mid-fifties I would characterize myself an atheist. My deity was rational thought, science, and the human mind. Certain experiences in my late thirties and early forties convinced me that there was more to reality than the physical world. I began to seek, I knew not what.

One day my wife brought a thick blue book home from work. A coworker had loaned the book to her, saying, "Here is a book I think Fred should read." I read the book for a couple of weeks, skipping here and there, sampling its flavor. My initial reaction was one of skepticism and disbelief. I rejected the book for its unconventional science (an *ultimaton?*) and its unfamiliar nomenclature. After returning the book to its owner, I mentioned it to my business partner and gave it no more thought.

On my next birthday, my 47th, I received a copy of the book as a gift from my partner and his wife, both of whom are interested in spiritual matters. With the book now readily at hand, I undertook to read it again, mostly out of curiosity. As I read, I began to perceive the spiritual fragrance of truth. I began to understand that the book contained a conceptual framework of reality which united the material world and science with a spiritual world and religion. Even more, I realized that I was a beloved son of a loving Universal Father. I began to see the way home.

LEE COLBERT: One day in 1983, my only brother, David, and I prepared for an outing. We perched his canoe atop his 1965 Ford Pickup truck and set out into the blazing sun for the six-hour drive from Albuquerque, New Mexico, to Bluff, Utah. The temperature was at least

110 degrees, and we soon were broiling in his unairconditioned, shock-absorberless bucket of bolts. My brother, a geologist and diehard adventurer, said he knew a perfect spot to camp that night, but I was beginning to doubt that we would ever get there. The last forty-five minutes of the journey were spent on a rugged dirt path that at times seemed to trail off into nothingness. By this time I felt as though every molecule of water had drained from my body. Delusional, battered and bruised, I began to imagine us lost in the desert, two more living organisms charred to a crisp by the relentless, baking sun.

Just about then the view suddenly changed. The dirt road gave way to a vista so beautiful I had to pinch myself to confirm that I was not dreaming. We had climbed a rocky plateau, three thousand feet above a valley that the spectacular San Juan River, a jumble of meandering goosenecks, called home. In the distant background the sandstone formations of Monument Valley and the Valley of the Gods loomed like fine sculptures. Mesmerizing sun rays danced upon the formations. Surely, God was directing a play that day!

The adventure I have just described parallels my search for truth and meaning in life, my search for God. On the road that day I had despaired of ever reaching my destination. But God woke me up out of my malaise and showed me that faith will always triumph over fear. All my life I had looked upon God as an external force only, the fearful creator and upholder of the world. From that day on I was consumed to know more about God.

To clarify my own beliefs about religion, philosophy and God, I set out to examine the sacred books of the world's major faiths—the Old Testament, the New Testament, the Koran, the *Upanishads*, the *I Ching*. I invested seven years of my life studying these texts. I became confused and discouraged. I saw gems of truth in each work but had a tough time subscribing to any one in particular. All my fundamental questions about life remained. Why did God create the universe? Is there life after death? Is there intelligent life elsewhere in the universe? Is reincarnation true? Do angels really exist? Is there really a heaven and hell? Does one need to empty one's mind to unify with God?

Frustrated at not really finding satisfactory answers to these questions, one day in 1989 I threw a Bible out of my bedroom window into a thundering rainstorm. That day I decided to ask God personally to lead me to the truth. On my knees I told God that I was sorry my search had failed, and that I would be depending solely on his guidance for further enlightenment.

Two weeks later, at work, I passed by the paper-strewn desk of my colleague Bill to ask him a technical question. Somehow I tripped and, trying to grasp his desk for balance, my hand swept aside a pile of technical reports, revealing a big blue book underneath. Curious, I asked Bill what this doorstop of a book was. He said it was an advanced book that integrated our highest concepts in science, philosophy, and religion, among other things. Intrigued, I began to thumb through the contents: "The Nature of God," "Energy—Mind and Matter," "The Early Evolution of Religion." I scanned the list of authors. What in the world is a Mighty Messenger or a Perfector of Wisdom? Although I was skeptical, I saw that the book was of a religious and spiritual nature so I asked Bill if I could borrow it for a couple of days.

After reading the Foreword I was blown away. This was either the manuscript of a mad genius or—could it be?—a revelation from celestial beings. I was on fire to either discount this book as a fraud or validate it as a revelation.

Consumed with the desire to read the whole thing, I spent many a night earnestly poring over this tome. I was amazed at the scope and consistency of its scientific and religious teachings. Fundamental questions were being answered satisfactorily: Yes, there *is* life after death! No, we are *not* alone in the universe! I came to understand that a fragment of the Universal Father lives and works within me, in addition to the outward ministrations of the angels and other spiritual beings. God is not just some aloof, impersonal being who created the universe; he personally shares my experiences! I learned that when the road seems bumpy and the path unsure I can always depend on the God fragment within me to lead the way—"not my will but yours be done on earth as it is in heaven." I now live with the assurance that the journey will be worthwhile.

SUSAN MOHR: In the early 1980s, newly divorced and having a great time living alone, I met an unusual character named Martin. He and his wife lived in my apartment complex. We all became buddies and partied a lot.

Sometimes our discussions would turn to religion and other serious topics. Martin was always making the most profound statements. He was a habitual liar, so hearing these spiritual concepts and phrases coming from his mouth was confusing. Finally I asked him, "Where are you getting all this religious stuff from?" He told me it came from the Urantia Book.

At the time I shrugged his answer off, but in late 1984 I asked him where I could find this book. Could it be bought at a store? From his description of the contents I had a vision that it was some huge reference book located in the National Archives. That afternoon Martin and I went to a Waldenbooks and bought the only copy they had, for $32. I was thrilled—for a day or so.

I was intimidated by its size. I didn't have much experience making commitments and I could sense this book required one. It was too much for me, especially since I was an alcoholic. I thought I would drink for a few more years before getting *that* serious. For the next eight years, I would occasionally glance at that monstrous book on my shelf and think, "One day I will read it."

In November 1992, at the age of 37, I surrendered my will to God and decided to get sober. Between my husband's ultimatum and just being sick and tired of drinking, I got some counseling and took the Urantia Book down from the shelf. Soon after that, a *Concordex* jumped at me from a shelf in a bookstore. I studied the Urantia Book alone for two years before coming in contact with other readers.

My life has continued to be transformed. I am grateful, happy, and I love Jesus! I lost track of Martin not long after I bought the Urantia Book. Several times I tried to locate him, but with no luck. It would be great to run into him again. If not here, then on the mansion worlds. . . .

Martin Madland, where are you?

TIMOTHY NICELY: Back in 1984 I owned an entertainment company called R. A. Chicken & Associates, which focused on corporate events, private parties, commercials and television specials. We would hire entertainers to perform at these functions. One woman who worked for us as a singer mentioned that she had a friend who had a book that was "very strange" and that used a lot of words that she thought were made up. She referred to it as a "space" book. Being a bit of a space cadet at that time, I was immediately interested. She borrowed it from her friend to lend to me for a few weeks. I randomly opened it to a page and read. At that moment I thought, "This is the book I have waited for all my life." That thought produced a chill in my body, which in some spiritual circles indicates confirmation of a truth coming from a divine source.

When the woman left the company she took the book with her. Shortly after that, a born-again friend of mine mentioned to me that her sister had that same book and was willing to sell it. Both women thought the book was the work of the devil. They were willing to sell it to me at a discount—I suppose they considered it a devil's discount. They never realized how important that book was to me. I thank them.

BARRY NORBY: The lacks in my early upbringing had left me with a tremendous need for a solid foundation of truth upon which to build my life. My search for truth did not begin as a search for God, but upon reading the Bible something registered as true in my mind. However, I saw that the Bible had been written by men. I could never accept it as the infallible, inspired "word of God." I was also aware of gaps in the Gospels.

As my search progressed, I joined one church after another. I often embarrassed church leaders with my questions. I also studied church histories and the writings of the early church fathers, gleaning what I could.

My mother had first learned of the Urantia revelation before it was published, through a man she was dating at the time. In 1948 he had taken her to a seminar in Washington, D.C., where the revelation was discussed. Several weeks later she went with others to Chicago to get more details about the Urantia Papers and came home all abuzz over this new revelation. The story she gave me then, about how the revelation was delivered, is not at all consistent with any other version I have heard since. The revelation, she was told, was to be put in book form, and she reserved several copies of the first printing.

In 1955, when I was 18, my mother sent me a copy of the Urantia Book. I opened it somewhere and read a paragraph. I thought, "This is weird!" I read another paragraph from a different part of the book. "It's talking about beings that don't breathe, and who live in atmospheres of 450° F. Wait a minute. I'm not ready for anything like this." I had a million reasons why I should *not* read this book. Deep inside what I really had was fear. I put the Urantia Book on the shelf, unread.

Life went on. One day, in a park, I met an old evangelist named Mike Peters, who spoke with a Ukrainian accent. He had a bed at the YMCA, an old tattered Bible, and one change of clothes. He was open and warm, always smiling with genuine happiness, and I attached myself to him. He preached on street corners, in the park, and in various churches when invited. From him I learned about the loving nature of God. He taught me that whenever there is strife, error, confusion, discord, violence or suffering, it is never from God.

Later I went to Iceland and studied the Talmud and the Koran; to Thailand to study Zoroastrianism, Gnosticism and Buddhism; and to Germany to study under a Baptist pastor who also taught me New Testament Greek so that I could compare different Bible translations. He also told me that I would not find the answers I wanted through such studies.

By this time, I had no problem trusting God, but I became more and more confused with man's presentations of how to find him. I could not accept the narrow-mindedness and, all too often, the meanspiritedness of the leaders of the various religious institutions, with their holier-than-thou attitudes. I was acutely aware of the tremendous contradictions between the knowledge of science and the teachings of the church. I was distressed by man's insistence on making God as imperfect as himself. And I was frustrated by my own inability to put it all together.

By 1985 I was without spiritual focus. I had given in to confusion and had become totally involved with the material world. I'd hopped on "the Greed Steed," and spent my days trying to keep up with the Joneses. Then something happened—I don't remember what—that made me stop for a while and get focused. I knew I had to find God again to re-secure for myself the peace I'd once had.

So I prayed. I read my Bible. Then I came across that blue book on the shelf. I remembered how difficult a read it was, and that it had some pretty far-out concepts. I looked over the table of contents and discovered it was broken down into four sections. The last section was "The Life and Teachings of Jesus." Since I knew quite a bit about this subject, I reasoned that if there was any truth there, I should be able to tell by reading it.

Wow! It said he didn't die as a sacrifice. This confirmed my own beliefs. So I finished the fourth section, then read the third section, then the second, and then the first. Then I read the book again from front to back.

The truth I'd been looking for was all there. The writers had put it all together, and everything made sense. Sure, the book introduced a lot of difficult concepts, but I could see that they were necessary to unify everything else. The Urantia Book took away most of my confusion and a whole lot of my fear. It gave me the ability to plot a course without being fearful that someone would tamper with the compass. The greatest thing it did for me was to teach me the value of communion with spirit.

So, I had the book for thirty years and didn't read it. I never said I was the smartest dude on the block.

JOILIN JOHNSON: When I was 14 years old I had my first "spiritual opening." From then on I became an active seeker, moving through many doors, gleaning the teachings that resonated as true and leaving the rest.

One evening in the late '70s I was about to be initiated as a Transcendental Meditator. I went to the house where the ceremony was to take place, and when I arrived the hostess was sitting at a table reading a huge book. Walking towards her, I asked what she was reading. She looked up at me with a glance that clearly said she did not want to tell me. I've always been an avid reader with a more-than-eclectic range of taste, so I continued to press her. Finally, she said, "Oh, all right, if you insist. It's a book about the history of our planet, the hierarchy of heaven, the beginnings of the world's religions, and has probably the best—no, *the* best—rendition of Jesus' life you'll ever find anywhere on this planet!"

I thought to myself, "Great! That sounds like my kind of book!" I looked at it, and since it was rather large I quickly figured that it would probably take me a few weeks to read it. "May I borrow it?" I asked her. She looked at me as if I had asked to borrow her husband, for goodness' sake! I assured her I was trustworthy and would bring it back in a timely fashion. She finally relented, saying, "Well, I guess I can do without it for one day." *One day?* "This must be some book!" I thought.

So I took it home and began to look at it, from the beginning. Let me tell you, the Foreword is the most complex piece of writing I'd ever attempted to read. I comprehended so little of it that reading further was out of the question. Then I skimmed through other parts of the book and read about the early human races. Hmmm, so there was a blue race, and a green one too, eh? Then I read about a Thought Adjuster, or Mystery Monitor.... Too much for me. I brought the book back the next day.

When I returned it I told her I thought it was the most way-out book I'd ever read. She looked me straight in the eye and told me that if I ever read the book straight through, my life would be changed; it would have to be; she'd never known anyone who'd read the book whose life hadn't been changed dramatically. Then she said I needed to know that it wasn't necessary that I understand the book; as a matter of fact, it was expected that we would not understand much of it. The important part was that we put the words into our minds; the Father would do the rest.

Those words stayed with me for the next three months. One day I found myself walking into a New Age bookstore, one I'd never frequented before, just to see if it had a copy of that big blue book. It did—one copy. So I bought it. It cost $30, and back then that was a lot of money to spend on just one book. I took the book home and put it on the bookshelf; it stayed there for almost six years.

One day I was reading a book about angels that claimed to be channeled just like the Urantia Book was. *The Urantia Book*? I have that book, I said to myself. So I scanned the bookshelves and sure enough, there it was. I took it down and began to read. Wow! I could read it now—it sort of made sense to me.

And I haven't been the same since that day.

GEOFF TAYLOR: Born and raised in an Anglican home, I was the stereotypical altar boy/choirboy—with a guardian angel working overtime to keep me from accidentally killing myself. Homemade model rockets (three-stage with a mouse payload), pipe cannons and fireworks tested the angel's ability to move shrapnel or place me where the exploding bits would least likely hit.

I matured to young manhood with a career in engineering, a family, wealth, and an ego that left little room for God. Science and logic left no need for a God, either. As executive VP of research and development for the largest turbine-engine overhaul company in the world, I pooh-poohed "metaphysical mumbo jumbo" and dismissed the people who were led astray by that stuff. I had taken religion back to its very base—the Big Bang—and decided that God was needed only to supply the initial energy. The natural processes of energy association and evolution would take over from there.

Then in 1985, when I was 37, I hired a creative genius, Dr. Irwin Ginsburgh. Irwin had a Ph.D. in physics, 45 patents, a brilliant understanding of everything, and a big blue book of answers, a book which he said combined science and religion into a logical whole.

A logical blend of science and religion? Impossible! Okay, maybe not impossible, but certainly improbable. I began reading as a skeptic but ended as a believer. Finally, the New Testament miracles and the death on the cross made sense; afterlife was logical, and there was a reason for my existence. I didn't need God; God needed me! He needed me to experience what he could not experience alone—relationships with others, learning, sympathy, empathy, love.

It was a sad day when I finished the book, and yet it is the last book I will ever need.

I find the Urantia Book to be internally consistent and scientifically credible. The probability of getting all those day/date combinations in Part IV correct staggers my mind. The big blue book that questions all answers and answers all questions has changed the ego *me* into the Supreme *we*. It's amazing how your attitude changes when your perspective is eternal.

RICK WARREN: I had been searching for meaning and purpose when, in 1985, after quitting an excellent job as a technician at Hewlett-Packard in Santa Rosa, California, I moved to Harbin Hot Springs. Just fifty miles north of Santa Rosa, Harbin is a New Age community nestled in an old volcano crater on the coastal mountain range. There I joined the Heart Consciousness Church, signed a vow of poverty and gave up my earthly belongings—all $300.

Living in that old crater with a hundred other seekers—mostly goodnatured, globe-wandering souls—taught me that people could exist peacefully and with a minimal impact on the earth. There was a garden and many community-owned amenities. Love and peace were the rule, but what was the purpose? The same questions plagued me even in that paradise.

The next spring, a beautiful terrestrial angel named Barbara drifted into the community and we fell in love. Under Harbin's moon we spent long nights luxuriating in each other's (albeit celibate) embrace. After three weeks of sweet romance and lolling in the warm pools, Barbara said, "Let's go to Boulder Creek and live with the Spirulina community. Besides, I want to go to UC, Santa Cruz." Without giving it much thought, I agreed.

After a couple of weeks in Boulder Creek, an apartment-sitter was needed by one of the community members Barbara had befriended. We moved our few things in and there we finally consummated our love. It was anticlimactic, and I began to have doubts about leaving Harbin and coming to this place.

On the bookshelf over the bed I noticed Big Blue staring down at me. All my adult life I had been looking for truth in books of many kinds. It had started with the New Testament while I was a rifleman in Vietnam, where I never knew if the next day would be my last. I had searched the East for divine knowledge. I had delved into the new age psychology and all that was swirling around during the '70s and early '80s. All I had found in my search was a scrap of truth here and a pinch there. I took the book down and began reading it. Now here was a book that spoke with authority and audacity! The Urantia Book was *all* truth, *all* the time! Finally, my hunting was justified, my thirst quenched, my soul engaged and attentive, and my Adjuster gratified.

Sadly, Barbara did not recognize the significance of this amazing book. Shortly thereafter, we split, she returning to L.A., I to Harbin, never to hear from her again.

An old friend, after hearing me rave about the book, gave me a copy for my birthday. I slowly read it over the next year, even taking three months off from work to permit my mind time to adjust. The teachings forced me to let go of erroneous philosophies that had accrued over the years. I felt like I had come home.

In l990, I moved to Texas. There I read the book two more times and began a study group which now has from twelve to fifteen regulars. Through the Foundation's library placement program, I have put more than 800 English and Spanish Urantia Books in Texas libraries. My life, my mind, and my goals have all been reorganized. I thank God and the revelators every day and my fondest wish is to have everyone know of this incredible written revelation.

LEE RAUH: I was born in Kansas into a strict religious faith. Part of the strictness came from my grandmother, a Swedish Baptist whose beliefs were something of a hellfire-and-damnation/Quaker/Puritan mix; the rest came from my grandfather on the other side of the family who had been an Episcopalian minister in Russia before arriving in the Midwest in the late 1800s.

At an early age I began displaying psychic abilities that could not be explained; I was able to perceive things from afar. As this phenomenon was seldom discussed openly in the '50s, my mother thought I was possessed. After high school I began seeking answers. I would read late into the night. I attended spiritual churches, study groups, and anything else that would open up the channels that had been closed down by the pressure and harassment I'd experienced as a child.

Later, when I was in my twenties, I found that I could diagnose medical problems in people. In my search for explanations I came across internationally known teachers who had great understanding of the "other" realms. Their knowledge helped me to develop my abilities, but it was not until I met a certain teacher and her long-time student that I began to get some answers. This teacher credited the Urantia Book for providing her with the basis of her insights.

I looked for the book and found one in a metaphysical bookstore. It was the store owner's personal copy. She had read some of it but decided it was too much for her. I purchased her book, which was in perfect shape, for the same price she had paid, a whopping $24.

This was in 1985. I began to read and soon found study groups to help me. Study groups are wonderful tools; as others share their understanding, one begins to see things from completely different angles, thus broadening one's understanding. I make notes in my book of others' interpretations, and today its pages are covered with sentences, scribbles, outlines, stars, highlights, and exclamation marks. At one meeting, when someone asked which printing of the book each of us was using, we discovered that I owned a first edition. Everyone was shocked to see how I treated it, but I wouldn't change a thing. This book has been the answer to my life.

GISELA FILION: My wide reading of Edgar Cayce books and assorted New Age materials reawakened me to the fact that God is real and Jesus was and is who he said he was. And yet I knew that there was more, *much* more. I knew that I was missing the really big picture.

I used to spend much time poking around in a certain New Age bookstore, where I had discovered Alan Watts, the *Seth* books and many others that piqued my curiosity. I well remember first seeing the Urantia Book lying face-up on a shelf in the same corner where I had found so many books that fed my interests. I recall looking at it and thinking, "I'll pass on that." I didn't even bother opening it; the front cover alone was enough to turn me away.

What followed was an amazing ritual that repeated itself over several months. I would be drawn to that same bookstore many times, and each time I left empty-handed. I knew that I was being guided there, that I was supposed to find something so spectacular that it would change my life and my view of the world. And yet I left disappointed every time. No matter what book I picked up, I knew it was not the one.

After several months of this strange searching, when I found myself once more bewildered in this store, I heard a voice loud and clear inside my head telling me to go to a particular library branch, adding, "You will find what you are looking for. This bookstore is just too big and overwhelming." Immediately I headed for this library branch. Walking over to its Occult section, the UB fell into my hands almost within seconds. I didn't even realize that I had discounted it before in the bookstore. I sat down, and looking through it I could only say yes, yes, yes, yes, this is it! *This is it!* I was in heaven. I read the book right from the beginning. The descriptions of the spiritual hierarchy in particular made so much sense to me. I was enthralled!

I talked to everybody I knew, asking if they were aware of this book, until finally somebody suggested writing to the publisher's address in Chicago. That resulted in my getting the phone number of a local study group. Meanwhile, I talked so much about the UB that several people got infected by my enthusiasm and rushed out to buy their own copies. I did not urge anybody to buy the book; it was my passion for it that aroused their appetites.

Did the Urantia Book change my life? You bet! I joined a Christian church to mix with fellow believers—just as the UB advises—and in my enthusiasm for the book I talked to another member about the great spiritual truth it contains. Ironically, that got me turned out in no time. The senior pastor told me, "Satan has got you!"

One of the great revelations that came to me through reading the UB is that love is not slavery. By temperament a people-pleaser, I used to bend over backwards to please others. I don't do that anymore. Being subservient to the spiritually lazy and morally indifferent is not what love and service are about.

When I first began reading the UB I was a member of a Rosicrucian Order, where several members were also UB readers. One woman said that she had picked up the book at a garage sale. When I asked another Rosicrucian if he thought the book was genuine, he said that he had meditated over that same question and had found that his feet were getting noticeably warm, which to him meant that the UB was on solid ground.

I keep remembering Jesus' saying, "I have other and better worlds," and I look forward to going there one day. I am forever grateful for this tremendous gift. I rely on it completely as I go through the day, through life.

JENNI DI BACCO: Being in the pizza business in Arizona in the mid-'80s, I used to trade pizzas for metaphysical books from Jan Ross Gifts and Books. One day I saw the Urantia Book sitting on one of the new-book shelves and asked the owner if she would trade pizza for it. My first Urantia Book cost me two large deluxe pizzas.

Even though I had to look up the definition of many words (and still do!), the Urantia Book was one of the few books—out of the hundreds of spiritual and metaphysical books I'd read—that really made sense to me. But before I'd had a chance to finish reading it, circumstances arose in my life that left me quite suddenly without the book. I had just gotten to the Jesus papers.

About ten years later, in June of 1997, I accepted a job promotion and relocated to Arcadia, California. When my family came to visit me over the 4th of July weekend, I took them to Venice Beach. We were strolling together down the boardwalk, passing the various booths and stands that lined the walkway, when I noticed a painting of something that looked like a galaxy. I excused myself, telling my family that I needed to take a closer look at this artwork. As I approached I saw that it was a large poster of the universe. It was leaning against a table at which two men stood conversing with others. One of the men had a Urantia Book in his hand.

"Oh, my God! It's the Urantia Book!" I exclaimed. I had neither seen nor discussed this book with anyone for the past ten years.

The man smiled at me. "Are you familiar with the Urantia Book?" he asked. I replied that I had read part of it many years ago in Arizona. He asked if I was visiting, and I told him that I had recently moved to Arcadia, whereupon he informed me of a weekly study group in Arcadia at the home of Hal and Lucille Kettell. I hugged both men goodbye and thanked them.

A few weeks later I contacted the group and have since been gifted with many new family members. I have also gotten to know the two men who were running the booth that day—Don Roark and Norman Ingram.

BILL KELLY: Converted to Christianity at age 19, I held strong evangelical beliefs for many years. I trained at Fuller Theological Seminary and San Francisco Theological Seminary, and served as a Presbyterian minister for eleven years before returning to psychology. My leaving the ministry had nothing to do with God, the Bible, or the Urantia Book; it was just a matter of preferring a different sort of ministry.

My introduction to the Urantia Book was through a fellow science teacher who was a Methodist. He and I had many discussions about faith. One day he told me he had a book that he thought might interest me, and lent me a copy.

I began at the beginning, reading the Foreword, despite his caution not to. I figured that with degrees in philosophy, psychology and theology, I should be able to handle it. I found it more or less incomprehensible and put the book down for about six months. When my friend asked how I was doing, I told him I thought it resembled Gnosticism because of all the orders of angels and other celestial administrators it presented. He asked if I wanted to return the book; I told him I would give it one more try.

I looked through the table of contents until I found Paper 189, "The Resurrection of Jesus." On a warm summer morning I read that paper with a cup of coffee in my hand. I was astounded. Never had I heard such a convincing story of the events of the Easter weekend, down to the final details. What impressed me most was the UB's explanation of the disappearance of the mortal body of Jesus—instantaneous decay by the speeding up of time, at the request of the "angels of the resurrection." I had never heard this explanation before, and it made sense.

I spilled my cup of coffee on the book and decided I had better buy my own copy and read on. This I did for about six months, every night for about thirty minutes. I read it with an attitude of open skepticism. I found as I read that I didn't understand some of the words or concepts, and that some of the information was completely new to me. Many of the teachings struck an immediate *Aha!* response, and the book—so mysterious and exciting—steadily grew on me. I began to wonder, could the book be true?

About halfway through the book I called up the friend who had loaned it to me and asked him if he believed the book was what it claimed to be, a revelation of truth. He said yes, and told me the story of how he had found it.

I am now in my tenth reading in about ten years. My habit is to maintain an almost daily reading schedule. My wife, Virginia Enfield Kelly, has joined me in the study and application of the book and has become just as convinced and enthusiastic about it as I am. We are active members in two Urantia Book-related study groups.

The book has transformed my life, my thinking, my perspective on

God, the universe, humanity, the afterlife and the purpose of life. The Jesus of the Urantia Book is, in my opinion, greater than, but not different from, the Jesus of the Gospels. He is more complete, believable, loving, human and—if you can believe this—more divine.

GARY MCSWEENEY: In 1986 my wife and I were blessed with the second of our two children, my career was on a fast track, childcare ruled our lives, and the future seemed bright in a materialistic sort of way. Everything but a clear sense of spiritual purpose was evident in our daily activities. Then, from my sister and brother-in-law, both long-time advocates, came the Urantia Book.

What started out as an attempt by me to humorously critique the book became instead a personal encounter with pure truth and wisdom. I was stunned by the clarity of the revelation despite its complex matrix of facts and figures. It was impossible to deny my transformation from UB skeptic to UB believer. Reading is believing, especially when the truth contained is indisputable and without equal.

I have truly been blessed in finding myself among those who have read and believe the fifth epochal revelation. When I hear someone ask, "Why are we here?" I can now smile and say: *"There is in the mind of God a plan which embraces every creature of all his vast domains, and this plan is an eternal purpose of boundless opportunity, unlimited progress and endless life. And the infinite treasures of such a matchless career are yours for the striving"* (p. 365).

Every day is now truly a bonus.

JERRY DALTON: My family has been faithful members of the Mormon Church for three generations. I am the first of three boys who all served missions for the Church, and my two younger sisters married former Mormon missionaries. (A Mormon missionary, in addition to proselytizing, is a full-fledged minister who conducts meetings, baptisms, marriages and funerals; he ministers to his assigned membership and is authorized to act in the name of the Church.) During my first twenty-five years I was very active in the Church. I was a missionary in Argentina, was ordained to the higher order of the priesthood, made sacred vows in one of the temples, and held various positions of authority and responsibility.

A few years after returning from my mission, before I was married, I was involved in a relationship that resulted in a pregnancy. I urged and supported abortion. Later, in order to rectify my standing in the Church I confessed these matters to the proper authorities, and was promptly excommunicated. I had known what the consequences of my confession would be, and had every intention of proceeding in the prescribed manner to gain rebaptism and return to the Church.

I decided to investigate alternative spiritual paths, anticipating that by doing so my belief in Mormon doctrine would be strengthened and reconfirmed. My spiritual quest lasted many years, and as I gained a different insight and understanding I gave up my original intention of gaining re-admittance to the Church. One of my nagging questions had to do with the atonement doctrine, that of God requiring the sacrifice of Jesus to atone for the sins of mankind, a cornerstone belief of most of Christianity. Through my study of *A Course in Miracles*, I learned a different and more satisfying way of understanding Jesus and his mission.

One evening in 1986 I was having dinner with a fraternity brother from college, Wally Ziglar, a long-time reader of the Urantia Book. My enthusiasm for the *Course* came up and Wally said, "If you think the *Course* is great, then you *must* read the Urantia Book." The following day I purchased the book and the rest, as they say, is history.

I found in the Urantia Book a convincing revelation of the life and teachings of Jesus on our world, as well as so much more. As my acceptance of the teachings of the Urantia Papers deepened, I summoned the courage to announce to my family that I would never return to the Mormon Church.

Many Mormon teachings coincide with those contained in the Urantia Papers. But since I can't accept certain beliefs of Mormon doctrine, I don't meet the requirements for rejoining the Church. Otherwise, I would satisfy my family's anxiety about my eternal life by becoming a member again.

The Urantia Book is a wonderful blessing to mankind and I strive to incorporate its teachings into my life so as to be an effective emissary of the revelation to my much larger family.

Part VIII

1987-1993

ARLEY GRUBB: On a cold starry night in the winter of 1974, with a hint of moon peeking over the horizon, I arrived at my destination—western Arizona, somewhere near a place called Bouse, between Interstate 10 and God knows where. I'd driven a few hours from Phoenix to visit a friend who'd gotten himself involved in mining for bat guano in a natural cavern. Someone had dynamited the entrance, so it was not an easy task getting to the product.

After relaxing from the drive and listening to some good music, my friend showed me a book he had come across that answered a lot of his questions. Since we were both searching for the meaning of life at the time, I was interested in what he had found. I glanced through this enormous tome for a while and was in awe of what I was reading. Much of it I couldn't comprehend, but I sensed something profound here and decided to keep the book in mind, live a little more, and hopefully find it again at a later date.

Some years later, in 1980, I was still searching for the meaning of life, mostly in the wrong places but searching nonetheless. A new friend had the Urantia Book boldly displayed in his foyer. Each time I passed by I paused for a little reading. I was almost ready to get serious with this book. My friend showed up one day in a drug-induced frenzy and said, "Here, this is for you." He handed me his Urantia Book and walked away. I never saw or heard from him again.

Seven years later—at last! Something finally provoked me enough to start a serious study of the revelation. Over the years I had tried many times to get into the Papers. Each time I sat down to attempt the task I would begin with the Foreword. I'd get through seven or eight pages and the smoke would start coming out of my ears. Each time I would replace the book on the shelf with a sigh.

Now, after a long and serious bout of an Asian variety of the flu, I was at last humbled to the point of submission. Having re-read every book in my modest library, unable to work or do much of anything but remain prone, I realized there was only one book in the house I had not yet come to know. And this time I was *not* going to read the Foreword!

I laugh now, thinking that that was all it took! From the moment I started reading Paper 1, on page 21, I was taken like never before. I must have repeated the expression *wow!* a hundred times. I had finally found something that was shot through and through with truth. By the time I had finished the first five papers I was a mess.

Something happened to me that night, and I'm not sure what it was. If I could put it into words, I'd have to say I felt the Spirit of Truth descend into my being. I was left emotionally depleted, shaking like a leaf and crying uncontrollably for the better part of an hour. Once that event had passed, I felt the most wonderful glow. The glow remains, as I grow in spirit. My life has changed in ways too numerous to mention. Praise God. May his will be done.

JUAN JOSE MARTINEZ AFONSO: Born in Argentina, I moved to Spain as a child. I lived in a Catholic community, went to Catholic schools, and attended Mass regularly.

As I grew older I became fed up with feeling guilty and fearful of hell. I needed some love and compassion. No matter how hard I tried to live as I should, I always seemed to fail. Was I therefore to be condemned? How could God condemn me so easily? Shouldn't he speak loving words to me, as a father would do for a hurt son? I believe it was such thinking that began leading me towards a personal relationship with our Father.

In 1969 I was 18 years old. I had a good friend who was deeply into yoga and was seriously trying to find God in his daily life. I admired his devotion, but for myself I still failed to recognize the truth; I couldn't find that soft and lovely embrace. I would become disappointed when, occasionally, I thought about God and my life. I look back on those days as a time when I was being prepared to be led to God.

One day in 1987, when I was working as a police officer, a friend came to me with some pages that he wanted translated from English into Spanish. As I was reading, I noticed the following:

"When fully perceived and completely understood, the righteous justice of

the Trinity and the merciful love of the Universal Father are coincident. But man has no such full understanding of divine justice" (p. 115).

O my God! There it was! When I was finished reading, I asked my friend, "Where did these papers come from?"

"From the United States," he told me, "from the Urantia Book." I immediately asked my father, who was living in the United States, to find me a copy as soon as possible. Back then there was no Spanish translation.

Since that time I have read the book through front to back twice, and various sections from "The Life and Teachings of Jesus" many times. The book helps clarify many ideas I had before, presents new ones which I suspect are true, and offers other concepts which I have not yet "swallowed." Nonetheless, it is the greatest written manifestation of truth I have ever found. Through reading the Urantia Book I've begun a new path. I've come back to God, my loving Father, and renewed my search for love and light.

I have since found out that the friend who sought my help in translating the pages of the UB actually reads and understands both English and French. What was his purpose in asking me to help him translate the English text? I haven't asked him that question, but next time I see him, I will!

ROB LAWSON: In 1987 I was at a birthday party for the one-year-old son of a client of my best friend. During the course of the afternoon, I struck up a conversation with a young couple I had never met before, who were sitting across from me at the table. After I mentioned that I had recently attended the Whole Life Expo in Pasadena, the conversation turned to spiritual matters, all of us realizing that we were on some sort of spiritual quest. They suggested I read the Urantia Book.

I couldn't grasp the word "Urantia" at first, even after they pronounced it several times. When they spelled it for me I wrote it down. They weren't able to tell me very much about the book, but they did impress upon me that they thought the book was truly unique and of biblical stature. They said it was available at a popular New Age bookstore close to where I lived. The following week I stopped in. I felt a strong connection to the few passages I read, and bought both it and the *Concordex* on the spot.

I have never seen that couple again nor do I know who they were, but I shall be ever grateful for that "chance" meeting.

MARY HUGGINS: At 15 I attended meetings of Young Life, an evangelical Christian group. For some time they had been telling me that I needed to give my life to Jesus, but I couldn't handle the emotionalism of the meetings. I felt a need to talk to Jesus one-to-one instead of proclaiming my faith so publicly. One evening, while walking from one end of my room to the other, I spoke to him, and I knew my life would never be the same again. Since then my beliefs about God have changed a great deal, but that first commitment was real, heart-centered, and is still the core of my relationship with the God that I've found through the Urantia Book.

I got married, had children, and became too busy with life to attend the mainline Protestant church in which I had grown up. But always, beneath my blasé exterior, there remained that silent core. During the '80s I felt the stirring of spiritual longing, but did very little about it. I was so preoccupied with teaching and raising a family that I had no time for religion.

In 1987, while still teaching, I enrolled in summer and night classes to get my Master's in French, mostly for the challenge and prestige. The first summer was spent taking an intensive class that met five to seven hours a day. The teacher, Dr. Jean-Pierre Heudier, was demanding, yet caring, loving and gentle. One of the girls in the class, his student secretary, had known him for several years and talked about what a wonderful person he was, that he'd been a real mentor to her. She also told us that he read a strange book that was like a bible to him. I was intrigued.

During the next semester, Jean-Pierre and I became personal friends, sharing light dinners together before the weekly class. We talked about many things, and in time we came around to religion. He eventually invited me to a Urantia Book study group in his home. When I arrived that first Saturday afternoon, he gave me a big blue book. We talked about fairies (or midwayers, as he called them) and Jean-Pierre explained how they came to be here: Invisible babies—hundreds per couple—grew to maturity and then mated with one another to have more invisible babies. It was really weird stuff.

But the example I saw in my friend's life drew me in more than the strangeness of his bible put me off. So I dug into the book. I was working full time, raising a young family, going to grad school nights, and yet I read the UB from cover to cover in less than a year. Whew! A couple of years later I began attending a study group closer to home, and I have been a core member ever since.

There are no words in this language to express my gratitude for the Urantia Book. Learning about how our universe really operates has totally changed my perspective on all within that universe. I have rediscovered the real Jesus of my teen experience; but now, not only do I know why he died on that cross, I know why he came to our poor, beleaguered planet. I also have a glimpse of what the future holds beyond this world. It puts all the suffering into perspective. We are little children, like babies, and we are here to learn.

LOREN LEGER: While living in Hyattsville, Maryland, between 1970 and 1976, I used to visit the public library and browse among the books. One day I found a religious book that described the boyhood years of Jesus of Nazareth. The information amazed me and I never forgot it.

My next encounter with the material occurred in Tallahassee, Florida, in 1987. I was at a singles club meeting when a woman passed a book around the circle of members for everyone to examine. I recognized the material I had seen some fifteen years earlier. The impact was immediate, and I have been an eager student of the Urantia Book ever since.

TOM CHANNIC: A lot of readers can tell you exactly where they were, who they were with, and what they were doing when they first came in contact with the Urantia Book. I cannot. The book slipped into my life like a secret agent on a mission.

I know my ex-wife bought one during the time we were married, but I believe I had heard of the book before then and had seen a copy on the bookshelf of a friend or two. The book had been under my nose for quite some time, but it was a time when I could scarcely see the nose on my face.

I had strange preconceptions about the book. My ex-wife believed it was some kind of oracle: You could ask it a question, and by opening to a random page, you would receive your answer—not necessarily a direct answer, but the answer your soul needed at that time. Right. Once, just to spite her, I opened it and started reading. I opened to a paper on Thought Adjusters. I figured a Thought Adjuster was a human teacher who actually knew something about spirituality. I remember wishing that I might find one.

Some time later, I was writing a play about God taking a vacation. I pictured God as a CEO and heaven as having more of a corporate than a lie-around-in-the-clouds-all-day atmosphere. Where these notions came from or why I found them worth developing, I have no clue.

While writing this play, I ran into a block in the scene involving the transfiguration of Jesus. According to the Bible, Jesus is visited by Moses and Elijah and, from the clouds, the voice of God bursts forth with words of approval for his Son.

The problem I had with this scene was: Why did God have to announce his approval? Jesus constantly referred to God as his heavenly Father. Moses and Elijah must have known that God approved. The apostles present wouldn't have been following Jesus if they didn't already believe that God approved. And, if God was omnipresent, why at this time did he become so localized? If God was within, why the big outward display?

I spent weeks thinking about these questions and was getting desperate, so desperate that I decided to read what the Urantia Book had to say about the transfiguration. I borrowed my wife's copy. I found out that Moses and Elijah weren't at the transfiguration; the two individuals with Jesus were actually Gabriel and Father Melchizedek, who were conveying testimonies of satisfaction from, respectively, the Eternal Mother-Son of Paradise and the universe representative of the Infinite Spirit.

So now I had a lot more questions. I had heard of Gabriel, so I looked him up in Part IV, and yes, he did appear to Mary, but he was also the Bright and Morning Star of the local universe of Nebadon. Uh oh! More questions. After several minutes of page turning and head scratching, I figured the book had worthwhile information, but if I were going to get anywhere I would have to start at the beginning. So I opened to the Foreword.

O my God . . . the Sevenfold?!

It took me well into the evening, but I managed to finish the Foreword, realizing I was on to something really big. That was on Sunday, February 28, 1988. Within eight months, I had finished reading the fifth epochal revelation to our planet and had no doubt that it was precisely what it claimed to be. Also, within that time the book brought me my partner and family co-creator, but that's another story.

SAGE WAITTS: During the summer of 1988 I was living at Breitenbush Hot Springs, a community/retreat center in the Cascade Mountains of Oregon. I was searching for a way to live in the world that was counter to the mainstream. My search for a spiritually alternative lifestyle had begun several years previously, when I spent four months at the Findhorn

Community in northern Scotland. Findhorn is an eclectic spiritual community that first became known for growing 40lb cabbages in the sand while working in cooperation with nature spirits. Dedicated to planetary transformation, it provides educational courses in spiritual disciplines, alternative energy sources, unique business approaches, and ways to get along with one another. In the years since my first visit to Findhorn I returned three times, each time with the intention to remain, but it never seemed quite the right time.

My spiritual exploration began in 1982, while attending my first Alcoholics Anonymous meeting. Even though I could barely utter the word God, I remained with the program, and as I became more committed to my sobriety, I grew more passionate about my spiritual life. It was this hunger that led me to read anything on spiritual topics I could get my hands on. My search took me on many adventures where I met many fascinating people. It eventually led me to Breitenbush, where I hoped to find integration of spirit purpose with mundane work.

After one year, I became a member of the Breitenbush community, which was operated as a worker-owned co-op servicing guests through workshops and personal retreats. It was not unusual for individuals to wander through Breitenbush and stay for a while, and it was one such person who turned my world around. This person was a Urantia Book reader claiming to be an Avonal Son on a mission to destroy the anti-Christ. She had a magnetic personality, as many slightly insane people do, and I found our frequent conversations about the Urantia Book fascinating.

One night, after a particularly intense discussion with her, I had a dream in which I saw the Urantia Book against a black background, as if it were hanging in a night sky. This might not seem so unusual except that I had never seen a copy of the book. The next morning I drove to the nearest town that had a bookstore and bought it. When I saw the cover of the book, its color and the way the title was laid out, I stopped breathing for a second. Except for the night sky, the cover was identical to the one that had appeared in my dream.

For the next six months or so I read it off and on. Breitenbush was a pressure cooker for personal growth, and by March of '89 I was ready for a break from the rain as well as from the growth opportunities. I packed up and headed south to Arizona, where I found a nudist camp (more sunshine per square inch!) and spent the next seven days, butt to the sun, reading the Urantia Book.

The moment of realization came on my way back to Breitenbush. I had driven all night and was in eastern Oregon, which is high desert country. I pulled onto a dirt road and found an open vista and a place to park, and had some breakfast. I was sitting on the floor of my van, eating, side door open, sun shining on me, birds singing, reading "The Attributes of God."

Boom! Boom, again! I got it! This was for real! I don't know why then—maybe my Adjuster was finally able to break through because of the open spaces—but I finally *got* it.

My enthusiasm was mainly self-contained during my remaining three years at Breitenbush. I would occasionally share what I was reading with a few friends, but I didn't seek out any other readers because I was afraid they would be as crazy as the person who'd introduced me to the book.

Finally, when the day came to leave Breitenbush, I knew it was time to meet other readers, so I got the name of our area coordinator and called him. He invited me over and we spent the afternoon in his back yard, within hearing distance of the Pacific Ocean, talking about the book. He was normal. Still is. And this was the beginning of a new chapter in my adventure with the teachings of the Urantia Book.

SUZANNE KELLY-WARD: In 1988 I moved to San Diego. I was hired by a woman from India who had lived in Australia from the time she was in high school. She and I became fast spiritual friends and I gave her a copy of my epic poem "Elan Vital," which at the time was 28 pages long. It was a compilation of truths I had gleaned from reading volumes of religious and metaphysical teachings in my lifelong quest for the real story of man and God.

She read it and beamed, "Oh, you've read the Urantia Book."

"What's that?" I asked.

"Everything that is your poem," she replied.

I don't know who looked more confused at that point, but needless to say, I ran to the nearest metaphysical bookstore to get the book—they just happened to have one copy.

The Urantia Book filled in all the blanks in my previous epic speculations—and then some! I was amazed.

"Elan Vital" is now 128 pages long. My study group compadres refer to it as the *Cliff's Notes* to the UB. I'm still amazed.

ROBERT SCHREIBER: As a child, then as a youth and an adult, I felt something was missing in my life. I was drawn to things religious, but had no idea what I was looking for.

In college I took a World Religions class, but found the way they were studied was too analytical. I read the Bible and found it helpful but lacking something. I read many religious books and studied Edgar Cayce, parapsychology and the paranormal, but nothing really spoke to me.

Gradually I settled into mainstream Protestantantism and was reasonably happy, but deep inside I was still unfulfilled. Then, in 1988, my colleague and friend, Bill Kelly, told me about the Urantia Book, which he had just discovered.

Though a skeptical person by nature and still smarting from a long history of disappointments, I quickly but unenthusiastically secured a copy. To my astonishment I knew from my first reading of the Urantia Book that it was what I had been looking for all my life. I felt I was home at last.

I am now in my fourth reading of the book. (I'm a slow reader.) I still find it the source of much satisfaction and continued enlightenment. In 1996 I founded The Correcting Time Ministry to introduce and promote this new revelation to my friends and relatives.

STEPHANIE FORBES: Since I was 17 years old I have been actively searching for God. In the first phase of my search, I was a Rastafarian. I know that God used that religion to reach my heart because no other religion would work. When I came to realize that it could not answer all my questions, I looked for something else.

In 1982 I became a born-again Christian and had a very close relationship with God again. My experience of God was very intimate; he was my closest friend. I would ask him questions and receive very strong answers. I guess he knew I would not "get it" if he wasn't very blatant. Later I came upon troublesome times and found that once again I could not get answers to some difficult questions.

I developed a close relationship with my earthly father, Larry Gwynn, who was very insightful and intelligent. One day I saw the Urantia Book on his table. When I started reading it I could not put the book down. It was so obviously true. I would read non-stop for six hours at a time, excited to find answers to questions that I had been asking for over ten years.

The first section I read was "The Meaning of the Death on the Cross." I found that all I read rested well with the spirit of God within me. I never doubted for a moment that what I was reading was the truth.

My then-husband was very unhappy with my choice of reading material. He demanded that I stop studying the book. When I refused he said he did not want to sit across the table from a demon-worshipper and even arranged a conversation between me and two pastors we knew. I was comfortable standing my ground in my belief that the Urantia Book was true, and felt as though the Spirit of Truth was helping me reply to the pastors' questions. I know they were displeased by my responses but I feel right about it to this day.

My belief in the God portrayed in the Urantia Book has enabled me to change my entire life. I have gone from a pathetic, beaten girl to a strong, loving, and comfortable woman. I never could have fully broken free from the bonds of my first marriage without the knowledge that God would love me no matter what. I now know that I have some wonderful gifts with which to serve my Father in heaven.

I love the fact that we have a divine purpose in this universe and that we are all treading the same road to the Father. We are never truly alone. We are surrounded by our God at all times.

WILLIS DAVIS: After visiting church after church and having none of my questions answered, I finally realized that the people I had been asking really had no more knowledge than I did. Their only source of enlightenment was the same as mine—the Bible.

As my frustration grew, I continued to wonder at how retarded our planet was. I felt that there must be something available that explained why God allowed this. I had an insatiable desire for facts about Adam and Eve, Jesus, and Lucifer. I wanted the real deal on creation and evolution.

While venting my frustrations with a friend, William Gainor, William said, "Davis, you're just searching for truth." Those were strange words coming from him. William is a great guy but a saint he was not. I would never have dreamed that he had the answers to my or anyone else's universal questions! But I decided to "listen to the message and ignore the messenger." He fed me enough data for me to ring my "truth bells."

William and I had a history of trying to "one-up" each other, and that pattern carried over into the way I got this revelation: He would copy a few pages at a time for me to read so that he could keep the upper hand by having something I really wanted but couldn't get until he was ready to give it to me. He gave me a few pages about Adam and Eve, which answered two decades' worth of questions. Then he gave me a few pages about energy and matter, which aligned science and religion in a way that confirmed what I had suspected for years. After about a week he reluctantly told me where I could get a book.

He and I have grown immeasurably since then, and since 1989 we have had a reading group. We have spun off two more study groups and have found numerous new students of the book.

MICHAEL D'AMBROSIA: I attended a Christian high school, going to Bible class every day for five years. I was a very disciplined, serious Christian.

In 1988, I began to experience an intense state of consciousness which lasted about a year and a half. During that time I was guided in my spiritual and emotional life by an inner wisdom which was not my own. I felt as if I were God. Although I logically denied that possibility, I still used that sense as a reference for what I was thinking and feeling. I felt secure until I began to search for conscious knowledge of what I was experiencing in my superconscious mind.

As this intense experience continued, I gradually became internally stressed because I could not understand or communicate the glorious feelings I was having. Looking back, I can see that I was becoming delusional and getting sicker due to the onset of schizophrenia, which runs in my family.

I began searching used book stores and libraries for books on metaphysics, pyramids, alchemy, and Rosicrucian thought. I found many interesting ideas about personal transformation, but eventually I gave up searching for an answer to my intimate questions.

Right before I had my emotional breakdown, I spotted the Urantia Book on a shelf in my local library. When I got it home and began to read it, I couldn't believe my eyes. I had actually found something that explained a big part of what life, the universe, and Jesus were all about.

On April 20, 1990, I had a breakdown and lost contact with my normal mind. Eventually I found help, became stable on medication, and am now basically back to normal. Throughout these experiences, I continued to read the Urantia Book when my mind would let me.

I am very thankful that the Urantia Book was written. I experience a great satisfaction in discovering new information as I read and attend study groups. The book is here to answer the many mind-boggling questions about life, God, and the universe.

PERI BEST: In 1989 my husband and his partner John were busy writing a film script loosely based on the life of James Dean. At the same time, I was working on a story set in ancient Crete. I was fixated on the Minoans because they were precursors of the Greeks, upon whose ethics and ways of thinking our present civilization is based. I felt that in studying the Minoans we would find out why we are the way we are.

My search for the answers to the big "whys" had been the driving force behind my leaving the Anglican Church as a teenager and submerging myself in all aspects of the occult—especially astrology, Aleister Crowley, Tarot, and Taoism. It also led me to Sufism and my spiritual teacher, Murat Yagan. Ten years and two children later, I considered myself an authority on New Age thinking and religions.

So when I told John that I was looking for more information on Crete and he suggested that I check out the Urantia Book, I was taken aback by the fact that I didn't know what he was talking about. I had to utter those famous words, "The what?" John suggested I look in the local library and, by golly, there it was. After checking it out for three consecutive months, I finally found a second-hand copy of my own.

Since I was eight years old, my reading material of choice had been science fiction; now, suddenly, I didn't want to read it anymore. Recently a friend asked me why I no longer read sci-fi after finding the Urantia Book. After much thought, I answered, "Truth is stranger than fiction."

After three years of studying the book for clues of its being a hoax, I finally had to cry "uncle" and admit that I could not conceive of it being anything other than what it said that it was—a revelation.

SUSAN KIMSEY: During an acrimonious divorce in 1985, I was encouraged to read *A Course in Miracles* as a means to heal my discouragement and bruised emotions. I found the *Course* to be compelling; it opened my mind to the possibility of spiritual guidance from sources other than the Bible.

In 1989 I joined a *Course in Miracles* study group, where I met Cheryl

Zents, who became one of my closest friends. Cheryl had been a reader of the Urantia Book for a number of years, and she never hesitated to introduce the book to anyone she sensed might be open to hearing about it. She perceived this openness in me.

One night she brought the Urantia Book with her to a *Course* meeting and plopped it in my lap. I was somewhat overwhelmed by the size of the book, but I trusted Cheryl. I began to look at the table of contents. As I skimmed the titles of the papers, I was seized with a strong curiosity. Just as the *Course* had given me a broad perspective on human relationships and human understanding, I sensed that this book would give me a broad perspective on the universe in which I lived.

Cheryl loaned me her Urantia Book for a few days, and I thumbed through its contents. I told myself that someday I would read the book. A few days later, I went to the local library just to browse the shelves, and the Urantia Book was the first book I saw, in the first book stack I approached.

This felt like too big a nudge from the universe to ignore, so I checked out the UB from the library and have been a reader ever since. I finally bought my own copy after I had borrowed the UB as many times as the library would allow.

FRED HARRIS: As a young boy, I seriously thought of becoming a priest. I was raised Catholic by my mother, but my father was not Catholic and so the religious training of the children was often a contentious topic in our household. Still, I might be a practicing Catholic today had it not been for my puppy love for a girl in one of my classes.

To be able to see her outside of class, I attended her church and made sure to sit where she would see me. After the service I spoke to her, but it turned out that she was not interested in me. In those days it was a sin for a Catholic to attend a non-Catholic church service. Although it was a minor sin from what I could tell, I took no chances and mentioned it when I made my next confession. When I informed the priest of my offense, he upbraided me as if I had murdered someone and gave me a stiff penance of twenty-five Hail Marys. Twenty-five Hail Marys! I was incensed. I walked out of the confessional, refused to do the twenty-five Hail Marys, and left the Church forever.

I embraced hedonism during my college days and for a few years thereafter, but by 1989 I was married to a wonderful woman, had a family and was practicing law in Tallahassee, Florida. At that time I was representing Butch Trucks, drummer for the Allman Brothers Band. As a favor to Butch I agreed to meet with a promising young musician who called himself T-Ray, to discuss the possibility of my becoming his lawyer. T-Ray had traveled from Utah to Florida to record an album of original songs.

Although T-Ray could not afford to pay for my legal services, he would not agree to become my client until I understood his philosophy of life. I assured him that I could represent him anyway, but he was adamant. Rather than argue with him, I said, "Okay, then. What is your philosophy?"

"All my life," he explained, "I've been a seeker, jumping from one philosophy or religion to another. But each time I felt that something was lacking and I continued to search. Then one day I was in a bookstore looking for a birthday present for my father-in-law, when I came upon a large blue book that looked interesting. I bought it for him. But while perusing it before wrapping it, I became interested in it and went back to buy one for myself. It is in that book that I found revelatory truth, and it is from that book that I get the inspiration for my music and life. I want you to read the Urantia Book," he said, reaching into his knapsack and pulling out a book that resembled the New York City phone book. He handed it to me.

I took one look at the huge tome and started laughing. I pointed to all the books littering my office, saying, "I read all day for a living! Do you think I want to spend my free time reading this book? That's unrealistic!"

After glancing around my office, T-Ray marked several key pages in Part IV of the book and suggested that I just read those. To humor him, I agreed and took the book home with me.

That night I lay in bed and began reading the Urantia Book. My first thought was that it was very well written, structurally and grammatically. Then I began enjoying the story. Then I couldn't put it down. For the next several weeks I was exhausted at work because I was staying up a good portion of the night reading this book. Being trained in logic, I had always had a problem with the irrationality of much of the dogma that I had encountered in institutional religions. The Urantia Book was the first document I had come across that presented spiritual concepts in a logical context.

Ultimately I came to the conclusion that this was indeed a revelation, and I began buying cases of books to give to friends and family. I was shocked that they weren't interested. I prayed to God to help me find a way to let people know about this wonderful revelation, and those prayers are beginning to be answered. The Urantia Book is not the exclusive source of truth or of the revelation of God, but it has opened my eyes to a spiritual path that continues to unfold. The Urantia revelation has been a blessing to me.

MIKE BAIN: It was my 18th birthday. I unwrapped my last present—a Urantia Book—and said, "Oh, ummm. . . ."

"It's for you," Dad said, "for when you are ready."

"Gee, thanks, Dad," I said. The book wound up in the back of my closet.

A year and a half later I was living with a buddy and slaving away in college, not really enjoying the courses. I had picked up the Urantia Book and was reading it, when something told me that this was *it*. The experience was beyond description. It was sublime.

I started with the Foreword. I didn't get much sleep that night. Or the next. Or the next. I think I was up every night that first year until 3 a.m. reading. I got so involved with reading and restaurant work that college suffered. I dropped all of my classes and devoted myself to my job and studying the Urantia Book. I finished the book in a year and a half.

Some papers were so beyond the scope of my mind—"Universe Levels of Reality" and "Deity and Reality," for instance—that I had to skip them. The rest of the book was so overwhelming that I almost went insane with the knowledge. I had to cut back and read just a little at a time.

When I went to the clubs and watched everyone dance and have a "normal" life, I imagined myself a prophet rejected by his generation. I had all this truth to share with them but was extremely disappointed by their lack of interest. I still try to help them today, but not in such a direct way. The Urantia Book has taught me that there are many paths to our Father and that everyone has their own level of spiritual receptivity.

I am overjoyed to have been blessed with a dad with whom I can communicate about all this Urantia stuff. We've spent many a lunchtime at Pizza Hut talking of cosmic things.

LEONARD ABLIETER: Growing up in an areligious household in a largely areligious society—Germany during World War II—had left me without any real religious convictions. It also had left me without any religious baggage.

Yet, there were always questions in my heart and mind, and occasional spiritual urges and longings. The former resulted in my investigating various religions, including Buddhism, Taoism, Mormonism and traditional Christianity. None of these belief systems inspired me to pursue them further. At one point I was led to peruse an atheist manifesto, which proved even less acceptable. The urges and longings were harder to ignore but seemed to generate an appreciation of beauty both abstract and physical. At times these sensitivities led to pantheistic musings, but such thoughts were fleeting.

So my life went on, dominated largely by career interests and demands. God remained a mystery, and Christ an interesting historical figure.

Erich Von Däniken's *Chariots of the Gods* opened up a new avenue, one that appealed to the intellect. Von Däniken's theory, that the gods of mythology were actually alien astronauts, was reinforced by a book by a NASA official which analyzed the prophet Ezekiel's visions. My interest then moved to reincarnation, chaos theory, and finally, to the ultimate intellectual challenge, quantum mechanics. Paradoxically the latter subject—a hard science one could easily believe in—opened a door to something intangible and tenuous, a reality or realities beyond what one can touch and see—a world beyond the world of Newton.

I was living in California on my sailboat when I met Karen, a woman from Florida who'd come for an interview about crewing for me. We had an intense intellectual weekend listening to classical music and discussing chaos theory and quantum physics, among other things. Before Karen left she told me about a book she thought I'd be interested in. She herself hadn't read all of it, but she was sure I would find it fascinating.

A year later I chanced to be in Florida and stopped to visit Karen at her home in Key West. Once again there was lots of discussion, and in the midst of it she pulled a big book off the shelf and put it down between us. I grabbed it and read the cover jacket. "The Central and Superuniverses"? Great, I thought. "The Local Universe"? Interesting. "The History of Urantia"?

"'Urantia' is the name of our earth," she said.

"Good—this might be something different," I said, looking forward to the prospect of widening my horizons.

But when I noticed Part IV, "The Life and Teachings of Jesus," the excitement drained away and was replaced by an I-should-have-known disappointment. Without opening the book, I laid it back down. "I don't want to read this; it's not what I'm looking for," I said, sad at what I perceived as another dead end. Quickly, Karen assured me that this was not the kind of book I thought it was. She was adamant that I would find it of value, and gave me a form for ordering the book directly from Chicago.

Months passed before I finally sent in my order. A few weeks later the big blue book arrived—with its 2,097 pages, a bear of a Foreword, and that Part IV that had bothered me so much. On the shelf it went But in the end, reasoning that since I trusted Karen's judgment and had nothing to lose but an investment in time, I decided to read it. Checking the total number of pages, I calculated that if I read ten pages a day, five days a week, I'd be able to finish the entire book in less than a year. That seemed to be an acceptable proposition. Then and there I went for it.

I had no expectations. I cleared my mind of any preconceived ideas and just read one page after another. Part IV was way down the road and I was prepared to let it take care of itself when the time came. In the meantime there were new worlds to discover, concepts that stretched the mind beyond anything I had encountered before, and historical information that was endlessly fascinating. I approached the book on a strictly intellectual level, the only level I was capable of at the time. And I was continuously pleased by how perfectly the Urantia Book communicated with me.

In due course I arrived at Part IV. I was sorry that Parts I through III were behind me. They had completely taken hold of my imagination and I could not envision Part IV being as interesting or exciting. But I went on, maintaining a three- to five-papers-a-week regimen until the end. And when I had finished I was able to accept, intellectually, the reality of Christ Michael.

Later, I read the Urantia Book again, front to back, and studied various papers independently. Although my first reading had been on a purely intellectual level and fully satisfying at the time, an emotional element, which grew more and more profound, entered into the second reading. As a result an entirely new perspective arose: Out of understanding grew the beginning of knowing, out of belief sprouted the first seedlings of faith, and out of intellectual acceptance ensued the early stirrings of religious experience. Parts I through III became the prelude to Part IV.

As I indicated earlier, I had great difficulty bringing myself to read the book initially because of the simple yet necessary reference to Jesus on the cover. Had the reference to Jesus been more prominently displayed on the cover, who knows how much longer my search for meaning might have gone on?

MICHAEL J. ZEHR: I was given the Urantia Book in a manner which I hope will be increasingly common in the coming years: my parents gave it to me.

I was exposed to several different churches when growing up—Mennonite and Lutheran the most frequented—but while my parents demonstrated their values through loyal living, they never tried to dictate to me which faith I should believe in. By the time I was ten years old, I knew enough about God to want to learn more. It was when I started asking questions that could be summarized as "How do I learn more about God?" that my parents started talking to me about the Urantia Book.

We began reading Part IV together on Sunday afternoons, and over the course of a couple of years slowly worked through the book. While doing that, I went along with them to conferences and study groups. By the time I went to college I was ready to read the book in order, on my own. It was during this second reading of it that many of the concepts and ideas clicked in place in my heart and mind and I became even more fully committed to it.

I am looking forward to the day when I have children who are mature enough to ask, "How do I learn more about God?" so that I can introduce the book to them.

CALVIN McKEE: On October 4, 1955, the same day the great Urantia Book was issued its catalog number by the Library of Congress, I was born in Tridell, Utah. It took thirty-six years, though, for me to find the UB.

I was raised on a large farm, one of fifteen kids in a Mormon family. Our home life was "dog eat dog"—too much stress and work, not enough harmony and loving service. My father was an alcoholic and "in the bamboo" a lot, so my mother had to do the work of ten maids and be the farm boss most of the time. I don't think there is a harder-working woman alive—to this day she still milks over a hundred head of cows daily, tends a big garden and does lots of church work. She and my dad divorced in the late '70s. Dad moved to Canada to escape drunk-driving penalties; he sobered up ten years before his death in 1997 and had rearranged his life to become a faithful, loving and serving person.

I was a very inquisitive kid. While the rest of my family were quite follow-the-standard-pattern Mormons, I drove my Sunday school teacher nuts always wanting to know the "why" of everything I didn't understand—who said what, why, when, where and how. I must have run out of satisfactory answers at about 14 because that's when I began putting my mind to deep study. I turned over a lot of rocks seeking truth and reason. Before I was 21 I went on a Mormon mission to the Tennessee area; while there did some serious study, highlighting passages in Scripture that either moved me or confused me. When I returned home I got married, took over the dairy farm and continued my search.

About ten years and plenty of good church business and community experience later, I found myself wanting answers that no church member could provide. Among my questions was, Where are the greater truths promised in our Mormon scriptures that would give us an understanding of the universe, our origins, the "gods" and the rulers of time and space? In this promised record to come were "the greater things Jesus taught the people," but I could find no one who was seeking such a record.

In search of answers, I went to the Mormon church headquarters and stayed outside the First Presidency's office until someone finally agreed to talk to me. I explained my quest, expressing my confidence that the head prophets had the real truth but were just waiting for the membership to become ready to receive it. The good man there told me, "I don't know what you are talking about and I don't know of anyone who does."

I walked out of that office feeling truly liberated for the first time in my life. I was now free to pursue my truth without fear of reprisal from either the church or my family. My new freedom caused my first wife to take the kids and run from her now "anti-Mormon" husband—she would never get to heaven with such a deserter. The whole community, my family and friends, now looked the other way when they saw me coming, fearing that I might taint them. A hundred and one rumors arose.

So, I sold the farm for just enough to pay off my debts, and moved out. What did I do next? I had bought a car from a Pontiac dealership in Salt Lake City, and one day I stopped in to have it serviced. To make a long story short, they offered me a job. The last thing I wanted was to be a car salesman, but something inside told me to give it a try, and I did.

One of my co-workers was a student of the big blue book. After listening to me telling about my search, he showed me the book, which he thought I might be interested in. Talk about falling out of my chair! I have devoured the book a few times since.

BILLY BURNETTE: After separating from my wife in 1990, I wondered what true purpose and value I had in my life. Having gone through the trauma of drug addiction and regaining a lost spirituality in 1989, I started praying faithfully for a sign, a fragment of truth. I had always known God to be my Father, but many questions remained to be answered.

I had studied all the great religions and all seemed to contain truth. Jesus was constantly on my mind because of the true faith and courage that he showed, but one thing about him bothered me—his anguished cry on the cross: "My God, my God, why have you forsaken me?" Since Jesus had such a sublime and absolute faith in his Father, how could he feel forsaken by Him? Every morning I would also pray for the knowledge of David and Solomon. I would fast for ten days at a time to try and hear from God, to allow the spirit to minister to my worn and tired soul.

It was at this time that a bookstore opened up in a mall near my home in Maryland. I went there looking for something interesting to read and noticed a big blue book. I asked the woman at the counter what the book was about. She didn't know, admitting she had never even seen the book before. Mind you, she was the owner of the store. She opened it up, started reading, and remarked that it seemed to be about God and the universe and some teachings of Jesus. She even commented that it looked very interesting. I asked her how much it cost and she said $36.

"Thirty-six dollars!" I exclaimed. "No way! That is too expensive!" I had about $600 in my pocket but did not yet feel called to the book. I put a piece of paper in the book, telling myself that if the book was still there the text time I came in, I would buy it.

For two months I tried to avoid that place, and when I finally walked in and saw that no one had touched the book, I knew that God had something in store for me. Since that summer day in 1990, I have been robbed of the book on three occasions, and each time I have run right out and bought another copy. I carry the book with me always and it has often been a beacon of light for people whose lives I touch on a daily basis. It has truly taught me that joy comes in the morning and that there is no greater service than to serve the Father by serving others.

GENE NARDUCY: I was raised in a Catholic neighborhood on the south side of Chicago. During the '60s I became steeped in the turmoil of social and spiritual change, embracing and then dropping every belief system I could find while growing my hair long and dropping out. I became an agnostic.

It took me twenty years to begin reading the Urantia Book after first discovering it 1970. In that year I was living in an apartment building on the north side of Chicago with a group of free spirits. Our days and nights were an endless celebration of peace, love and brotherhood—and, of course, drugs.

Many unusual people passed through, but one day, as I was sitting alone in the music room, a tall, gowned figure with long blond hair placed in front of my eyes a blue book. I opened to a page with very detailed print that bore the title, "Paper 74—Adam and Eve." I read a little, turned to the figure, and said, "I'm not ready yet." The person left with the book and I didn't think much of it at the time.

Years later, in 1990, after completing a marathon in Napa, California, I was with some friends in a bookstore in downtown Calistoga. Leafing through a book called *Dolphins, Angels and ETs*, I came upon a page that described the Urantia Book. I showed it to my friend. It turned out that he knew of a Urantia Book study group in the area and gave me contact information, but I never got in touch with them.

As things in my life became more chaotic, I thought, "I'd better get that Urantia Book." I went to a bookstore, picked up a copy, saw the price, and put it back down. After going home I reconsidered and went back for it but it was gone. When I came across it again later I bought it immediately. I eventually found my way to a study group in Santa Monica, and have now begun my Paradise ascent!

SHERIE CROSBY: I cannot remember how old I was when I was first blessed with spiritual thirst, but I do remember, as a child, being alone in a room watching a movie on television about the life and death of Jesus. The scenes of this man loving everyone and teaching wonderful things about God held me in rapt attention. Nothing could prepare my young mind for the sorrow that overcame me as I watched Jesus being nailed upon the cross. I had no knowledge of the theory that he was dying for anyone's "sins." I felt sad and cried genuine tears.

Later, learning the "blood of the lamb" theory, I began to reject the concepts of Jesus as presented by the popular churches. I was repulsed by the dying, bloody image of Jesus. I desired the truth, the missing links that would bring him to life.

Another milestone in my spiritual searching came when I was a teenager. We belonged to the Christian but non-denominational Unity Church in Lees Summit, Missouri. I often went into the prayer chapel to meditate and pray for guidance in the direction of my life. One day, after a deep, longing prayer to know more, I walked over to the Bible that sat on a pedestal and opened the book to "any answer." The words jumped out at me and seared into my heart: "Ye shall know the truth, and the truth shall set ye free."

Much time and many experiences passed until the Urantia Book came to me. In the summer of 1987 I befriended a drummer who had come to Kodiak with a band to play at a nightclub. Because he was from Los Angeles, I was surprised by his answer when I asked him what he liked most about Kodiak. He said, "I feel closer to God." During a discussion about Jesus, he alluded to a book that contained a fuller presentation of Jesus' life than the Bible. He said it spoke of universal truths and revealed the true concept of the Trinity. Thinking this book was yet another New Age version of sci-fi, I was skeptical. But after devoting a summer to reading the Jesus papers, I knew I had discovered the Truth.

I understand that the Urantia Book came into my life as a divine gift, at a time when I was most ready to receive it. Reading the book is a never-ending story. Never will I think that I have learned every truth it contains. I will continue to read and study it as long as I live on this planet.

MARGO LEWIS-SUTTER: Living in Western New York, approximately sixty miles from Lily Dale, a Spiritualist camp, I spent many summers over the course of thirty years at the camp with friends. Occasionally I would get readings from the mediums. In 1983 I befriended one of these medium-teachers, a woman with whom I had a lot in common. She moved to another state but continued to come to Lily Dale for the summer.

In the summer of 1990, during a reading with this friend, she came through with the name "The Urantia Book." She told me I had to get it and read it, and mentioned that it had something to do with the history of creation—a hot topic for me. About three years later I walked into a bookstore and saw the Urantia Book on display. Because it was expensive I decided to try to get it from the local library. I was successful and renewed it several times after my interest was engaged.

Deciding to buy it, I went back to the store. While there I picked up a copy of an alternative newspaper. Inside was an advertisement for a Urantia Book study group. After a few days I called the number and was enthusiastically greeted by the group's host. That was in the mid-'90s, and I have been a member of the group ever since. So, regardless of the Urantia Book's negative comments about mediumship, it was through this avenue that I first found out about it. I'm very grateful that I did.

HAMID REZA MAZDEH: I was born and raised in Tehran, Iran. Since the age of 15, I have been fascinated with our immense universe and its numerous known and unknown phenomena. I spent a good portion of my late teenage years reading astronomy and science books. Another area of interest for me was the supernatural. I read books on telepathy, reincarnation, and the spirit world.

The revolutionary crisis in Iran prompted my parents to send me to America to pursue my academic education. I began attending university in the United States in 1978. I majored in aerospace engineering and got my B.S. degree. I was also a political activist and wanted to help transform Iran into a democratic society. Unfortunately the Shah's fall did not result in bringing about democracy in Iran. The ruling Mullahs were worse than the Shah and caused much destruction. Being opposed to the Mullahs, I was not allowed to return to Iran.

I was hired as an engineer by a major aerospace company in Southern California. But living an average day-to-day life was not satisfying to my hungry soul. I had many unanswered questions about life and was desperately looking for answers. I wanted to know: Who is God? Why am I here? What is my role in the total picture?

As a Muslim, I had read over one hundred books by progressive Iranian Muslim thinkers, but found many of their answers unsatisfying. So, I decided to go back to the source, and read the Koran in three languages: English, Farsi and Arabic. I concluded that although a beautiful work of inspiration, exquisitely narrated in poetic style, the book was obviously of human origin. I also read the entire Bible. This book was very inspiring as well, but its tribal God concept and its message of the atonement of Jesus made me very uncomfortable. The real God, I thought, must be far more loving, merciful, and universal. More importantly, he must have a solid plan for human growth and evolution.

In October 1990, while visiting an Iranian doctor in California, I started sharing my scientific knowledge about celestial objects and the possibility of other life in the universe. At the time, I was writing an astronomy book in Farsi called *A Comprehensive Survey of the Universe*. She told me she had a book I might be interested in. As she described the book, I became so captivated that the next day I went to a local bookstore and bought my own copy. It was the Urantia Book. I found it to be by far the most fascinating and intriguing book I had ever read. It confirmed my personal belief that we live in a loving and orderly universe, that there is a divine purpose for our lives, and that we are not placed on earth in vain.

In 1999 it occurred to me that it would be a good idea to translate the book into my native language, Farsi (Persian). I took up the challenge, and have since found a few other Iranian Urantia Book readers to help me with the translation.

The Urantia Book has made me a much more loving, caring and service-oriented person. I love the teachings, and try to implement them in my personal life and share them with other searching souls.

EVELYN HAMMOND: One day in 1990 I was in a different branch of the public library than the one I ordinarily patronized. I checked out the spiritual/religious section and saw a big blue book on the shelf, one that I'd never seen before. I started to read, then sat down and opened the book to some pages that talked about the administration of the universe. I was hooked.

I checked it out along with my usual bagful of books, but the other books never got read. All that winter I read the Urantia Book, first dipping into parts that interested me, then reading it straight through from the beginning. After that, I contacted the publisher for local readers and found a study group. Our hostess was the one who had placed the book in the local libraries.

In my second reading, I discovered many new things and suddenly grasped concepts I hadn't understood the first time. And for every question answered, ten new ones presented themselves. It seemed, as I read, that I was "remembering"—that my mind would say, "Yes, that's how it is . . . or was!" In the process of reading, I came to feel like a cosmic citizen.

The book found me late in life, and I agree that it is probably meant for the coming generations. With that hope I have placed a copy in each of my three daughters' homes. They are daunted by its size, and are all very, very busy; but I know the day will come when they and my grandson will discover it for themselves.

ANGEL SANCHEZ ESCOBAR: Although I grew up Catholic, I had always been a truth seeker. Before finding the Urantia Book, I believed in reincarnation, channeling, spiritualism, the faithful protection of saints from physical dangers, and so on. At that time I was an exultant, euphoric person. I felt that nothing seriously bad could ever happen to me because I was well protected by spiritual agencies.

I remember in 1990, when I was 37, how happy and proud I was to share one of Conny Mendez's metaphysical books with my friend Josefina, a former partner in spiritualism sessions. It was my latest find in my favorite subject of positive-energy thought. But Josefina also had a gift for me: the Urantia Book in English.

Being an English professor, I expected to have no problem reading it, but the book stayed on the shelf for around six months until one day I picked it up and decided to read "The Lucifer Rebellion." After that, I read many more papers and finished the whole book in less than six months. Since then I have read it four more times and have helped to revise the faulty 1993 Spanish edition.

When I left my old beliefs I felt completely alone. But the Urantia Book awakened me to the fact that I have a fragment of God within me, and this realization dispelled my sense of loneliness. Further, many things have happened in my life—disappointments, frustrations, and other setbacks—that have forced me to grow. I no longer feel as if I'm in seventh heaven or Nirvana. No, I am not so exultant as before but more realistic and sober-minded. I feel I am being more truthful to myself, more faithful, and more capable of following the non-easy path to Paradise.

PAT PORTER: My first encounter with Big Blue was in the early '80s, when my ex-husband brought it home and then forbade me to read it. He said it was "magic" and that it was so deeply written that I wouldn't understand it anyway. The challenge was delivered. I accepted it. One night I picked it up and started reading from page one.

The timing wasn't right, however. I was just returning to graduate school and working full time, and we were starting to make contacts to adopt a child. My husband, having become deeply depressed, had to be hospitalized. I had no time to concentrate on the book, but I did get very positive feelings about what little I had dipped into. Ten years later, the book had become a distant memory, and vanished along with my by-then ex-husband.

Living in Denver, I made a new friend named John. I enjoyed his company and the company of his friends. I learned that one of John's friends, Eric, frequently flew in from the East Coast to attend a "Urantia group" in Boulder. Hearing the word "Urantia" brought back vague recollections.

Eric became someone I could talk to like family. We would discuss John's problems and how I could help him. The subject of the Urantia Book was never brought up until an awful thing happened. John committed suicide. Eric was a great help during this difficult time. He spoke about the morontia worlds, and the beauty, the peace, and the love that are on the other side of our present life. He convinced me that John was all right, that he was in the care of wonderful, loving beings who would help him find himself.

I was given the book for my 50th birthday. I read it. I study it. I try to live it as my understanding grows.

KARRIE HUMMEL: In August of 1991 I signed up for an Anasazi weaving class that was being offered at the University of Utah extension school at Moab. It was a small group—three students and the instructor. We spent three days trying to duplicate a mat woven out of yucca cordage and reeds. The mat had been taken out of a Grand Gulch site and placed in the museum in Blanding because it was very fragile and had been disturbed too much at its original site.

During those three days I spent a lot of time talking with Penny, another student who, like me, was in her late forties. We discovered that we lived only fourteen blocks from each other in Salt Lake City, had both grown up in Illinois, and had many of the same interests, as evidenced by the obscure class we had both signed up for. We continued our friendship when we returned home. We talked together about many things, eventually getting around to religion and spiritual matters.

In Illinois I had attended the Lutheran Church of my dad's family, had taken the catechism classes, and was confirmed. When I was 14 we moved to Salt Lake City, Utah, the home of my Mormon mother. During my junior high school years, I signed up for a Mormon seminary class in lieu of a free period so I could learn about my mother's church, and ended up graduating from seminary after attending from eighth grade through my senior year in high school.

I enjoyed learning about God, whether it was from the Bible or *The Book of Mormon*. I often kept the seminary teachers after school answering my lists of questions. However, my Lutheran and Mormon educations never gave me satisfying answers. I had learned that God was fearsome and punishing, and that I could never be good enough for him. I would say my prayers of thanksgiving, but never dared ask for anything. So I continued searching. Over the years I looked into New Age religions, Native American folklore, and many other creeds and doctrines, but something was always missing.

One day, about a month after the class ended, Penny said, "You might be interested in a book I've been reading for a long time." The next time I saw her she gave me a copy of the Urantia Book. I started reading it from page one but was very discouraged by my inability to grasp much of its teachings. At her suggestion I began attending a study group with her. This offered me a chance to ask questions and have discussions with like-minded people who were seeking to understand the book better themselves. Thus a whole new world opened up for me.

After attending the study group for several months, I began to find the Urantia Book to be more than I had ever expected. My mind was reeling from all the information I was digesting. I was finding the answers to questions for which I had never been able to find acceptable answers before.

The book began to speak to my heart and soul. It led me to what I believe has been the greatest realization of my life—that my Father in heaven loves me just as I am. It's a simple thing to say, but experiencing the reality of that love was very new to me. Discovering the Urantia Book marked the beginning of a period of incredible changes and intense learning experiences in my life which continue even today, and will continue on through eternity. I look forward to this growth with great excitement and joy.

TERRY: In early 1992 I was studying at a local library, doing some work on my dissertation. At some point I was interrupted by an intrusive thought—not a voice, mind you, but an intrusive thought: "Go get the book." The idea was an extreme annoyance, since as a wife, mother, grad student and full-time nurse my time was very precious and not to be wasted. Nevertheless, the thought would not pass.

I got up from my desk, wandered down a particular aisle and stopped at the end. On the bottom shelf—a shelf I generally avoided because of its inconvenience and my nearsightedness—I saw a huge book with a white cover. On the cover was a blue, tri-circled insignia. I opened the book out of curiosity and spent the remainder of the afternoon enthralled, feeling as if I had "come home." Synchronicity? Maybe, but I choose to believe that my Thought Adjuster was redirecting the course of my life. And to think, I never even knew I had a Thought Adjuster!

JUDY TUTTLE: I was in Egypt during the month of Ramadan in 1992. Sitting alone on the deck of our small tourist boat, drifting down the Nile, I was mesmerized by the call of the muezzin echoing from the tall minarets stretching lazily against the sky. Every sunset, night, dawn, noon and afternoon the faithful are summoned to worship—man reaching out to God, God reaching out to man—an endless loop. The sun was beginning to go down, quenching itself in the great river, exuding a coral sheen on the water and far distant horizon, as if setting fire to the papyrus beds. The graceful feluccas glided silently along the Nile, like the wings of long-forgotten water birds glistening in the last rays of sunlight.

As if in a poetic trance, I asked myself, How did I find myself here? From what distant call was I summoned and allowed to place my hands on each of the Holy of Holies, participating in ancient, mystical initiations in Abu Simbel, Aswan, Philae Island, Kom Ombo, Edfu, Luxor, the Valley of the Kings, Dendara, Abydos, Tell el Amarna, Beni Hasan, El Mina and finally, the Giza plateau. Just where and when did my pilgrimage begin?

I was on tour with a group of Rosicrucians, having been a member for the past eighteen years. The Rosicrucian Order is an ancient, metaphysical organization that traces its roots through Akhenaton to the days of Atlantis. During the '70s, when others were experimenting with psychedelics and drawn to New Age religions, I, too, experienced the restless urge to open the doors of perception. As a child, I was intrigued by the advertisements of the Rosicrucian Order in popular magazines. The attraction for me was their promise to expand one's psychic ability; since early childhood I had had psychic experiences.

When I joined the order, I was told that, upon the completion of our studies, we would be allowed to remain as social members if we so wished, but that each would embark on a new course of study, directed by an unseen hand. After eighteen years, I was finished with my weekly monographs and had no desire to participate in social activities. My time as a Rosicrucian would culminate in this final, three-week pilgrimage to Egypt and two-week stay in Israel.

As I sat on deck, listening, thinking and waving to the beautiful children who threw kisses to us from shore, I was joined by a German woman who lived in Ottawa. She was a curious woman who had caught the attention of all, because of her insistence upon wearing white dresses of Battenberg lace and carrying a white lace parasol while the rest of us wore running shoes, T-shirts and our cleanest pair of dirty jeans as we trudged through the hot, dusty desert. Resembling a character from an Agatha Christie novel, Eva proved to be a charming and enchanting companion with whom I shared many conversations. She told me about her horrific time in Russian-occupied Germany during Hitler's final hour, her escape to Paraguay as a Mennonite, and how she had cleared the fields and given birth to her three children on the dirt floor of her hut.

One day I confided to her some of my own private hypotheses, one of which was that the Adamic default had nothing to do with eating forbidden fruit but rather with an inadvertent transmutation of the human DNA.

"Uh oh!" she whispered in her child's voice, "That's the Urantia Book!"

"What's that?" I queried.

"It's a great secret! A big, blue book!" She said in hushed tones, half covering her mouth with her wispy fingers.

"Who wrote it?" I asked.

"No one knows! But a group of people were given the book and they want to keep it a secret! At this moment," she added, "my friend, Joseph, who lives in Ottawa, is translating the book into Farsi for his wife, so that she can share it with him. Maybe he can give you an address."

When I arrived back in the States I was determined to find the "secret" book recommended by the little gingerbread lady, but in the days before Windows and Amazon.com it was not an easy task. I enlisted the help of my friend Pam, who was endlessly dabbling in New Age religions. Within two weeks Pam came bounding over to my house, a big blue book securely held in each arm. She had found the book at a New Age fair in nearby Long Beach. The warm and loving Urantia folks that she met not only openly sold her the book, but also gave her flowers and a gold pin with concentric circles, one for each of us.

And that is how I found the Urantia Book, or rather, how it found me, or better still, how we found each other!

LEE AND MILDRED MAXTON: In September of 1992 my wife Mildred and I went to California for a vacation and stayed with my son in Santa Ana. Shortly after our arrival we noticed a big book on his coffee table. When we asked him about it, he told us that he had discovered the book while on a trip to Albuquerque, New Mexico. We also asked some questions regarding its authorship. Mildred became intrigued by the book, and she and my son selected various papers to read together. We all became so deeply absorbed that instead of visiting the various tourist sights, most of our visit was spent just reading the Urantia Book.

After returning home to Tempe, Arizona, we looked for local study groups and found one in Scottsdale, hosted by Larry Bowman on Thursday evenings. Larry welcomed us and we have been going there ever since. In the summer of 1993 we joined the Grand Canyon Society and became very much involved in its activities, Mildred serving as secretary and vice-president, and I as treasurer and navigation chairman. Presently I am the publisher of our quarterly newsletter.

These past few years have been very rewarding for us. Both of us had always had so many unanswered questions regarding our religious beliefs, and we discovered the answers we were searching for in the Urantia Book. We have not found the book to conflict with our individual religious backgrounds—Millie is a Mormon and I am a Presbyterian. Rather, the teachings of the Urantia Book have greatly strengthened our religious life. We have also met many interesting and dedicated Urantians. Now in our senior years, we are so thankful for the peace and beauty the Urantia Book has brought into our lives.

ALLENE VICK: I first saw the Urantia Book in 1985 when a friend got out her copy to look up the Lucifer rebellion, which three of us had been discussing. I took some time to page through the book, knowing that someday I would have a copy of my own, but at the time I didn't have $38 to buy one.

I next came across the Urantia Book when I was visiting my mother for three months in Florida while she was awaiting surgery. It was about the only stretch of time I'd had since I was 16 that I wasn't working. I went to a small branch library and, to my amazement, there it was. For three months I couldn't put it down. I read the Jesus papers, and in between flipped through the first three parts, stopping at various passages that caught my attention. Being a fast reader, I covered most of the book, but it was at times overwhelming.

Later, when my brother asked me several times what I thought of it, I found myself saying that I didn't need to know the hierarchy of heaven. That seems strange to me now, because since the age of 14 I have had a compelling desire to understand how the universe works. I had been seeking answers for over thirty years, following a lot of different paths, studying Eastern religions, metaphysical and New Age material, philosophy, science—you name it. But I had accumulated so much knowledge by then that I was more interested in learning how to apply it than learning any more.

In 1992 an acquaintance, Chris Hart, came over to talk to me about polarity units, and as we got to talking, we discovered many mutual interests. She asked me if I had read the Urantia Book. When she found out I had read most of it, she invited me to join a small local study group. I began attending classes twice as week with a wonderful teacher, Patije Mills, who helped to bring the book to life for me. I have been reading and studying it ever since.

When I think of what I like most about the book, two things stand out. First, its portrayal of the Universal Father. The God I'd learned at church was either highly judgmental, or omnipresent but impersonal. The UB's first five papers describe God in terms that make sense to me;

I love the fact that I can have a personal relationship with him. Second, its story of Jesus. I believed he lived as portrayed in the Bible, but I always sensed he was much more and had put him on hold. Thanks to the understanding gained from the Urantia Book, I now have a very intimate, loving, personal relationship with Michael.

Over the years I had acquired kernels of truth from many sources, but always they were found amidst a lot of mythology and distortion. I didn't know what to do with these truths or the truths I had learned from my own personal experiences, as they didn't fit any system. The Urantia Book is like a giant oak tree, where all the truths I've gleaned over the years find a place to belong—a leaf here, a twig there, a branch over here. My lifelong desire to understand how the universe works has at last been satisfied, and it has been pleasing to see the magnificent order of the whole. Now I can focus my full attention on learning to live the truths of the Urantia Book.

DON ROARK: When I was 16 years old, I was standing with others in a traditional Christian church reciting the Apostles' Creed when it occurred to me: I don't really believe what I am saying, so I'd better leave until I find out why.

Thus began a long adventure looking for the meaning of life, why we are here and what we should do. This search included altered states of consciousness, Eastern philosophy, Science of Mind, the 12-Step Program, *A Course in Miracles*, and many blind alleys.

Then in 1992 I went to the Whole Life Expo in Los Angeles. After wandering around not seeing anything of interest, I found myself standing in front of a beautiful, blue, awe-inspiring booth. A tall, distinguished, older man (older than me) smiled and said, "This is quite a book—you might want to read it!" So, I bought the Urantia Book from Duane Faw, and my life has never been the same.

At first I bounced around for months, reading bits and pieces, and concluded that this was either the greatest science fiction story ever written, or it was indeed a revelation of truth. I preferred the first alternative, and decided to read one whole paper every night without fail. Soon I was reading the book "religiously." Halfway through my second reading I concluded that the book was, indeed, a revelation.

I am now on my fifth reading and it is truly amazing that concepts continue to emerge; words that were "not there" during the first four readings suddenly appear. The things that I do remember are suddenly magnified as if they are in neon lights. Part IV is illuminated in vivid 3-D and I sometimes believe I am immersed in a virtual reality environment with surround sound.

The Urantia Book is not merely the most amazing book I have ever encountered, it is the most amazing source of truth this planet has had in the last two thousand years!

ALBA TERESITA ROJAS AGUDELO: In the early '90s, every eight to fifteen days I would travel nine hours by car to Tabio, Santa Fe de Bogota, Colombia, to assist two groups in their study of the *Enneagram*. Each study session lasted three days. During one session I saw, among several books on a table, the big blue Urantia Book. I picked it up and leafed through it. It looked very interesting. One of the speakers for the *Enneagram*, Juan Osorio, sat down next to me and we talked about the book. He told me of its wonders, and my heart opened with a joy that I couldn't explain.

That afternoon I was asked to assist at a meeting. During this time I wrote down questions I had about the Urantia Book and then discussed them with Juan. I was beginning to fall in love with the book. Then Juan took me to a bookstore in Bogota and I bought a copy to take home with me.

Sometime later, when I could no longer attend the meetings, I studied the book alone at home. I searched for a group to study with, but couldn't find any. I tried to form a group of my own but people treated me as if I had lost my mind, as if the Urantia Book were a strange religion. Still I continued reading at home, but that got me in trouble, too. I had to hide my book for fear it would be burned.

One day I faced my family and told them that for me the Urantia Book came first. I put the book back on my bookshelf, although not without fear, because if they were to burn it I would have to go to Bogota to get another one, as there was no place to buy it in my hometown. In reply, my family told me to leave home and go live with my book.

That was in 1996. At a later *Enneagram* meeting, someone invited me to another gathering to talk about the Urantia Book. At first I was nervous, but I took control of my emotions and finally was able to discuss the book at some length. The next Tuesday a Urantia Book study group began and I have been in charge of it ever since.

I like everything about the Urantia Book. It has totally situated me in life. I now know things I didn't have the slightest idea about previously. I have learned not only to live with others but also to forgive, to understand, and to love them even more. By the way, most of those who had treated me like I was nuts now ask me to let them read the book. It's bewildering!

HOLLY: At the age of eight I was already having prayer time with God. My prayer was simple, "God, please let me be like Jesus." I had learned about Jesus from my grandmother—together we would pray the Lord's Prayer. At nine I attended a Church of Christ summer Bible school where I accepted Jesus into my heart. When I learned that as he was dying he said, "Forgive them, for they know not what they do," I knew that he understood our spiritual ignorance and loved us in spite of it.

For the next ten years I had a deep desire to know God intimately. I attended Baptist revivals, Lutheran retreats, Methodist Bible schools, and Young Life meetings. I gravitated to friends who would talk about God and were involved in church. But somehow I wasn't getting the big picture, the big truth—the daily personal experience of knowing God. By the time I began college, I was starting to drift away from my search.

In November of 1992, at the age of 32, I began having spiritual talks with a friend. Knowing how much I loved Jesus, he mentioned the Urantia Book to me. He said it contained a more complete version of Jesus' life. I was curious and skeptical. I thought it was probably channeled and therefore not to be trusted.

A year later I was in Ruidoso, New Mexico, in a candle shop that had a small selection of books. How excited I was when I saw that one of the books was the Urantia Book! I read through some of the Jesus section and liked what I read. I wasn't yet ready to buy the book, but I did purchase a pamphlet entitled "The Birth of a Revelation, The Story of the Urantia Papers" by Mark Kulieke. Its description of the way the book came into existence—through a unique interaction between spiritual beings and human beings—sat well with me. This sort of process made more sense than channeling.

A few months later I was in a New Age bookstore in Austin, Texas, where I saw a high-quality magazine entitled *The Jesusonian*. The "Jesus" part of it caught my eye. I read through it and soon realized that its material was based on the Urantia Book. I bought it. The bookstore's owners said they held a meeting each week to study the UB with other readers. At one of the meetings I met a reader named Mary Huggins, whom I had previously met through my brother. Wow! What serendipity! She and I got together a few times after that, and she loaned me a book. Since I was still investigating. I read my borrowed UB diligently every day for two weeks, as well as the supplemental UB material I'd purchased through the Jesusonian Foundation in Colorado. A few months later, the UB softcover came out, and I bought it.

I have received so much inner peace and freedom from the truths in the UB. The book's narratives completed the partial biblical accounts I had been questioning. They answered my questions about Jesus' crucifixion, Adam and Eve, the Lucifer rebellion, Melchizedek's purpose and identity, and Paul's Christian religion. I had not been in complete agreement with the Christian view of these subjects, and the UB confirmed my gut feelings about "the rest of the story." I was relieved to learn that true religion is personal and experiential and is not necessarily derived through associating with a church. I was also relieved to find confirmation of the fact that absolute rejection of God is the only way we don't survive into the next life. I experience sanity and unity in my thinking due to the support I receive from the Urantia Book.

JORDI SOLSONA I ESTRADA: I've long been reading books that attempt to explain the reason for our existence. I began with Teilhard de Chardin, continued with Rosicrucian literature, and discovered the revelations of Paiporta. Paiporta is a town in Valencia, Spain; the revelations were given by angels to some local teenagers. I then began to search for other angelic revelations. As I studied and compared these revelations, it struck me that all their various teachings contained truth.

One day, I asked a friend who was traveling to New York to try to track down a book entitled the Urantia Book, which supposedly talked about extra-terrestrials. I had just learned of the book's existence but wasn't desperate to get a copy as I wasn't particularly interested in ET's. When my friend returned he reported that he couldn't find the book.

Two weeks later I was searching through a bookstore in Barcelona when I suddenly saw the Urantia Book. I felt it was ironic, and figured that my friend would be glad to know he could buy it right here in Barcelona. I was surprised by its great size and the logo, but as soon as I read the table of contents and saw "The Life and Teachings of Jesus," I bought it and began to read it.

That day I felt that all my urges and searching for truth had led me to that book; I found it at the precise moment when I needed it. It answered all my desires for integration of the different ways of telling truth that I had been finding up until then.

NORA AND SAED MOAKHER: I [Nora] was living in a refugee camp in Sweden, the country I had fled to when the war in Bosnia broke out. I was by myself most of the time, and had countless questions without answers. I volunteered in two youth organizations, teaching jewelry-making, a craft I had taught myself years earlier.

In Sweden I met Christel and Sandy Garrick, long-time Urantia Book readers, who were just about to start a gospel choir. Christel was interested in my jewelry and I was interested in her oil paintings, so she invited me over for a cup of tea and also to show me her work. The first thing I asked her was, "Where does artistic inspiration come from?" Sandy just looked at me and in a matter-of-fact voice said, "From God, of course."

That evening Sandy played the opera he'd composed, the words based on the Urantia teachings, and I just sat in the rocking chair and couldn't stop crying. My soul was shaken like never before. After the recital, Sandy and Christel brought out their Urantia Books, and we began to read: first, "The Inevitabilities" section on page 51, then the "Morontia Mota" section, and finally the beginning of Paper 100. That was all it took—it became *my* book.

Soon the Garricks invited me to move into their home, a kindness I will never forget, and I pretty much became a member of their family. The choir was a success; it attracted a great number of people, Swedes as well as immigrants. There I met my husband Saed, an Iranian Muslim, who was at the time working in the same office as Christel. It was quite unusual for Muslims like us to sing in a gospel choir, but the Garricks were so charismatic and loving, our fascination with them was infinite. Many other Bosnians joined in, mostly young people, many of whom were also intrigued by this couple. Probably one third of the choir— those who asked questions—learned about the Urantia Book, and we soon had a study group.

That was in 1992, just as the war in Bosnia was at its worst. The Urantia Book played a great part in helping me preserve my hope and faith throughout that difficult time. Soon I began to translate the revelation into Serbo-Croatian, in part to help other study group members understand what they were reading about, in part to share my wonderful discovery with my family, and in part to better understand the book myself. At the time I did not imagine that one day the translation would turn out to be a serious project. But if you were fluent in a language other than English, wouldn't you naturally want to see this book translated into your language, and made available to your closest family and friends?

Saed and I love the Urantia Book. Many of the things it speaks about are self-evident, and yet I often wonder, "How come I never thought of it?"

Recently I found a quote by Emily Dickinson that says, in essence, "Maturity only enhances mystery, never decreases it." This aphorism can certainly be applied to my experience with the UB. The book has helped me arrive at a more mature way of looking at things, and has assured me, better than anything else, that a meaningful design underlies our lives. And if you wonder how the book has been able to do that, well, start reading!

DONNA BROWN: I found the Urantia Book while attending a Whole Life Expo in Pasadena, in March of 1993. I was wandering around looking at various booths when one with a picture of Jesus and the words "Jesusonian Foundation" caught my eye. I've always felt drawn to Jesus.

At the booth I talked to a very nice lady named Ann Garner. I asked her some questions, such as, "What is this about?" and "Is this a church?" She told me it was about a book. She then showed me a copy of the Urantia Book and gave a brief description of it. She asked me what I did for a living, then recommended some chapters in the book that I might be interested in as a marriage and family counselor. I asked her if there was anything to join, and she said no. Lastly, I wanted to know where I could get the book to read before buying it. Ann suggested I try my local library, and that if I had any trouble obtaining the book to contact her.

That was my introduction to the book. I was skeptical about finding it in my local library, since I had read most of the books in the Spiritual/Metaphysical section and had never noticed it there before. Ann assured me that it could always be found through an inter library search.

I took some pamphlets and brochures from the booth and went home determined to track the book down. I was successful. My local library ordered it for me and I had it in my hands within a week. First I read the parts I was most interested in, then quickly perused the table of contents and the chapters Ann had pointed out that pertained to my profession.

I loved what I read. The literature I had received contained information on study group meetings, where you could read together and learn more about the book from experienced readers. Being a people person, it didn't take me long to find a group nearby. I first heard of the book on March 20, 1993, requested a copy from my local library on March 22, wrote the Urantia Book headquarters in Chicago on April 21, and attended my first study group at Hal and Lucille Kettell's in Arcadia on May 17, 1993. I've been there ever since.

I also held an experimental study group bimonthly in my own home in Temple City two years later, beginning with an "Introduction to The Urantia Book" party on March 19, 1995. In my introductory talk to some twenty-one friends and family members, I said:

"If you have ever wondered, as we all have, who we are as human beings and what our place is in the larger scheme of things, how we got here and why we are here, what our purpose is on earth, this source answers these questions—the big questions—in a most eloquent and comprehensive manner. It is inspiring, enlightening and enlarging. It will augment and expand your concepts of divinity and the physical creations of the whole grand universe as nothing you have read before. I encourage you to read it and to judge it by its content and how it speaks to your heart."

I continue to enjoy my study of the book as well as my association and fellowship with many other readers at meetings, conferences, and retreats, including a pilgrimage to Israel in 1994.

If you are a spiritual seeker, open the book, open your heart and open your world.

DIANA ELWYN: As a teenager in the mid-'70s I was always lurking in the Religion and Philosophy section of the library. I was desperately seeking higher meaning. I grew up in an alcoholic family but was ever the hopeful optimist. I was the vegetarian with the Earth shoes (anyone remember those?). I started doing TM at age 14. Somewhere along the line I lost the desire to find the faith that kept eluding me.

I was practically an atheist when in 1993 I went to the Spring Fair and happened across a Urantia Book booth. A man I had worked with, Lee Smith, was in the booth. I knew that Lee was into some strange UFO religion—at least, that's what people at work would say when they teased him! He had shown me the book about a year before but it looked like too big of a task. I only stopped because I knew him to be one of the nicest and most sincere people I had ever met. So I asked some of the questions I'd had for a long time, and darned if his answers didn't make sense! At that moment the spirit moved.

Sometimes I wish my hometown library had had a copy of this divine revelation during my teens. Mostly I'm just grateful I finally found it.

JEANNIE SCOTT: When I was a toddler my mom took me to church, and I loved Jesus. At 12, I went to Bible camp and was saved by Jesus Christ. Then, as a teenager, I gained a stepfather who was an atheist. I adopted his beliefs, namely, that religion is a crutch for those too weak to face the truth that this life is all there is. I certainly didn't want to be identified with those weaklings, and sided with my stepdad, much to my mother's dismay.

In the ensuing years I searched and wandered, wandering right into alcoholism, where I stayed for thirteen years. Throughout this period, I continued to search for truth. New Age looked good to me, especially the reincarnation bit—I loved the idea of having been famous in a previous life!

I tried repeatedly to quit drinking. Every morning I awoke with yet another hangover, despite my best efforts to stay sober the day before. Where was my willpower? One Friday night I hit bottom, and hit hard. Two days later, I was packing for a drinking vacation, still hung over from the Friday before. How and when would I get off this hellish merry-go-round? In anguish I cried out, "God, I can't do it alone!"

I was immediately transformed. My desire for alcohol left me and was replaced with the most sublime feeling of peace and serenity I'd known in all my forty years. God has had me in the palm of His hand ever since.

Although there was a major shift in my soul, New Age still provided the bulk of my diet—it was filling, yet lacking substance and value.

Fast forward three years to 1993. Serving tables at Red Robin, I waited on a man named JJ Johnson who had his Urantia Book strategically placed on the table. When I asked him about it, he shared just enough to intrigue me, wisely refraining from answering my question about the UB's teachings on reincarnation. I later found the Urantia Book in the library—the *other* Big Book. I got it home, glanced at the Foreword and thought, "Yeah, right!" I decided to read the book just to spot errors—an easy thing to do, I thought, in such a large volume.

I was hooked immediately and fell in love with the book. I read it three hours per day, renewed it, and continued until I had to return it to the library. The next morning, I felt as if I'd lost my best friend, or worse. I called bookstores until I located a copy and immediately drove down to buy it. Ah! the pure joy I felt when I left the bookstore with *my* book in my arms!

It's been a rough and rocky seven years since the Urantia Book entered my life. The book has been my anchor in the choppy seas of life. It has lifted me up, yielding the most sublime peace and joy I could ever imagine. It saved me. God, I love your book!

DOUG HUNTZINGER: My big question during the early '90s was, "What is a human being?" I searched many places for the answer, trying everything from different religions to literature about extraterrestrials, but no real answer was forthcoming. Then in 1993 my mother handed me a big blue book that had been sitting on her shelf since 1955, mostly unread. I must have passed by that book thousands of times! This book—the Urantia Book—explained to me just what a human being is and what his origins are. It also revealed the celestial realm, and that spirit entities are right here and can be contacted.

During the summer of 1995 I finished my first reading. Wanting to contact the spirit realm, I asked a fellow UB reader, Fred Smith, if he knew how to get in touch with the Holy Spirit, and on his recommendation I joined a Pentecostal church. Watching Rev. Benny Hinn on TV I saw many people filled with the Spirit of Truth, which he called the Holy Ghost, and I had never seen people so happy. I had to have that touch.

It was during the first night's service at one of their Men's Retreats up in the high mountains near Los Angeles that I was "baptised by the Holy Spirit." As I stood in the middle of the dining hall of the camp, I felt the Spirit enter me through the top of my head. It energized inside of me for about thirty minutes, feeling like a thousand volts of spiritual electricity filled with love. A white mist seemed to form around me and I was enveloped by golden spirit fire. As I looked up, the ceiling drew away to reveal thousands of stars and galaxies in full color, all in silence and in slow motion. It was during the first five seconds of this awesome event that the Urantia Book became real for me. Being indwelled by the Spirit of Truth was like being held in the arms of Jesus. The love I felt was cosmic and eternal. I now see each person as a child of God.

Part IX

1994-1996

JOHN MCKINNEY: My story begins in 1994 when my best friend, whom I had not seen for twenty-five years, came to town for his mother's birthday. Our reunion was short, and as we were giving parting hugs I heard the wonderful phrase, "May God bless you," coming from my friend's lips. I can still vividly hear those words. I was in shock because twenty-five years earlier my friend was a professed agnostic.

He said he was going to be back in town in a few months and suggested we get together for a longer visit. I was thrilled to have this opportunity to visit again with my treasured friend. When the time came, we settled into the usual discussion of life's adventures. Then the conversation drifted to religion. I was glad this topic had come up because I was curious to know what had changed my friend's beliefs. I was a Roman Catholic who did not agree with a lot of the doctrines of the Church, but I loved God; and although I didn't realize it at the time, I had a parching thirst for truth.

He told me how he had come upon this 2,097-page book called the Urantia Book, and how, once he'd started to read it, he couldn't put it down. He told me of the book's teachings about Jesus being the creator of our world and about the resurrection of the soul on the morontia worlds. Although I didn't tell him so, he had whetted my appetite for truth and I made up my mind that I was going to find this book.

I searched the local libraries for the UB and found three copies listed, but all were long overdue. Months went by but the books were never returned. I found a bookstore that could order the book for $50, but I wasn't going to spend that kind of money on a book I wasn't sure I would like.

But my Thought Adjuster was lovingly urging me on, for I had a constant desire to read the Urantia Book. Then one day the idea popped into my head to search the Web. I typed "Urantia" into my favorite search engine and was led to The Urantia Book Fellowship's site, where the full text of the book could be accessed. It only took a reading of the Foreword and I was hooked. While reading Paper 1, I couldn't keep the tears from flowing as I learned about our Father's love for us. By Paper 3 I knew this to be the truth.

This story will end when, after having been swept by the currents of life to the bosom of our Father, I will touch the face of God. Then a new story will begin.

BEU'LAH MARY OMAR: We are all familiar with the term "heart attack." Well, this is my story of the day I almost had a brain attack. It all began back in February of 1994 when I first started to read the Urantia Book. I became obsessed. I would wake up in the middle of the night with the irresistible urge to get up and read it. Then my first thought in the morning was to sit up in bed and start reading it again. For six weeks I spent every spare moment reading this big blue book. I was not especially interested in the book's science and history, but I was strongly drawn to the papers on the nature of God. I skipped about and read such chapters as, "The Attributes of God," "The Universal Father," and "God's Relationship to the Individual."

My religious background was diverse, to say the least. I was raised Catholic, became a Jehovah's Witness, then went on to Judaism, Buddhism, and Islam, to name just a few. My names for God changed as rapidly as people change their socks. I was determined to gain a full understanding of God if it was the last thing I ever did, which it almost was that near-fatal day in April.

I was sitting on my front room sofa, reading, and I really felt that I could not accommodate one more concept. "I can't take it anymore!" I yelled out to God as I keeled over, onto my left side. I was on the verge of breaking into uncontrollable hysteria, but the Spirit in me would not let up. "Just finish this last chapter," it admonished me. "I cannot!" I screamed out, holding my head, which felt as if it were about to burst open at any moment.

"I promise you," the Spirit pleaded, "if you just finish this last chapter you will have the understanding that you seek."

Seeing that the Spirit would not release me, I finally sat back up, regained some amount of composure, and resumed my reading. Several minutes later, having finally finished that particular chapter, I ran into my bedroom and fell flat down onto my bed. I felt myself sink into something like an altered state of consciousness. I may have actually fallen unconscious for a few minutes.

I suddenly envisioned a form of God standing in mid-air before me. I saw, coming out from his seven circles (*chakra* centers), the seven heavens, the first heaven being the mansion worlds, or bottom circle; then Jerusem came out of his second circle, and so on . . . Edentia, Salvington, Uversa, Havona, and finally Paradise out of his seventh center. The Spirit said to me, "Everything that you see in the outside world has come from within me." Now, at last, I felt I understood the saying, "As above, so below; as within, so without."

BUD HUGHES: Born in 1935 into a dysfunctional family, I became a ward of the State in my pre-school years and moved from one loveless home to another. I was taught a smattering of fundamentalist religion at an early age, dropped out of school, and walked on the wild side of life until 23—not a good background for religious learning! Things went somewhat better after I started a family—I have now been married for 43 years and have three healthy and reasonably happy children and six grandchildren. But more was to come: a triple bypass at 48, then another at 57. Could disability and forced retirement due to a degenerative lumbar be a wake-up call from God or one of his many helpers?

In March 1994 I was on my annual book trade-in at my local used book store, having run out of religious and metaphysical reading material. As I coursed through the bookshelves, up on the top a big blue hardback, bigger then any surrounding it, caught my eye. I left the store with my armload of books and when I got home I picked up the biggest book to examine. After reading the introduction and deciding I had no idea what I had just read, I paged through to the back and—yes!—came to the story of Jesus. Once I started it I never stopped. I completed my first reading of the book in August '94, and it is my constant companion to this day.

CALVIN MATTHEW GORMAN: I found the Urantia Book in the summer of 1994, while working as a letter-carrier for the US Postal Service. At the time I considered myself agnostic but open to truth. A co-worker of mine, who was into the Modern Huminds material, decided that I probably had an open mind, and introduced me to the MH literature and booklets.

It did not take long to see that MH was not for me. However, in reading a bound pamphlet of various articles, I came across an article entitled "Evaluating the Urantia Book," by Stephen F. Cannon. In its efforts to denounce the Urantia Book it actually piqued my curiosity, specifically because it alleged that the book contradicted some of the very issues that were stumbling blocks for me—the atonement doctrine, eternal punishment in hell for sinners, and a heaven of automatic perfection and bliss.

I decided that this book was something I had to read. A couple of months later I was in Austin, Texas, and came across a small pamphlet on the Urantia Book in a metaphysical shop. It contained an order form for the book, and as soon as I got home I sent in my order.

I read the Urantia Book once, read it again, and am now reading it for the third time with a local study group. The Urantia teachings are what I was looking for. They have given me a strength of faith that will serve me to Paradise.

BOB FONTANA: I was led to the book during a bridge game, by a fellow player who had been introduced to me by a mutual friend. My first impression of this person was not favorable. I found him to be antagonistic and overly competitive; however, as bridge players go, he was not unique in this respect.

Some time later, when we got together for a game at this individual's house, I noticed that he had a mess of papers all over the table. While clearing the papers away, he began talking about them briefly—that they had to do with "a group of readers" that he was associated with.

"Readers of what?" I asked.

"Oh, this book that we all read," he replied, and said that he would tell me about it after the game.

I was slightly intrigued by a bunch of people who all read the same book, but didn't give it much more thought. After the game that evening, he invited us into another room where he had some drawings and other material relating to this book. He proceeded to explain some of the concepts the book explored, illustrating his lecture with interesting artwork that depicted the universe in a way I had never seen before. What he was saying wasn't really registering with me; what I was noticing was the remarkable metamorphosis that was taking place in this person as he spoke. I was suddenly witnessing a most generous, giving, honest, and confident person speaking to me. I began asking myself, How could this be the same person that I had just tangled with at the bridge table?

In the days that followed, I remembered almost nothing about what he had said, but I did recall how blown away I was by how much he seemed to change when he was talking about this book. I began considering looking into it, thinking that if this book could have such an effect on this kind of person, there might be something to it.

During a break in our next game, I asked his opinion about a dream I'd had many times in the past, which had to do with a friend who had died years earlier. I remembered that he had spoken about life after death when he talked about this book. As soon as I asked him about it, I saw this same generous, caring, confident person emerge again. I can't express how remarkable that transformation in his character was to me. He invited me to the next Urantia meeting and I accepted, but with misgivings. Some years back I had been involved with a fundamentalist organization, and had left it because I could no longer abide its intolerance of individuality. I feared a situation where everyone would be of "one mind."

At my first Urantia meeting I was apprehensive. After a brief and relaxing meditation, a conversation between two of the people began. This discussion immediately escalated into a disagreement, with others beginning to join in. Within five minutes, it became a heated argument. It was the best thing that could have happened for me. My fears of "one-mindedness" were tossed out, and I suddenly felt at home there. That was six years and a lot of reading ago, and I'm happy to report that our meetings are as colorful now as they were at my first exposure to them. We definitely have "unity without uniformity" down pat.

I have undergone so much growth since then that it is difficult for me to recall how I used to look upon things before coming in contact with the Urantia Book. Perhaps the biggest eye-opener for me was reading about the ascension journey to Paradise. The UB's depiction of life after death expands on the Christian concept, and is so beautiful and logical that it struck me as an epiphany.

SYBIL W. MORGAN: Raised in a traditional Protestant home, during and after college I delved into Eastern philosophy, Egyptian beliefs, and the metaphysical arts. I spent thirty years teaching elementary school, and in the midst of my teaching I always made time to work on my spiritual quest. I discovered that I could relieve people's pain and heal their ailments by using crystals and gemstones and working with the guardian angels of the light. I also spent a number of years studying Native American spirituality.

I was introduced to the Urantia Book in December of 1994. I had been discussing spirituality, philosophy, and faith healing with a teacher friend, a Christian Scientist, when she asked me if I would be interested in looking at a book her father had given to her, one that she had not actually read herself. I said yes, and she brought it to school. I took it home, began reading the Foreword and knew immediately that I had to have my own copy of the book. A few days later—the beginning of the winter holiday break—I purchased one and began reading. I was a bit obsessed during the entire year of 1995, spending every spare moment reading the book. By the end of the year I had read the UB from cover to cover three times! I realized after reading it that my prior exploration of the evolutionary religions of mankind was necessary so that I might more clearly understand my kinship with all my brothers.

GONZALO AND MERCY BANDERA: Since we were married in 1971, and especially since we had our children, my husband and I have been on a constant search to find answers and identify our purpose in our earthly life. Our commitment grew out of a desire to provide a home environment full of love, compassion, kindness, and progress—a "speaking without words." Sadly, few of the answers we sought were available in Catholicism, and the examples set by many of the Catholics we knew closely were not too impressive. We deeply needed the encouragement, advice and inspiration of a group—a study group where we could increase our spiritual awareness and education.

One night, through our children, we had the good fortune to meet a lovely couple, Dr. Hal and Mrs. Lucille Kettell. Their genuine care, the peace they radiated, their kindness and compassion were truly a personal inspiration to me. I wanted to know, what had motivated them to act the way they did, without knowing me? That night in 1994 represented a turning point in my life and consequently in my husband's life.

We started spending more time with the Kettells, and they kindly invited us to attend their Urantia Book study group in their home. Actions speak louder than words, and one's daily performance can be more inspiring than any intellectual discussion or lecture. The actions and reactions of the people we've met in the study group are truly enlightening, and brotherhood is what we share with the other readers.

Our awakening came after search and faith, and this we have found through the Urantia Book.

EDUARDO GUELFENBEIN: January 1995 is when the Spirit of Truth found me and led me to my sister's bookshelf in Milan, Italy, where I discovered an unread Urantia Book. The Divine Monitor had been valiantly preparing me with biblical teachings, making me very spiritually hungry.

The Urantia Book has enlightened me from beginning to end. It is a very delicate celestial gift, for the mind and the heart. It is what it claims to be.

I study the Urantia Book in Spanish and French, and will soon be reading it in Italian. The UB inspires me to pray, worship, paint, sculpt, create art videos on *Revelaçion*, and further my knowledge 360 degrees. Sharing the Urantia Book is paramount, like sharing a beautiful experience.

I was born a Russian/Polish Jew in Santiago, Chile, in 1953. I attended English boarding schools and the Brera Art Academy in Milan, Italy. I lived in Australia for six years, in Paris for five, and now I live in Italy by the foot of the Alps on Lake Varese, with my loving wife and two children.

Viva Jesus! He challenges us today and tomorrow!

ALICIA SATTERTHWAITE: When I was young I went to different churches with my mother. I was never seriously involved in any church, but I did "believe." For example, I have always known that death is not just the end of life, but the beginning of something new as well. I knew there was something more out there. But I didn't think I'd find it in the various books that so often consume the minds of different religionists. I maintained a somewhat half-hearted search for something greater than the church experience, or the beliefs and philosophy of my mother. My father, brought up a Mormon, no longer believed Mormon doctrines, nor did he ever express an opinion about any other faith. For many years I never found anything to take my breath away, or even to interest me enough to pursue it. Until . . .

In 1995, when I was 20, I went to a club with friends to listen to a band that performed the music of Pink Floyd. The band was so great that I returned a second night. It was that second time that I met the lead singer and guitar player. I couldn't figure it out, but there was a connection between us so spiritual, the likes of which I had never felt before. We started to talk and became friends. I remember he said he'd noticed a glow about me. He himself was very involved in a "spiritual journey" at the time.

We'd known each other for about a year when he said he thought I was ready to check out this book. He'd waited to show me the Urantia Book until he no longer worried that it would scare me away. Ever since then I have been reading the book little by little, and I have become involved with so many spiritual, kind, wise, and very good people who also read it.

One of the best things about the Urantia Book is that it has helped me become a better, more loving person. Being nice towards our brothers and sisters and learning as much as possible in this lifetime is also a fun, happy, wonderful way to live—the best way of life I can ever imagine.

This book provides a glimpse into the way things will eventually be once everyone realizes and begins living the way of God. I hope to introduce more and more people to this way of life and to inspire them through my own life here on Urantia

JULIE SUGA: Born in Russia in 1952 during the Soviet era, I lived there until I was 25 when I left for Japan to marry a Japanese man. Culture in the USSR consisted of Communist ideology—anti-religious and anti-God-knowing—and times were particularly hard for the young because of the personality cult surrounding Brezhnev. Even so, it was not easy to leave my country for Japan.

Arriving there in 1977, I found Japan to be very complicated, with a difficult culture and language. But the big attraction for me was its large number of traditional religious shrines and temples.

I had been living in Tokyo approximately three years when I decided to have myself baptized in the Russian Orthodox Church. I was 27. The night before my baptism, I received a strange power in my body, as if someone unseen were revealing himself within me. And from this time on, I have always felt joined with someone who is like me. In the beginning I was scared, but I made up my mind that I would find out who this was and what he wanted. From the start I felt this power was male.

My search to understand what this power could be led me to study various Buddhist concepts, and introduced me to many individuals and groups of believers. It was all very interesting, peaceful and spiritual, but still the goal of my search was not revealed to me. I began to grow bored with the very-close-to-true, but not-exactly-true, concepts of Buddhism.

In March of 1995, after mastering certain meditation techniques, I believed myself to be in verbal communication with the one within me. Very often I would hear his voice, and I knew it was not me talking. So many times I was angry with him. Why would he not come and talk to me directly? One day in March he told me that we would meet soon, and that then I would understand who he is and who I am, too. So, for the time being, I put him out of my mind.

I began to suffer from health problems that the doctor could not diagnose. A friend in Hawaii suggested that I travel there to consult a local doctor, and that September I went to Honolulu. The doctor diagnosed a thyroid condition and set up a treatment program. For the first time in my life I enjoyed the beach and the sun.

Every day I would take walks around in the city. One late afternoon I walked into a marketplace with lots of small shops. There were not many people. In the center, astrologers were performing their services. I bought some orange juice and continued my walk. A black lady was sweeping around some chairs. As I approached, I tried to step over her broom, and my feet stopped right in front of her. I tried to walk but my feet wouldn't move. The lady looked down at my feet and said, "Go ahead, please." I said that I wanted to but I just couldn't move. She then looked into my eyes and invited me to sit down in front of her.

"How can I help you?" she asked me.

"I have no idea, " I replied, "but there must be something you can do for me."

She was a meditation and spiritual consultation master named Palmela Waiolena, and it is through her that I heard about the Urantia Book. The day I met Palmela was September 22, 1995. After telling me about the book and its concepts, she gave me the name of the Foundation in Chicago so that I could order a copy. When I returned to the hotel, I immediately realized that the promise to meet my divine mind was soon to be fulfilled. I was very happy.

When the book arrived, I opened it and was shocked by its length and difficult language. Before I started reading, I did not speak English.

I said to my divine mind, "Master, who is going to read it?" The voice replied, "Worry not, little one. I will help you." And then I started to read, not by my direct mind, but by intuition.

Today I have very little stress, and when I do I can deal with it easily. In my day-to-day life I don't take things personally the way I did before. I now understand unconditional love; before it was mostly emotional. But the best thing I've gained is great peace and security. I know that many opportunities are given to me to better myself, to be more aware, to be stronger, to conquer my animal nature, and to resist being a slave to my own ego and emotions. I do not feel the limitations of time. I have no more health problems. I feel young again. It is wonderful to know my true self.

The daily life struggle becomes a simple and funny and interesting journey. Thank you, Universal Father. I hope all readers of the Urantia Book will be as happy as I am.

SANTIAGO FLORES: In early 1995 I read an article in a magazine here in Uruguay entitled "Does God Break the Silence?" which briefly described three revelations—the Urantia Book, *A Course in Miracles*, and *Talks to Awake*—and a novel, *The Ninth Revelation*. After reading it, I made up my mind to read the Urantia Book. I began to look for it in bookstores but nobody had heard of it.

Nearly four months later, passing by a bookstore, something caught my attention at the bottom of the window: a big blue book with golden letters—it was the Urantia Book! Eureka!

My wife bought it for me as a gift weeks later. I began reading the Foreword, understanding almost nothing. I then continued through the table of contents; the Lucifer rebellion and its lessons on true and false liberty; the life of Jesus until the beginning of his public ministry; and the history of Urantia until the time of Andon and Fonta. It was then that I felt it was truly a revelation, and that an intelligent purpose lay behind the orderly arrangement of the text. Once I realized this, I went back to the beginning and read through to the end. This took me eight months.

When finished, I returned to the Foreword and said to myself, "Well, let's look at this revelation now in the light of the revelation itself." I read it through another time, which took another eight months. I'm absolutely convinced that the Urantia Book is a revelation, and even though it doesn't contain all the truth that there is, I truly believe it is the most complete, harmonious and coherent compilation of universal truth available to our generation and those to come.

PHIL KAVA: I was born in 1966, the youngest of eleven in a quasi-Catholic family. Refusing to participate in my first confession, I turned away from Catholicism. The church made no sense to me, so I quit going. I continued to be a rebel until I was 20. Smoking dope and dropping acid since I was 12 and using cocaine for most of my teens, I saw a great deal of life in the real world in a very short time. Shortly before I was 21 I knew I had to change or die, so I changed.

On May 10, 1987, I was "saved" at a Southern Baptist church in South Carolina. I truly experienced a spiritual awakening. Enveloping myself in the church, I finished reading the Bible in a few weeks and grew hungry for more. I felt the call to preach, but I met a girl from the church and within a year we got married. My preacher tried to warn me against marriage but I wouldn't listen. In September of 1991 my wife left and I have not seen her since. I was now a 24-year-old single father with sole custody of two boys and a girl ranging in age from six months to two-and-a-half years.

The next several years of my life were very trying. I quickly got involved in another challenging relationship which led to marriage. It was around that time that I first heard about the Urantia Book from a job placement counselor. All I was told was the name of the book and Christ's actual birth name. At the time it sounded evil to me as I was leery of anything which strayed from my limited Southern Baptist religious views. Because of some prior childhood experiences, I believed in aliens and other paranormal phenomena, but I was too afraid of the Devil to delve into those topics.

After my second divorce the kids and I moved to Georgia so I could finish my Bachelor's in social work at the University of Georgia in Athens, but I had to quit when I could no longer afford school and daycare costs. We went through even tougher times after that, even briefly living in a homeless shelter. At times I got extremely angry at God, asking him, "Why?" I knew the Bible and lived a good Christian life as a single father, but I felt there had to be more and I began to pray for it. Then, when it seemed I was out of prospects and with no one to turn to for help, a book found me and gave me hope.

It was in September of 1995 that the Urantia Book was again brought to my attention, this time by my brother's friend's wife. When I tried to find a copy at the local library in our rural Georgia town, the librarian said she had never heard of it, but searched for it anyway. They had five copies, all checked out, but one was on order that was due to arrive the following morning. The next day I got to the library just as the delivery truck was leaving. The five librarians at the desk were all looking at the book, wondering what it was and where it had come from. They could not believe that none of them had known the book was in the library. I told them I'd heard it was a modern version of the Bible.

That evening I read the Foreword and the first five papers. Wow! I went to bed in awe. As I lay there almost asleep a sudden sensation came over my whole body. It was as if I were plugged into a high-voltage power line. I jumped up and shook it off. I lay back down and it happened again. I prayed to God for guidance to help me understand if the Urantia Book was my next step. What I'd read so far seemed to be what I'd always believed—as if somehow I knew. I'd prayed for the answers and found them.

CHARLIE BARDEN: I came to find the Urantia Book through an organization called the Miehi Family Church. Actually, the Miehis are my in-laws.

My wife and I were moving into our own place for the first time. Both of our families met at the Miehis' to help us move. I had been up to my in-laws' home in the mountains of California many times but had no idea that they read such an incredible book. At one point my father, who is a Lutheran/Episcopalian priest, and my father-in-law and I were outside taking a break. We were discussing religion and philosophy, and my dad-in-law mentioned how he used to read science fiction until he found a book that just blew him away. He said that no human being could have written it, and that this was the only book he read anymore.

So, I went to the library, checked it out, and was hooked. Following my mother-in-law's advice, I read the sections in reverse order, which is a good idea for new readers, especially those with a Christian background. To this day I still owe the Kern County library system over $50 in late fees.

Now I understand things that people never dreamed of comprehending and it's really cool!

JEFF ABERCROMBIE: One day several years ago a friend and I were talking over philosophy and religion, and he said some really neat things. When I asked him where he'd gotten his ideas, he pointed to a large blue book on his bookshelf. I had passed by it many times but had never noticed it before. I looked it over, and was immediately struck with a compulsion to read it.

I asked if I could borrow it for a while. He responded that the book was very important to him, and this was his only copy. He stated he had never let anyone borrow it before. He then said it would be fine if I borrowed it. This was a week or two before Christmas, 1995.

A few days after that Christmas, my friend's house and everything in it burned down to the ground because of an electrical short in the Christmas lights. Everything he and his young family had owned was lost. He had built the house by hand, over several years' time. Nobody was inside at the time, thank God. Now his only possession—besides the clothes on his family's backs—was a big blue book he previously had not let anyone borrow.

A special smile comes over me every time I see that book still in my friend's possession. It sits with all the other stuff he has accumulated since the fire—the only "tattered" thing he owns!

PATRICK MALOY: I grew up in a small town in South Texas where I attended parochial school and church six days a week. I enjoyed learning about God, Jesus, Mary, the angels, and the saints. In my twenties my spiritual beliefs fell by the wayside while career and money became my focus. I kept looking for material things to fill that emptiness inside me. I knew that something was terribly wrong but I couldn't figure out what it was, and in time I became suicidal. Trips to numerous psychiatrists provided little help. I didn't realize that my drinking had become an addiction that disconnected me from a oneness with God. In a final act of desperation I asked God for help. I soon found myself sitting in an AA meeting on St. Patrick's Day and I've been sober ever since.

When my mind began to clear from the effects of alcohol, I realized that divine guidance had led me there. My newfound friends in AA helped open my mind and heart to new ideas and concepts. I was spiritually famished and wanted to know more about the divine force that led me. The phrase I kept hearing was, "Let go and let God."

Later, finding myself at another spiritual/mental crossroad, I sought professional help from Steve Farrell, a psychologist and friend. Steve had been given a copy of the Urantia Book by another colleague. Having had time to read only a paper or two, Steve suggested that I start reading from anywhere in the book to see what I thought of it. After reading a few sentences I knew the big blue book was the source of information I had been looking for. I had to have my own copy and I wanted it right away.

After making a futile search of the local bookstores in Corpus Christi, Texas, I finally found the book in a large bookstore in Boulder, Colorado, a couple of days later. The bookstore had an end-cap display of Urantia Books.

My Urantia Book became a constant companion providing a source of truth, knowledge, wisdom, strength and hope. The big blue book had come to me when I was ready for it, during a time when I was experiencing the transitions of five of my closest relatives, all of whom were dying of cancer. It was also a period when many of my friends were dying of AIDS. I called upon the book's beautiful truth while attending the dying and I often read it aloud to them.

I longed to study the book with people who had a better grasp of it than I did from self-study. When I moved to the Northwest, to Portland, in 1996, I received a list of local names and phone numbers from the Urantia Foundation. I started calling everyone on the list until I was able to reach someone. That someone was Joy Brandt. She and the people I met through her became a new family for me, and being a member of that family has added a new and joyful dimension to my life. It made me realize that I am truly part of something incredibly large, that my role is important, and that I'm exactly where I am supposed to be.

SCOTT SMITH: During a conversation about things spiritual with a man and his daughter one Friday night in a little roadside bar outside Massillon, Ohio, the man asked me if I had ever heard of the Urantia Book. My reply was the usual, "Huh?"

Both he and his daughter had read various parts of the book and recommended that I look into it. He had questions about the book's authorship (who doesn't?) and some reservations about the celestial hierarchy described in Parts I and II and about the book's historical narratives in Part III. But he thought the part about the life of Jesus was absolutely great.

For several months afterwards, I scoured all the bookstores I could find, with no luck whatsoever. In August of that year, my older brother passed away as the result of a traffic accident. It was a tragic blow to my entire family, even though he had been estranged from us for several years. Little did I know what real significance his death was to play in my immediate future.

Questions about what was in store for my deceased brother and for the rest of us still living now began to dominate most of my conscious thinking. It was at this time that the Urantia Book found me in a local bookstore—a store I must have been in once a week for four months! Alongside the new softcover edition was a copy of the third edition of Clyde Bedell's *Concordex*.

With a delight and surprise that I cannot find words to explain, I went straight to the *Concordex* looking for clues to my brother's future welfare. Honest to God, life has not been the same since! Although it took me over a year to read the Urantia Book from cover to cover the first time, my relationship with the Father within and my desire to be a more God-knowing person have deepened with each passing day. Knowing that my brother's future is really safeguarded and that the "brass ring" is always in our pocket, that all we have to do is dig deep enough to find it, really makes life worth living.

I find it most unfortunate, though, that I have lost touch with the man and his daughter. Long ago I decided to stop going to bars and clubs. But someday I will have my opportunity to thank them for opening the door to true living.

RODGER BENJAMINS: My eldest brother, Enno, began reading the Urantia Book when I was 16. Nine years separate us, so in those days I had little to do with him. I recall in my early twenties telling some friends about "this book that my brother reads," that it was "the bible of the future" and that there would one day be a new religion based on its teachings. So, while I knew the book existed, I never tried to read it and did not know what it was about.

The turning point in my life came in 1994. What sparked it was the Los Angeles earthquake in January of that year. At that time I was a devout materialist, and feeling on top of the world because I had recently been able to buy myself a condominium. I already had a great car and now I had real estate to park it in! What more could life give me than this kind of happiness? Well, thirty days after escrow closed, *Whamooo!*—the quake hit. I remember lying in my bed, clinging onto the mattress to keep from falling off, knowing, *knowing*, that I was going to die. I would soon learn if there was a God or if I was doomed to nothingness. I survived the quake, but I will never look at "things" in the same way again.

I believe this shock was the catastrophic event I needed to force me to look within and begin the great search for truth. I committed myself to weekly talk therapy, a trying but life-changing experience. I was relieved to learn that my parents were not gods but truly human, and I discovered a great deal about myself—mostly, just how wrong I had been.

One of the issues I had to resolve was my anger at society for the injustices heaped upon me by its intolerance of a young gay man. I held this anger deep within me and it controlled every relationship I had. I was especially harsh with my sister who, being closest to me in age, had been my mentor. When she left to get married I felt that my only true friend had abandoned me.

It was during this time of learning how to become self-supporting and self-contained that I first became aware of the currents of the spirit in our lives. When I began to ask my therapist questions she could not answer, I realized it was time to stop. Little did I know that I was getting ready to embark on a path I didn't even know existed at the time, the path to God.

After finishing therapy I felt better than I'd ever felt before, but I was still not free from spells of anxiety and anger. Then something wonderful happened. I met Gerald, the person with whom I wanted to spend the rest of my life. We wished to sanctify our love before our family and friends with a "Union Ceremony." After many phone calls we finally found a minister who would perform our ceremony, and invitations went out.

To our great disappointment, my sister, one of my brothers and all of Gerald's family refused to attend, and they all made their biased feelings known to us. While I was intensely wounded by my sister's decision, I knew that deep down she loved me, and that it was her own hurt feelings that prevented her from attending. For the first time in my life I saw her point of view rather than mine. I began to see the spirit of her actions, and I was humiliated by my own.

On the day I learned of my sister's decision I told my brother Enno that I believed that all of the world's problems were caused by this unknowing of other people's true intentions, that at the core of almost everyone's being is the desire to love and be loved. That was when he said to me, "You should read the Urantia Book."

Yes! The sudden, unyielding urge to get the Urantia Book stunned and excited me. It was too late in the evening to find a copy, so it would have to wait until the next day. I slept restlessly, anxious for the morning, and woke up with one thing on my mind: Find a copy of that mysterious book! Locating one was easy, and soon I was sitting on my couch with the Urantia Book on my lap. It was not long before I started to recognize the significance of what I was reading.

Intending to find out what ugly things the Urantia Book had to say about sexuality and homosexuality, I went straight for the marriage papers. The beauty of those papers truly inspired and relieved me. In all that the book says in glorifying the marriage institution, it never resorts to lowering those like me who cannot participate. But I was still not convinced. My next stop was "The Lucifer Rebellion." In therapy I had asked, "What is the cause of all the confusion in the world?" By the end of this paper, I had received my answer. I've been hooked to this revelation ever since.

This all took place in August of '96. For the first couple of weeks I read so intensely that I developed a headache, yet I had never felt more alive in my life. At first the idea of reading the Jesus papers frightened me, so I read "The History of Urantia." With the turning of each page, I felt myself coming closer to the realization of life's true purpose. By the following spring I had read the entire book (except for the Foreword!).

The Urantia Book confirmed for me that God loves us unconditionally, and that to worship him is to love others as he loves them. The Father's love for us has brought my entire family back to me. I have living proof within me that God can do it all.

CURT DAY: One day while in college in 1996, my girlfriend (now my wife) and I were at a local bookstore here in Lexington, Kentucky. This was a store we often went to, but on this occasion I felt something was different. My wife and I were standing in line to purchase our stuff when I felt compelled to turn to my right. It was almost as though someone or something was looking at me. I turned, and directly in my line of vision on the neighboring shelf was the Urantia Book. I took it off the shelf and bought it without even opening it or looking at the price. I had never heard a thing about the Urantia Book before—nothing! My wife turned to me and asked, "What is the Urantia Book?" I very confidently replied, "Everything. Existence."

In the coming months I found that it was everything I knew it to be. Yet, it has been more than I ever imagined.

LINDA BARNETT: I was standing in a New Age bookshop. I had just finished *A Course in Miracles*. I saw a brown box on the shelf, glued shut, with a book inside and the price on the outside. I felt too guilty to open it, so I bought the box. When I got home and opened it I got the surprise of my life. That was 1996. I still can't read too much of it at one time—tears blind me.

HOLLY CARMICHAEL: One day, my years-long search for truth finally landed me in a little church just up the road from where I live. It happened like this:

Earlier that morning, I had become extremely but inexplicably anxious to go out—but to where? I decided to go to the store. But for some odd reason, I was overdressing myself and the kids, too. As we set down the road to the little store nearby, I tried to figure out what my problem was. Why was I in such a tizzy and in such a hurry to go to the store? I must be crazy, I thought. This staying at home with the kids has finally taken all my brain cells away, and I am completely nuts.

While thinking these thoughts, I scooted past the store and up the road a little further, where I approached two churches whose parking lots became my target for turning the car around. Suddenly, the steering wheel seemed to be turning itself into the parking lot of the first church.

Instead of turning around, I found myself parking and walking the kids up to the pastor's entrance. I knocked. The pastor was a wonderful woman who told me of the church's Sunday school for children and its adult Sunday school class which would be starting in a few weeks to study the different Christian denominations. Stunned by this answer, on the spur of the moment I decided to attend the classes and had great hopes of finally learning the answers to my many questions.

I remember thinking that an angel must have guided me there. I had just caught the minister as she was literally on her way out for a couple of weeks. The classes were scheduled to begin on her return. I thanked God over and over for all his help.

After a few weeks in the church, I was invited to sing in the choir. I soon became friends with the choir director and we began to have lots of talks about our families. As our friendship grew, I told him of my concerns about another family member's spirituality. My friend told me about a big blue book called the Urantia Book, and suggested that my family member read it. I myself was infinitely curious about this book, and if it could help my loved one, then I was all for it.

So, one Sunday after church, the choir director came to my house and thoughtfully presented a copy of the Urantia Book to my loved one, who received the book graciously but over the next few weeks came to reject it.

But *I* didn't. I read the book voraciously from start to finish. I read it twice in one year. Not long after that, when I finally got a computer in my home, my choir director friend introduced me to some electronic study groups for Urantia Book readers. I am now on my third go-round with the book. I still sing in the choir and attend the little church, and with new fervor I seek to gently and quietly spread the truth around by doing good.

SHANE BOROWSKI: All my life I have been a dreamer and a romantic who loves to ponder the unknown. As a child I would observe nature and always try to guess her next move.

Shortly after college I married a beautiful Native American girl. From her I learned about the world and the incredible power of truth. After our separation—in slight part because of spiritual differences—I began to look hard for God.

I started by the reading *The Celestine Prophecy*—a great beginner's manual for general awareness. After finishing that book I went on a sojourn of sorts, alone, to the Four Corners area, staying mainly in Utah. Using my newfound knowledge from the *Prophecy* book, I began to really pay attention to the world around me, listening to the trees, the birds, the wind, and just generally picking up on signals. Signals I found, and by following them, I met all sorts of great people. Each person seemed to have the answer to a thought I was holding on my trek to meet them; each answer led me to another train of thought, which in turn led to another chance meeting and another answer. It was beautiful.

In the year or so after the trip, and still lonely from my breakup, I started scanning through the Bible again. I had been raised pretty much a Christian, but had never found satisfaction in the Bible or in the church. Friends of mine who were Christian missionaries had traveled to remote places in hopes of converting natives who were unaware of the Bible to Christianity. "As good a person as a native may be," said one friend, "if they don't know who Jesus is, they are condemned to suffer." I just couldn't come to grips with this philosophy. Aside from that, I found things in the Bible that seemed so true, but expressed in such obsolete terminology. I thought, "What if it could be rewritten for us?"

I then discovered the works of Zechariah Sitchin. He spoke of celestial creatures—aliens—who had visited earth before the birth of civilizations, and had given the human race a boost. His amazing claims were all substantiated by legitimate evidence. The Sitchin books opened my eyes to a whole new world. I had always felt there was more to our history than we had been taught or preached. Still, these claims were not quite the answer for me. They satisfied the science end of my quest but left my spiritual curiosity dangling.

Then along came the Urantia Book. During one of my weekly visits to Borders Books I went to my usual sections—Spirituality and Metaphysics. I was desperately looking for some new truth. Then I saw a little white box with three blue concentric circles on it. It was sealed shut and said only "The Urantia Book." I pondered it a bit and picked it up, but was afraid to open it. I left the store intrigued and, in a weird way, "touched."

A week went by, and I couldn't stop thinking about that little white box. In all the times I had gone to the bookstore, I had never seen it before. What was in it? What is Urantia? So I went back, and there it was, virtually untouched since I had last put it down a week earlier. I braved up and unsealed the box (it was only $10—I'd buy it if they made me) and took out a thick, blue book. I opened it up to Part I, which talked about the Superuniverse, and—*Whammo!*—I knew this was my long-sought answer.

I pummeled through each page—especially Part III, our history—and fell in love. Everything inside me told me *Yes!* This is *it!* Every question I had had seemed to be dealt with in the UB. Never had I been so sure about something. What a great feeling! Even better, all my thoughts and concerns about Christianity were addressed in a way that made perfect sense, and my relationship to God and Jesus/Michael was solidified for good. I had found what I was looking for.

CATHERINE HEYNEMAN: In June of 1996 I had been divorced for about a year and was looking for something to plug up the big empty hole in my life. Silly me, I thought I needed a man. Pocatello, Idaho, is a place where the men you meet in bars believe the size of their belt buckle is commensurate with their virility. So, desperate but not *that* desperate, I decided to answer some personal ads in the local paper.

One ad in particular intrigued me—it was from a vegan. A vegetarian myself, I was really excited to meet this person. We dated for a while, and he introduced me to the Urantia Book as well as to a group of local readers. A very smart man, he didn't shove the book in my face and say, "This is truth!" He simply left it out on his coffee table where I eventually picked it up and "discovered" it for myself. He warned me, "Whatever you do, don't start with the Foreword!" So what did I do? Yup. Put the book down and didn't pick it up again for three months.

But in the meantime, I was attending the Pocatello meetings and was completely blown away by some of the people there, mainly Debbie Roberts and Nancy Kelly. The spiritual energy in that room just took my breath away. It was as though I'd found home. And it was about then that I realized that that big empty hole wasn't a relationship vacuum—it was a *spiritual* vacuum that desperately needed to be filled.

I'd been tromping all over the country, going to Esalen and to Body and Soul conferences looking for something that would tie together my readings (I'm a big fan of Alan Watts, Fritjof Capra and Carolyn Myss) and my experiences. That something was the Urantia Book and the group of readers, both of which I found in my own back yard. The UBook is the only thing I've ever come across that resonates within me as pure truth. Thanks to all the members of the Pocatello group, past and present, I now have a functional "family of choice" as opposed to the dysfunctional "family of chance" I was born into.

DAVID LINTHICUM: Growing up, I visited my friends' churches and became exposed to many different denominations. Not having been indoctrinated into any one religion, I was free to find my own way.

As part of my search, I spent fifteen years reading the *Seth* books, authored/channeled by Jane Roberts. I first came in contact with the *Seth* material when I was in the Navy, stationed in Meridian, Mississippi. I had gone into town to do some shopping with a girlfriend when my eyes landed on a *Seth* book. I picked it up, read the dust jacket, and bought it. When I returned to base I started reading and couldn't put it down. I read for hours, totally forgetting about a date I had. I look back at the years I spent reading the *Seth* books and wonder if it was time wasted. I really don't think so. If anything, I feel that I was led to that material as sort of a stepping stone to the next level.

In the summer of 1996 I was visiting an old friend named David who had moved to the quaint little town of Medicine Park, Oklahoma, nestled in the foothills of the Washita Mountains. David and I had similar tastes in life and had shared some memorable experiences. It was during a discussion we were having about the Kennedy assassination that he motioned toward his bookshelf and told me to look for a particular book on Kennedy. While I was searching I stumbled onto this big—and I do mean *big*—book, and pulled it out of the bookcase. As I plopped it down on the coffee table, I asked, "What is this? It weighs a ton."

The next hour or so was a revelation about The Revelation. He told me a story he had heard about how the Urantia Book came into existence as well as the little that he remembered about the contents of the book. It turns out that David hadn't gotten through much of it before "shelving" it. He suggested I read the last part of the book first and then go back and read the beginning. The whole thing sounded a bit too strange but I decided to read a little of the Foreword and get a flavor of it. Wow! It claimed to answer all of the questions that had nagged me for years. The more I read the more fascinated I became.

When I returned home from my trip that summer I was determined to find this Urantia Book and take a closer look at it. In the neighborhood of the office where I worked was a bookstore called Peace of Mind, which carried a potpourri of New Age, mystical, and religious literature and trinkets, and where the smell of incense was overpowering. One day during my lunch break I went in. I found the Urantia Book prominently displayed, but was surprised to see that it was boxed. Never before had I bought a book in a box.

I didn't follow my friend's advice. Being the stubborn sort I was determined to start at the beginning and work my way through. That plan didn't last long. My curiosity got the better of me. I had to get some answers to my most burning questions, so I tore through the table of contents until I found the listing for Adam and Eve. That is where I would start. It is still one of my favorite sections of the book, along with the Lucifer rebellion. Those were the biggest mysteries in my mind, the ones that had forced me to question what I had been taught and had heard for years. I could never buy into the Bible's version of these events, but the Urantia Book solved these riddles and set my mind at peace. I found my peace of mind at the Peace of Mind bookstore in Tulsa, Oklahoma.

Since then I have found a study group in Tulsa where I enjoy sharing with other students of the Urantia Book. Yes, this book has changed my life. I feel a sense of calm now that comes from knowing there is an exciting future ahead for us all—if we choose it.

RICARDO FRANCO: The first lessons from the book came to me when I was 16 years old while reading the first volume of *Caballo de Troya (The Trojan Horse)*, a novel written by J. J. Benitez, based on teachings from the Urantia Book. This series of five books describes the life of Jesus, and it came to me when I needed it most. I felt that the conventional way of seeing God offered by the church was leaving out something essential. I had always been rebellious about it and had problems finding support for my point of view. The refreshing new life of Jesus of Nazareth told in these books was like an answer to my prayers.

The Trojan Horse came into my hands by chance, and after devouring it, I eagerly awaited the next volume of the series. The same author later wrote *La Rebelion de Lucifer (The Lucifer Rebellion)*, which recounts the story of the creation of our galaxy, the organization of the universe, the planting of life on our planet, the birth of Andon and Fonta, and the evolution of man, climaxing with the story of the Lucifer rebellion.

This particular book made me feel new things, because my soul knew the instant I was reading it that it was more than a fantasy. I decided to look for the source of these books. When at last I found the Urantia Book I could finally begin to read from the beginning.

The Urantia Book has given me an enormous, wonderful vision bigger than that taught by any other religion. This revelation has shown me a new dimension of God's love; it has changed and continues to change my life from its foundations. Imagine the incomparable sense of joy that comes from knowing that God wants us to love him voluntarily and not because of fear! Thanks to the teachings of the Urantia Book, I've become a freer human being and therefore able to be more worthy of his love.

PRADHANA FUCHS: I live in the south of South America, in a city in Chile. Years ago a man told me about an incredible book called the Urantia Book. That was all. Then I received a message from the sky, given to me in a dream. They were telling me to go north, so I packed. My first destination was Machupicchu, the hidden city of the Incas, in Peru.

I had almost reached Machupicchu when I stopped in a small town called Pisag. Up on the hills of this town were some Inca ruins. After the bus left, I noticed in a corner of the town a small hotel, so I went in. Sitting inside were some gringos who looked like kind men. As I was walking by, one of them stood up and said, "Hi," and asked what I was doing there. "Just visiting places," I replied, and asked them what *they* were doing there. One of them responded, "We have a book and we are sharing it. It's the Urantia Book." My ears heard and my eyes were shocked. I said to him, "I want one!"

The next morning my new Urantia friend and I went on a strenuous pilgrimage to the ruins together. Then we made an agreement to travel together on a Urantia Book sharing mission. This decision was taken under a big tree, and from that moment on, I called my friend "Big Tree." I want, through these words, to express my love for this friend, Norman Ingram. We were in so many countries, shared so many experiences together—Norman, me and our celestial Father. It's amazing how so many people got interested in our small blue treasure. I have a beautiful study group here now, and we want to spread our love to the universe.

KINDA FORD: I had a Christian upbringing but could never bring myself to believe that there was a devil in the wings, just waiting to lead me astray. Nor could I comprehend that Jesus died for the sins of mankind, and that to avoid hell I had to become "saved." To me it all sounded like make-believe. I chucked it all, including God, and became an atheist. It made much more sense.

My husband had always had an interest in New Age books, and after much prodding he finally got me to read some of them. For the first time in my life, I was reading things about God that made so much sense that I decided God *did* exist after all.

My quest for finding out all I could about God had begun. I read every New Age book I could get my hands on. At the bookstore one day

I came across a volume entitled *The Handbook of Metaphysics*. My husband tried to talk me out of buying it, saying that I should get some other book that he had in mind, but I wouldn't budge.

It turned out that this book devoted a whole chapter to the Urantia Book. What it said about it made me so curious that I checked the UB out of the library and began reading different sections. I was amazed that anyone could have this much knowledge about God, and believed that the information had to have come from a higher source.

In 1996 I eventually bought a copy of the book, but soon found out that we needed two because my husband and I were always fighting over whose turn it was to read it. I devoured every page, managing to read it through in about two months. While reading one page, I couldn't wait to see what it had to say on the next one!

The information in the UB has transformed my life. I have truly found God—or did he find me? I have dedicated my life to doing God's will, not out of fear of being cast into hell if I don't, but because I truly love my Father in heaven. And the angels cheered—for little ol' me!

JEFFREY MASON: I first learned of the Urantia Book when my father and I were visiting my sister, who was attending seminary in Lancaster, Pennsylvania. She introduced me to a classmate named David Pendleton, a hypnotist studying to become a pastor in the United Church of Christ, where most of my immediate family were members. David was seeking to supplement his professional credentials with a seminary degree. Finding him sincere and knowledgeable without being a slave to convention, I immediately felt that I could discuss anything with him.

It was late spring and a singularly radiant day. As our conversation developed, David's two children and my nephew ran back and forth around us yet we stayed focused on a truly unusual exchange that lasted for two hours. At one point I confided that one of my goals was to create a progressive kind of school, utilizing the most advanced concepts and knowledge to design the courses and train the instructors and students.

He looked at me for a moment, then told me about a book that addressed some of the issues I had raised. He cautioned me that it was not your usual book. He further stated that although he'd been reading the book for several years, I was the first person besides his wife with whom he'd shared it. I took that as a challenge.

When David began telling me about his unusual book, I was reminded of an early childhood experience: As a six-year-old, sitting in the sun in the middle of the street, I felt the beauty of everything around me, and was strongly aware of the presence of the Creator, both inside and outside of me. That moment of peace had been the most intense experience of my life thus far. Listening to David describe the book evoked the same sense of spiritual communion.

Then he showed me the book. I don't recall what I opened to first, but something inside me vibrated like an internal Geiger counter, like a seismograph alerting me of a coming earthquake. It was as if an inner alarm had gone off—and yet I was not alarmed.

JAIME ANDRES CUELLO: In 1996 I was reading J. J. Benitez's *The Trojan Horse*, a book based on the Urantia Book. A friend, also a Benitez reader, told me, "I know of a little book that J. J. uses as a source for his books. Are you interested?" A few days later I was asking for the Papers in a bookstore, but when I saw the UB for the first time, for US$80, I said, "Naaaa! Too long, too expensive, and maybe full of lies!" I left the bookstore.

Five minutes later the salesman in the bookstore was handing me the book in a bag, and that was all. Since that day I feel I am a different guy—a better guy!

VICKI MILLER NEWBY: One Sunday evening in February of 1995 I met an interesting man named Steve Newby. A light seemed to shine from him, and as I got to know him, I marveled over the things he would say. One day, after he'd told me something particularly amazing and beautiful, I asked him, "Where did you get that?"

"Have you ever heard of the Urantia Book?" he asked me in return.

"The what?"

As he explained a little bit about it, he produced his copy of Big Blue.

"Who wrote this?" I pressed him, thumbing through the thick book. Given my penchant for seeking out and studying spiritual works, I couldn't believe I hadn't come across the book earlier in my life. What he showed me, however, went straight over my head. It all seemed pretty weird to me. I wasn't ready for the Urantia Book just yet.

I could tell Steve read this book a lot when I wasn't around. Days rolled into weeks, and weeks rolled into months. He continued to share beautiful and spiritually moving concepts from the Urantia Book with me, so much so, that I no longer needed to ask him where the ideas came from.

In the summer of 1996, to celebrate his birthday, I invited Steve out for a steak dinner but he declined, preferring to celebrate by studying this strange big blue book with a group of like-minded others. When he asked if I'd like to go along, I saw that light that had first attracted me to him, and I agreed to accompany him. I'm glad I did.

And so it was that I began reading the book in the company of the Spirit Jazz Study Group. I had a thousand questions and the group was very patient with me. The first thing I looked up when I got home that first night was Paper 38, "Ministering Spirits of the Local Universe," as I was curious to know more about the unseen help that we receive. Next I read Paper 93, "Machiventa Melchizedek." I had always been interested in this mysterious Melchizedek character who was mentioned in the Bible. One of the study group members had talked about the Thought Adjuster papers, so I read them and fell in love with that little spark of God that loves me so. "The Consecration of Choice" is one of the most moving and meaningful messages I have ever received. What a gift not to have to wrestle my will against God's, to be able to say, "It is my will that your will be done," and mean it!

Having been put off of religion by well-meaning but dogmatic twentieth-century Christians, I might never have read the Jesus papers if the study group hadn't been reading them. My thinking is now open to Jesus and all who love him. These bits and pieces of study have given me a whole new perspective on this life, on humanity, and on my part here.

I've noticed an interesting thing about Urantia Book readers. They still have human problems, but in each UB reader I've met, I see that same light that I saw in Steve the first time I met him. My consciousness of this light in UB readers has encouraged me to look for it in others, and seeking, I have found.

JOSEFINA DE MARTINEZ: One day, while looking for some postcards and magazines in a bookstore in Cancun where I live, I found *El Testamento de San Juan (Saint John's Last Will)* by J. J. Benitez. It appeared to be the last copy in the store and I wanted to buy it because I had already read his *Virgin de Guadalupe* and had seen him interviewed on TV. While I was paying for it, I asked the clerk if the store carried any other works by the same author. He called the manager, who informed me that he had never heard of Benitez. I showed him the book I'd just bought, and he told me, bewildered, that the book I had in my hands was not for sale at his bookstore. "It doesn't have our special marks," he said. "Maybe somebody forgot it and left it here." He told the clerk to return my money in case the owner came back asking for the book. I finally convinced him to let me keep it and gave him my phone number in case that someone returned. No problem, since nobody has called me yet.

Later, I went to the dentist and told him the story, and he asked me if I had read *The Trojan Horse*. Since I hadn't, he offered to lend me his own copy. I read *Last Will* first, finished it quickly, then began *The Trojan Horse*. It all was so interesting that I read day and night, till later that week, when a friend and I left for Cozumel to attend a series of lectures on "Superior Consciousness."

In Cozumel we stayed for three days at the hotel where the lectures took place. On the second day, I noticed a table full of books on one side of the room. During the next intermission I went over to that table and was informed that those books had been brought over for the hotel tourists by a woman named June. In that heap of all sizes and subjects I found the Urantia Book—the same book J. J. Benitez had talked about in *Last Will*. I located my friend, and together we went looking for June. When we found her and asked her about the Urantia Book, she told us to keep it, saying, "I haven't really read it. Somebody left it at my home."

So came the Urantia Book, in English, into our hands. For me it is a wonderful book and I believe in it completely. The account of the life of Jesus answers most of the questions I had asked my parents and the Catholic priests in my youth. I wish to thank J. J. Benitez from the bottom of my heart for bringing the UB to my attention. It is important that this major revelation from the Most Highs be disseminated around the world, and that we all learn what we can from it.

JUAN PAULO VEGA: My encounter with the Urantia Book came at a most opportune moment in my life and in a unique way. For some years I had been looking for the answers to my many questions, and this led me to investigate various religious beliefs and to become associated for a brief time with several religious organizations. However, I never found answers that left me feeling satisfied.

Earlier I had left Chile, forsaking my job, my family and my friends to try my luck in another country. Things abroad did not turn out the way I'd hoped, and I was obliged to return to my family after six months. I came back somewhat defeated, but happy to reacquaint myself with my world—my Andes Mountains, my Pacific Ocean, my Spanish tongue and the love of all the people I knew. The first days back I was quite content, but I soon began to worry because I could not find work in my city and would soon be needing money to pay the bills.

It was then that I felt an urgent need to search for something. With little else to do I began navigating the Internet and came upon the Urantia Book. The name riveted me. I felt an imperative need to investigate what the book was about. Looking for more information, I came to the summary of its four parts. The more I read the more astonished and surprised I grew; I became convinced that I was facing something much larger than a book. I was certain that this was what I'd been searching for.

The next day I called the Urantia Foundation in the United States and was given the address and telephone numbers of two people, Nina Bravo and Oly Tartakowsky, who each conduct a Urantia study group in the capital of my country, Santiago de Chile. They have become my good friends and, in a certain way, spiritual guides. Incredibly, at the same time I was notified of a job opportunity in Santiago. Transferring to that city, I was welcomed by Oly into her study group. Oly gave me my Urantia Book in Spanish, one of five thousand copies of the 1991 first edition. I then began to explore this wonderful revelation that has since transformed my life.

The revelation has broadened my horizons and changed my beliefs. It has quenched my thirst for answers. It has brought me closer to God and to Jesus in a very special way. It has made me understand the reality of the brotherhood of man and the Fatherhood of God. It has opened my eyes to the fact that we're not alone, that we are part of a vast plan of evolution and perfection. Through this book I have met wonderful people, not only in Chile but also in other countries in the Americas and the rest of the world. I'm grateful for that. My desire and challenge for the future is to be able to share this revelation with many people and to lead a study group, to do my share towards the dissemination and recognition of the Urantia Book's marvelous contents.

DIEGO GONZALES MUNOS: Having studied at an Anglican school in Chile, a predominantly Roman Catholic country, I had the opportunity of learning and experiencing tolerance. I was very curious about UFO phenomena and paranormal activity, and an insatiable thirst for truth led me on a search through several religions. One day, a friend told me about *The Trojan Horse* by J. J. Benitez. I soon read all of the books in the series, devouring them one after the other. I began to read other books by Benitez, including *The Lucifer Rebellion, Visitors (The UFOs)*, and *St. John's Last Will.* The latter book talks about the Urantia Book; the author says he has drunk from its waters. But it was not yet the hour.

I was studying at the university in the city of Santiago, three thousand kilometers from home, when one day I saw the Urantia Book in a bookstore, inside its box. Its look was powerful, mysterious. Unfortunately, it was very expensive and I didn't dare buy it. It was not yet the hour. Two months later I made up my mind to purchase it, but I couldn't find the book anywhere. Was somebody playing me the fool?

I was out for a walk with a friend, near a commercial center, when I saw it again. I called my father and very subtly told him about the book I wanted, mentioning that I had not received any Christmas gifts or birthday gifts from him. Mission accomplished!

With money in hand, I took a bus across town to buy my book. After two minutes, I felt an irresistible pull to jump out of the bus, which I did. Feeling embarrassed and foolish for jumping out without a real motive, I began walking a few steps to a bookstore, and there it was in the middle of the table—the Urantia Book, Spanish version. I talked with the bookseller and began to understand that "the hour had come."

I don't believe in chance. For example, I will tell you about a person who came to our study group and told us how he'd found the Urantia Book. He was anxious for us to learn of the strange and seemingly supernatural nature of his encounter. He asked, "Well, what do you think? Isn't that strange?" To which I answered, "It would have been strange if the encounter had *not* been strange."

GUSTAVO PROANO: From 1976 to 1982 I belonged to a brotherhood that met weekly to discuss esoteric matters. We would often get into trouble because we couldn't find a logical or rational explanation for something. One of our members used to say, "Surely it must be explained in the Urantia Book," as if the book were the last word. This happened many times, and just as many times I would ask him, "What *is* that book?" He couldn't answer me, since he only knew about it from other people. On several occasions I asked for the book in bookstores and libraries, but no one had heard of it. They asked me for the author, the name of the publishing company, or any other information that would help to locate the book, but I couldn't give it to them.

Many years later, in October 1996, I was in a bookstore looking for a book on marketing. Nearby, in the Esoteric section, a fat blue book caught my eye. I moved closer and saw the name on top, *El Libro de Urantia*. I remembered the title instantly. It was unbelievable to me that almost twenty years after I had first heard of the Urantia Book, I could finally touch it, feel it, and begin reading it.

What an absolutely extraordinary vision it portrayed of God and the universe, sparking almost as many answers as questions! I must say that when I began reading, I found the book strange and hard to understand, with so many different and unfamiliar names—it was almost impossible to grasp them all; but I did manage to make charts to establish relations among these different concepts and personalities. Even after reading the same things over several times, it seems as though I'm reading a different text each time. But, proceeding slowly and carefully, I try to understand as much as I possibly can.

ROGER IN HAWAII: One day in the summer of 1992 I was painting in front of my gallery in Haleiwa, Hawaii. Around closing time a homeless person, an adventurer, entered the gallery. I could see that he was lonely and hungry, so I asked him to stay the night at our house, which he was very happy to do.

We talked into the night, and talk turned to God, as a good conversation must. At the time I was studying with the Jehovah's Witnesses and was preaching to him. He kept telling me, "God doesn't kill people!" Inside I knew this made sense; I had been struggling with parts of the Bible, and had many unanswered questions such as, "Who was Nod?"

Christopher stayed in Hawaii for two years before returning to the mainland. He told me about the Urantia Papers as well as the *Paramony*, a book that his friend Duane Faw had put together. Christopher had attended some study groups and a national convention of Urantia Book readers. Although he really hadn't read that much of the book himself, he seemed very confident that the Urantia Book was superior to the Bible.

The Witnesses teach that the Bible warns us that all other books about God—and there are many—are from demons. The day finally came, however, when the Jehovah's Witnesses and I parted. The Bible seemed to have only a part of the truths that I needed to know. One of the last conversations I had with the Witness friend I'd been studying with went something like this: "Roger, the Bible is the Owner's Manual for Life," and my instant reply was, "I believe it may be, but I want the Repair Manual!"

All I can say is, angels do listen to us. I had just read the first *Conversations with God* book, and at the time it made a lot of sense to me. When I went to the bookstore to buy my own copy, it was sold out. However, on a nearby shelf I spotted the Urantia Book. Was this a book of truth or was it a demon book? I opened it up. The first thing I read was "Our Religion." I didn't know who wrote it, but it sure sounded like something I would say. I put the book back on the shelf, still unsure of its true origin.

Some time passed, and then I had a family crisis. I found out my kids were not vegetarians as I thought they were—they had been eating Big Macs for a long time! I was so hurt by this discovery that I was ready for a divorce. I had been deceived by my own family!

Feeling lost and hurt, I went again in search of that *Conversations* book. Once again—this time at a different bookstore—it was sold out. I started to leave, but turned to look one more time. It was definitely not there, but up on the top shelf was another huge copy of the Urantia Book, priced at around $75. I looked at it again and this time I wanted it, but not at that price—not today.

Ready to leave, I took one more look, and then I saw the little blue softcover Urantia Book that I now love, and for only $20. I went to a park and read for the next four hours, crying and laughing at this beautiful little blue Repair Manual! When I read the section, "The Talk with Nathaniel," where Jesus says that our Father does not send out armies to kill people, especially women and children, I knew that Christopher had been right, that "God doesn't kill people." I had finally found the God that I had been searching for my whole life—a God of love!

The book saved my marriage and my family when I realized that I was just one of the many mortals of Urantia who are trying to get rid of their animal inheritance, and that we all must do this in our own time. I often think about how the Father works. My friend Christopher was an alcoholic and homeless person who was often abused by society even though he had never hurt anyone; he was looked down upon by most, and yet he had the keys to life on Urantia. I'm glad he shared them with me.

NEL BENJAMINS: I grew up a Dutch girl in Amsterdam, the third of five children. At six I was enrolled in a Christian school. Since my parents were of modest means, I felt privileged and honored to be in such a beautiful school. The first hour of every school day was dedicated to religious teaching, mainly Bible reading. I loved those old Bible stories, although I often found them brutal. As I learned about the life of Jesus, it gave me great joy to realize the love he brought us, but the story of how he died so cruel a death on the cross for my sins troubled me. It didn't make sense, but then who was I to question the adults? The guilt and fear created great confusion within me, but oh, how much I loved Jesus!

Then something big happened. A new teacher, Mr. Keyl, came to our school. He seemed to come straight from heaven, like Jesus incarnate, because he loved us so much. In science class he took us out into the field around our school, to teach us about bugs and other creepy-crawlers, and to pick wildflowers which we kept in empty jelly jars on our desks. He brought in containers with caterpillars so we could observe them transforming into butterflies. The experience of having this teacher in my life made me believe in the possibility of a great love existing somewhere out there. As I grew to young womanhood, while having this conflict about the story of Jesus, I tried to live as much as I could like Jesus and to do the will of the Father.

At 17 my special guy came into my life. We were married and in no time had three children, two sons, Enno and Robin, and a daughter, Sharon. My husband, a Dutch-Indonesian, loved Holland but did not want to live there, so we emigrated to the United States where, after three years, our "native American" Rodger was born.

For me the move to a foreign country was difficult. I did not have a feeling of belonging and began to isolate myself more and more. For many years, while raising my family, I struggled with depression. Now I know that even in my darkest days our Father was always there, lifting me up, guiding me along, compelling me perhaps to see a movie that had an important message for me, to help me visualize his beautiful silvery light in my mind; but at the time I wasn't aware of it.

Some time after Enno got married and had a family of his own, he found a big blue book and started telling us about it. He talked about celestial beings and "Thought Adjusters." My husband and I thought, "What is happening? Is this some kind of cult?" While it was somewhat frightening, at the same time I was fascinated. After a while, however, Enno stopped talking about the book.

Later, when Rodger grew up and faced his own troubles and difficulties, Enno suggested to him that his answers could be found in the Urantia Book. Rodger dared to buy it, and within a few weeks I noticed a great change in him and in Enno, who had started reading again. Now both of them were bugging me to read this book.

Still leery, at the same time I became more intrigued. The two of them conspired to get the book into my house by giving it to me for Christmas 1996. "Oh, no!" I thought, "Not that book again!" I put it in my desk drawer and, although I was aware of it being there, I did not attempt to read it for five months.

Then one day I took the book out, put it on my lap and said to myself, "It's just a book. It's not going to eat me. I will throw it out if I don't like it." As advised, I started with the Jesus papers. Oh, my God—how wonderful it was! I was on the phone a lot asking my sons, "What is Nebadon?" and "Who is Melchizedek?" I had so many questions and it was all so exciting!

Now, after several complete readings, I am a different person. I am freed of my old fears and confusion. I feel as if I am being carried on the wings of the Spirit of Truth, thrusting forward to serve in the kingdom of God—the adventure of eternal life.

Part X

1997-2000

TIMOTHY W. MORRIS: I was raised in a devout Mormon family in Virginia, my parents having converted to that faith while in their twenties. I was the tenth of fourteen children, and although our family life was hectic, my parents had a wonderful, loving relationship which aided greatly in keeping the family close-knit. From a very young age I was devoted to the Mormon faith; I read the entire Bible, *The Book of Mormon*, and other religious works.

At 19, like many young men in the Mormon religion, I did two years of missionary service. During my mission in southern Spain, I came face to face with a lot of questions concerning the absolute truthfulness of *any* religion. Although I served an honorable mission and assisted many people in joining the Mormon faith, I was beginning to distance myself from my religion. Towards the end of my mission I lost my belief in Mormonism.

While at a family's home in Seville, I came upon a copy of the fictional Spanish-language work *The Trojan Horse* (first volume), by J. J. Benitez. I read only a small excerpt but found its description of Christ tremendously appealing. I did not buy the book while in Spain, thinking that there would be editions in the United States; but upon my return in 1988 I could not find a copy anywhere.

During the next six years I attended Brigham Young University and got married. I let no one know of my loss of belief except my father, whom I told immediately upon my return from Spain. I went through the motions of being a Mormon throughout those six years, becoming more spiritually removed with each passing year.

In 1994, after finishing my schooling, I was hired by a banking software firm and given the responsibility of overseeing their sales in

Latin America. I began heavy travel throughout South America, and while in Bogotá, Colombia, I came upon the *Trojan Horse* books again (then numbering four volumes). I bought all four and began reading them on my flights to and from South America. The content of the books was too realistic to be fiction and I was continually fascinated.

At the end of 1996, I found another book by J. J. Benitez, *The Testament of John*, at the same bookstore in the airport in Bogotá. This book portrayed the apostle John giving a final declaration to the body of Christian believers in which he admits to errors that he and Peter had made in organizing the church. It then went on to provide an in-depth portrayal of the afterlife, describing the mansion worlds, the superuniverses, Havona and Paradise. At the end of the book was a disclaimer from the author admitting that much of his material had been derived from a book which was in the custody of the Urantia Foundation. My first thought was that this foundation must be a group of dedicated monks hidden somewhere in the Italian Alps guarding the holy writ. I searched for the foundation and repeatedly came up short.

I knew that I had come upon something very important and wanted to share it with one of my brothers, who I knew was questioning the Mormon faith as well. So I began translating *The Testament of John* from Spanish to English for my brother's benefit. In early 1997, after finishing the translation of the first three chapters, I contacted the Miami office of the editors of the Planeta publishing group and asked whether the Benitez works were available in English. They told me that they were not. I then asked if they had ever heard of the Urantia Foundation. They said yes, that it was located in Chicago and that it published a book over 2,000 pages long that I could buy at any bookstore.

I immediately went out and bought it and read close to 400 pages in the first night. I was amazed by the content and detail and could not stop reading, continuing until around four in the morning. When I finally put it down to go to bed I felt incredibly calm and serene.

I have since read the Urantia Book twice and have shared it with my brother and two close friends, all of whom have devoured it in amazement.

ANDREW GAMEZ: Over the past ten years I have read a lot of literature on metaphysical themes and practices. I was fortunate enough to have a sister who led me to books by Edgar Cayce, Ramtha, Arthur Ford, Ruth Montgomery, Sutphen, and R. Monroe, to name just a few. However, none of these books had quite the impact on me that Courtney Brown's *Cosmic Voyage* had. To an amazing degree it validated a lot of metaphysical teachings I had been exposed to.

What still shakes me up is the section in *Cosmic Voyage* titled "The Midwayers." Courtney Brown and others in the military who are adepts in a technique called remote viewing confirmed the presence of "subspace entities" whose role is to uplift mankind by providing information and aiding in its evolution. Later on in the midwayer chapter, Courtney said that he and his researchers were influenced in their understanding of the midwayers by a document entitled the Urantia Book. That prompted me to look up the Urantia site on the Internet, get on the mailing list and eventually download the MS-Word document version of the UB.

Now I spend a lot of time shuttling back and forth between *Cosmic Voyage* and the Urantia Book because many of their ideas and claims about the universe, heaven, God, and humanity correlate. I most appreciate the section where Courtney converses with Jesus and reveals a being with a great personality, confirming the Urantia Book's descriptions of God and Jesus as warm, caring, and real.

JACOB DIX: By the age of 21, in 1997, I had already faced many personal failures and defeats. I had been through half a dozen different religions but none of them ever seemed to satisfy me. I found myself in an unhappy family, with a monotonous job, and without a single friend who could possibly understand my sadness. I was alone.

In the midst of my depression, a strange idea popped into my head: "Go to Arizona." For five minutes I stood on a ladder in the stockroom where I worked, aromatherapy products in hand, and weighed the pros and cons. Finding no cons, I decided to quit my job and bought a one-way bus ticket from Los Angeles to Sedona. I didn't know a thing about Sedona. I had a hiking pack, some money and no clue what I was going to do there. What an adventure! I was there two days when things started happening. Through a conspiracy of events I met Wilcy Haas, the man who would introduce me to the Urantia Book, and his wife Leah, both of whom I considered very wise.

After ten days I left Sedona with some hippies from Mississippi and we headed out to Oregon for a rainbow gathering. When our car broke down in Central California everyone decided to go home. I was broke, but I had made new friends and had shared some great experiences.

A year later, the same thought popped into my head: "Go back to Arizona." I returned, this time staying in a tent up on a nice little hill at the foot of a red rock mesa overlooking the beautiful desert. One day near the end of July, I went to visit Wilcy and Leah, but they were not home. They always left their door unlocked for visitors, so I went inside. I noticed this really big tome on the table with an old leather cover with three circles on it. My eyes got wide as I stared at it. I would never have looked through their things but this time curiosity got the better of me. I took a deep breath and scanned the table of contents: "Government on a Neighboring Planet," angels, evolution, Adam and Eve—and a huge section about Jesus whom I regarded at the time as a master, but not *the* master. When Wilcy came home I asked him, "What is this book?" He then started telling me about it and answering all my questions, like a father to a searching child.

That night when I went to back to my tent to sleep my mind was filled. I dreamt of an angel taking me through space and showing me the different states and planes of reality. Had I been to the morontia worlds? The next day, enthused, I went to a used book store and found a copy of the Urantia Book. A couple of days later I had saved enough money to buy it. Every night for the next two months, I ran home to my tent to read, by flashlight, "The Life and Teachings of Jesus." One day, while walking down the hill from my tent, a surge of spirit went through my being, a knowing smile came across my face, and the words passed so smoothly through my head: "I am a Jesusonian."

JIM PATTEN: Born in 1953, I received an excellent upbringing in a small town in Southern Missouri. My mother and father were involved in almost every organization and activity in the area, and insisted that all five of their children be likewise involved. They taught us excellent moral and ethical values and the basics about God and Jesus. During my younger years, when I was often extremely ill with hay fever, allergies, and asthma and could hardly breathe, my mother would lie down with me and we would pray to Jesus. In 1971, after high school, I joined the Army.

That brings us to a cold, clear day—December 10, 1997—at Fort Douglas, Utah, where I was a battalion commander for the 9th Support Battalion. My sergeant major and I had decided to go out and eat lunch at the Training Table downtown. On the way we witnessed a man being hit by a car at a pedestrian crossing and, assuming he was dead and with the ambulance on the way, we continued on.

During our meal we discussed what happened to the man's soul after death. The sergeant major expressed a few of his thoughts, and then it was my turn. After years of reading the Bible and attending various churches—from Methodist to Baptist to Mormon to Catholic—you would think I could come up with an intelligent answer. Thinking back to my Baptist days, I mentioned that Jesus would return some day and take us back out of the grave. I said something about the 144,000 people who would get special recognition early on, but at this point I became really vague, remembering little. My next thought was: "Go to the bookstore and buy a book!" It was like a voice speaking in my head.

Somewhat embarrassed, I suddenly said to the fellow Army infantry airborne ranger sitting across from me, "Is there a bookstore around here? I'm supposed to buy a book now. Someone is telling me to buy a book." He gave me a queer look and laughed, "You're joking, right?" I replied, "No," and smiled back.

We finished lunch and he steered me to the Barnes & Noble bookstore which happened to be directly across the street, all the while giving me a weird look and smiling.

I rarely visited bookstores. Upon being greeted at the door I asked one of the employees, "Will you help me find a book?" He asked me for the name of the book, and I replied, "This is going to sound pretty stupid, but I don't know the name." With a serious look on his face he asked, "Do you know the name of the author?" "I don't know that either," I admitted. At this point the clerk and my top NCO both started laughing, increasing my embarrassment and frustration. I thought it would be easier to look for the book myself, so I asked the clerk if there was a Religion section in the bookstore. He led me to it.

Standing in the middle of a long row of bookshelves, I thought, "God, if it's you speaking to me, show me the book." From left to right I started scanning the titles, but nothing happened. "This is really stupid!" I said to myself. Then a box sitting at the end of the shelf caught my eye. "This is it!" went through my head. I walked over, reached up and touched it, and said, "I know this is the book. What's in it?"

"It's the Urantia Book," said the clerk.

"What's Urantia?"

"I don't know," he said. "I've never read it, but I think it's about God."

"Good enough for me!" I said, "Wrap it up!" I didn't realize what I had in my hands at the time, but I would soon learn that the Urantia Book would change my perspective on life.

That same night I started reading the Foreword and did not understand a single word. After reading the front section a thought came to me again: "Read the book seven times from front to rear without stopping." I immediately scanned through the book and checked how many pages it comprised. I thought, "Oh, no! This thing is long!" Nevertheless, I read every single day and finished the first reading less than two months later.

About this time, when I took my final Army retirement physical, some problems were detected and I was rushed into surgery. First the doctors removed a tumor from my prostate and bladder; five days later my back went out and I was airvac'd to Fort Lewis; a little later the doctors burned seventy-nine pre-cancerous skin spots off my body, and a few months after that they cut a cancerous tumor out of my ear. My wife was worried, but I had no fear, no anxiety, no concerns—just pure joy with God and his son, Jesus. I thank God I listened to him—or one of his representatives—and read the Urantia Book.

Today I'm a car salesperson, with nobody to be in charge of, but with greater responsibilities—*spiritual* responsibilities—to my family, friends, co-workers and customers. Most customers treat me pretty badly when we first meet; later, the majority will drop their guard a little and make a connection spiritually. I've learned that whatever you do or whatever position you hold, you *can* make a difference.

MONTE PAGNI: When I was younger, I had several disabilities that made me question God and life itself, so I started reading books on theology. At 18 I spent a lot of time studying the *Seth* material, which I found heavy but enlightening. Little did I realize that it was preparing me for something even bigger much later.

After a while, though I had read many books about God and the universe, I found nothing that matched the feelings I had in my heart about such matters. I'd reached many dead ends and a lot of unconnected puzzle pieces. The *Seth* material explained many things, and some of it felt right or nearly so. The Bible offered some relief but not enough; too many things were out of place and out of sequence, and its centuries-old information always left me feeling disjointed and incomplete. I needed more!

In 1997 I was watching an episode of a weekly show TV show called "Strange Universe," in which a gentleman was talking about a book called Urantia. What caught my attention was the way he delivered himself. Right then and there I felt that that was the book I needed to continue my search for the truth.

I have been reading the Urantia Book ever since. I also attend a local reading chapter and enjoy our chats and questions. The Urantia Book could conceivably help the human race to achieve a better life. It's now up to us to do the Father's will.

SHAUNA HARDWAY: As a child, I thought heaven was a gigantic cathedral with millions and millions of pews. The better you were in life, the closer you got to sit to the podium where Jesus and God would take turns giving long-winded sermons. If you were really good, they might even toss you some padding so your butt wouldn't get sore sitting for eternity on those wooden benches. I really wasn't sure that I wanted to go to heaven. And when I would question my Sunday school teachers about what heaven was really like, they would answer, "It's a beautiful place where you worship God forever." That didn't really change my vision of heaven because to me, being a Southern Baptist, worship was a big church service with an occasional amen thrown in.

In 1997 I was in my senior year of high school and had recently outgrown my teenage rebellion. Although I felt very spiritual at the time, I thought I fit nowhere since my life was no longer defined by the church. One evening my boyfriend and I were sitting in front of his TV, bored. It was raining outside. He suddenly got up and said, "I've got a book I think you might like." He pulled out a big blue book. "My dad got this a long time ago," he explained. "It's kinda like the Bible, but with a twist of sci-fi. It's called the Urantia... uhh... I've never read it, though." He went on to say that his dad had shown the book to a Catholic priest who told him that the book had good messages, and that basically it taught us how to live.

By this point my curiosity was piqued. I opened the book and started reading. In my excitement, I flipped from page to page hoping to absorb it all.

From then on, whenever I went over to my boyfriend's house, I'd end up reading the Urantia Book. My favorite parts were the mansion world and morontia life papers. My erroneous interpretations of heaven were finally being turned around and I began to see that the worship my Father in heaven had always intended was creative and glorious, ever-changing and joyous!

But my enlightening reading days didn't last long. My boyfriend got jealous of my reading all the time. He said I was using him to get to the book, so I was forced to buy one of my own. At the check-out, the clerk stated, "You're in for a good one. I've heard interesting things about this book."

The skeptic in me answered, "Well, we'll see . . . I'm going to read it before I pass judgment." It didn't take long for me to fall totally in love with the Urantia Papers.

I'm grateful that my journey started at 18. My mother's journey did not begin until she was 45. Now an ALANON member, she seeks the same personal God I do. We have different ways of going about it but it's amazing how many times our visions of God coincide. She reads the Big Book, I read the Urantia Book, and we have both found our loving Father. I now believe that the Christian church is not the only way to God. There never was only one way, or one person with the authority to tell me how to experience my spirituality. Why would a God who created such an eclectic group of people create only one way to find his love?

TOM GREAVES: From the ages of eight to 15 I served as an altar boy at an Episcopal church. I was very devoted to the church and participated in services several times a week. But when I asked the questions that were always on my mind, I never got any answers. My questions were: What is the purpose of life? Who created God? Why is God so mean? Finally I quit going to church because I couldn't believe in something that no one could explain.

In 1975 I saw a magazine ad put out by the Rosicrucians. It claimed to offer a way to "improve your ESP." I had no ESP, but wanted to have it, so I became a Rosicrucian. After five years I still had no ESP, but I had been introduced to esoteric teachings. From that point on, I read everything I could find about mystery schools, religions and cults.

In 1985 I discovered the Association for Research and Enlightenment (A.R.E.), which published the Edgar Cayce readings and books inspired by them. Most of what I read struck harmonic chords in me. After seven years of study I felt I had all my answers except one: "What is my purpose in life?"

The A.R.E. didn't provide that answer.

In 1992 I discovered the Internet. I was in heaven. All the knowledge in the world was at my fingertips. I joined all the spiritual mailing lists I could find. On one of the lists, someone posted a reference to the Urantia Book. I had never heard of it, so I did a search, found the full text of the book online, and started reading. I read for about an hour and stopped. It was too complex, and the writers used too many names and words I had never heard of. I've got a Master's in nuclear engineering, so it isn't as if I had never seen a big word before, but none of this stuff found any resonance in me.

In 1997 I saw another reference to the Urantia Book on one of the email lists, this time in connection with Adam and Eve. Adam and Eve? I hadn't seen anything about them before when I had started reading from the beginning of the book. So I accessed the online text again and found the table of contents. These topics looked very interesting. At first I jumped around the book, reading only the parts that appealed to me. Finally, I bought a hard copy and started at the beginning, determined to read every word, from cover to cover.

I've now finished my second complete reading. I believe that the book is either of divine origin or was written by a collection of people with an incredible breadth of knowledge, writing skills, and imagination. I am leaning toward the "divine" theory.

My life's purpose is to learn to do God's will in every situation I encounter and that is what I am now striving to do.

JUDY KROLL: I left the Jehovah's Witnesses in 1987. Bitter and miserable, I was starting to doubt the Bible and had begun to think that maybe there was no God. Ten years later I got a computer. I was interested in anything and everything. I joined a newsgroup that discussed government conspiracies, UFOs, and so on. It was cool.

One day some comments were made about religion, and one fellow said, "Judy, you need to read the Urantia Book." What could this be? Being Watchtower-indoctrinated for 35 years, I immediately thought this must be the work of demons. My cyber friend, Dr. Byron Weeks, offered to send me the book. When I found out that he had been teaching the book for over twenty-five years, I reluctantly accepted.

What a surprise I got when I received the book! My husband and I devoured it. In fact, my husband grabbed the book from me—at first we had only the one book that Byron had sent—and started reading it aloud.

When he got into the papers describing the mansion worlds, I can still remember that my comment was, "I can't wait!" It was totally different from what I had been taught all my life. You see, The Watchtower teaches life on a paradise earth forever. That appeals to me too, but this message from the Urantia Book made me finally "see" beyond the normal earthly realm of life.

My husband and I consider the Urantia Book to be the most reasonable book we've ever read. It answers all the questions we had about Bible passages that didn't make sense to us before. For instance, the Flood: we never could believe that God would destroy all people and wildlife, and that the whole earth could be repopulated with billions of people just a few thousand years after Noah. The Urantia Book addresses this subject very logically, as well as many others. Its teachings help us to keep on trekking to find everlasting truth in our universal home.

FERNANDO MULDONADO: Around 1990 I was in a transpersonal psychology group which focused on Gurdjieff's teachings and the *Enneagram*. I had been in that group for about three years when I first heard of the book *The Trojan Horse*, by J. J. Benitez, which was said to provide a superior description of the life of Jesus. I was so interested that I bought the book within a few weeks and began reading it with intense concentration and emotion. The book's portrayal was so much more beautiful than anything I had ever heard during my Catholic upbringing.

After finishing that first book, I spent the next several years reading all the other books of the series, through *The Trojan Horse IV*. I knew inside me that the information in these novels was based on another source. I wanted to find that source but had no idea where to begin looking for it. In 1997 I found *St. John's Last Will*, by the same author, and after reading it with passion, I learned that the source was the Urantia Book. After that, I read another Benitez book called *The Lucifer Rebellion* and understood everything in it.

While my work as an electronic engineer had taken me to the Internet since 1988, it had never occurred to me to search for the Urantia Book via an electronic library until ten years later. First I found a website, and some days later, the English-language discussion group. That led me to the Spanish website and subsequently to the discussion group to which I now belong.

That is the story of how *El Libro de Urantia* came into my life, beginning with a vague idea to the book that finally got into my hands, which I now read with tears of endless happiness. The Spanish version may have mistakes—typos, misspellings—and may even be a bad translation, but I know that the heart of the book is real and wonderfully truthful. I know it, I feel it, and I am sure of it. I am certain that Jesus is our Master-brother and the Creator-ruler of this universe, and that together with him we are sons of God our Father.

OLGA LOPEZ: Since the day I began to reason, I have been interested in all that is beyond the reality that we can experience with our five senses. I've always been passionate about knowledge, and it wasn't long before I realized that scientific explanations on one side and those from the Catholic Church on the other didn't fully answer my questions.

I thought it was impossible for life to have emerged from nothingness as a result of haphazard and highly improbable chemical reactions—not intelligent life! I knew that something was lacking in that theory, namely the hand of a Supreme Intelligence who was able to give sense and coherence to the whole known creation. I was also not convinced by the image of the God of the Catholic Church. The idea of sin and the atonement doctrine were, for me, a barbarism. A vengeful God did not sit well with me.

I learned about the Urantia Book through the books of J. J. Benitez. The first of his books reflecting the teachings that came into my hands was *The Lucifer Rebellion*. I read it in 1993 and was so impressed that I traveled to the little Spanish town of Sotillo del Rincon near Soria. For those who have not read the novel, this is the town where the story begins—a beautiful town in which peace and calmness reign.

Three years later, in the summer of 1996, I bought *The Trojan Horse I* by the same author. I was so moved that I read it straight through and didn't stop until I had completed the entire *Trojan Horse* series, to number IV, which was the last one published at that time. You cannot imagine how badly I felt when I finished the fourth book. It ended so abruptly. I needed to know more.

I then read *St. John's Last Will*, which contains many concepts from the Urantia Book. I couldn't read too many pages at once because I was dizzy with all those new ideas. It was like attempting to hold the entire ocean in one's arms. I was trying to understand the nature of God and the immense infinity of the whole creation, but it was impossible. Our poor human mind isn't able to comprehend all that greatness.

However, I had received my share of good vibrations; I had begun to see my existence and that of others with new eyes. By "chance," thanks to my work as a computer analyst, I got on the Internet in 1996 and began surfing. One day I searched the word "Urantia," and what a surprise! I discovered an electronic edition of the book and the URL of a group of UB readers from around the world. I joined the list, made regular contact with other readers and finally got my Spanish translation in 1997.

FERNANDO RISQUEZ: In December 1991 a close friend who does Zen meditation and other spiritual practices received as a gift the book *St. John's Last Will* by J. J. Benitez, which draws from the well of the Urantia Book. This friend in turn gave the book to me, in order to get rid of something he didn't like and still do well by me that Christmas. I began to read it in February of 1992. In that book I found important revelations and deeper teachings than those presented in the New Testament Gospels. I was impressed with the explanations and visions that, in a brilliant and holistic way, integrate science, philosophy and religion. It was there that I first heard about the Urantia Book.

I reread *Last Will* many times, as well as books by Fritjof Capra, Teilhard de Chardin, C. G. Jung, and many others. Three years after reading *Last Will*, I saw the Urantia Book for the first time here in Caracas, but it was not until 1997 that I could afford to buy it. Since then it has become a rich and important source of knowledge and revelations for me. It helps me tremendously with the lectures I give at the Central University of Venezuela, where I present the different models of the universe, including the artistic vision of the master universe according to the Urantia Book.

Since March 1998 I have been in contact with the Urantia community, thanks to the Internet. Now daily I receive lots of Urantia posts, one of which was an invitation to submit my story for publication in this book, *How I Found The Urantia Book*.

GABRIEL LARA: Even though I had a well-organized and comfortable life, I felt there had to be something more profound and important. In 1997 I began to search for new paths. One day I read about a forthcoming lecture on reincarnation in the town where I lived. With the money I had won in a lottery, I went to that meeting. I was very skeptical. In the middle of the lecture the speaker began to talk about a big spacecraft, and some people there expressed their doubts and incredulity.

I heard someone mention the name, "the Urantia Book." An urge I cannot understand even today led me to buy the book that same day, without even looking at its pages. Since then, it goes with me everywhere. It is my guide, advisor, and counselor. Now I am beginning to feel really happy.

Curiously, the money I had won exactly equaled the combined price of the book and the meeting. Coincidence? I believe it was a gift from our Father.

ALBERT OLIVER: I was born in 1952 and was raised in Torrance, California, not far from the beach areas where I spent most of my weekends and summers surfing.

My mother basically had to drag me and my brothers to church while my father stayed home working in the garage listening to the Mormon Tabernacle Choir. We belonged to the Church of Religious Science, but I never felt a part of it. I always believed in God, though for most of my life I did not communicate with him or his Son in a personal way. I never felt that structured Christianity spoke to my soul.

When I was 14 my father had a heart attack and died in my presence. I had prayed to God to please let him live but he died anyway. For many years afterwards I blamed God for not saving him although the blaming was mostly on a subconscious level.

Years later I met my wife and we had two beautiful children. She had been reading the Urantia Book since she was 16 years old and always felt a personal relationship with God. In our twenty years of marriage we had many good times and a few problems, but we always seemed to pull through. I now know how much my lack of spirituality really bothered her.

I had known about the Urantia Book from my wife and had spent twenty years avoiding it. I guess my resistance to it was a reflection of my religious past and my fear of change. In 1998, because of her frustration with me and because of other problems we were having, she left me. I had nowhere to turn but to the one truth, the word of God that I knew was so near. I went to the bookstore and found a softcover copy of the Urantia Book. I discovered truth through the story of Jesus' life.

When I first started reading it I couldn't believe how foolish I had been all those years in refusing to share this treasure with my wife and my children. I realize, though, that every man has his time and that God is ever waiting to minister to his heart and soul.

It is a real charge for me to read the Urantia Book every day and I feel very blessed.

RAY NATHAN STEPHENSON: I was introduced to the Urantia Book twice. I don't always "get it" the first time.

My good friend Karen told me about a woman she'd met in Sedona, Arizona, who had introduced her to the UB. When Karen asked me if I'd heard of it, I confused it with a different book that I thought little of, and suggested she'd be wasting her time. When a few weeks later another friend mentioned it, warning buzzers started going off in my mind. However, I still wasn't moved enough to go looking for the book.

Not long after, in 1997, I was searching the Internet for "Melchizedek." I found that most of the references to Melchizedek were connected to websites related to the Urantia Book. I soon found the Urantia Papers online and began to read them. Having been a student of metaphysics for over thirty years, I found the material interesting and challenging to my many beliefs; but reading on the screen was a drag, and printing up the chapters was time-consuming. Tired of the downloading, I went to the Mayflower Bookstore and found a copy of the book in the Christian section.

I first read the chapters that looked interesting to me, and then I read all of Part IV. This part touched my heart deeply, but Christ always has; even the distorted version passed down in the New Testament gives enough of his words to steer us straight, if we but listen to his words and not to another's interpretation.

Now I understood what John was trying to convey in his "First there was the Word" passage. Christ as our creator is a shocking revelation—and humbling. The Urantia Book has put a face on all of God's creation for me.

SHANE COTNER: For about four years, my family regularly went to Baptist churches and my brother and I attended Christian schools. Much of the religious instruction I received was true and helpful. I am very thankful that I was taught to talk with the Heavenly Father and Jesus, and grateful to my mom for always telling us kids to listen for the "still, small voice" of the Holy Spirit. At times I found the Bible inspiring, but the God it portrayed was too much like my dad: someone rarely pleased with me.

One verse in particular always discouraged me—something to the effect that backsliders are doomed. I finally did a big backslide away from religion and went for another form of sliding that truly made sense to me: skiing. I focused my spiritual longings on this material joy all through high school and college. Skiing was immediate food for perfection hunger and it brought many beautiful moments. In the end, of course, it fell far short of filling that God-shaped hole in my heart. So I spent more and more time reading philosophic and metaphysical books, searching, struggling, wondering. I knew there had to be some way everything made sense.

One cold night, I decided that I deserved to meet God in person. Sad and frustrated, I walked to the edge of town and lay down in the snow. If God or Jesus wanted me to live, they could personally send me back to life with more information and a clear mission, just like in the near-death-experience stories. Well, I did get a response; it was loving and tender but also like a nuclear shock-wave that leveled every thought and left me power-washed, happy, and ready to get on with life. All the life-mission information I'd ever wanted and plenty more was just around the corner.

My last summer in college, 1997, I was in California visiting my grandma. She had been exploring assorted approaches to spirituality for many years, and there wasn't nearly enough time for me to read all of her wonderful books. I skimmed them and got the basic message from all but one—a large blue book with a strange name. My grandma had never mentioned this one to me. I thought the foreword would be the best place to get a feel for it. I was impatient; it took me far too long to read one sentence. It turns out that my grandma hadn't read much of the book herself. She liked *A Course in Miracles* and had bought the Urantia Book because Marianne Williamson had mentioned it.

Two years later, I finally knew it was time to find out more about *"Absolute perfection in some phases and relative perfection in all other aspects."* Had I known what was in the book I sure wouldn't have waited two years! I never dreamt that I would be so eager to help with "the work of the world," nor did I imagine how much fun it would be, not to mention the peaceful wonder of "striking step with eternity"! The whole experience of finding the Urantia Book makes me wonder what other amazing truth-gifts are out there, in some unexpected form, just waiting for us to be ready and willing to accept them.

BETSY BERNA: Recently I have become aware that we in the Spanish-language world must thank J. J. Benitez for having sparked interest in the Urantia Book. I, as have others, learned about the Urantia Book through the works of this author.

I didn't really like reading until a friend told me about *The Trojan Horse*. I began with the five-book *Trojan Horse* series, then read *The Lucifer Rebellion, St. John's Last Will*, and finally *Talking with God at 33,000 Feet*. Thus I began my adventure in the world of books. I liked the Benitez style of science fiction mixed with religion, and I wondered where he could have gotten all that information about the life of Jesus and the structure of the cosmos. My friend also told my father, who is addicted to books, about the Benitez books and he subsequently bought the series.

One day, in the spring of 1997, I was searching through my father's books when I discovered that he already owned the Urantia Book. I was stunned. He told me he'd bought it in 1996. He had noticed it on the shelves of a bookstore and took it down, not knowing what it was about. As he was looking through it, the bookseller came over and advised him to buy it, and he did. He then put it in his bookcase, unread, where it stayed until I found it. I began to read it from the very beginning, finding answers to questions I had long asked myself about God and other mysteries, such as: Who was Jesus? Do angels really exist? What is the soul and the spirit?

My ideas were clarified. I now see life with a new perspective, another meaning; now life is not merely growing up, studying, eating, working, having children and dying. I now know that I have an inner guide who tells me that I must learn to forgive; to be patient with those around me; that I must try to understand why some people are so hostile; that I must try to awaken in others an interest in enriching their own spiritual lives; that there must be an equilibrium between the material and the spiritual life. The most important thing—before all else—is to love. Love has no barriers. If you love you know how to forgive, as our Father on high does with us, his sons. And our goal is to be like him.

THERESE LOGAN: I guess you could say I am a displaced American living in Canada, having been born in Virginia and brought to Canada when I was seven. For as long as I can remember I was on a quest for truth. I studied everything I could get my hands on and attended every class that piqued my interest. I belonged to many churches and study groups, from Christian to New Age to Eastern religions, and made a thorough study of reincarnation. I delved into UFOs and crop circles and had psychic readings. In many of the books I read I kept coming across references to the Urantia Book, and one day in 1992 I found it on the top shelf of a secondhand-book store in Peterborough, Ontario. The bookstore owner told me it was heavy stuff and that I wouldn't like it. It was also old-looking and battered and cost $10, so I didn't buy it. I spied it a few times after that, still up on that top shelf, and still didn't buy it.

In January of 1994 I moved away to take care of my terminally ill mother, then moved to yet another city, and returned to live again in Peterborough in 1995. And the book was still up there. By now I was studying Edgar Cayce. In 1995 I moved away again, and when I came back to Peterborough in 1996 the book was still there, but now there was a *Concordance* with it and the price was now $40 for the pair. I still didn't buy. In the summer of 1997 I became seriouly ill, so ill that I had to retire from my career in the health care field and move in with my family in Cambridge. Yes, I left the book behind.

Just before Christmas I came across yet another reference to the Urantia Book, in a series by Joshua Stone. *Now I wanted that book.* I called long distance to Peterborough and asked if it was still there. Yes! My lucky day! And the owner of the bookstore said he was coming to Cambridge for Christmas and would bring it to me himself! It arrived on December 23, 1997, and I plunged in right at the beginning. I devoured it nonstop, then started over again. I had come home at last!

My precious old battered blue book, absolutely beautiful to my eyes now, had not only found me but waited patiently on that top shelf for over five years! I have never looked back, and only wonder why it took me so long! It may have to do with that old saying, "When the student is ready the teacher will appear."

CYNTHIA TAYLOR: I live about 50 kilometers east of Johannesburg, South Africa, in a town called Springs. As far back as I can remember I was a seeker, questioning my reason for living, my purpose for being on this planet, why God allowed people to kill each other, to fight wars, and allowed them to go to hell. Having been raised a Catholic, I had many questions that the Church could not answer. Later I began searching among the various Christian faiths, but none of them could answer my questions either.

Deep inside I had a feeling that there must be more to this life than the Christian concept. How could God save only Christians and allow millions with different religions—people who were good, kind, understanding and caring of their fellow man—to go to hell because they didn't believe in Jesus? That a loving God could condemn these people for all eternity just because through ignorance they did not know Jesus did not make sense to me. How could God be limited, as people limit his abilities, sanctioning only one religion when there were thousands of different belief systems and understandings of the cosmos? I came to the conclusion that to realize God in all his glory was to honor God in all of his creation, to see and experience God in all people of all walks of life, philosophies, races, religious persuasions, and cultures. I also felt that we were not the only inhabited planet in the universe. It seemed ludicrous to me that God would create all those planets and populate only one.

In 1998 I joined the Internet and subscribed to a list called Bridge-L, a busy email discussion group of people who shared their various spiritual beliefs and philosophies. There I met Lee Armstrong and Susan Sarfaty. At the bottom of Lee's messages he always quoted a passage from the Urantia Papers. I asked him about these Papers and he mailed me a copy of the Urantia Book all the way from America.

Susan Sarfaty then invited me to join the PorchSisters, a women's corps of Urantia Book readers headed by Julianne Clerget. Never before had I come across such a group of people who truly care about one another! A wonderful illustration is when my father was diagnosed with a brain tumor. These women were a shining example of ministry in action when they took up a collection to pay for plane fare for my husband and me to visit my father in a hospital in another city. I would not have been able to get through much of the drama of my life without their support. Even before I had read much of the Urantia Book the people connected to it had become a blessing to me.

Soon after I received the book I had it sitting on my desk next to my computer when one of my clients, Reverend Jacob Freemantle, came to give me some typing work. He picked the book up and glanced through it, then asked where he could get a copy. I made arrangements with Julianne, and she kindly sent a book to me to present to the Reverend, who ministers to a large African Methodist congregation in Kwa-Thema, Gauteng Province, South Africa.

I found trying to read the book by myself very difficult, especially the introduction and the sections about the universes. In January 2000 I joined the JUMP train on UBRON (Urantia Book Readers Online Network, started by Susan Sarfaty), and together we began a project of reading six pages per day together and discussing them online. What a difference it makes doing something like this with others! For the first time I have been able to read the Foreword and start understanding it. It's wonderful to get other people's insights!

The Urantia Book gives a more enlightened view of the life of the great teacher and Master, Jesus. It makes sense of the Satan/Devil/Lucifer story—the UB's account talks to my soul. Its version of the Adam and Eve story and narration of the beginnings of world history have confirmed my own understanding. It shows how the other planets are being used by God. Many of the teachings in the Urantia Book correspond to the teachings of other world religions; if one looks one can find these parallels.

I was fortunate in having the Urantia Book missionary Norman Ingram stay in my home on his way back from his first trip to Africa in 1998. Norman continues to be an inspiration to me; I love his enthusiasm, commitment and dedication to the spreading of this revelation. Also, in December 1999 I worked in the Urantia Book booth at the Parliament of the World Religions. Seeing the number of people who were interested in the book was a revelation in itself! I am so grateful that I was fortunate enough to find this revelation and will continue to promote it to all.

COSTAS DIAMANTOPOULOS: I was born in Greece and moved to England in 1973 for college and university studies. I completed my Marine Engineering degree in 1978 and moved to London after a brief sojourn in Africa and Northern Ireland for training. My London job took me to many places in the world, including the Far East, South America and North America.

After moving to Britain, through a series of events I became interested in Spiritualism, Magic, UFOs and the whole New Age movement. I studied all relevant literature and sat in mediumship séance circles. This background made me thirsty for Truth. I knew that every ism was providing only a small fragment of the whole truth which was still evading me. Even *OAHSPE*, a supposed revelation which inspired me to become a vegetarian for five years, was not the real thing for me.

My experiences in both in the material world and the spiritual realm led me to change jobs. Under the guidance of the angels of health (as I know now) I struggled with the establishment of a new multi-wavelength semiconductor diode device which triggered healing processes into cell structures, especially in soft tissue injuries and wounds. As a result of this effort more than two thousand devices were spread around the world, including the USA, although I failed miserably to obtain FDA approval for more widespread use.

After ten years of hard effort I stepped out. My family was demanding more time at home and my exhaustive worldwide placement of the project was taking its toll in my marriage. We lived partly in Greece and partly in Poland whilst I maintained a London base. By November 1998 I had lost a fortune. One by one my material assets were starting to evaporate, and my marriage was on the rocks.

In London around that time I met, through opposite sex attraction, a beautiful female Greek-American banker working in London. We discussed many things, and when I mentioned the book *The Celestine Prophecy*, she told me that this was McDonald's compared to the Urantia Book. The first thing I asked was, "Who is the author?" She smiled and said, "Read it and decide for yourself."

When we went to her apartment the next evening I saw the blue book and started reading parts of it. I was immediately impressed by the language, the authoritative tone, the wide breadth of subjects. She saw how absorbed I was, and although she herself at that stage had not even finished the first paper, she gave the book to me as a present. What a marvelous present for life! Though she moved on with her life and I with mine, our brief interaction in time had an impact on my life for eternity.

I finished the book in the spring of 1999, reread it immediately after with equal absorption to finish again in the following September, then started a third in-depth study. I noticed the transformative power the book had in every aspect of my life from work to family, and the knowledge of my cosmic citizenship made me a very happy, secure person trying to listen to the friend who has chosen to be my Thought Adjuster.

To help others experience the same joy as I did, I have planted the seeds for a presentation of the book in Greece. I also hope that a translation core will be created. The Greek language will hold many challenges to be solved in a fair and accurate translation, but I trust the midwayers and all other seraphic friends attached to the task will assist

GEORGE BENAVIDES: In 1998 I read a book by J. J. Benitez called *The Trojan Horse*. It was essentially about an astronaut who went back in time to meet Jesus Christ. It was a very interesting story that put the character of Jesus in a whole new light. I began searching more after that.

One day I walked into the Barnes & Noble bookstore and happened to see the Urantia Book on a shelf. It was a big, white book with many questions on the outside cover, such as, Who are we? Where are we going? Where do we come from?—all questions I was curious about. When I opened the book I immediately zeroed in on the part about Jesus' early childhood. I was instantly excited. I knew what I had in front of me, so I bought it. I kept reading *The Trojan Horse* books for quite a while, then began to compare Benitez's books with the Spanish edition of the Urantia Book I had recently purchased. I realized at once that *The Trojan Horse* books must have been inspired by the Urantia book.

When I first started reading about Jesus in the *Trojan Horse* books, I felt him come alive for the first time. I saw him for what he truly was here on earth. After reading the Urantia Book, I saw him for what he truly is in heaven. I bought all five of the *Trojan Horse* books, but I only got halfway through number three. I lost interest in reading them when the Urantia Book became a superior book to me. However, I still appreciate J. J. Benitez for opening the doors that so many people wish to enter.

Ever since I found the Urantia Book my life has steadily improved. I can only thank the celestials for making this revelation possible. I hope one day that the whole world can unite in spirit.

FAYE LOSKAMP: In early 1998, while watching the evening news on FOX-TV in Los Angeles, I saw a promotion for the magazine show "Strange Universe." They mentioned something about a secret alien bible which caught my interest. I wrote a little note to myself to be sure to watch the show, then went about my chores and forgot all about it.

Just about the time the show was to go on I looked up at the television to see my note hanging there and was reminded to turn it on. During the beginning of the show I didn't pay much attention because I had many distractions, and then the telephone rang. I realized that I was going to be on the phone for a while and decided to record the rest of the show to watch it later.

The next morning while having my coffee I turned on the VCR and found that about sixty seconds from the "alien bible" segment had been recorded, but in that time they never mentioned the name of the book. However, the book was displayed on a table, and I had to play the tape over and over again until I was able to pick out the words "Urantia Book."

I called around to find where I could buy a copy and picked one up the following Wednesday. I began reading. I couldn't put it down throughout the entire weekend. On the following Monday morning, I called the Urantia Foundation in Chicago to get a list of other readers, and heard about a brand-new study group for beginners that was starting that very night, only a mile away from where I lived, at the home of a long-time reader named Saskia. She shared her understanding and enthusiasm for the teachings and helped me to locate those parts of the book I was most interested in. It was also wonderful to meet other readers and discuss these new and mind-boggling concepts with them.

As a child, my first conscious thoughts were such questions as, Where am I? Who am I? Where I am going from here? What is the purpose of life? I had always assumed the Bible was written in a mysterious code and that one day, as I matured, I would automatically know the answers. In the meantime my job was to question and search for these answers. I was confident these answers would come to me some day. The Urantia Book has brought me these answers.

AL LOSKAMP: My wife Faye and I had been searching for many years for something to give us a spiritual foundation. We were both believers in God but found it difficult to relate to the various religious organizations that we had experienced.

I had been a successful attorney for thirty years and very active in the Burbank community. I had been president of the Chamber of Commerce, the YMCA board of directors and the Burbank Bar Association, and chairman of the Burbank Planning Board. Then came a very dark period. I was wrongfully sued for millions of dollars by a client. It looked as if we might lose everything. This experience brought us to the deepest depths and made me ask what was really important in life.

While this was going on I became aware that Faye had stopped watching television and instead had her nose buried in a big blue book. In addition, she started going to weekly meetings to discuss the book. Finally I asked her what was so intriguing and she replied that all the answers she had been seeking were in that book. I decided that when I got around to it I would check it out, and went about my business.

Faye occasionally answered my office telephones. One day in April 1998 my longtime poker-playing friend called to remind me of our monthly game. Faye had picked up the phone and told him I could not attend because I would be busy that night. I asked her what was so important that I could not attend the game, and she replied, "I go to a lot of your meetings with you, and on this particular night you are going to one with me."

Leaving me no choice, we went to a Urantia meeting in Topanga Canyon. I was fascinated with what I heard. The following week I went with Faye to the local study group she had found for new readers. The first evening we read about life on other planets; the second week, Adam and Eve. I was hooked right away. The hostess happened to have the audiotape version of the book, which I borrowed and listened to all the way through, and I have been a serious student of the Urantia Book ever since.

After three years of litigation I finally won all the lawsuits. The combined experience of the legal hassles and the Urantia teachings have helped us to re-evaluate our priorities and have given our lives new meaning and value.

INGE SCHEUMANN: The book came to me in 1998. I consider it an answer to years of prayer for light and truth. I went to our local bookstore for yet another "New Age" book to get information and maybe find a bit of the truth I was looking for. On the shelf was a cardboard box, no title to be seen. Something told me to pick it off the shelf, open it up and take a look at it. It was a softcover edition of the Urantia Book. I sat down and started to read, and I think I left that store three hours later—with the book, of course!

It's been the best thing that has happened to me since my dedication to Jesus. I cannot express the joy I feel when reading this revelation. It is as if my soul is jumping for joy and my Adjuster is breathing a sigh of relief after all I have put them through in order to find my God and Father.

Because I am a novice reader I feel I do not yet have the knowledge to share the book with others and give intelligent answers to forthcoming questions, but one day I will and then I hope the Father will use me to help others to find this book.

LONITA MURTO: I first heard about the Urantia Book early in 1998 on a TV program called "Strange Universe," which claimed that the book had been channeled through an unnamed person by alien spirits. Never having believed that God made this whole wonderful universe just for us humans, this rang true with me. I wrote down the information from the show and found the book on the Internet the next day.

I was glad that it referred to itself as being given to us by higher celestial forces, an explanation that I preferred to the show's ET-type theory. I started reading the Foreword that same day and knew that this book was something I needed to know more about. The next day I printed up "The History of Urantia." It was what I had read in that section that kept me coming back; my husband is science-minded and I am a lifelong spiritual searcher, and the subjects in those history papers provided us with much-needed common ground.

Throughout my life I attended many different churches and denominations, never really feeling that any of them had the answers I was searching for. Nor did I believe that those answers could be found anywhere. I will say now, for the record, that I believe I will find what I've been seeking within the pages of this wonderful book. It has made me long for fellowship with like-minded thinkers.

Still reading on-line, I then began delving deeply into Part IV, "The Life and Teachings of Jesus." Anyone who wants to feel and understand Jesus' love for us should be able to enjoy the simplicity with which his story is written. His love has never been so easy for me to see. I recommend reading it to anyone seeking to know our savior. It has changed me in several ways. I plan to study and learn from this book for the rest of my life here on earth. I wish the peace and enlightenment that I've received to all who may read this.

WENDY: What if I could open up to the secrets of the universe? If I could connect with God? Could I become more than I am? Who am I? What have I been? What is my purpose? These were the questions that were swirling around in my head at the time I discovered the Urantia Book. I was worried about my life, my health, and my job.

It was May 28, 1998, when I ran into Saskia in the kitchenette at our workplace. She was making tea. She began to share some exciting information with me. She told me about a book of stories she was compiling about another book that had changed many lives, including her own. Suddenly something inside me opened up. "What book is that?" I asked, "I want to read it, too!"

She invited me into her office where she showed me a picture of the unfinished book cover, a work in progress that depicted our planet, evolution, Adam and Eve, Jesus, and the entire universe.

"You have a book that describes all that?" I asked.

Although I had studied metaphysics, I had never heard of the Urantia Book. The more she told me about the book and the impact it had had on her life—an impact that had endured for over twenty years—the more interested I became. What compelled me to learn more was her enthusiasm. What could there be in this book that could change someone's life so dramatically and have such long-lasting effects?

The next day she called me into her office and gave me a copy of the Urantia Book as a gift. Together we combed through the table of contents. I wanted to go straight for the last section of this magnificent book, to the Jesus papers. Being Jewish I had never read the New Testament and I had never really had a desire to read the Bible, yet lately I had wondered about Jesus and wanted to learn more about him.

I've been finding the answers to my questions in this book. Already I'm beginning to feel more relaxed about my life. From the moment I started reading it I felt at home. I even went out and bought the softcover edition so I can carry it with me wherever I go. I've only just begun my Urantia reading adventure yet I look forward to going home every night and sitting with my book.

MARK UNDERWOOD: Though my parents were agnostics, my mother had our family of six kids attend Sunday school, and I was confirmed into the church at age 13. But the religion I learned at church was never a meaningful part of my life.

It was in college when my interest in spirituality was piqued. It happened like this. I and a mob of about six hundred other students were eating supper as usual in the canteen of a notoriously riotous co-ed residence, when I accidentally dropped my fork on the floor. A guy by the name of Randy, a fourth-year engineering student, reached down to pick it up and then handed it to me. Our friendship began with his unusual act.

Randy was an evangelical Christian, involved with a Christian outreach ministry on campus. He persevered with me despite my stubbornness, engaging me in discussion and Bible study. He even got me to pray with him occasionally, a prayer to an invisible God that I did not quite believe in yet. Finally, after several months of being continually asked the question, "How close are you?", I clued in to the fact that I personally had to *do* something, either believe this stuff or not. Finally, after a three-day struggle in relative isolation, I gave in. I then told every Christian I knew that I had become a believer. That was in early 1982.

The period from 1982 to 1994 was a time of religious growth for me and my wife Marlene. We studied the Bible and were devoted to our semi-fundamentalist, evangelical church. I taught Junior High Sunday school and served on the deacon's board. Theologically minded from the start, I rode many doctrinal hobby horses.

In 1994 I was personally touched by the charismatic renewal movement within Christianity. This movement was, and still is, a worldwide phenomenon, and one of its primary epicenters was a little Vineyard church near my home in Toronto. The nightly meetings consisted mostly of worship, testimony, some preaching and, most conspicuously, something called "ministry time," during which a small band of people would go around to pray for the hundreds who were standing to "receive the blessing." Often spiritual, emotional and physical phenomena would ensue. I first went because I was curious and hungry for something more in my Christian experience. I wasn't disappointed. Soon I was experiencing an intimacy with God as a loving Father that I had never known before. The stern, vengeful, hard-to-please God idea was evaporating from my outlook. The senior pastor there had many sayings, one of which was, "You must have more faith in God's ability to bless than Satan's ability to deceive."

Late in 1997 my wife and I and some friends left our Baptist church to start a simple home church. One of our friends had discovered the home church idea on the Internet; it was appealing to us to get back to what we saw as New Testament basics, away from the program-driven, authoritarian, spectator type of institutional church mentality. My interest in doctrine subsided, and I became much more interested in the "spirit" of a believing fellowship and worship.

During this time I got hooked up to the Internet and quickly found a major Christian apologetics discussion board where I discovered even wider divergences in Christian opinion. I began toying with "deviant" doctrines like Preterism and Universalism, and to seriously question biblical reliability. But now, with a personal experience of God to hold me fast, my faith remained intact despite the tremendous uncertainties I was going through.

Then, in February of 1999, someone at the Christian discussion board mentioned a book he had just discovered online—the Urantia Book. He gave us the address of the site and asked us to look at the text and provide feedback. After linking to the online version of the book and reading various sections, within a couple of days I posted back to the discussion board something like, "This is either the most incredible written revelation from God ever, or else the most intelligent devious doctrinal scheme ever assembled."

Within a few weeks I had devoured Part IV and then proceeded to other chapters that interested me. Finally my tired eyes convinced me to buy the book.

Words cannot describe the sheer thrill I had on reading this new material. It just felt right. I had been thinking along many similar lines, and here the ideas were presented in far greater scope and magnificence than I would have dreamed of. Along with the content, I was struck by the book's consistency and egoless, matter-of-fact narrative style. It was very compelling to one who was used to reading reams and reams of obvious theological speculation.

I have remained with my Christian fellowship and continue to enjoy it. I still have much to learn about sharing and living the truths of the revelation. But I realize now there is so much more than before. My worldview has been forever rocked. The very real spirit-fellowship of all believing humanity is starting to grip me. I truly believe now, as the prophet Isaiah said, that "the knowledge of the Lord shall cover the earth, as waters cover the sea!" Let it be.

BRAD TRAINHAM: In order for this story to make any sense, a few introductory details are in order. First, I'm a computer programming instructor for the Internal Revenue Service, and so of course I spend a lot of time on the computer. Next, I'm totally blind, and have been all my life. I use synthesized speech to access the computer and to "read" what you would normally see on the computer screen. And like many computer users, I probably spend way too much time on the Internet. The increased use of the World Wide Web has given me access to information and literature I formerly had no means of finding or reading.

Finally, and probably most important is the issue of my spiritual development. My childhood was spent within the Church of Christ. It was assumed I would become a preacher within that denomination. Since perhaps a little too much force was used in the imparting of doctrine, I rebelled with everything I had when I reached adolescence. As an adult, I made superficial studies of several religious and spiritual disciplines, but I always secretly wished for an honest way to live and grow within the teachings of Jesus as I understood them.

I found the Urantia Book quite by accident one day at work. I had taken lunch at my desk that day, and thought I'd briefly search the Web for traditions related to Lucifer's transgressions and subsequent expulsion from heaven. I use a program that checks several of the popular search engines, so I entered /"Lucifer"+"Michael"/ in the search field and sat back to see what would happen.

When launching similar searches in the past, I had always come across several condensed theological texts and commentaries, and a few times I'd seen some of the Theosophist writings related to their concept of Lucifer. This time, however, I kept getting sites with the word Urantia. I finally opened one of these, and found the text of Paper 53, "The Lucifer Rebellion" being read to me. I read this paper, and then Paper 54 as well. At that point, I realized I'd probably want to read the whole book, but I couldn't do that right then. A student called me, and I was soon back to work.

That night I had a fortuitous bout of insomnia, and back to the Web I went to read some more. I finally decided to start from the beginning, and ordered the CD-Rom version of the book so I wouldn't be tying up a phone line quite so much.

I've never had such a positive reaction to a course of spiritual study as has happened with the Urantia Book. I found a local study group in Austin, and went to a meeting. Some of the people there had spiritual histories somewhat similar to mine. We discussed sections of the book and as I drifted off to sleep that night, I thanked God for this book and the people it has influenced. I want to learn everything I can from this book; I just can't believe I'd never heard of the Urantia teachings until just recently.

Available in bookstores everywhere!

INDEX

Abdo, Roger J. 150
Abercrombie, Jeff 327
Ablieter, Leonard 290
Adkins, Forrest 100
Afonso, Juan Jose Martinez 276
Agudelo, Alba Teresita Rojas 307
Aldo, Al 250
Anderson, Kermit 42
Armstrong, Lee 124
Ascher, Jean 178
Ayers, Claudia 116
Bain, Dick 28
Bain, Mike 289
Balnicke, Janelle 88
Bandera, Gonzalo and Merci 320
Baney, Tonia 32
Barden, Charlie 26
Barnett, Linda 332
Bartley, Beth 156
Beckner, Fred 259
Bedell, Clyde 1
Bedell, C. Barrie 6
Begemann, Henry 47
Belitsos, Byron 142
Bell, Glenn 120
Bellman, Sheryl 165
Benavides, George 369
Benjamins, Enno 247
Benjamins, Rodger 329
Benjamins, Nel 347
Berna, Betsy 364
Best, Peri 286
Beyer, Charlie 191
Biek, Christilyn 241
Blackstock, Sara 34
Block, Matthew 176

Borowski, Shane 333
Bowen, Angus 120
Bradley, David 61
Brandt, Joy 139
Bright, Betty 179
Brooks, Scott 67
Brown, Nancy 197
Brown, Virginia 256
Brown, Donna 311
Bruyn, Robert F. 56
Bryan, Bill 18
Burnette, Billy 294
Burns, Robert 153
Calabrese, Philip 78
Caoile, Mario 155
Carmichael, Holly 332
Carriker, Bruce 216
Channic, Tom 279
Clerget, Julianne 175
Cocking, Eldred 20
Colbert, Lee 259
Cotner, Shane 362
Coutis, George 69
Cratty, Liz Engstrom 219
Crickett, Rob 117
Criner, Darlene Sheatz 134
Crosby, Sherie 295
Cuello, Jaime Andres 340
Dalton, Jerry 273
D'Ambrosia, Michael 285
Daniels, Karen Farrington 166
Davis, Willis 284
Day, Curt 331
De Martinez, Josefina 341
Defourneaux, Paul 212
DeToy, Jon 196

INDEX

Di Bacco, Jenni 271
Diamantopoulos, Costas 367
Dinsmore, Delores 136
Dix, Jacob 351
Downs, Jim 68
Dupree, John 217
Ebben, Mary 188
Eichmann, JoAnn 34
Elder, Dorothy 40
Elstrott, Kelly 85
Elwyn, Diana 312
Escobar, Angel Sanchez 299
Estrada, Rob 240
Faul, Ardell 111
Faulk, Ron 184
Faw, Duane 95
Fearey, Pat 36
Feller, Joe 162
Filion, Gisela 269
Flores, Santiago 324
Fontana, Bob 318
Forbes, Stephanie 283
Ford, Kinda 338
Franco, Ricardo 337
Freeman, Mark 97
Friedman, Polly Parke 21
Fuchs, Pradhana 338
Galvin, Terry 151
Gamez, Andrew 350
Gawryn, Francyl 51
Geiger, Philip 65
Geis, Larry 58
Ginsburgh, Irwin 208
Girard, Pierre 243
Glass, David 110
Glazer, Daniel Love 203
Goodwin, Lynn 133
Gorman, Calvin Matthew 317
Greaves, Tom 356
Green, Marilyn Hauck 45
Greenhut, Marty 70
Greer, Mark 211
Groh, Martha 122
Grubb, Arley 275
Guelfenbein, Eduardo 321
Gustafson, Russ 76
Gwynn, Laurence 218
Hall, Ila and Loren 17
Hall, Gary 48
Hall, Paul 215
Hallock, Virginia Lee 27
Hammond, Evelyn 298
Hanna, Donna Maria 210
Hansen, Jess 126
Hardway, Shauna 355
Hardy, Thea 73
Harlan, Stacey 84
Harney, LuAnn 227
Harries, Katharine J. "Ticky" 7
Harris, Fred 287
Harris, Jim 103
Harrison, Gerald 91
Harvey, Sioux 152
Hayes, Michael 254
Hayman, Peter 257
Hazzard, Bill 26
Healy, Ed 247
Hecht, Steven 55
Hemmingsen, Susan 129
Heyneman, Catherine 335
Holt, Dave 206
Horton, Tammy 109
Howell, Barbara Jo 237
Hoy, Emy 119
Huggins, Mary 278
Hughes, Bud 317
Hummel, Karrie 300
Hunt, Bob 76
Huntzinger, Doug 314
Ingram, Norman 89
Irwin, James 24
James, Wesley R. 4
Jameson, Gard 107
Jeppeson, Karen 171

INDEX

Johnson, Peggy M. 102
Johnson, JJ 161
Johnson, Joilin 265
Jones, Cathy 207
Joyce, Gene 14
Kava, Phil 325
Kelly, Bill 271
Kelly-Ward, Suzanne 282
Kettell, Hal 21
Keys, Jeff 32
Kimsey, Susan 286
Klimesh, Michelle 149
Konstas, Christos 181
Krasny, Lorrie Shapiro 157
Kroll, Judy 357
Kubik, Mike 148
Lachance, Luc 243
Lara, Gabriel 360
Lawson, Rob 277
Lear, Lyn Davis 79
Lee, Jim 160
Leger, Loren 279
Lewis-Sutter, Margo 296
Lieske, Rosey 159
Linthicum, David 335
Livingston, Doc 38
Lockett, Al 106
Logan, Therese 364
Lopez, Olga 359
Loskamp, Faye 369
Loskamp, Al 370
Maloy, Patrick 327
Mann, Michael 135
Mark, Michael 244
Markellos, Helen 245
Martin, Patricia Bedell 35
Mason, Jeffrey 339
Maxton, Lee and Mildred 304
Mazdeh, Hamid Reza 297
McCarty, Ginny 258
McCollum, Jerry 64
McCormack, Gregory 233

McKee, Calvin 292
McKinney, Jamail 81
McKinney, John 315
McNelly, Pat 48
McSweeney, Gary 273
McWhorter, Steven 253
Megow, Daniel 213
Michael, Mary J. 31
Moakher, Nora and Saed 310
Mohr, Susan 261
Montgomery, Chick 43
Morgan, Sybil W. 319
Morris, Timothy W. 349
Muldonado, Fernando 358
Mullins, Larry 39
Mullins, Joan Batson 221
Munos, Diego Gonzales 344
Murto, Lonita 372
Narducy, Gene 295
Newby, Vicki Miller 340
Nice, Dolores 168
Nicely, Timothy 262
Nicomede, Dennis 189
Nilsen, Janet Quinn 126
Norby, Barry 263
O'Guin, Robert 249
Oliver, Donna 128
Oliver, Albert 361
Omar, Beu'lah Mary 316
Omura, Richard 141
Orjala, Thomas 54
Outerbridge, Tommy 173
Owen, Ed 75
Pagni, Monti 354
Parker, Doug 93
Patten, Jim 352
Pawlitsky, Larry 131
Pearson, Denver 62
Pike, Karen 223
Pike, Kathryn 225
Pitzel, Michael 104
Poppel, K. Brendi 108

INDEX

Porter, Pat 300
Praamsma, Saskia 199
Proano, Gustavo 344
Raphael, Daniel 115
Rauh, Lee 268
Rayl, Mike 233
Rehnstrom, Joel 29
Reinecke, Kris 130
Religa, Stella 118
Renn, Ruth 2
Risquez, Fernando 360
Roark, Don 306
Robertson, David 190
Rohrsen, Craig 230
Roper, John 72
Roper, Jane A. 147
Sadler, Sharon 229
Sarfaty, Susan 52
Satterthwaite, Alicia 321
Schach, Denie 80
Scheumann, Inge 371
Schneider, Sonny 109
Schreiber, Robert 283
Scott, Jeannie 313
Seklemian, M. (Sek) 201
Sherwood, Will 49
Shinall, Steve 234
Siegel, Mo 41
Smith, Sue 145
Smith, Chrissy Palatucci 169
Smith, Fred 187
Smith, Scott 328
Solsona i Estrada, Jordi 309
Spang, Bill 66
Sprunger, Meredith 12
Steach, Ruth L. 156
Stephenson, Ray Nathan 362
Suga, Julie 322
Sutton, Paula Lynn 180
Szabados, Sandor 226
Tallqvist, Stefan 30
Taylor, Geoff 266
Taylor, Cynthia 365
Thompson, Paula Garrett 182
Thorburn, Stephen 251
Tibbals, Les 86
Tibbets, Dave 186
Townsend, Irving 45
Trainham, Brad 375
Traylor, Kitty and Tim 231
Tuttle, Judy 302
Tyler, Don 114
Underwood, Mark 373
Vega, Juan Paulo 342
Vick, Allene 305
Vinson, Kathleen 215
Waitts, Sage 280
Walker, Grace 3
Walstrom, Gus 15
Warren, Rick 267
Watkins, Larry 163
Wattles, Jeffrey 82
Weber, Dave 209
Weimer, Buck and Arlene 112
Weiss, Jacques 11
Wellen, Charlotte 195
Whelan, Laurence R. 165
White, Bruce 229
Wold, Beverly 23
Wood, Esther 144
Woodward, James 100
Wortendyke, Brad 220
Zabielski, Lamar 223
Zehr, Michael J. 292
Zendt, Stephen 88
Zents, Cheryl Ashiqa 91
Zeringue, Henry 252
Ziglar, Sharon 172
Ziglar, Wally 16
Terry 302
Holly 308
Roger in Hawaii 345
Wendy 372

BOOK ORDER FORM

To order additional copies of *How I Found The Urantia Book*, please fill out the following form:

NAME_____

ADDRESS_____

CITY_____

STATE /PROV._____ZIP/POSTCODE_____

Email_____

_____# COPIES AT $15.00 ea._____

CALIFORNIA RESIDENTS ADD 7% TAX___

$3.20 SHIPPING FOR FIRST BOOK_____
(Outside USA please check our website for shipping prices.)

$1.00 FOR EACH ADDITIONAL BOOK___

TOTAL____

Would you like to be on our mailing list? YES____NO____

Send check or money order to:

SQUARE CIRCLES PUBLISHING, INC.
P.O. BOX 251194
GLENDALE, CA 91225

Books can also be ordered online at:
http://www.squarecircles.com